T0312061

# The Informal American City

**Urban and Industrial Environments**
Series editor: Robert Gottlieb, Henry R. Luce Professor of Urban and Environmental Policy, Occidental College

For a complete list of books published in this series, please see the back of the book.

# The Informal American City

Beyond Taco Trucks and Day Labor

edited by Vinit Mukhija and Anastasia Loukaitou-Sideris

The MIT Press
Cambridge, Massachusetts
London, England

© 2014 Massachusetts Institute of Technology

All rights reserved. No part of this book may be reproduced in any form by any electronic or mechanical means (including photocopying, recording, or information storage and retrieval) without permission in writing from the publisher.

This book was set in Sabon LT Std by Toppan Best-set Premedia Limited.

Library of Congress Cataloging-in-Publication Data
The informal American city : beyond taco trucks and day labor / edited by Vinit Mukhija and Anastasia Loukaitou-Sideris.
    p.   cm. — (Urban and industrial environments)
Includes bibliographical references and index.
ISBN 978-0-262-02707-6 (hardcover : alk. paper) — ISBN 978-0-262-52578-7 (pbk. : alk. paper)
1. Informal sector (Economics)—United States. 2. Social interaction—United States. 3. Cities and towns—United States—Social conditions. I. Mukhija, Vinit, 1967– II. Loukaitou-Sideris, Anastasia, 1958–
HD2346.U5I554   2014
330—dc23
2013035292

To our families and students

# Contents

Part II Responses

# Acknowledgments

We wholeheartedly acknowledge the intellectual collaboration of our contributors and thank them for their participation in this endeavor, which included a speaker series hosted by the UCLA Department of Urban Planning during the Winter quarter of 2012. We also appreciate the financial support of UCLA's Institute for Research on Labor and Employment and its director, Chris Tilly, for his enthusiastic encouragement. We are indebted to the faculty, staff, and students of the Luskin School of Public Affairs for their support, and thank Dean Frank Gilliam for financial help to pursue this inquiry through the Dean's Social Justice Grant. We wish to thank Waiyi Tse and Marsha Brown, who provided valuable support for the organization of the speaker series, and Yasmine Diaz, who helped us prepare mock-ups for possible book covers. We are very appreciative of the support of the Lewis Center and the Department of Urban Planning at UCLA, and would also like to acknowledge the editors and staff of the MIT Press, especially Robert Gottlieb, Clay Morgan, and Matthew Abbate, for their support and wise counsel. Last but not least, we acknowledge the excellent assistance of Alex Schaffer, our graduate student researcher, in copyediting these chapters, and our amazing students in the Informal City seminars. Our students have allowed us to share our thoughts and deepen the ideas presented in this book.

# Introduction

Vinit Mukhija and Anastasia Loukaitou-Sideris

A street vendor pushes a cart with ice popsicles down the sidewalk. Periodically she rings a little bell to make her presence known. At the street corner, some day laborers solicit work by raising "labor for hire" signs each time a motorist drives by. In the next block, passersby gaze at the array of clothing, tools, and toys displayed on the front lawn of a home. Some stop, check them out, talk with the homeowner who has organized the sale, and buy an item. In another block of single-family homes, an extended family has converted their garage into an unpermitted apartment to expand the available living space. Such informality, comprised of a multitude of activities taking place beyond the regulations of the state, is typically associated with cities of the developing world. But the neighborhood scene just described is not from Quito, Lagos, or Ahmedabad but from a city in the United States, one of the most industrialized, regulated, and economically developed regions of the planet.

There is ample evidence that informality is an integral and growing part of cities in the developed world. Partly a result of globalization, deregulation, and increasing immigration flows, partly a response to economic instability and increasing unemployment and underemployment, and partly because of the inadequacy of existing regulations to address the complexity and heterogeneity of contemporary multicultural living, informal activities have proliferated in U.S. cities and are clearly reflected in their built environment. In the United States and other regions of the affluent and developed world, however, informal urbanism is understudied and often misunderstood. Planners and policymakers usually see informal activities at best as unorganized, marginal enterprises that should be ignored, and at worst as unlawful activities that should be stopped and prosecuted. Similarly, the physical settings that host such activities—the sidewalks and street corners, front lawns, garage apartments, parking lots, community gardens, and taco trucks—are equally understudied, though they have become an increasingly visible and relevant part of the city for a number of social groups.

In this volume, we question the commonly held but narrow conception of informality as a space of marginality and irrelevance, and empirically and comprehensively examine the burgeoning informal urbanism of U.S. cities together with its settings. Our key objectives are to focus attention on the wide range of informal activities prevalent in U.S. cities; to theoretically elaborate on the nature and underlying logic of these activities, including the organizing strategies of the involved stakeholders; to explicitly argue for a spatial understanding of informality and its settings; and to discuss how planners, policymakers, urban designers, and communities can respond to the emerging landscape of opportunities and challenges.

In previous research we have examined various aspects of informality in the United States, particularly in the context of access to affordable housing (Mukhija and Monkkonen 2006, 2007), and in the conflicts over public spaces, including the typically overlooked sidewalks (Loukaitou-Sideris, Blumenberg, and Ehrenfeucht 2005; Loukaitou-Sideris and Ehrenfeucht 2009). As Southern California residents, we are at the epicenter of what many consider the "informal revolution" in the United States, and the scholarly work of a number of our friends and colleagues with ties to Los Angeles has influenced us. Among these scholars are Abel Valenzuela and Margaret Crawford, and both have contributed more than their chapters to this volume. Abel Valenzuela's important research on day laborers on urban street corners has highlighted the instability and exploitation often inherent in informal work, and the need for institutional arrangements that add stability, security, and fair compensation for workers (Valenzuela 2003; Valenzuela et al. 2006). Margaret Crawford's intellectual contribution to the idea of everyday urbanism (Crawford 2008) has highlighted the significance of the usually ignored everyday life, particularly informal, unplanned, and spontaneous activities, in the social life of cities. Ordinary, everyday life in Southern California is at the heart of Crawford's and Valenzuela's work and highlights the paradoxical need both to be wary of informality's precariousness and to celebrate its vibrancy.

To elaborate on such paradoxes of informality, we have adopted a case study approach in this volume. We include detailed studies of informality in U.S. cities, with examples from across the country including Los Angeles, Sacramento, Portland, Seattle, Phoenix, Kansas City, Atlantic City, and New York City. The chapters on informal actors (street vendors, day laborers, neighborhood residents, homeless denizens), their settings (food carts and sidewalks, garage apartments, front lawns, community gardens), and public policy responses (legalization, mediation, provisional guarantees, and so on) are original pieces contributed by some of the leading and emerging scholars of urban studies in the United States. The chapters focus both on the theoretical basis and nature of informality in U.S. cities and on the practical question of planning and policy responses, interventions, and regulations. Additionally, the chapters employ an explicit spatial lens and social justice frame in comprehending and addressing informality.

## The Need to Comprehend the Informal City in the United States

The conventional wisdom is that planning standards and requirements neatly structure, regulate, and define the built environment, economic activities, and housing opportunities in U.S. cities (Ben-Joseph and Szold 2005). Unregulated or informal activities, while widespread in developing countries, are not usually expected here. Most planners and policymakers assume that informal activities are either limited in scope, and therefore safe to ignore, or criminal in nature, and thus need to be opposed. A regulatory response to informal activities is often challenging. Surprisingly, the scholarly planning and design literature rarely focuses on informality despite its increasing presence. This volume departs from the conventional wisdom; but rather than romantically celebrating informality, our purpose is to explore more sophisticated ways to recognize, understand, and address it.

In addition to demonstrating through a wide range of case studies that informal activities are prevalent in U.S. cities, one of our main intentions is to reveal the complex nature of such informality. Collectively, the chapters in this volume show that informal activities are not rare but widespread and varied. Most of them are not criminal in nature, nor are they limited to instances of economic survival. And while informality has often been associated with immigrants, informal activities are pervasive and spread across different social groups, diverse urban settings, and different geographical regions of the country. The case studies show that formal and informal activities may at times conflict and at times overlap or depend on one another. The cases also help reveal the logic and underlying rationality of informality, and the structural linkages between informal activities and the larger political economy of cities and regulations.

Finally, our cases show the contradictory nature of informality, with both potential winners and losers associated with it.

An area of urban design where the idea of informality has struck a chord is the growing enthusiasm for pop-up or temporary installations and interventions in the built environment. In many ways, they are welcome insertions in the strict order and monotony of many U.S. cities. At times, however, there is a glib superficiality in the rising fervor for pop-ups. A serious examination of informal urbanism should not only be aesthetic in nature but must include a comprehensive understanding of the serious economic and equity issues underlying its activities. To address informality in sophisticated ways, and to recognize its implications for cities, their built environment, and spatial justice, it is necessary for planners and policymakers to have a more comprehensive understanding of such activities, and this volume attempts to provide that.

We also hope that the revelation of urban informality in U.S. cities will lead to a new openness on the part of American planners and policymakers to learning from the richer experiences of developing countries, which have a longer policy history of recognizing and responding to informal activities. Correspondingly, we also anticipate that a grounded and sophisticated understanding of informality in the affluent developed world will provide constructive insights for scholars and planners addressing informal activities in developing countries. It is likely that lessons from the informal city in the United States may put the conventional literature, which is focused on developing countries, in sharp relief and suggest new policy avenues for developing countries. Thus, research on informality can be an intellectual area of inquiry for the active exchange of ideas between scholars of developing and developed countries. In the next section, we briefly summarize our interpretation of the existing literature and place the contribution of this volume in its context.

## What Do We Know about Informal Activities?

Keith Hart, a British anthropologist, was the first to use the term "informal sector" to characterize unaccounted employment opportunities in Ghana (Hart 1973). Hart's concept built on Nobel prize-winner W. Arthur Lewis's (1954) work on economic development and the dual-sector model, as well as on previous research conducted by economic development experts in the United States (Averitt 1968) and by the International Labour Organization (ILO) in developing countries (ILO

1972; Moser 1978). Like earlier researchers, Hart distinguished self-employment in the informal sector from regular wage earning in the formal sector, which he described as rational, planned, organized, and regulated. Unlike most previous approaches, though, Hart stressed the potentially productive value of the informal sector, and questioned both the feasibility and desirability of conventional economic development policies focused entirely on shifting employment from the informal to the formal sector. He recognized that in most developing countries the informal sector was too big to be easily formalized, and that poor countries lacked the institutional capacity to adequately monitor informal activities. Moreover, as Hart noted, the informal sector provided the poorest and the neediest with much-needed opportunities to earn a livelihood.

At about the same time that Hart introduced the notion of the informal sector, Patricia and Louis Ferman used the term "irregular economy" to describe similar activities in the United States (1973). Just as Hart described unaccounted and unenumerated activities, the Fermans pointed to unmeasured and unmonitored economic activities in inner-city neighborhoods. While Hart and other dualists focused on structural economic issues to explain the informal sector, the Fermans identified race as the key structural social issue responsible for the irregular economy in U.S. cities. They argued that because of racial discrimination, inner-city residents were denied access to typical services and licenses to provide such services. Consequently, both suppliers and consumers of services such as plumbing, electrical repair, taxis, etc., resorted to the irregular economy. Where Hart noted that the informal sector included both illegitimate and legitimate activities, the Fermans similarly argued that while all the activities in the irregular economy were illegal, few were criminal (Ferman and Ferman 1973). Although the Fermans' scholarship did not gain as much attention as the economic development work of Hart, their insights on informal activities in the context of inner-city U.S. neighborhoods were noteworthy for their emphasis on race.

In the following years, Hart's concept of the informal sector gained currency as the conventional wisdom in international development planning (Peattie 1987), and was expanded beyond employment and livelihood to include forms of urban development, particularly shelter (Turner 1976, 1978). Consequently the broader term "informal economy"—sometimes called the "underground economy"—became more common (Peattie 1987; Portes, Castells, and Benton 1989). And while the concept of an informal economy is more readily associated with the developing world, some scholars have emphasized its presence and relevance in the developed world, particularly within the lives of minority and immigrant groups (Hondagneu-Sotelo 2001; Gowan 2009; Morales 2010; Venkatesh 2009; Ward 1999). This literature has grown with the increased scholarly emphasis on globalization and immigration from poor countries to rich (Sassen 1991; Valenzuela 2003).

Additionally, scholars have noted, on the one hand, the withdrawal and weakening of the welfare state—evidenced in the decline in social welfare spending, such as deinstitutionalization of facilities for the homeless (Hopper 2003)—and on the other hand its strengthening, particularly through more rigid regulations in the public sphere and stricter public space ordinances (Loukaitou-Sideris and Ehrenfeucht 2009). These simultaneous trends have contributed to the increase of informal activities and the ensuing academic literature on informality.

Informality in developed countries is not limited to the poor. For example, tax policy scholars of the underground economy in developed countries point out that informality, which they examine through a study of tax evasion, is common among the wealthy (Schneider 2011). Some estimates suggest that up to two trillion dollars of the U.S. economy goes unreported (Cebula and Feige 2011). As the scholarly understanding of informality has expanded, critics have also challenged the logic of economic dualism inherent in Hart's conceptualization (Bromley 1978; Moser 1978; Rakowski 1994). It is now generally accepted in the literature that although informal activities are unregulated by government institutions, informal and formal activities are linked to each other, integrated in the larger economy, and often overlapping, which makes it difficult to narrowly define informality (Peattie 1987; Portes, Castells, and Benton 1989; Portes and Sassen-Koob 1987; Sanyal 1988). This suggests that future scholarship should explain in detail the connections between informal and formal activities and the larger economic context, including the institutional framework of regulations (Peattie 1987).

How informality should be addressed is more contentious. We categorize three broad approaches in the literature. Scholars following a *structuralist approach* argue that informal activities are linked to the deepening of global capitalism, the abundant supply of labor, the weakening of government enforcement of regulations, and employers' interest in avoiding state regulations governing workplace conditions and wages (Bernhardt et al. 2008; Portes, Castells, and Benton 1989; Portes and Sassen-Koob 1987; Roy 2005; Roy and AlSayyad 2004; Sassen 1991;

Sassen-Koob 1989). They therefore emphasize the need for structural changes in the economy, a new social contract with laws protecting workers' rights, and better enforcement of regulations.

In contrast to the structuralist approach, scholars following a more *neoliberal approach* argue that the underlying problem is too much regulation, which increases the costs of doing business (De Soto 1989). They blame excessive state regulation and unrealistic standards for growth in the informal economy. They also emphasize human agency and its entrepreneurial spirit and argue for deregulation policies.

A third, *reformist approach* sees structural economic reasons for the existence of informality, does not expect informality to disappear, and advocates an active role for government and civil society in supporting and upgrading informal activities (Iskander and Lowe 2010; Peattie 1987; Piore and Sabel 1984; Sanyal 2008). The reformist approach recognizes the possibility of entrepreneurial activities and maintains the need for their support through state programs of training, credit, and marketing assistance. A substantial body of scholarly literature on informal housing policies in developing countries follows this approach (Mukhija 2003; Payne 1977; Peattie 1979). Peter Ward's (1999) seminal research on informal housing efforts in Texas also falls in this category. Ward noted the importance of the informal housing market in making home ownership accessible for poor families and argued for corresponding changes in land development regulations and housing finance rules. He also argued, however, for the strengthening of infrastructure requirements to address health and safety concerns in informal settlements. Broadly speaking, in addition to its emphasis on active government support, the reformist approach suggests the need for a careful balance between the strategic strengthening of some regulations and the loosening of certain policies. Our intellectual position on the policy responses to informality is closely aligned with the reformist approach.

Finally, although the scholarship criticizing the overwhelming emphasis on order in urban design is not typically regarded as literature on urban informality, we consider it relevant, as it emphasizes the importance of informal activities in cities. Scholars arguing for less emphasis on order and more space for unplanned activities in the built environment of cities include Jane Jacobs (1961), Margaret Crawford (Chase, Crawford, and Kaliski 2008), Simon Sadler (1998), Richard Sennett (2008), and Elizabeth Wilson (1991), among others. These scholars appreciate the contribution of informal, spontaneous, and everyday activities to the richness of urban environments and argue for a change in the conventional way in which cities are planned to accommodate and encourage such activities.

Similarly, we conclude that the prevalence of informality in cities suggests that conventional city planning and urban design regulations should be reevaluated, as they are failing to meet the complex needs of society. This, however, is not a call for a laissez-faire city. Certain informal practices may raise serious public health and safety concerns, and regulations are necessary to safeguard from such risk. Nonetheless, we do argue for different kinds of regulations. A passage from Richard Sennett's classic *The Uses of Disorder* (2008, 81–82) succinctly captures our position:

The process of change . . . could easily be misread, along what someone has called "slum-romantic" lines. I am not arguing that we return to the old ways of city life when times were hard; rather I have tried to show how the emergence of new city life in an era of abundance and prosperity has eclipsed something of the essence of urban life—its diversity and possibilities for complex experience. What needs to happen is a change in the peculiar institutions of affluent city life, in order to create new forms of complexity and new forms of diverse experience.

## Intellectual Approach and Organization

Drawing from the existing literature, our intellectual approach is defined by four key premises. First, instead of seeking to redefine informality, we simply follow the lead of Castells and Portes (1989) and operationalize informality in practice as activities unregulated by the state. Previous research suggests that robustly defining informality, which we consider an epistemological approach, is neither an easy exercise nor a particularly productive or useful endeavor. Such attempts invariably find it difficult to avoid following a dualist approach. Consequently, we are keener to explore and elaborate on the nature of informality, developing a clear and theoretically sophisticated understanding of its characteristics in U.S. cities. We consider this an ontological approach to comprehending informality.

Second, as urban planners and urban designers we are interested in the spatial characteristics of informality, the locations and physical attributes of settings hosting informal activities. One of our key premises is that the articulation and use of the built environment is likely to be important not only in understanding how informality functions, but also in developing responses to it. Thus, we expect this volume to make the case that, in addition to the conventional emphasis on legal responses, the spatial lens of physical planners and urban designers can also play an important role in interpreting and managing informality.

Third, we recognize and accept the contradictory or paradoxical nature of informality, including its ability to be either productive or exploitative. Although we are concerned about the possibility of informality hurting the poor, we also recognize the importance of informal strategies in helping the poor survive. Our intellectual strategy is to explore under what conditions the poor are more likely to benefit from informality, and what kinds of policy actions in response to informality might privilege the poor.

Fourth, we are driven by a policy-oriented interest. One of our primary motivations for this project is to explore the practical question of how planners, policymakers, and urban designers can better understand and respond to urban informality and its spatial settings.

Given these intellectual foundations, we have employed a case-study-based, inductive approach to understand the nature, complexity, and potential of informality in American cities. Each chapter responds to the following questions:

1. What is the nature of informality in U.S. cities, including its prevalence, characteristics, rationale, advantages and disadvantages, and sociospatial implications?

2. How should planners, policymakers, and urban designers address or regulate instances of urban informality?

3. How should conventional regulations and planning practices change in response to informality in U.S. cities?

Guided by these questions, our contributors focus on the nuanced details and corresponding policy and design implications of informality. In the following section, we share a brief preview of their case studies.

## The Case Studies

We have organized the chapters under the two rubrics of "Settings" and "Responses." The chapters in the first group emphasize the physical settings of informality in U.S. cities and explain how the informal actors organize such activities, including their spatial strategies for leveraging and adapting the built environment for informality. The chapters in the second part of the book elaborate on the planning and policy challenges of informality and focus on how planners, policymakers, urban designers, architects, and communities can respond to them. To a large extent, all chapters address both the spatial settings of informality and the strategies of key stakeholders in organizing and regulating it. Nonetheless, there is a difference of emphasis between the case studies in the two parts.

## Settings

Our first three chapters focus on informality in settings associated with domestic environments. Margaret Crawford focuses on the understudied American institution of garage sales, which homeowners regularly organize on their front lawns and in other private spaces. Estimates suggest that there are over 10 million garage sales every year. Crawford emphasizes the social interactions that characterize these exchanges, and how normally private spaces become public and open to strangers. As she notes, "Domestic qualities pervade the sale, turning interactions between strangers into a form of hospitality, with the seller as host or hostess and the buyer as guest." She also suggests that the collective wisdom of sellers and buyers provides clues for planners on how mixed land uses can help to expand the public life of residential neighborhoods and ordinary spaces.

Vinit Mukhija focuses on urban informal housing in the form of second units on single-family lots in Los Angeles. These units are colloquially known as garage apartments, granny flats, companion units, backyard cottages, and in-law units (among other names); Mukhija calls them "outlaw in-laws" because they are often unpermitted or illegal. Because second units are usually not formally allowed, their informal supply tends to meet the strong demand for such housing. Mukhija's research suggests that a substantial number of unpermitted second units exist in Los Angeles; they are distributed all over the city, not just in poor neighborhoods; and they include units with very good housing conditions. He argues that these insights indicate the need for upgrading and legalization strategies, and for changes in the conventional regulation and zoning of single-family housing.

The chapter by Peter Ward explains how informality is a rational response to housing needs and broader market and institutional conditions. His case study focuses on self-help housing efforts in so-called "colonias" of the U.S.-Mexico border region and other "informal homestead subdivisions" found in the hinterland of many U.S. cities. Ward shows that informal housing is rational and dynamic but not temporary or aberrational, and needs appropriate policy responses. Informality, he suggests, often exists because of structural conditions of poverty, the lack of formal market avenues, and innovative workarounds by stakeholders.

He argues, however, against a laissez-faire approach and notes the need for the state to be involved in reducing the risks faced by the poor who live in these colonias.

The next two chapters focus on less studied urban public spaces. Jeffrey Hou's chapter on community gardens examines their growing popular appeal but typically provisional institutional support, characterized by temporary and precarious land agreements. He draws lessons from Seattle, one of the few cities to adopt community gardens as an integral part of its formal open space network. Hou shows how informal social practices continue to thrive in Seattle's community gardens thanks not only to grassroots labor but also to institutional support from the city's administration and local nonprofits. He argues that Seattle's community gardens demonstrate the potential for such successful partnerships for placemaking in contemporary cities.

Anastasia Loukaitou-Sideris and Renia Ehrenfeucht's chapter focuses on the informal property rights exercised on urban sidewalks by abutting property owners and tenants, whose actions may have both positive and negative consequences for other sidewalk users. The authors use evidence from the four largest cities in California—Los Angeles, San Diego, San Jose, and San Francisco—to show how the expectations of abutters, due to their physical proximity to sidewalks, are exacerbated by formal obligations of maintenance and surveillance imposed by cities, and how sidewalk property claims are at times regularized as formal property rights. Loukaitou-Sideris and Ehrenfeucht emphasize the need for creative urban design and policy that can accommodate the needs of abutting property owners and sidewalk users, as well as for caution in privatizing rights to the public realm.

The following two chapters focus on the creative but unsanctioned and informal use of various spatial settings in cities. Thus, Nabil Kamel in his case study of suburban Phoenix focuses on unsanctioned everyday practices, which he describes as placemaking "tactics." This grassroots humanizing of an otherwise harsh built environment, according to Kamel, is driven by the need both for economic survival and human belonging. Examples include yard sales, vending in public spaces, street basketball courts, impromptu skateboard parks, community gardens, and home improvements and additions. Kamel argues that these informal tactics highlight the shortcomings of formal regulatory visions, suggesting that the conventional built environment and land use regulations are inadequate and poorly designed to respond to the cultural needs and diversity of contemporary cities.

The final case study of the first part focuses on the settings of homelessness in Atlantic City. Jacob Avery uses ethnography to examine the "chronically unhoused" in this city, building on Mitchell Duneier's (1999) understanding of urban spaces as "sustaining habitats." Avery identifies the sociospatial attributes of Atlantic City settings that allow homeless denizens to creatively hustle and make money, locate sleeping spots in bus terminals, stairwells, and sidewalks, and find decent food through the courtesy of tourists. Atlantic City thus provides the basics of food, shelter, and social life for marginal citizens to overcome their material hardships. As Avery notes, this may also enable severe chemical addictions among the unhoused inhabitants.

## Responses

The first chapter in this part also focuses on homelessness in U.S. cities, but with more emphasis on its regulatory framework. Renia Ehrenfeucht and Anastasia Loukaitou-Sideris discuss the "irreconcilable tension" between dwelling in public and conventional regulations, arguing that cities must do more for the homeless. Planners often support spatially decentralized approaches as a strategy to address undesirable individuals or activities. Ehrenfeucht and Loukaitou-Sideris, however, disagree with Robert Ellickson's (1996) well-known recommendation to decentralize decisions regarding homelessness by allowing neighborhoods to accommodate or ban dwelling in public based on resident preferences. They are concerned that the rights of homeless individuals and other minority groups may be ignored in decentralized decision-making, and argue for more active and accommodating responses from cities. They highlight efforts in Seattle to provide shower and laundry facilities for the needy, and in Portland to increase access to public restrooms, as steps in the right direction.

Michael Rios's chapter is based on an urban design studio he organized for his students in the neighborhood of South Sacramento and explores how informality can inform urban planning practice. Many scholars of informality worry that planning mostly focuses on questions of normative order and aesthetics in the city. The conventional wisdom is that an emphasis on aesthetics hurts the poor. Rios, however, argues that planners must actively engage with the issue of aesthetics because it is an important political issue. He suggests that understanding how minority groups use the city, particularly through informal practices, can provide lessons for progressive urban design and planning responses.

The case study by Matt Covert and Alfonso Morales examines the typically informal activity of urban agriculture as distinct from domestic gardening and commercial agriculture. They document a successful social movement that reformed land use regulations in Kansas City, Missouri, to allow urban agriculture and recognize the legitimacy and identity of small-scale urban farmers. The chapter shows how framing the narrative about informality can play an important role in creating support for it, and also how negotiation and compromise can help reduce fears about informality. It also discusses the constructive role local government planners can play in offering advice, sharing information, and making discretionary decisions in support of informal activities.

The following three chapters focus on street vendors and regulatory responses in Los Angeles, New York, and Portland respectively. Mark Vallianatos examines street food in Los Angeles in the context of the rise of the city's now famous gourmet food trucks. Los Angeles is one of the few cities in the United States where sidewalk vending is illegal, although, as Vallianatos notes, it is "forbidden but ubiquitous." His research finds that the majority of street vendors favor formalization and are interested in paying for vending permits. Vallianatos argues that street vending should be legalized and that policymakers should use the opportunity to create incentives for vendors to increase access to healthy food in inner-city neighborhoods.

Gregg Kettles's legal analysis focuses on street vending in New York City based on an examination of over 127,000 citations of street vendors over a five-year period. Scholars typically distrust police power and discretion in law enforcement and conventionally argue for clear, or "crystal," laws rather than "muddy" laws open to subjective interpretation. Kettles, however, finds that in New York the overwhelming majority of citations are for crystal laws that vendors find impossible to follow. Moreover, an overwhelming majority of citations are for spatial laws, dealing with location restrictions, rather than for health laws dealing with food safety. He concludes that regulatory responses may not need to be clearer but should be less burdensome on street vendors.

Ginny Browne, Will Dominie, and Kate Mayerson share the case study of innovative street vending and regulatory workarounds involving food carts in Portland, Oregon. They describe how the vendors take advantage of land use regulations that allow mobile food carts on private lots, as long as they have wheels and in theory can move. In addition to showing the difficulty in defining formal and informal

activities, this case study illustrates how food carts have helped transform downtown Portland's parking lots into pedestrian-friendly areas
with cafés and retail activities. The authors also emphasize the positive
role played by local planners in fostering opportunities for economic
development through the food carts, mediating conflicts, and educating
the food cart vendors about the regulations, thus empowering them to
work around the restrictions.

Abel Valenzuela's case study focuses on informal day laborers, who
have become ubiquitous in many U.S. cities. Valenzuela describes two
civil-society-based responses that have emerged in recent years to improve
the precarious working conditions of day laborers. First, worker centers,
most of which are organized by community-based organizations (CBOs),
help day laborers in wage setting, job allocation, conflict resolution,
training, and education. These worker centers have succeeded in creating
an informal system of regulation to address some of the worst violations
in the day labor market. Second, many of the CBOs managing worker
centers have collaborated to form a national network, which is advocating for immigration reform with the support of organized labor. Valenzuela praises these innovative responses, but also notes their limitations
and calls for more sustained efforts from the federal government to
protect day laborers' rights.

The final case study by Donald Shoup focuses on informal parking
practices. Although there is no academic literature on informal parking,
Shoup shows that it is a common practice. For example, dispersed informal parking on private lots can help meet the heavy parking demand for
regular but infrequent events like big sporting events in college towns
and in neighborhoods near college sports venues. Not all informal
parking, however, is benign. Shoup is particularly critical of illegal
parking on sidewalks through "apron parking," which impedes public
movement, particularly for wheelchair users. He argues that market-
based responses with curb parking can help address the demand for
parking spaces and curtail the practice of apron parking. Shoup also
suggests that the growing use of shared cars, which is inspired by informal social practices of sharing, can help reduce the need for private cars
and parking spaces.

Collectively, the chapters that follow sketch the contours of informality and informal urbanism in U.S. cities. And while the book does
not cover all settings of urban informality or offer all-encompassing
recipes to address every issue or challenge, we hope that the variety of
contexts, scales, and responses presented in the case studies takes the

first step toward acknowledging, understanding, and responding to the informal city.

## References

Averitt, Robert T. 1968. *The Dual Economy: The Dynamics of American Industry Structure*. New York: W. W. Norton.

Ben-Joseph, Eran, and Terry S. Szold, eds. 2005. *Regulating Place: Standards and the Shaping of Urban America*. New York: Routledge.

Bernhardt, Annette, Heather Boushey, Laura Dresser, and Chris Tilly. 2008. *The Gloves-Off Economy: Workplace Standards at the Bottom of America's Labor Market*. Champaign, IL: Labor and Employment Relations Association.

Bromley, Ray. 1978. "Introduction—The Urban Informal Sector: Why Is It Worth Discussing?" *World Development* 2 (9/10):1034–1035.

Castells, Manuel, and Alejandro Portes. 1989. "World Underneath: The Origins, Dynamics, and Effects of the Informal Economy." In Portes, Castells, and Benton 1989: 11–37.

Cebula, Richard, and Edgar L. Feige. 2011. "America's Underground Economy: Measuring the Size, Growth and Determinants of Income Tax Evasion in the U.S." MPRA Paper No. 29672. Munich Personal RePEc Archive.

Chase, John L., Margaret Crawford, and John Kaliski, eds. 2008. *Everyday Urbanism*. New York: Monacelli Press.

Crawford, Margaret. 2008. "Introduction, and Preface: The Current State of Everyday Urbanism." In Chase, Crawford, and Kaliski 2008: 6–15.

De Soto, Hernando. 1989. *The Other Path: The Invisible Revolution in the Third World*. New York: Harper and Row.

Duneier, Mitchell. 1999. *Sidewalk*. New York: Farrar, Straus and Giroux.

Ellickson, Robert. 1996. "Controlling Chronic Misconduct in City Spaces: Of Panhandlers, Skid Rows, and Public-Space Zoning." *Yale Law Journal* 105 (5):1165–1248.

Ferman, Patricia R., and Louis A. Ferman. 1973. "The Structural Underpinnings of the Irregular Economy." *Poverty and Human Resources Abstracts* 8 (1):3–17.

Gowan, Teresa. 2009. "New Hobos or Neoromantic Fantasy? Urban Ethnography beyond the Neoliberal Disconnect." *Qualitative Sociology* 32 (3):231–257.

Hart, Keith. 1973. "Informal Income Opportunities and Urban Employment in Ghana." *Journal of Modern African Studies* 11 (1):61–89.

Hondagneu-Sotelo, Pierrette. 2001. *Domestica: Immigrant Workers Cleaning and Caring in the Shadow of Affluence*. Berkeley: University of California Press.

Hopper, Kim. 2003. *Reckoning with Homelessness*. Ithaca: Cornell University Press.

ILO (International Labour Organization). 1972. *Employment, Income and Inequality: A Strategy for Increasing Productive Employment in Kenya.* Geneva: International Labour Office.

Iskander, Natasha, and Nichola Lowe. 2010. "Hidden Talent: Tacit Skill Formation and Labor Market Incorporation of Latino Immigrants in the United States." *Journal of Planning Education and Research* 30 (1):132–146.

Jacobs, Jane. 1961. *The Death and Life of Great American Cities.* New York: Vintage Books.

Lewis, W. Arthur. 1954. "Economic Development with Unlimited Supplies of Labour." *Manchester School* 22 (2):139–191.

Loukaitou-Sideris, Anastasia, Evelyn Blumenberg, and Renia Ehrenfeucht. 2005. "Sidewalk Democracy: Municipalities and the Regulation of Public Space." In Ben-Joseph and Szold 2005: 141–166.

Loukaitou-Sideris, Anastasia, and Renia Ehrenfeucht. 2009. *Sidewalks: Conflict and Negotiation over Public Space.* Cambridge, MA: MIT Press.

Morales, Alfonso. 2010. "Planning and the Self-Organization of Marketplaces." *Journal of Planning Education and Research* 30 (2):182–197.

Moser, Caroline. 1978. "Informal Sector or Petty Commodity Production: Dualism or Dependence in Urban Development?" *World Development* 6 (9/10):1041–1064.

Mukhija, Vinit. 2003. *Squatters as Developers? Slum Redevelopment in Mumbai.* Aldershot, England: Ashgate.

Mukhija, Vinit, and Paavo Monkkonen. 2006. "Federal Colonias Policy in California: Too Broad and Too Narrow." *Housing Policy Debate* 17 (4):755–780.

Mukhija, Vinit, and Paavo Monkkonen. 2007. "What's in a Name? A Critique of Colonias in the United States." *International Journal of Urban and Regional Research* 31 (2):475–488.

Payne, Geoffrey. 1977. *Urban Housing in the Third World.* London: L. Hill; Boston: Routledge and K. Paul.

Peattie, Lisa. 1979. "Housing Policy in Developing Countries: Two Puzzles." *World Development* 7 (11–12):1017–1022.

Peattie, Lisa. 1987. "An Idea in Good Currency and How It Grew: The Informal Sector." *World Development* 15 (7):147–158.

Piore, Michael, and Charles Sabel. 1984. *The Second Industrial Divide.* New York: Basic Books.

Portes, Alejandro, Manuel Castells, and Lauren Benton, eds. 1989. *The Informal Economy: Studies in Advanced and Less Developed Countries.* Baltimore: Johns Hopkins University Press.

Portes, Alejandro, and Saskia Sassen-Koob. 1987. "Making It Underground: Comparative Material on the Informal Sector in Western Market Economies." *American Journal of Sociology* 93 (1):30–61.

Rakowski, Cathy. 1994. "Convergence and Divergence in the Informal Sector Debate: A Focus on Latin America, 1984–92." *World Development* 22 (4):501–516.

Roy, Ananya. 2005. "Urban Informality: Toward an Epistemology of Planning." *Journal of the American Planning Association* 71 (2):147–158.

Roy, Ananya, and Nezar AlSayyad. 2004. *Urban Informality: Transnational Perspectives from the Middle East, Latin America, and South Asia.* Lanham, MD: Lexington Books.

Sadler, Simon. 1998. *The Situationist City.* Cambridge, MA: MIT Press.

Sanyal, Bishwapriya. 1988. "The Urban Informal Sector Revisited: Some Notes on the Relevance of the Concept in the 1980s." *Third World Planning Review* 10 (1):65–83.

Sanyal, Bishwapriya. 2008. "What Is New in Planning?" *International Planning Studies* 13 (2):151–160.

Sassen, Saskia. 1991. *The Global City: New York, Tokyo, London.* Princeton: Princeton University Press.

Sassen-Koob, Saskia. 1989. "New York City's Informal Economy." In Portes, Castells, and Benton 1989: 60–77.

Schneider, Friedrich. 2011. "The Shadow Economy and Shadow Economy Labor Force: What Do We (Not) Know?" IZA Discussion Paper No. 5769, Institute for the Study of Labor (IZA), Bonn, Germany.

Sennett, Richard. 2008. *The Uses of Disorder: Personal Identity and City Life.* New Haven: Yale University Press.

Turner, John. 1976. *Housing by People: Towards Autonomy in Building Environments.* New York: Pantheon Books.

Turner, John. 1978. "Housing in Three Dimensions: Terms of Reference for the Housing Question Redefined." *World Development* 6 (9–10):1135–1145.

Valenzuela, Abel. 2003. "Day Labor Work." *Annual Review of Sociology* 29 (1):307–333.

Valenzuela, Abel, Nik Theodore, Edwin Melendez, and Ana L. Gonzalez. 2006. *On the Corner: Day Labor in the United States.* Los Angeles: UCLA Center for the Study of Urban Poverty.

Venkatesh, Sudhir Alladi. 2009. *Off the Books: The Underground Economy of the Urban Poor.* Cambridge, MA: Harvard University Press.

Ward, Peter M. 1999. *Colonias and Public Policy in Texas and Mexico: Urbanization by Stealth.* Austin: University of Texas Press.

Wilson, Elizabeth. 1991. *The Sphinx in the City: Urban Life, the Control of Disorder, and Women.* London: Virago.

# Part I

## Settings

# 1

## The Garage Sale as Informal Economy and Transformative Urbanism

Margaret Crawford

On any given weekend, somewhere in the United States, someone is preparing for a garage sale. Collecting and sorting used possessions and unwanted household items from their basements, garages, attics, and closets, they evaluate and price them before displaying them on their lawn, driveway, porch, or front steps. Potential buyers stop to look, just passing by or attracted by flyers posted across the neighborhood or notices on Craigslist or in specialized advertising publications such as the *Pennysaver* (figure 1.1). Inspecting and discussing the goods, buyers come and go. Many will bargain over already low prices. By the end of the day, depending on what hasn't been sold, the seller either repacks the leftover items to return to storage or dumps them in the trash.

This familiar scene is played out thousands of times, weekend after weekend, across the country, according to a rhythm of climate and events. In Southern California, the mild climate and absence of rain make garage sales a year-round activity. In other places, spring cleaning and warm weather mark the beginning of a selling season that ends with autumn rains. In college towns, yard sales cluster at the beginning and end of the academic year. In exceptional circumstances, entire neighborhoods, towns, or even multiple states, such as those along the 630-mile-long Highway 127 corridor (from Michigan to Alabama), hold collective garage sales on designated days each year (DeCaro 2000).

These sales are one of the most ubiquitous yet little-studied dimensions of the informal economy. Although they probably number in the millions each year, no public or private entity has taken the trouble to count them. The few estimates that exist, from the 1980s, claim that nationally there are more than 10 million garage sales every year, generating more than a billion dollars in revenue (Herrmann and Soiffer 1984).[1] Since the numbers of sales rise and fall with the economy, these numbers are almost certainly higher now. In some places, the garage sale

**Figure 1.1**
Sign advertising garage sale. Photo credit: Margaret Crawford.

economy involves enormous numbers of people as buyers and sellers. A
1996 survey in Southern California found that more than half the population had attended a garage sale in the previous year (Curtiss 1992;
O'Reilly et al. 1984). Yet, in spite of their pervasive presence, garage sales
are economically invisible. Their very ordinariness allows them to exist
largely under the radar as a form of commercial exchange that takes
place outside of the formal economy and is largely unrecorded by official
economic statistics. Sellers are not required to obtain business licenses
or pay sales tax, and sales are conducted on an all-cash basis. Although
some municipalities attempt to control garage sales by limiting the
number of sales per year and requiring permits, these rules are widely
disregarded and rarely enforced.

Once examined, however, garage sales challenge a surprising number
of economic, social, and spatial conventions. Hidden within ostensibly
commercial exchanges are alternative economies: recycling, which allows
used objects to acquire a second life, and gifting, a form of generosity
that establishes social bonds between strangers. The objects for sale,
although often mass-produced commodities, also have social meanings.

They are biographies acquired through use that can be shared between seller and buyer. Held in ordinary settings such as front yards and driveways, the sales invert these areas' usual meanings, making spaces that are normally private extremely public and open to anyone. These reversals of daily life, like carnival customs that turn the world upside down, are officially tolerated and even celebrated when they occur within a limited time period. Once they become more permanent, they threaten the spatial categories that structure American cities. This chapter argues that, once understood, the garage sale has the potential to reshape urban values and urban space.

My own interest in garage sale urbanism began in Los Angeles during the early 1990s, a period of economic recession. Doing research in East Los Angeles, a largely Mexican area, I discovered many creative uses of front yards and driveways to sell both new and used items (Crawford 1994). At the same time, the expanding number of continuous garage sales in affluent Beverly Hills prompted the city to regulate them. This intriguing coincidence suggested that garage sales might have a broad urban and economic significance, leading me to investigate further. Since then, I have attended dozens of garage sales all over Los Angeles and in Cambridge, Massachusetts, as a participant-observer and interviewer of both sellers and buyers. The interviews were conducted informally, as casual conversations without set questions. I also held several garage sales myself, a convenient way to conduct fieldwork and get rid of excess household possessions at the same time!

## Garage Sale Economics

In terms of the official economy, the garage sale is a small part of an extensive network of recycling. Unlike the best-known forms of recycling, which transform existing items into forms that can be reused, and which usually involve complex manufacturing processes, garage sales simply recirculate existing goods. They constitute the amateur end of a commercial network of for-profit and nonprofit resellers of clothing, books, and household goods and equipment that range from charity thrift stores like Goodwill, to flea market and swap-meet vendors, to high-end "vintage" and antique stores. Within this system, depending on their perceived value, cast-off items can move up or down a commodity chain that extends from throwaways, one step above garbage, to still functional items, to "collectibles" and valuable antiques. As used items move up the value chain, quality replaces quantity. Out of the millions of used items sold every year, only a very small number reach these rarefied settings. Nonetheless, the possibility of adding value generates opportunities for small-scale entrepreneurship like that of the Afghan refugees depicted in the novel *The Kite Runner*, who scour suburban California garage sales for items to resell at flea markets.

Unlike garage sales, these diverse outlets all operate in an official commercial context that must conform to state and local requirements for registration and taxation. The state of California, for example, requires even the most casual flea market vendor to register and declare sales (California State Board of Equalization 2010). Swap-meet operators often establish flat rate payments to the city in lieu of taxing individual sellers (Kaliski interview). In recent years, the Internet has offered new outlets for selling used goods. Craigslist functions as digital classified advertisements, accessible to an extremely broad regional audience. On eBay, sellers market individual items, often collected in online "stores" analogous to stalls at a flea market. So far, with the exception of occasional announcements on Craigslist, the Internet has not penetrated the garage sale. Although electronic marketplaces are easily accessible, they still require computers, advance planning, official registration, photographs, and extensive follow-up for sales.

In contrast, the garage sale has few barriers to entry. All you need is a physical space, usually but not always in front of your residence, and goods to sell.[2] It is a strictly amateur enterprise, unlike tag sales (sales of the entire contents of a house) or estate sales, both of which are typically operated by paid dealers. Avoiding the selectivity and ordering involved in higher-level reselling, most garage sales offer a random and heterogeneous collection of items, brought together by the accident of ownership and the owner's decision that they are no longer needed. These objects are offered at low prices, which can become even lower during the sale through bargaining ("haggling" in garage sale parlance) or the seller's desire to get rid of the goods. The sale is usually bound by strict temporal limits, typically a day or a weekend, although some may be quasi-permanent. Although it is modeled after a store, involving advertisements, goods priced and arranged for sale, and payment expected in cash or check, all profits represent a windfall, since the items for sale have already been bought, paid for, and used.[3]

### Commodities or Gifts?

Although the garage sale is explicitly based on commercial transactions, the flexibility of pricing and the nature of the objects produce a continuum between purchasing a commodity and receiving a gift. Here, use value frequently trumps exchange value, or the two are inextricably mixed. The practice of garage sale sellers simply giving away sale items to shoppers is widespread. "Free boxes," filled with items that anyone can take away with no payment expected, are common (Herrmann 1997: 910). In addition, Gretchen Herrmann argues that since garage sale prices are often so low—"giveaway prices"—the items are quasi or partial gifts. In these cases, the payment of money is primarily symbolic, a way of saving face for the buyer by making the transaction formally a commercial exchange rather than a charity handout, allowing the buyer to retain a sense of dignity and not feel indebted. Both parties maintain the commercial facade while actually participating in a gift economy (Herrmann 1997). Spontaneous gifting or lowering prices to nominal amounts often occurs in garage sales, particularly during the last hours of a sale. Typically, these gifts are the result of personal exchanges, such as conversations where shoppers reveal that they need or want specific items.

My fieldwork garnered numerous examples of giveaways or sales at minimal amounts to buyers who expressed a need or a purpose for different items. For example, one seller lowered the price of an entire bolt of fabric to one dollar for a woman who said she wanted to make curtains with it. Conversely, sellers may project these desires on shoppers. As a child, my daughter was the recipient of many unsolicited garage sale gifts, typically offered by the seller with a personal statement such as "I loved this when I was your age" or "you look like you would enjoy this." The age difference eliminated the need for the face-saving fiction of commerce. These gifting practices, unlike those analyzed by anthropologists such as Mauss (1925) or Sahlins (1972), do not require reciprocity; objects are freely given to strangers with no expectation of obligation. Another practice, typical of regular shoppers at garage sales, is to buy items not for themselves but as gifts for friends or family. Such purchases, based both on their evaluation of the worth of various items for sale and their knowledge of what others can use, mix the two economies. Recognizing a bargain, they buy it and then pass it on as a gift to someone they think can use it.

## History of the Garage Sale

In contrast to many informal practices that are modern versions of age-old activities, garage sales are a recent invention. Before the 1960s, used items, particularly clothing "hand-me-downs," were passed on through kinship and friendship networks. Other items were donated to charitable organizations that held rummage sales to raise funds. The origin of the garage sale lies at the intersection of two contradictory economic dynamics. During the affluent 1960s, people began to acquire far more possessions than in previous times, eventually accumulating enough items to start divesting themselves of some of them. As the name garage or yard sale suggests, this was closely associated with the suburban single-family house, where the garage serves as a repository of unused items, and the front yard is rarely used. Similarly, the types of goods sold represent the consumption patterns of middle-class suburban households, the kind of mass-produced items bought in increasing quantities beginning in the late 1950s. If the prosperity of the 1960s created the goods and habits of consumption, the economic crisis of the 1970s produced the incentive to sell them. As the incomes and purchasing power of households declined, the number of garage sales increased. Reduced spending power affected both sellers, who realized additional money for their unused possessions, as well as buyers, who were able to purchase goods for much less than their original cost.

During the 1960s, in a changed cultural context, used objects also acquired a cult value. As some young people attempted to live off the leftovers of consumer society, they valorized concepts of recycling and reuse. No longer expressive of poverty or charity, used items acquired new and positive associations. In the 1970s, as the economy contracted and the counterculture aged, these concepts filtered down into the society at large. Greater ecological awareness as well as an increasing aesthetic appreciation of "vintage" and retro styles accompanied a generalized loss of faith in progress, with its promise of an infinitely expanding economy and profusion of new and better products. Similarly, the spread of a camp sensibility, previously confined to gay subcultures, produced a new appreciation for a wide array of kitsch products. Aficionados revalorized many categories of used items, including clothing (such as Hawaiian shirts) or household items (such as Fiestaware). These selected items became collectibles, creating a secondary market for garage sale purchases. Even the readymades and junk incorporated into sculpture and collages in 1960s art supported this new ethos of recycling (Herrmann and Soiffer 1984). By the 1980s, the garage sale was an established part of mainstream American life.

### Representing

In spite of such widespread acceptance, garage sales rarely appear in literature and art. When they do, they are largely represented in reductive terms, as convenient symbols of loss and abjection. In Terry MacMillan's novel *Waiting to Exhale*, the betrayed wife scatters her husband's expensive and valued possessions on the lawn, selling them for insultingly low prices. One of Raymond Carver's most famous short stories, "Why Don't You Dance," describes a disconcerting encounter between a single man, who places all of his furniture and household goods on the front lawn, and a young couple interested in buying them. Carver's minimalist prose does not reveal the background or the outcome of this exchange, but compellingly conveys the bleakness and desperation contained in apparently ordinary circumstances. In contrast, photographers focus on objects rather than people. Adam Bartos's book *Garage Sale* (which includes the text of Carver's story) employs detailed close-ups that transform the random juxtapositions of objects for sale into surreal collages. Karen Geiger's photographs of Los Angeles garage sales focus on the unexpected beauty of carefully arranged items disposed in a wide variety of front yards, illuminating the diversity of the city.

The artist who has explored the garage sale most fully is the installation and performance artist Martha Rosler. The garage sale functions as a key theme in her work, beginning with her original *Monumental Garage Sale* of 1973, for which she installed a complete garage sale, with the typical array of secondhand goods, records, books, clothes, toys, costume jewelry, and personal letters and mementos in an art gallery at University of California, San Diego, allowing visitors to actually purchase the items. Since then, Rosler has staged other garage sales, the most recent at the Museum of Modern Art in New York. In each city, she solicits used items from the public and the museum. Advertised as both a garage sale and an art event, it exists on two levels: one questions the art object by bringing the everyday into the "art" space of the gallery; the other highlights the multiple and contradictory meanings contained in such an ordinary event.

An audiotape that ran during a Rosler installation asked, "What is the value of a thing? What makes me want it? I paid money for these things—is there a chance to recuperate some of my investment by selling them to you? . . . Why not give it all away? . . . [A quote from Marx:] 'A commodity appears, at first sight, a very trivial thing, and easily understood. Its analysis shows that it is, in reality, a very queer thing . . . in it the social character of a person's labor . . .' She wonders, is it sacrilege to sell the shoes her baby wore? . . . She wonders . . . Will you judge me by the things I am selling?" (Rosler 1999). In a subsequent interview, Rosler described the multiple "masquerades" sellers and buyers can assume: "homeowner as recycler, as idiot, as predator, as business-wise householder, as neighbor, as parent of rapidly growing children, as empty nester simplifying the home. The buyer is not a sucker but a smart deal maker, a connoisseur with secret knowledge, a neighbor helping out" (Rosler 2002).

## The Social Life of the Garage Sale

Rosler's installations underline the garage sale's paradoxical nature: these are public events that take place in private, social events masquerading as a commercial activity as well as its opposite. They simultaneously celebrate and undermine consumption, and are economic exchanges where meaning and significance change hands along with used goods. However, Rosler's transposition of the garage sale from the front yard to the art gallery, if necessary to challenge the conventions of the art world, eliminates a central constituent of its meaning: the domestic setting. Taking place in a garage, driveway, carport, front yard, or porch,[4] whether of the single-family house or of an apartment complex, the sale is located in the private space of the individual, the family, or the household. Yet for the duration of the sale, this private space becomes public. Although organized by a private individual, garage sales are public events, open to all. Flyers posted around the neighborhood, notices on Craigslist, or newspaper ads announcing the sale constitute an open invitation for anyone to attend, testifying to their public nature. Interaction between strangers or partial strangers is an accepted part of the event; in the numerous accounts of garage sales I found, none mentioned anyone being turned away. It is likely that the sale's presumption of commercial exchange mandates, at the very least, politeness. Although social markers such as gender, race, and ethnicity clearly affect transactions, these social distinctions are muted by what Herrmann (1997: 920) identifies as a "garage sale ethos" that includes a generalized friendliness and an overall egalitarian style of exchange.

Such public uses can temporarily transform urban space. In many places, garage sale shopping mixes classes, races, and ethnicities in surprising ways, often crossing the prevailing boundaries of residential segregation. There is evidence that poor people often travel to affluent areas to find garage sales, believing that the quality of the merchandise offered there is higher and the seller's need to make a profit lower than in their own neighborhood (Herrmann 1996, 2006a). In dispersed, car-oriented cities like Los Angeles, shoppers often drive long distances to search for sales. Taking advantage of this, some well-located neighborhoods have established themselves as the equivalent of garage sale strips or malls, with multiple individual sales lining the streets, a magnet for bargain hunters from across the city. These "chance encounters" produce a casual form of social mixing, bringing people together who would rarely meet under normal circumstances.

The sellers' residence as the site of the sale imbues the sellers and their goods with a personal quality. The sellers' place in society is approximately identified by the size, location, and appearance of their house. This specific location establishes their legitimacy, which extends to the provenance of the goods for sale, making them more acceptable to buyers. Domestic qualities pervade the sale, turning interactions between strangers into a form of hospitality, with the seller as host or hostess and the buyer as guest. This makes interaction far more intimate and friendly than in conventional shopping. Mixing the commercial and domestic alters the function and meaning of the front lawn or driveway, transforming it into a liminal space. For a few hours or days, the sale inverts the usual meaning of the house, making what was the private space of the front lawn into a site of public display for items that recently resided in the most private places of the house, the insides of closets and drawers or basements and attics. Arranged on the lawn or driveway, they become available to be inspected or bought by any passing stranger. In many respects, this is an everyday version of "defamiliarization," the same modernist artistic strategy used by Martha Rosler in her garage sales. Presenting something common in an unfamiliar way, the garage sale renders it strange and thus open to new interpretations. At the same time, the objects create what I call "refamiliarization," a process that domesticates spaces like the front lawn that are usually empty and largely symbolic.

## Sellers and Buyers

Both strange and familiar, the domestic setting structures highly personal interactions between buyers and sellers. The motives of both sellers and buyers are extremely varied. Although it would be easier and in many cases more financially remunerative to donate cast-offs to a charitable organization for a tax deduction, sellers often choose to have a garage sale because they want to see where their possessions are going (Herrmann 1997). A man clearing out items from his earlier years said, "it will be fun to see the people who get the things and can actually use

them" (Herrmann 1997: 919). Sellers offer their no-longer-needed possessions for sale for different reasons. As MacMillan and Carver suggest,
this can be a significant moment in the passage of lives, such as death,
divorce, children leaving home, or moving. But the most common reason
is housecleaning, getting rid of unwanted and unneeded possessions,
whose accumulation has become a very real problem for millions of
middle-class American families (Leu 2012).[5] The proliferation of inexpensive goods from China in recent years has added to domestic inventories. Cleaning usually occurs in regular cycles, accounting for the
intensity of sales during the spring season. Others hold garage sales for
the revenue, including people who have a pressing need for money as the
result of the loss of a job or pressing bills. The number of garage sales
increases significantly in times of economic recession and in regions
undergoing economic crises. In rural areas, poor people often use sales
to supplement the income of marginal occupations. At the far end of
the continuum is the perpetual garage sale, held so often that it is necessary to replenish it with new or used merchandise. A largely commercial
enterprise, it is more like a domestic store than an occasional event
(Herrmann and Soiffer 1984).

Most buyers are looking for bargains, useful or interesting items at
low prices. The large cost differential between a new item purchased in
a store and a used one bought at a garage sale produces considerable
savings for people who want or need to economize, particularly on items
like children's clothing and household goods. In some cases this is driven
by economic necessity, a helpful survival strategy for low-income households. Others are driven by political or ecological ideologies or cultural
styles that reject mainstream consumerism for recycling. Students and
other young mobile populations use garage sales as a low-cost method
of furnishing temporary households, often reselling their household items
at another garage sale before moving again.

Not all bargain hunters shop from necessity; many middle-class and
even upper-class people frequent garage sales for entertainment and what
one magazine called "the joy of cheap finds," the pleasure of discovering
unexpected and, occasionally, valuable items. For some, garage sale shopping is a hobby or even an obsession.[6] Every weekend, Rocky Behr, the
owner of the Pasadena shop The Folk Tree, wakes up early to visit garage
sales. Her professional eye has located amazing finds, for example a
two-dollar pot worth 1,000 dollars, but she acknowledges that "the
hunt" itself is what lures her (Behr 2008: 4; Gregson and Crewe 2003).
Her purchases are eclectic, whatever catches her eye, but collectors also

haunt garage sales in search of specialized items. Some of these represent highly personal tastes (their own or their friends'). Others are actively engaged in the expanding marketplace of collectibles, where the value of each item has been established by collectibles guides or eBay.

Many sellers and buyers fit traditional gender roles, although this is changing. The fact that an estimated two-thirds of both sellers and buyers are women is not surprising, since both selling and buying are extensions of traditional female domestic roles (Herrmann 1996).[7] Since women manage the household, and often its budget, they also make most of its purchases, becoming experts in the quality, condition, and price of goods to sell or buy. For the seller, cleaning, folding, and arranging of goods for sale is an extension of housework and home decoration. Even sellers interested in profits can be seen as part of the traditional female labor market of part-time employment and supplemental income (Landman 2003). For the buyer, bargain hunting is an extension of household shopping. Much garage sale sociability has female overtones, structured by chatting and informal discussion.

Gender roles identify some categories of shoppers. "Sailers," savvy buyers who frequent garage sales as a hobby, are women. They establish friendships and create social networks with other regular shoppers. "Early birds," the first to show up at sales, are almost always men. Also knowledgeable shoppers, they seek out garage sale finds as professional restorers or resellers. Unlike the sailers, they are all business and drive hard bargains. Younger people, especially couples, less invested in gendered roles, tend to participate together on a more equal basis. In cities like Los Angeles, entire immigrant families often shop together. The children are available to try on clothes, and their English language skills help their parents to bargain and buy.

### The Language of Things

The variability of price and profit makes garage sales one of the few places in our society where bargaining is normal and even expected. According to scholars like Richard Sennett, bargaining shapes our experiences of public life. Sennett (1974) argues that the replacement of bargaining with fixed prices in retail shops in mid-nineteenth-century Paris marked the end of an important form of face-to-face sociability. Instead of an active participant in shopping, the buyer became a passive consumer, transforming public behavior into private contemplation. This, Sennett believed, opened the door for a form of commodity fetishism that stimulated buyers to invest objects with personal meanings beyond their utility.[8] Following Sennett's logic, the garage sale not only reinstates bargaining but also makes personal meanings an inescapable part of the exchange of goods, investing with significance even the mass-produced products he considers to be inherently devoid of meaning (Sennett 1974).

The sale of garage sale items is qualitatively different from a normal exchange of goods for money, far more laden with meaning beyond the use value of secondhand goods. Used objects come with meanings attached to them in various ways, but during the process of exchange buyers and sellers also construct additional meanings. As anthropologist Igor Kopytoff (1984) points out, things have social lives. Through use, personal possessions acquire biographies that transform anonymous and interchangeable commodities into unique items. In addition to physical signs of wear (nicks, stains, or scratches) that evoke the original owner, they also transmit emotional associations or a sense of subtle contagion imbued with the identity of their owner (Herrmann 1997). Each time they change hands, they become "singularized" again (Herrmann 1997: 919; Kopytoff 1984). With their purchases, buyers take away something of the previous owners. In a garage sale, these meanings are specific, attached to a particular individual or household.

Sellers add to these meanings in the conversational exchanges that typically accompany negotiations and sales, passing personal memories and associations along with their goods. Sellers often personalize items by mentioning "these were my daughter's favorite pants" or "I bought this fabric to make curtains but never got around to it." These stories link buyers and sellers by establishing a shared past for the object being sold. Buyers often respond by assuring the sellers that these meanings will be appreciated, and the object treated with care. They may also add to the object's biography by telling the seller what they plan to do with it. Later, buyers may include these meanings in the stories that describe their purchases, adding additional chapters to the items' biographies. Furnishing information can also be a form of bargaining, in which the buyer exchanges the story for a lower price. There are many accounts of sellers lowering prices or giving away goods when offered a personal explanation or appreciation (Selvin 1996).

## Planning For and Against the Garage Sale

Planners have already recognized the usefulness of the sociability generated by garage sales by adopting them as a "community-building" technique, with the goal of increasing "social capital." They organize block, street, or entire neighborhood garage sales with the explicit purpose of connecting neighbors through a common endeavor. Residents share the set-up and advertising expenses, and often a portion of the receipts is devoted to neighborhood projects or local charities (Herrmann 2006a).[9] Some city governments also encourage garage sales to eliminate the amount of solid waste generated by residents (Herrmann 2006b). Planners' positive assessment of the garage sale depends on its frequency. They consider a garage sale held once or twice a year a wholesome event but quickly perceive more frequent sales as "blight," an ominous but elusive term describing a visual condition predictive of urban decline. Most threatening are sales held so regularly that they become off-the-books retail stores, with a garage often used as a warehouse and sales room.

The visual chaos produced by the garage sale furnishes the ostensible reason for many of the planners' objections. In skiing, the term "yard sale" indicates a particularly messy fall, strewing legs, arms, and skis all over the place. In some places this perceived chaos has led to restrictions that limit the number of garage sales to no more than two a year and require city permits. The sponsor of one New Jersey ordinance asserted that such regulations protect the town's aesthetics and keep tacky flea markets out of residential neighborhoods (Chen 1995). The blurring of categories that are supposed to be separate, such as residential and commercial uses, alarms planners and officials, since it undermines the basic principles of land use and real estate. Even garage sale enthusiasts often draw a line between sales organized to eliminate excess possessions and those for serious commerce.

But these more permanent sales are not without redemptive social and economic aspects (figure 1.2). For example, artist Leda Ramos's MFA thesis described her mother's garage store in the Los Angeles neighborhood of Echo Park. After exhausting all of her used garage sale items, her mother, a native of El Salvador, started buying wholesale clothing in the downtown garment district and reselling it to other Salvadorian women from her garage. Her "store" offered credit, transactions in Spanish, and interaction with other women, and became an important social space in the neighborhood (Ramos 1993). Not too far away, another local woman held regular garage sales in her tiny front yard to augment her income. She kept a permanent accumulation of used clothing in her house, welcoming anyone who knew her, including garage sale regulars, to stop by, look, and buy at any time. Familiar with her ongoing

**Figure 1.2**
Garage store in Hollywood, California. Photo credit: Margaret Crawford.

sale, neighbors, friends, and acquaintances would donate their old clothes to her to sell. She specialized in children's clothing, a useful product in a poor but populous neighborhood.

If the one-time garage sale offers a kind of temporary heterotopia, the permanent garage sale serves as a bottom-up challenge to the functional segregation that characterizes American suburbs and cities. By bringing commercial activities into the domestic environment, garage sales break down the rigid barriers between the home and the neighborhood. These illegal sale variants often make imaginative use of the single-family house, showing that the concept of "mixed use" is not the sole property of the architects and urban designers who have popularized it. Professionally designed mixed-use buildings for middle-class users, ground-floor retail with apartments above or live/work lofts with space for studios or offices, are expensive and require zoning and code changes. In comparison, the garage sale store costs almost nothing and offers extremely flexible spaces (Bowden 2009; International Council of Shopping Centers 2006). Such small-scale informal businesses offer an easier and potentially more creative way of introducing new and mixed uses into neighborhoods without vacant land, new construction, or high-income buyers. As suburbs densify, legalizing garage stores and businesses could provide a flexible way to transform the stock of single-family houses and add complexity and opportunity to single-use residential neighborhoods. In a volatile real estate market, they offer residents in danger of foreclosure part-time opportunities to supplement incomes, opportunities particularly adaptable to women's household roles (Bawden Davis 1998; Curtiss 1992).

This analysis suggests that planners need to rethink their attitudes toward garage sales and other informal practices. Rather than seeing them as a problem of order to be controlled with regulation, they might regard them as positive additions to the planner's toolkit. Produced by collective wisdom, the dynamics of the garage sales, once recognized and understood, has the potential to improve and expand, in both functional and symbolic ways, ordinary urban and suburban spaces.

## Notes

1. This is Gretchen Herrmann's estimate, made in 1984.

2. A small but recognized category of garage sellers, called "squatters," conduct sales in highly trafficked areas not on their own property (Wikipedia 2010).

3. This chapter is indebted to the pioneering work of anthropologist Gretchen M. Herrmann, the only serious scholar of garage sales. In a series of articles she has analyzed and theorized the garage sale from a remarkable range of different perspectives. In particular, see Herrmann (1997).

4. A recent development has been the "stoop sale" held in denser urban neighborhoods such as Manhattan and Brooklyn, often by young people who grew up with garage sales in the suburbs (New York Times 2009).

5. A multiyear ethnographic study of 32 middle-class families in Los Angeles revealed that controlling excessive clutter had become a serious problem in many households (Ochs and Kremer-Sadlik 2013).

6. Every observer of garage sales has drawn attention to the surprising numbers of regular shoppers or "intensive participation" buyers. One even characterized the sales as potentially addictive in nature (Olmsted 1991).

7. Herrmann (1996) estimates that two-thirds of both sellers and buyers are women, a figure backed up by my own fieldwork.

8. This understanding of commodity fetishism is somewhat different from Marx's use of it to describe the worker's alienation from the product of his labor.

9. Herrmann describes "planned" sales in Ithaca, New York, organized by nonprofit community organizations. I encountered several of these in 2004 in low-income neighborhoods in Boston. See also Dylla (1987).

## References

Bawden Davis, Julie. 1998. "Cash In Your Clutter." *Los Angeles Times*, May 24, K1.

Behr, Rocky. 2008. "This and That." *Las Noticias* 89:4.

Bowden, Marilyn. 2009. "Live Work Condos Offer Dual-Purpose Space." *MSN Real Estate*. http://realestate.msn.com/article.aspx?cp-documentid=13108477 (retrieved July 14, 2012).

California State Board of Equalization. 2010. "Operators of Swap Meets, Flea Markets, or Special Events." Publication 111, California State Board of Equalization. http://www.boe.ca.gov/formspubs/pub111/.

Chen, David W. 1995. "The Garage Sale: Loud and Tacky, or Suburban Imperative?" *New York Times*, September 3, NY Region.

Crawford, Margaret. 1994. "Mi casa es su casa: The Politics of Everyday Life in East Los Angeles." *Assemblage* 24:12–19.

Curtiss, Aaron. 1992. "Ubiquitous Garage Sales—Big Business, Big Problem." *Los Angeles Times*, November 2, A1.

DeCaro, Frank. 2000. "The Mt. Everest of Yard Sales." *New York Times*, August 31, D1.

Dylla, Doug. 1987. "Collective Bargaining: How to Organize a Neighborhood Yard Sale." *Grapevine* (Ithaca, NY), August 13, 9.

Gregson, Nicky, and Louise Crewe. 2003. *Second-hand Cultures*. New York: Berg.

Herrmann, Gretchen M. 1996. "Women's Exchange in the U.S. Garage Sale." *Gender and Society* 10:703–728.

Herrmann, Gretchen M. 1997. "Gift or Commodity: What Changes Hands in the U.S. Garage Sale?" *American Ethnologist* 24 (4):910–930.

Herrmann, Gretchen M. 2006a. "Garage Sales Make Good Neighbors: Building Community through Neighborhood Sales." *Human Organization* 65 (2):181–191.

Herrmann, Gretchen M. 2006b. "Special Money: Ithaca Hours and Garage Sales." *Ethnology* 45 (2):125–141.

Herrmann, Gretchen M., and Stephen M. Soiffer. 1984. "For Fun and Profit: An Analysis of the American Garage Sale." *Urban Life* 12 (4):397–421.

International Council of Shopping Centers. 2006. "What Exactly Is Mixed-Use?" International Council of Shopping Centers, New York. http://www.brokersedge online.com/uploads/Mixed_use_Development_Definition.pdf.

Kopytoff, Igor. 1984. "The Cultural Biography of Things: Commoditization as Process." In Arjun Appadurai, ed., *The Social Life of Things*, 64–91. New York: Cambridge University Press.

Landman, Ruth H. 2003. "Washington's Yard Sales: Women's Work, but Not for the Money." *City and Society* 15 (1):45–49.

Leu, Melissa. 2012. "Clutter and Other Family Problems of the 21st Century." *Los Angeles Times*, July 20.

Mauss, Marcel. 1925. *The Gift: Forms and Functions of Exchange in Archaic Societies*. New York: Norton.

New York Times. 2009. "In a Recession, There's Still Sidewalk Chic." *New York Times*, May 17, D6.

Ochs, Elinor, and Tamar Kremer-Sadlik, eds. 2013. *Fast-Forward Family: Home, Work and Relationships in Middle-Class America*. Berkeley: University of California Press.

Olmsted, A. D. 1991. "Collecting: Leisure, Investment or Obsession?" *Journal of Social Behavior and Personality* 6:287–290.

O'Reilly, Lynn, Margaret Rucker, R. Flint Hughes, Marge Gorang, and Suzanne Hand. 1984. "The Relationship of Psychological and Situational Variables to Usage of a Second-Order Marketing System." *Academy of Marketing Science* 12 (3):53–76.

Ramos, Leda M. 1993. "In La Garage." MFA thesis, Rutgers, The State University of New Jersey, 1993.

Rosler, Martha. 1999. "Traveling Garage Sale." In *Martha Rosler: Positions in the Life World*, ed. Catherine de Zegher. Cambridge, MA: MIT Press.

Rosler, Martha. 2002. "Artist Questionnaire: 21 Responses." *October* 100:12.

Sahlins, Marshall. 1972. "On the Sociology of Primitive Exchange." In Marshall Sahlins, ed., *Stone Age Economics*, 185–276. New York: Aldine de Gruyter.

Selvin, Molly. 1996. "Saying Goodbye to the Stuff of which Memories Are Made." *Los Angeles Times*, August 10, B1.

Sennett, Richard. 1974. *The Fall of Public Man*. New York: Knopf.

Wikipedia. 2010. "Garage Sales." Wikimedia Foundation Inc., December 2010. http://en.wikipedia.org/wiki/Garage_sale (retrieved September 5, 2011).

Interviews
Kaliski, John, May 2010.

# 2

## Outlaw In-Laws: Informal Second Units and the Stealth Reinvention of Single-Family Housing

Vinit Mukhija

Informal housing is usually associated with the poor in developing countries. It is often seen as a euphemism for slums and substandard housing, and is likely to remind readers of Dharavi in Mumbai, Kibera in Nairobi, the *favelas* of Brazil, and the *gecekondular* of Turkey. Contrary to public perception, informal housing also exists in the United States. It is, however, surprisingly understudied. Colonias, the infrastructure-poor subdivisions typically associated with the border region of Texas, may be the best-known example of informal housing in the United States, but there is limited scholarly literature about them (Mukhija and Monkkonen 2006; Ward 1999; Ward in this volume). Similarly, there are only a few studies examining unpermitted second units developed on lots with single-family housing or unpermitted apartment subdivisions in multifamily housing (Baer 1986; Gellen 1985). My chapter adds to this limited literature and focuses on second units with single-family housing. In land use planning regulations, second units are customarily referred to as secondary dwelling units (SDUs) or accessory dwelling units (ADUs), but colloquially they are generally known as backyard cottages, granny flats, companion units, and in-law units. Since they are often unpermitted or illegal, I also call them *outlaw in-laws* in this chapter.[1]

According to the urban studies literature, second units are an underappreciated housing typology, as they offer many potential social, economic, and environmental benefits. More specifically, scholars argue that, given the country's changing demographics, a second unit offers the possibility of independent housing for elderly parents, grown children, extended family, and care providers (Chapman and Howe 2001; Folts and Muir 2002; Liebig, Koenig, and Pynoos 2006; Pollak 1994). Others make the economic argument that these secondary units provide affordable rental housing, with the rental income allowing middle-class households to own single-family homes in more expensive neighborhoods

(Downs 1991; Liebmann 1990). Advocates also argue that second units utilize the existing urban infrastructure more efficiently, and that the extra density can be accommodated within the built fabric of single-family neighborhoods without altering their visual character (Cuff et al. 2010; Duany, Plater-Zyberk, and Speck 2000; Friends of San Diego Architecture 2005).

In California, the state government acknowledges these potential advantages and has repeatedly passed enabling legislation to make it easier for local governments to allow second units within single-family neighborhoods. But most of the local governments in the state remain unconvinced of their value. They assume that their constituents are opposed to second units because of doubts about existing infrastructure capacity, particularly parking; worries about absentee owners and unreliable tenants; fears of losing the single-family character of neighborhoods; and the apparent lack of viable policies for addressing existing, unpermitted second units—the outlaw in-laws.

There is, nonetheless, a strong demand for second units. Research conducted by the AARP (formerly the American Association of Retired Persons) suggests that many of the advantages of second units discussed above are valued in the housing market. The AARP's surveys of seniors indicate that "80% or more of older households would like to remain in their current homes," and "over one-third would consider modifying their home to include an ADU if they needed assistance" (AARP and APA 2000: 9). Similarly, the *Wall Street Journal* (Fletcher 2002) noted that in the experience of KB Homes, the Los Angeles-based suburban homebuilder, "generally a third of its new homebuyers want a granny flat." Legal permits for second units, however, are difficult to obtain. Consequently, the informal supply dominates the market, but the unregulated homes it provides are not always safe.

As in developing countries with informal housing, it is not entirely clear how many unpermitted second units exist, where they are spatially distributed in a city, or what kind of housing conditions they provide. Nor is it evident how planners and policymakers should deal with these informal units. In 1987, the *Los Angeles Times* conducted a rare and comprehensive survey of illegal garage conversions to second units in single-family homes of Los Angeles County, which includes the city of Los Angeles and has a population about two and a half times larger than the city (Chavez and Quinn 1987). The newspaper used data from the Los Angeles County Assessor's office to develop a simple random sample of 500 single-family addresses in the county and surveyed these homes for the presence of unpermitted garage units. Its survey suggested that there were over 42,000 unpermitted garage units in the county. Although the newspaper acknowledged that these units were distributed all across the county, its narrative focused on garage conversions within poor immigrant communities and emphasized their slumlike conditions.

The *Times*'s study is over twenty-five years old and needs to be updated, but its field-based sampling methodology is expensive to replicate. As an alternative approach, I draw from past housing research in developing countries, where researchers often use real estate sales information to better understand informal housing markets (Jones and Ward 1994). Taking advantage of the publicly accessible data from the multiple listing service (MLS) of homes for sale in the city of Los Angeles, I sampled all the single-family homes for sale in spring 2012 and reviewed the sales listings for clues to the presence or absence of a possible second unit. The underlying premise of my methodology is that sellers are likely to advertise unpermitted second units in their listings to get higher sale prices from buyers. Some sellers, however, are likely to be concerned about regulatory authorities, and may not disclose such information. Another important limitation of my approach is that it only reveals second units that represent an investment by owners in permanent construction, particularly kitchens and toilets. But as the *Los Angeles Times* survey demonstrated, unpermitted second units in the informal housing market include seemingly temporary and impermanent arrangements, such as residents sleeping in ad hoc garage conversions and using toilet and kitchen facilities in the main dwelling unit. Thus, my research methodology should be seen less as an update of the previous survey than as a complementary approach that adds nuance to the understanding of informal housing in the United States.

In this chapter, I estimate the number of unpermitted second units in the city of Los Angeles, analyze their spatial distribution across the geography of the city, assess the typology of these units, and consider their conditions. I also discuss the planning options for addressing these units. Californian cities, with the state government's support for second units, are ideal sites for this research, and among them Los Angeles provides an exemplary case. Single-family housing dominates both the physical landscape and the mental image of the city. The city and its region are the global archetype in the romance of single-family living. Public regulations and political support for protecting single-family housing are fierce. But Los Angeles, like California and the United States, has an aging population, and access to affordable housing continues to be a challenge for many in the city. As a result, it is not surprising that outlaw in-laws meet the demand for second units.

In the section that follows, I discuss the history and institutional context for second units with single-family homes in the United States, then focus on the specific context of California and Los Angeles. The next section is the heart of this chapter, in which I present and analyze my empirical data on unpermitted second units in the city of Los Angeles. In the conclusion, I review the theoretical and policy implications of the evidence and discuss the complexities involved in addressing illegal second units. I also argue for a reinterpretation of the single-family house and flexibility in single-family zoning based on contemporary practices and needs.

## The Outlawing of Second Units: The History and Institutional Context

Second units with primary dwelling units have historically been associated with housing for domestic help. The mews houses in Britain, which were built on mews (or alleys) as stables with living quarters for staff on the second level, and the carriage houses and coach houses built on alleyways in the United States, are among the best-known historical examples of accessory units (Antoninetti 2008). In the United States, in the era before emancipation, such units were also used for housing urban slaves (Jackson 1985). Two-family homes were a common feature of the late nineteenth-century streetcar suburbs (Warner 1969). Nationwide, exclusive single-family neighborhoods in metropolitan regions "were quite rare until the 1940s" (Gellen 1985: 119), and only the very wealthy could afford to live in them (Flint 1977). But the single-family detached houses of the suburbs were emerging as "the ultimate rung" in housing and the sacred goal for "fulfilling both the American Dream and the American Creed" (Perin 1977: 47). Culturally, the privacy of these homes was touted as necessary to protect children from inappropriate role models, but their shortcomings are by now well recognized (Hayden 1984).

As early as the 1930s, federal institutions discouraged two-family homes through prejudiced mortgage-underwriting regulations (Gellen 1985). The Federal Housing Administration, fearing that the rental incomes from the second units would be unpredictable, demanded higher insurance rates from buyers of two-family homes. At the local level, single-family neighborhoods were seen as vulnerable to the risk of redevelopment at greater density and thus in need of protection. Initially they were protected by private covenants organized by homebuilders; later, zoning regulations enforced by local governments became the norm. While early zoning had focused on height and bulk controls—driven by concerns about fire and inadequate light and ventilation—as tools to protect the "health and safety" of citizens, later planners also aimed to maintain the character of exclusive single-family neighborhoods. As Martin Gellen (1985) pointed out, there is no good planning-based justification for preventing two-family homes on single-family lots that are twice the size of a typical lot. Nonetheless, modern zoning regulations do not typically allow this flexibility. Local governments have been able to justify zoning restrictions mandating residential-use districts that separate housing of varying densities as a way to protect the "welfare" of their citizens. In the social construction of the single-family ideal, accessory units are perceived as an indicator of a neighborhood's decline.

### The Informal Market

Although most postwar zoning regulations did not permit second units in single-family neighborhoods, a *New York Times* story on the suburbs in New York's metropolitan area in the late 1970s—"Legal or Not, Single-Family Homes Adding Apartments"—brought attention to the presence of outlaw units (Brooks 1979). The story quoted Paul Davidoff, who is well regarded in planning history for his opposition to restrictive zoning practices that prevent smaller, more affordable homes from being built in suburbs. Davidoff welcomed the informal supply of unpermitted housing: "It's beautiful. These apartments are a magnificent answer to the tremendous shortage of less expensive housing in the region. They are to everybody's advantage" (Brooks 1979).

Not everything about informal housing, however, is beautiful. Local governments typically fail to collect property taxes and utility connection fees. State and federal governments are likely to lose income taxes on rents from unpermitted second units. And tenants, most significantly, can also face unsafe housing conditions without any legal recourse. But land use regulations did not change substantially in the New York region to address the growth in informal housing. One notable exception was a seemingly successful, although unreplicated, amnesty program in the early 1980s to legalize unpermitted second units in Babylon, a town on Long Island (Rudel 1984).

### The Institutional Framework in California

California has been a national leader in considering second units as a viable option for affordable housing. The state's first initiative in 1981,

Senate Bill 1160, was geared toward seniors and allowed cities to grant variances from regular zoning restrictions for second units on single-family lots (Kyle 2000). The following year, the state approved SB 1534, proposed by State Senator Henry Mello and generally known as the Mello Act, to leverage second units as a source of affordable housing. It enabled local governments to develop ordinances allowing second units in single-family neighborhoods. Subsequent minor amendments were approved in in 1986, 1990, and 1994 (Bobrowsky 2007). Following the state's initiatives, many local governments made it possible for second units to be approved in single-family neighborhoods through discretionary reviews. However, the discretionary process was time-consuming. Cities continued to enforce strict standards, and permits were rarely granted.

To counter the reluctance of local governments and address the lack of progress in granting permits for second units, the state of California approved Assembly Bill 1866 in 2002. The bill was proposed by South Los Angeles-area Assembly Member Roderick Wright and took effect in July 2003. It prohibited discretionary reviews by local governments, recommended lower standards, and directed cities to allow second units by right. AB 1866 had wide-ranging support. Its advocates on the right included the California Association of Realtors, and on the left the California Rural Legal Assistance Foundation. Most cities, however, were not pleased by the new law. While many of them now allow second units by right, the standards mandated for approval of such units, particularly parking requirements, are so stringent that permits are still difficult to come by.

One of the few jurisdictions in California to follow both the letter and spirit of the state law is the city of Santa Cruz. Its second unit program, approved in 2003 to be consistent with AB 1866, has received significant media attention and noteworthy awards from the American Institute of Architects, the American Planning Association, the Environmental Protection Agency, and the League of California Cities (Bernstein 2005; Planning 2005; El Nasser 2004). The news reports on the program suggest that the city successfully built support for its more liberal second unit policy, including lower parking requirements, through extensive public outreach and workshops. Its innovations include a step-by-step manual, a design guidebook with prototype concepts, technical assistance, and access to affordable construction loans through the Santa Cruz Community Credit Union (City of Santa Cruz 2003). While other jurisdictions in California have been reluctant to follow Santa Cruz's lead, more liberal second unit policies have started to emerge in other cities across the country, including in Seattle, Portland, Arlington (Virginia), and Madison (Wisconsin).

Critics of second units worry typically about their adverse impacts on the single-family character of neighborhoods and the additional pressure on local infrastructure and municipal services. An article—"Invasion of the Granny Flat"—in Los Angeles's alternative newspaper, *LA Weekly*, fiercely criticized the city for considering zoning revisions in 2009 to make it easier to obtain permits for second units (Morris 2009). The city had initiated a public process to develop an ordinance consistent with AB 1866 for second units. The newspaper argued that instead of making it easier to obtain permits for second units, the city should follow the example of some of its neighboring jurisdictions, "resist the effort to increase granny flats," and consider banning them to protect the character and openness of the city's single-family communities (Morris 2009). Comments from readers on the article's website were mixed, but a strong majority agreed with the newspaper's critique and denounced second units for causing a decline in the quality of their single-family neighborhoods. Many commentators also cautioned that liberal policies would lead to an explosion of slumlike housing, echoing the conventional wisdom and the sentiment of the 1987 *Los Angeles Times* report that second units were likely to concentrate in certain neighborhoods and provide substandard and unsafe housing. In the following section, I take a closer look at unpermitted second units in the city of Los Angeles to examine such concerns.

## The LA Story

The *Los Angeles Times*'s survey developed a simple random sample of 500 of the 1.3 million single-family addresses in the county, and surveyed these homes for the presence of unpermitted garage apartments (Chavez and Quinn 1987). It concluded that 16 homes, or 3.2 percent of its sample, had illegal garage conversions.[2] The newspaper extrapolated from its findings that there might be 42,288 illegal conversions in the county. Using a generous average household size of five, it concluded that some 211,440 people were housed in these garages. (According to the 1990 census, the average household size in Los Angeles County was 2.96.) Experts approached by the newspaper to interpret the results pointed out that the suburbs had more garages than apartments to meet the region's growing housing needs. Other research, based on interviews with public officials, also suggests that there was a sharp increase in garage conversions in the region during the 1980s (Leong 1991: 47).

The *Times* article—"Substandard Housing Garages: Immigrants In, Cars Out"—gave the questionable impression that unpermitted housing was more prevalent in poor, immigrant communities of the county. It also suggested that the dominant strategy in the informal market for supplying housing was through garage conversions, and that one of its adverse consequences was the loss of parking spaces for everyone. Finally, the article emphasized the slumlike, substandard conditions of outlaw housing. Its narrative suggested that many converted garages were firetraps and highlighted the health concerns and risks of contagious diseases spreading due to the lack of adequate plumbing. Although the reporting caught public attention, it did not lead to any significant policy initiatives in the city of Los Angeles. But two tragic garage fires almost a decade later forced the city to revisit the issue (Los Angeles Housing Department 1997). In December 1996, a garage fire in the neighborhood of Watts killed five children. A few months later, in March 1997, two children and their grandmother died in a garage fire in the city's Sun Valley neighborhood. At the City Council's direction, the Los Angeles Housing Department assembled a Garage Housing Task Force to study the issue. The Task Force recommended a three-step plan, including (1) immediate hazard reduction, (2) interim occupancy permits, and (3) permanent legalization. But these recommendations were both controversial and daunting. They were buried by the more immediate affairs of the city.

Ignoring informal housing, however, may not be the best policy option. With this research, I hope to revisit the question of upgrading and legalizing informal housing. My goal is to increase the empirical information on unpermitted second units in Los Angeles, use the evidence to develop a richer understanding of the nature of informal housing, and suggest informed policy recommendations.

## Methodology

I used publicly available real estate sales listings data from Redfin, an online real estate brokerage, for this research. Redfin's database includes sales information from the multiple listings service and public property records from the County Assessor's office. I developed my sample by including all single-family homes for regular sale in the city of Los Angeles in Spring 2012, a total of 3,113 homes.[3] I searched in the listings, property descriptions, and photographs for clues to the presence of unpermitted second units. I also looked for discrepancies between the advertised size of the house and its formally recorded size in the Assessor's database. At times, sellers explicitly noted the presence of a "converted garage" or an "unpermitted second unit" (or granny flat, or some other synonym); sometimes they acknowledged a second unit but recommended that "buyers verify permits"; sometimes they suggested the possibility of "additional rental income" and provided a photograph of the additional unit. To be conservative, I did not include in my estimate of unpermitted second units seemingly illegal work spaces, playrooms, or guesthouses that have toilets but lack kitchens. Many of these, however, could be easily converted to second units.

As noted in the introduction, it is likely that some second units without permits are not publicized in the real estate listings, so that my estimate is an undercount. Moreover, my methodology is not designed to capture the many temporary second units in the informal market. To partially address this weakness, I draw lessons from previous research on unpermitted units in San Francisco. Estimates of informal housing in San Francisco suggest that the number of unpermitted units found through a field examination of a sample survey is about twice the number uncovered through an analysis of real estate sales data (SPUR 2001).[4] Intuitively this makes sense, as the sales data only partially reveal the extent of informal housing in a community. Therefore, I expect that the total number of unpermitted second units in Los Angeles is likely to be closer to twice my estimate from the for-sale listings.

### Prevalence and Distribution
As table 2.1 shows, my review of the for-sale data indicated that 168 of the 3,113 single-family homes for sale in the city of Los Angeles most likely included an unpermitted second unit. Thus, the research suggests that in 5.4 percent of the single-family homes in the city, owners have made significant investments in permanent construction to add outlaw units to their properties. This extrapolates to almost 25,000 single-family homes with such units in the city. However, following San Francisco's experience that the total number of unpermitted second units in the city, including less permanent arrangements, is likely twice the estimate from sales data, I conclude that there are closer to 50,000 informal second units in Los Angeles.[5] This estimate does not include unpermitted units in the city's multifamily housing stock.

**Table 2.1**
Unpermitted Second Units and Their Distribution in the City of Los Angeles

| Area Planning Commission (APC) | Number of Single-Family Homes | Number for Sale | Median Home List Price | Unpermitted and Likely Unpermitted Second Units | Proportion for Sale with Unpermitted Second Units (%) |
|---|---|---|---|---|---|
| Central | 31,941 | 434 | $1,117,000 | 32 | 7.4 |
| East LA | 42,465 | 258 | $420,000 | 18 | 7.0 |
| South LA | 64,675 | 551 | $202,250 | 21 | 3.8 |
| Harbor | 22,973 | 82 | $345,200 | 3 | 3.7 |
| West LA | 63,623 | 612 | $1,722,500 | 32 | 5.2 |
| South Valley | 119,955 | 726 | $627,250 | 47 | 6.5 |
| North Valley | 117,012 | 450 | $424,450 | 15 | 3.3 |
| Totals | 462,644 | 3,113 | $879,000 | 168 | 5.4 |

Sources: Author's research derived from for-sale listings in Spring 2012; Los Angeles County Assessor's records.

Table 2.1 also shows the spatially disaggregated distribution of informal housing in the city. The spatial units of analysis are the city's seven Area Planning Commissions (figure 2.1) under the Department of City Planning. As the median home list price in the respective APCs indicates, there is tremendous variation in wealth across the seven areas. (Because the sample size is smaller at the disaggregate level, the findings are less reliable in terms of their margin of error, but still indicative.) According to this indicator, the West Los Angeles APC is the wealthiest area, with a median list price almost twice the city's overall median, while the South Los Angeles APC is the poorest, with a median list price less than a quarter of the city's overall median. Unpermitted second units are spread all over Los Angeles, and their incidence does not perfectly match the distribution of wealth in the city. The data suggest that unpermitted second units are most prevalent in the Central, East Los Angeles, and South Valley APCs; there is no clear link between home price and the presence of a second unit. At the same time, three of the four APCs with the lowest median home list price—South Los Angeles, Harbor, and North Valley—have the lowest percentage of unpermitted second units. It may be unwise to read too much into these data. It is possible that

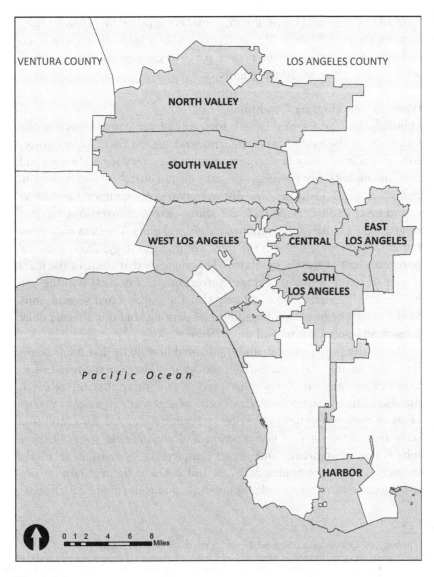

**Figure 2.1**
The seven Area Planning Commissions of the City of Los Angeles. Source:
Department of City Planning, City of Los Angeles. Cartography: Erin Coleman.

more ad hoc, informal housing arrangements are prevalent in less wealthy parts of the city. Nonetheless, it seems fair to suggest that there is no evidence in my data that the poorer parts of the city have more illegal housing than their wealthier neighbors.

## Typology and Housing Conditions

Although the *Los Angeles Times*'s focus on garage conversions and the popularity of the name "garage apartments" suggest that garage conversions or additions may be the most common strategy for adding second units to single-family housing, the data do not match this expectation. In my sample I identified six distinct spatial possibilities for adding second units (table 2.2). As table 2.2 shows, garage conversions account for less than a tenth of the unpermitted second units. The data also show that detached construction is the most common strategy, accounting for more than half of the second units.[6] This suggests that some of the fears of loss of parking due to garage conversions in informal housing are exaggerated. Nonetheless, it is likely that the unpermitted second units do not make any provision for additional parking, and this affects public opinion and policy on second units (Shoup 2005).

The conventional wisdom about informal housing is that it has slum-like, substandard, and unsafe living conditions. The periodic fires in Los Angeles's garage apartments substantiate this concern. But my research also shows that in many instances, homeowners make significant investments in their properties to develop unpermitted second units, and it is likely that the quality of construction and amenities in some of these units is not substandard. One such example of a second unit from my research is shown in figures 2.2, 2.3, and 2.4. The figures show a converted garage from the outside (figure 2.2) and inside (figure 2.3), as well

**Table 2.2**
The Typology of Unpermitted Second Units in the City of Los Angeles

| Category | Garage Conversion | Addition to Garage | Above Garage | Addition to Main Unit | Carve-out | Detached Construction | Other | Total |
|---|---|---|---|---|---|---|---|---|
| Unpermitted and likely unpermitted | 15 | 12 | 6 | 23 | 7 | 97 | 8 | 168 |
| Percent of total | 8.9 | 7.1 | 3.6 | 13.7 | 4.2 | 57.7 | 4.8 | 100 |

Source: Author's research derived from for-sale listings in Spring 2012.

**Figure 2.2**
The outside of an informal second unit in the Central Los Angeles APC. Photo credit: Ned Brown.

**Figure 2.3**
Living area in an informal second unit in the Central Los Angeles APC. Photo credit: Ned Brown.

**Figure 2.4**
Kitchen of an informal second unit in the Central Los Angeles APC. Photo credit: Ned Brown.

as its kitchen (figure 2.4). Although these images are from a single-family home in a relatively wealthy part of the city, and are not necessarily representative, they help illustrate the heterogeneity of informal housing conditions and suggest that it is a mistake to dismiss all informal housing as substandard.

**Implications and Conclusion**

The data in this chapter offer a nuanced portrait of Los Angeles's informal housing. My research suggests that as many as 50,000 single-family homes have outlaw in-laws in the city. These unpermitted second units are distributed all over the city, not just in poor neighborhoods. Moreover, not all of them offer substandard living conditions. I discuss some implications of these findings next.

First, the considerable scale of informal housing suggests the need for the city to reconsider the policy option of legalization. The research also indicates that many of the unpermitted units are in decent condition, and that the conventional fears about legalizing and incentivizing slumlike housing conditions are exaggerated. Previous research has also suggested that the illegal housing stock often follows the standards and safety provisions of the building code (Gellen 1985). Bringing them into the formal fold will allow the city to regulate them and collect taxes. Owners would gain the benefits of predictability and access to formal finance. Legalizing such housing will also help the city to focus on the more limited category of unregulated housing with substandard conditions. The substandard units can pose safety risks, and need to be improved and regulated. Some of them may need to be shut down. But more research is needed, and it is possible that the majority can be upgraded with public policy support, including flexibility in meeting regulations, technical assistance, fee exemptions, and access to affordable-housing improvement loans. Although there is not much experience with conditional amnesty programs for unpermitted housing in the United States, there are examples of such initiatives in Babylon, New York (Rudel 1984), Daly City, California (Cabansagan 2011), and Marin County, California (Chapple et al. 2011) that offer the opportunity for research and policy lessons.

Second, the scale, distribution, and housing conditions of unpermitted second units in the city also throw into relief the conventional wisdom on informality. Informal housing is relatively unexpected in the United States, and not typically studied. The substantial scale of informal housing in Los Angeles, however, emphasizes the need for serious academic and policy attention. Informality is usually equated with poverty and poor housing conditions, but the evidence on second units challenges this. In addition, the informal governance of Los Angeles's unregulated units also suggests a need to question accepted beliefs on informality. In anarchist-inspired literature, informality is sometimes portrayed as a virtue of good social regulations (Turner 1977). On the other hand, Marxist-inspired critiques suggest that the selective enforcement of regulations in informal activities is state-centric, allowing the state authoritarian influence (Roy 2005). However, in single-family neighborhoods of Los Angeles, the enforcement is society-centric but not necessarily benign.

When neighbors complain to the Department of Building and Safety, the department sends inspectors to intervene and check for infractions. If owners are caught, they face the risk of demolition and reconversion of their unpermitted housing units. Although the city enforces the regulations, its role is passive until it receives complaints. Neighbors may be more inclined to complain if they are bothered by the lack of street parking and by noise from the unpermitted units. They may be less likely to protest substandard housing conditions within unpermitted second units. As a consequence, tenants are vulnerable to unsafe conditions and lack viable options to address their living conditions. To ensure that the basic housing standards of the poorer residents of Los Angeles are met, the city's administration needs to be actively involved in regulating the informal housing stock.

Finally, if the nature of informality in the built environment is a lens for critically examining the prevailing regulations and formal development patterns, the city also needs to consider the limits of dogmatic models of single-family living. Even though Los Angeles is the poster child of urban single-family living, it may be time to modify this dream to better respond to contemporary needs. If the city can change its single-family model and allow for some flexibility, it will have more success in addressing its housing needs. Although cities like Santa Cruz, Seattle, and Portland may have taken the lead in this reform, Los Angeles can build on their lessons and offer a new model of contemporary single-family living.

## Acknowledgments

I gratefully acknowledge the financial support of a UCLA Academic Senate grant, and the excellent research assistance of Clarrissa Cabansa-gan, Erin Coleman, Katie Gladstein, Kate Mayerson, and Mark Simpson. I also thank realtor Ned Brown for allowing me to use his photographs in this chapter.

## Notes

1. I owe this usage and my chapter's title to Michael Litchfield's brilliantly illustrated and titled manual, *In-laws, Outlaws, and Granny Flats: Your Guide to Turning One House into Two Homes* (Litchfield 2011).

2. The estimate of 3.2 percent from a 500-home sample had a margin of error of ±1.5 percent, indicating that the percentage of garage conversions in the county could range from 1.7 to 4.7 percent.

3. I did not include homes under foreclosure or in short sale, because their sale listings are typically not detailed enough and often fail to include photographs or property descriptions. Removing the foreclosure and short sale listings reduced my sample size by about 40 percent.

4. In the mid-1990s, San Francisco's Planning Department examined a sample of single-family homes in the city and concluded that 23 percent had illegal units. About a decade earlier, a survey of sales records of single-family dwellings in the city indicated that 10–15 percent had an illegal second unit (SPUR 2001: 4).

5. Because of the lack of previous research, it is difficult to triangulate these findings. In comparison, the *Los Angeles Times* survey of illegal garage conversions in the county estimated around 42,000 cases in the county (Chavez and Quinn 1987). Although this estimate cannot be directly used to estimate the frequency of illegal garage conversions in the city of Los Angeles, the city accounted for about two-fifths of the population of the county, so it may have included close to two-fifths, or 16,800, of the garage conversions. It is unclear how garage conversions may have changed in the city since 1987. Between the 1990 and 2010 census counts, the city's population grew by about 8 percent. Although demand for housing has grown, there is some evidence that enforcement has also increased. Unless the number of unpermitted garage conversions in the city has dramatically changed, my results seem consistent with the *Times*'s research.

6. Previous research on second units in the Bay Area had similar findings, with detached construction accounting for almost a third of the informal second units (Chapple et al. 2011).

## References

AARP and APA. 2000. *Accessory Dwelling Units: Model State Act and Local Ordinance*. Washington, DC: AARP.

Antoninetti, Maurizio. 2008. "The Difficult History of Ancillary Units: The Obstacles and Potential Opportunities to Increase the Heterogeneity of Neighborhoods and the Flexibility of Households in the United States." *Journal of Housing for the Elderly* 22 (4):348–375.

Baer, William. 1986. "The Shadow Market in Housing." *Scientific American* 255 (5):29–35.

Bernstein, Fred. 2005. "In Santa Cruz, Affordable Housing without Sprawl: Granny Flats for Cool Grannies." *New York Times*, February 6.

Bobrowsky, Joshua. 2007. *Second Units: The Experience of Local Jurisdictions in Los Angeles County in Complying with AB 1866*. Los Angeles: UCLA Law, Public Policy Clinic.

Brooks, Andre. 1979. "Legal or Not, Single-Family Homes Adding Apartments." *New York Times*, June 3.

Cabansagan, Clarrissa. 2011. "Project Homesafe: From the Bay to LA. Lessons of Granny Flat Legalization in Daly City." M.A. in Urban Planning comprehensive project. UCLA.

Chapman, Nancy J., and Deborah J. Howe. 2001. "Accessory Apartments: Are They a Realistic Alternative for Aging in Place?" *Housing Studies* 16 (5):637–650.

Chapple, Karen, et al. 2011. *Yes in My Backyard: Mobilizing the Market for Secondary Units*. Berkeley: Center for Community Innovation, University of California.

Chavez, Stephanie, and James Quinn. 1987. "Substandard Housing Garages: Immigrants In, Cars Out." *Los Angeles Times*, May 24.

City of Santa Cruz. 2003. *Accessory Dwelling Units Manual.* Santa Cruz: City of Santa Cruz Housing and Community Development Department.

Cuff, Dana, Tim Higgins, and Per-Johan Dahl, eds. 2010. *Backyard Homes LA.* Los Angeles: cityLAB, UCLA.

Downs, Anthony. 1991. "The Advisory Commission on Regulatory Barriers to Affordable Housing: Its Behavior and Accomplishments." *Housing Policy Debate* 2 (4):1095–1137.

Duany, Andres, Elizabeth Plater-Zyberk, and Jeff Speck. 2000. *Suburban Nation: The Rise of Sprawl and the Decline of the American Dream.* New York: North Point Press.

El Nasser, Haya. 2004. "Granny Flats Finding a Home in a Tight Market." *USA Today,* January 5.

Fletcher, June. 2002. "Your New Neighbor: Mom." *Wall Street Journal,* December 20.

Flint, Barbara J. 1977. "Zoning and Residential Segregation: A Social and Physical History, 1910–1940." Ph.D. diss., University of Chicago.

Folts, W. Edward, and Kenneth B. Muir. 2002. "Housing for Older Adults: New Lessons from the Past." *Research on Aging* 24 (1):10–28.

Friends of San Diego Architecture. 2005. *Accessory Dwelling Units Design Competition.* San Diego: Friends of San Diego Architecture.

Gellen, Martin. 1985. *Accessory Apartments in Single-Family Housing.* New Brunswick, NJ: Center for Urban Policy Research, Rutgers.

Hayden, Dolores. 1984. *Redesigning the American Dream: The Future of Housing, Work, and Family Life.* New York: W. W. Norton.

Jackson, Kenenth. 1985. *Crabgrass Frontier: The Suburbanization of the United States.* New York: Oxford University Press.

Jones, Gareth, and Peter Ward, eds. 1994. *Methodology for Land and Market Analysis.* London: UCL Press.

Kyle, Selena. 2000. "There Goes the Neighborhood: The Failure and Promise of Second Units as a Housing Source for the Midpeninsula." Undergraduate thesis, Program on Urban Studies, Stanford University.

Leong, Dora K. 1991. "The Conversion of Garages to Residential Use in Los Angeles County: Impacts and Potential as a Housing Resource." Master of City Planning thesis, Massachusetts Institute of Technology.

Liebig, Phoebe, Teresa Koenig, and Jon Pynoos. 2006. "Zoning, Accessory Dwelling Units, and Family Caregiving." *Journal of Aging and Social Policy* 18 (3–4):155–172.

Liebmann, George W. 1990. "Suburban Zoning: Two Modest Proposals." *Real Property, Probate, and Trust Journal* 25 (Spring):1–16.

Litchfield, Michael. 2011. *In-laws, Outlaws, and Granny Flats: Your Guide to Turning One House into Two Homes.* Newtown, CT: Taunton Press.

Los Angeles Housing Department. 1997. "Garage Housing Task Force Report." Los Angeles Housing Department.

Morris, Steven Leigh. 2009. "Invasion of the Granny Flat." *LA Weekly*, December 10.

Mukhija, Vinit, and Paavo Monkkonen. 2006. "Federal Colonias Policy in California: Too Broad and Too Narrow." *Housing Policy Debate* 17 (4):755–780.

Perin, Constance. 1977. *Everything in Its Place: Social Order and Land Use in America*. Princeton: Princeton University Press.

Planning. 2005. "Not Your Grandmother's Granny Flat." *Planning* 71 (3): 8–9.

Pollak, Patricia B. 1994. "Rethinking Zoning to Accommodate the Elderly in Single Family Housing." *Journal of the American Planning Association* 60 (4):521–539.

Roy, Ananya. 2005. "Urban Informality: Toward an Epistemology of Planning." *Journal of the American Planning Association* 71 (2):147–158.

Rudel, Thomas K. 1984. "Household Change, Accessory Apartments, and Low Income Housing in Suburbs." *Professional Geographer* 36 (2):174–181.

Shoup, Donald. 2005. *The High Cost of Free Parking*. Chicago: American Planning Association.

SPUR. 2001. *Secondary Units: A Painless Way to Increase the Supply of Housing*. San Francisco: San Francisco Planning and Urban Research Association.

Turner, John F. C. 1977. *Housing by People: Towards Autonomy in Building Environments*. New York: Pantheon Books.

Ward, Peter M. 1999. *Colonias and Public Policy in Texas and Mexico: Urbanization by Stealth*. Austin: University of Texas Press.

Warner, Sam Bass. 1969. *Streetcar Suburbs: The Process of Growth in Boston, 1870–1900*. New York: Atheneum.

# 3

## The Reproduction of Informality in Low-Income Self-Help Housing Communities

Peter M. Ward

In this chapter I explore one key area of informality in the United States today: the production and consumption of housing among low-income groups. My focus is on the extensive self-help housing efforts in so-called colonias of the U.S.-Mexico border region and in other similar, but less widely recognized, informal homestead subdivisions (IfHSs) that may be found in the rural hinterland of many U.S. cities. All embrace important elements of informality and are rational responses to the aspirations of home ownership among low- and very low-income populations. The chapter has two main goals: first, to describe that rationality and demonstrate how informality is articulated through the production of housing in these settlements. Second, I wish to explore how, once entrained, informality may recast and reproduce itself as a response to evolving household dynamics and life course changes; housing and land market (under)performance; cross-generational property transfers; and the unintended consequences of well- (and not-so-well-) intentioned public policies. Far from being a temporary or aberrational construction, informality is both highly rational and dynamic. It is, therefore, important to fully understand this rationality and design sensitive policies that help, rather than hinder, people's creativity and sweat equity embedded in self-help and self-managed housing provision.

### Colonias and Informal Homestead Subdivisions

There is relatively little systematic research concerning how low-income urban populations in the United States adopt informal mechanisms to gain access to residential land and participate in the American Dream of home ownership. An exception since 1990 has been the growing public policy concern with and scholarly analysis of so-called colonias in Texas and other border states (Davies and Holz 1992; Donelson and Holguin

2002; Larson 1995, 2002; Mukhija and Monkonnen 2006; Ward 1999, 2003). Almost always this has been construed primarily as a rural and border housing phenomenon. In fact, however, the majority of these colonias do not house rural populations, even though their actual locations are often in the rural outskirts of cities, from which low-income (largely Latino) workers commute to low-paid food-processing, construction, or service-sector jobs in urban areas.

Nor are colonias and informally produced housing exclusively a border phenomenon, although many are indeed concentrated outside of U.S.-Mexico border cities, where they comprise some of the worst housing conditions. Colonias and similar types of IfHSs are widespread in the periphery of many cities (Ward and Peters 2007). Today, these informal subdivisions have been identified in places as diverse as Austin, Dallas/Fort Worth, Houston, and Lubbock in Texas; Albuquerque and Santa Fe in New Mexico; Tucson and Phoenix in Arizona; in so-called "gateway" cities such as Charlotte and Greensboro in North Carolina; and in Dalton and Atlanta in Georgia. And while these communities in the interior of the United States do not show the extreme poverty levels and impoverished housing conditions often associated with classic border colonias, they follow the same logic and rationale.

Not everyone who is low-income aspires to home ownership: rental trailer parks, mobile home subdivisions, low-cost apartments, and residential sharing remain important options for many households. However, for those who wish to build an asset through property ownership, colonias and IfHSs are often the only viable option, given low household incomes, the irregularity of workers' earnings, and their subsequent ineligibility for formal finance (mortgage) assistance.

Two-thirds of households in the United States are classified as home-owners, but poorer people are less likely to own their homes. Indeed, of the 12.5 million households living below the poverty line, 65 percent are renters.[1] Thus, the creation of new opportunities for home ownership among the poor can be an important vehicle to reduce this inequality. And for many low-income households, "manufactured" (trailer) housing offers an important lower-cost alternative to home ownership, whether in trailer parks, mobile home communities, or in subdivisions described below (Ward 2003).[2]

### The Rise of Colonias and Informal Homestead Subdivisions

Few people have a clear notion of what constitutes a colonia, let alone comprehend the large numbers of low-income households that reside in them. In Texas alone by the early 1990s, an estimated 400,000 people lived in some 1,600 or more colonias (Ward 1999), and densification and infill during the past 15 years have substantially added to the numbers, even while federal and state policies have successfully prevented the creation of new colonias.[3] In New Mexico and Arizona, the numbers are lower than in Texas but are nevertheless substantial: in Arizona, the 1990 census indicated that approximately 162,000 people lived in 77 so-called "*colonia* designated areas," while in New Mexico 70,000 lived in 141 settlements.

Three main types of colonias and IfHSs are identified in this chapter, all of which embrace different degrees of informality in their development (financing, production, and construction) as well as in their consumption and use.

1. *Classic border colonias* are located mostly in the border region, almost always beyond the city limits, buried in the rural hinterland, and contain almost exclusively very low-income Mexican-American or Mexican-born populations. Dwelling types are mixed, comprising self-built homes on a slab or hybrid arrangements often showing considerable innovation, as a trailer unit melds with a self-help extension, or a false second roof is added above the structure to provide shade and protection from the elements (figures 3.1 and 3.2).

**Figure 3.1**
Section of El Cenizo alongside the Rio Bravo in Webb County (20 miles south of Laredo). Source: Google Earth™.

**Figure 3.2**
Typical self-building in Starr County. (Note original house at rear serving as a temporary dwelling.) Photo credit: Peter Ward.

2. *New (post-1995) border colonia subdivisions* are identified in some Texas border counties such as Hidalgo and El Paso, and appear as large subdivisions with basic infrastructure developed under model subdivision rules required by the state since 1995 (figure 3.3). Given that they have basic infrastructure from the outset, the state does not define these subdivisions as colonias, although they share many of the worst housing characteristics traditionally associated with colonias (figure 3.4). The paradox is that they are the product of legislation intended to prohibit informal settlement and colonias, but which has led to new forms of informality.

3. *Non-border periurban informal subdivisions* are very similar to colonias, but are rarely perceived as such. Non-border informal subdivisions can be readily observed from the air, several miles outside of major cities. Compared to the other two types, a higher proportion of homes are manufactured, although one also finds a mix of trailers, self-built homes, and hybrid arrangements (figure 3.5).

**Figure 3.3**
New subdivision developed with full infrastructure. Pueblo de las Palmas, Hidalgo County. Source: Google Earth™.

**Figure 3.4**
New colonia housing in a settlement developed under "model subdivision rules": the shape of informality to come? Note the camper home that can be removed (as can the washer and refrigerator). Photo credit: Noah Durst.

**Figure 3.5**
Typical trailer homes in new colonias and subdivisions. Photo credit: Peter Ward.

### The Dimensions and Reproduction of Informality

Informality is embodied along various dimensions in the production of colonias and informal homestead subdivisions.[4] I discuss these drawing upon two studies: a 2002 survey of ten colonias outside Rio Grande City in Starr County, Texas, on the Mexican border, and a follow-up study done ten years later (Durst and Ward 2013).[5] The second study analyzed the prevalence of informal contracts for deed as a principal form of land conveyance and route to title provision, and assessed the ways in which informality remains a significant feature in colonia home sales. In this case some 1,200 households were surveyed in 65 colonias and subdivisions across eight counties (six on the border and two in central Texas), making this one of the most extensive surveys of its type ever undertaken (Ward, Way, and Wood 2012).

The essential backdrop to informality in housing and its reproduction are the low and very low incomes of these households. In border colonias, household incomes of less than a $1,000 a month are commonplace, and few households earn more than $20,000 year. Household incomes in non-border colonias and IfHSs are typically $15,000–25,000 a year. Most households have at least one worker, and the most common forms of employment span a wide range of low-paid service, agricultural, and haulage jobs, sometimes supplemented by part-time work. After 20–30 years of residence, an increasing proportion of colonia residents comprise "vestige" households of elderly couples living off modest pensions and Social Security.

Two principal mechanisms of informality make colonia and IfHS housing affordable to these populations: the low cost of land purchase and mechanisms of seller financing, and the opportunity to reduce the costs of housing construction. These informal options offer the only means for these low-income households to enter the housing market, albeit at considerable social costs: the hardship of living in relative isolation, with high transportation costs, poor housing conditions, and neighborhoods lacking adequate infrastructure and access to social services.

### Land Sales and Titles in Informal Subdivisions

In these developments, the primary way housing is made affordable is through the informality of the land acquisition process. Developers acquire tracts of (usually) poor-quality agricultural land at low cost and plat it into lots ranging from a third of an acre to an acre. The plat is recorded in the county courthouse, but there are no requirements to provide services and infrastructure. Thus, developers can immediately start selling lots to buyers with the promise of future services, or with clear notification that the purchaser must make arrangements for service provision, septic tank installation, etc. Not surprisingly, with few or no services, many people wait several years before occupying their lots. But the process is affordable: unserviced lots in the past have sold for as little as $8,000 (in current prices), with $100 down payment and monthly payments of $120–200 over several years (Ward 1999). The interest rate is likely to be 15–18 percent, so the eventual cost is significantly higher than the sale price.

Traditionally the most common form of purchase was through a contract for deed (CfD)—an informal method of seller financing sometimes called "a poor man's mortgage." These contracts are an agreement between the vendor and the purchaser to defer any delivery of title deed until the debt is paid in full, at which point the deed is handed over, and the buyer becomes the de jure owner. However, the contracts are often problematic: they are written in English for people who primarily speak Spanish, and do not always show the interest rate or final cost. More importantly, there are default clauses that permit the developer to rescind the contract without any compensation if more than three consecutive payments are missed. Sometimes there is no written contract—simply an oral agreement and receipts given for each payment. One study found that two developers sold lots through a mixture of informal means: CfDs and receipts, and lots allocated by "metes and bounds," so that residents had to guess where their lots began and ended, invariably incorrectly. These two developers sometimes sold the same lot several times over. Ultimately it became necessary for the state to step in to sequestrate the land developments, "regularize" lot ownership, and provide clean titles to the occupants or claimants (Ward et al. 2004; Ward 2012).

Because of the purchasers' vulnerability and the egregious exploitation by some developers, legislation after 1995 (in border areas)[6] and 2001 (elsewhere in Texas) required that these CfDs be recorded in the county clerk's office. This requirement has reduced the use of recorded CfDs in preference for more formal and secure property sales such as warranty deeds, which give some protection to the purchasers and can only be rescinded through formal foreclosure. A recent University of Texas study on behalf of the state's Department of Housing and Community Affairs contains data for over 15,500 recorded CfDs in ten counties of Texas. Figure 3.6 shows how the number of CfDs increased from around 620 in 1995 to over 1,200 in 2000 as new CfDs were recorded along with the backlog of unrecorded ones. Thereafter, the number declined to around 500 each year, but this latter figure indicates that CfDs continue

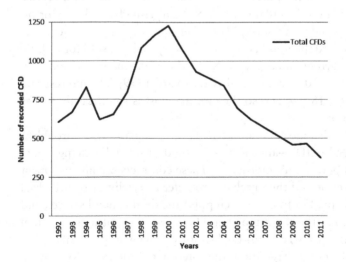

**Figure 3.6**
Trend in use of recorded contracts for deed across eight counties, 1989–2011.

to be important, especially in colonias and low-income subdivisions (Ward, Way, and Wood 2012).

In addition, unrecorded CfDs remain commonplace. The aforementioned study estimated that, of the 46,300 colonia owners holding deeds today in six border counties, some 5,400 (12 percent) had unrecorded CfDs, and around 20 percent of current holders of full property deeds had acquired their lots through unrecorded CfDs (Ward, Way, and Wood 2012). In short, informality in the form of CfDs (recorded and unrecorded) remains a major feature of self-financed housing in both border and non-border regions.

As a response to the 1995 border legislation that prohibited further unserviced colonia development, developers have shifted their portfolios into newer subdivisions that also target the poor, and which mostly eschew CfDs in favor of warranty deeds with vendor's lien and other deeds that skirt the need for conventional foreclosure procedures. Elsewhere, however, owners in the older colonias who need or wish to sell their properties invariably find that they must use seller financing and CfDs, many of which go unrecorded and are highly informal (see figure 3.7).

### Financing

Informality of financing is the key that unlocks the process of property sales in colonias. Because most colonia households are very low-income, they are rarely able to secure formal financing via mortgages or bank loans and acquire property through a deed or deed of trust. Thus, any sale must be seller-financed, usually at high interest rates of 15–18 percent, and with provisions that allow the lot to be repossessed if the buyer defaults. Low-income households often use the same method to buy their manufactured home, sometimes starting with a low-cost unit that may already have gone through one or several repossessions. These financing mechanisms add to the vulnerability of residents trying to survive, let alone thrive, in their home ownership endeavors.

### Housing Conditions, Housing Choices, and "Consolidation"

The lack of services such as water and power, while lowering the initial price of the land, creates major costs associated with informality. Water has to be hauled in, and drinking water must be purchased. Septic tank systems cost $1,200–2,000 to install and require periodic pumping at a cost of around $120 every 12–18 months. Garbage collection costs $30 per month for a weekly formal collection, or a little less with informal

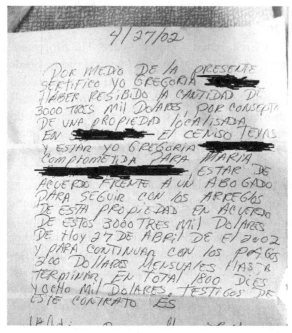

**4/27/02**

With this letter I Gregoria ***(redacted to ensure confidentiality) certify that I have received the total of 3000 three thousand dollars as part of a purchase of a property located at ***(address redacted) in El Ceniso (sic) Texas and being Gregoria *** (name redacted) swear before a lawyer that Maria ** * (name redacted) is in agreement to continue with the sale of this property and payment of these 3000 three thousand dollars, dated today April 27, 2002, and that she will continue to pay 200 dollars monthly until she completes the total of 1800 eighteen thousand dollars . Witness of this contract is:

Names, addresses, and phone numbers of the two parties (redacted) follow.

**Figure 3.7**
Handwritten contract—unrecorded contract for deed. Photo credit: Peter Ward.

entrepreneurs. Others carry and dump their garbage, while a few also burn their trash.

Electric companies run service through most settlements, and users pay both standing charges as well as metered consumption. Where two or more households share a lot, the electricity will often run through a single meter, and households must make informal arrangements with each other to pay the bill. Those without electricity use gasoline lamps and propane tanks for cooking and heating—a more expensive option. Social and other health services are rarely provided locally and require a trip into the city, usually by private transport from a family member or a neighbor. The only residents well served by formal transportation are schoolchildren, who are served by school district buses.

In Latin America, the classic process of self-build housing after land capture is to start with a shack or provision structure and gradually build out the dwelling over a number of years, adding a room as family needs demand and as resources permit. This process is called "consolidation" (Ward 1982). Housing consolidation in colonias and IfHSs in the United States is rather different. Self-building is commonplace in border areas (figure 3.2) and can cover a spectrum of informal arrangements, including the construction of a complete home on a slab or on cinder block pylons; extensions to an existing home or trailer; internal fitting out of modular homes; self-made decoration, as well as garden work and decking. Away from the border, manufactured homes are more widely used and offer fewer opportunities for self-help, at least within the primary housing unit (figure 3.5). But everywhere the housing process is predominantly self-managed and therefore largely informal, and often shows a trend toward home "consolidation," albeit in different ways.

While the process is different, both in Latin America and in Texas one observes an improvement in housing conditions (through self-help) in the substitution and/or addition of housing units over time. A common trajectory is that of a homeowner starting residence in a camper or in a low-priced manufactured home, and later substituting a newer single- (15 by 60 feet) or double-wide unit, sometimes keeping the older structures as overflow sleeping space, storage, etc. Traditional self-build housing construction and extensions are more typical along the border, but in all areas it is common to find hybrid arrangements where self-built sections are added to the primary unit. The relatively large lot sizes also allow for shared lots and for multiple units.

Even in Starr County, one of the poorest in Texas and the nation, colonia households have made significant improvements since 2000, largely through informal self-build. In a 2011 survey, three-quarters of households across ten colonias had made significant improvement to their homes during the previous ten years, investing an average of almost $9,500 during that period (Durst and Ward 2013). Very rarely were these improvements paid through formal sources of credit financing (20 percent), although a further 23 percent of the households did receive microfinancing support from the nonprofit organization associated with the title-cleaning program in Rio Grande City. Most people used savings and/or annual tax rebates, the latter being an especially important source of home improvement financing—a sort of informal savings fund.

Self-help provides a sweat equity approach to home acquisition and asset creation. In 2011 in the Starr County colonias, the estimated average property value was just under $51,000, up from $36,750 ten years earlier—a 38 percent increase. For most households, this is a significant potential asset, but its use value is most important since few wish to sell or use their properties as collateral on a loan, contrary to what Hernando De Soto (2000) and his adherents have argued. Most (84 percent) considered this to be too high a risk, although just under one-half said that they might do so in the future. But for those wishing or needing to sell, the lack of financing makes it difficult to find a buyer. Effective sale prices are depressed, lots go unsold, and further reversions to informality abound. Some abandon their properties by walking away; others rent out their lots and erstwhile homes; and others lend or sell to kin using oral contracts or unrecorded CfDs.

### Informal Household Structure Arrangements, Household Extension, and Inheritance

The opportunity for household extension is another important and often underappreciated advantage afforded by colonia and IfHS residence. As children grow up and need separate or more sleeping space, additional rooms can be built or they can move to a separate trailer or camper to sleep. Household extension can be vertical, i.e., adult children living with parents and grandparents; or horizontal, where siblings and in-laws share property, or accommodate friends or *paisanos* from their region of origin in Mexico. Such social capital is widely understood and lauded in Latin America and elsewhere, but such exchanges and social support are also important in Texas. Increasingly, as owners age or need to look after their own aged parents, large lots offer a relatively safe housing environment in which to accommodate an elderly or frail parent—probably the only option given the prohibitively high costs of formal residential and nursing care for the elderly (Ward 2007).

Our Latin American housing studies have alerted us to the importance of considering what will happen to these homes as the original buyers age and eventually die (Grajeda and Ward 2012; Ward et al. 2012). In Texas, as in Mexico, our data show that less than 10 percent of colonia homeowners have a will, which means that inheritance and succession will take place either through an informal arrangement or under intestacy law. The latter is a formal process that usually provides equal shares to the spouse's children and descendants. But informality is also common when it comes to inheritance: owners make verbal agreements with some of their children, or wish to favor one particular child, and so on. If challenged by other legitimate claimants *post mortem*, such informal agreements will not stand up, which means that until the matter is resolved it will be impossible for titles to be reset in the name of the inheritor. Without a will to determine inheritance and succession, problems with "clouded" titles appear to be a certain outcome of informality in the future.

## Public Policy Responses to Informality

As this chapter has amply demonstrated, housing informality is alive and well in the United States, and is invariably a rational response to structural conditions of poverty, low incomes, and the inability of the formal market to respond adequately to a need for affordable housing. Such informal responses are often innovative adaptations and workarounds to market dynamics and government policies, especially where the latter are obstructive rather than facilitative. Outlawing or criminalizing self-help housing is rarely successful, and experience shows that making a practice illegal often leads to a raft of unanticipated consequences that reduce housing access and self-help endeavors. But this is not a call for laissez-faire: public policy interventions are required to minimize exposure to risks and hazards in the home and the environment; to protect would-be homeowners from nefarious practices and from the excesses of predatory lending; to prime the market so that owners may take advantage of their sweat equity and sell their properties for the full value; to encourage clean titles and minimize "clouding" of titles through improper property transactions and conflicts over inheritance; and to respond to aging populations and new constituencies living in new or old colonias.

### Policies to Promote Clean Titles
Without formal financing support, seller financing is likely to remain the order of the day. But seller financing promotes informality, and many deals and transactions still go unrecorded. Policies should seek to ensure full recording of CfDs and facilitate the preparation of contracts by making available a no-cost standard template in Spanish and English that can substitute for handwritten notes for sales; confirmation of completion of contracted payments; affidavits of inheritance; and waiver of claims. These forms should carry clear instructions about witness requirements, notarization (if necessary), and filing—at minimal cost

(with the cost made transparent), or at no cost. Similarly, mediation services should be encouraged to advise on the use of these documents and intervene with conflict resolution, if necessary. These policies recognize informality and the inevitability of seller financing, and seek to work within the realms of informality, not exclusively outside it.

In anticipation of a new generation of title conflicts born of intestacy, homeowners should be encouraged to make a will assigning their property to a specific named beneficiary. In the past decade, Mexico City had considerable success in promoting wills through campaigns that helped the owners draw up wills at low or no cost, as well as minimize the costs associated with probate (Ward et al. 2011). The key issue is to recognize that often those who inherit a share of their parents' home also reside on that lot, and wish to continue doing so. Thus, if probate requires significant payments to be made (taxes, legal fees, etc.), or if other beneficiaries need to be paid a share in settlement, these payments cannot easily be made through liquidation of the deceased's property.

**Policies to Improve Market Functioning**
Banks and mortgage companies are unlikely to provide buyer financing to low- and very low-income households in colonias and IfHSs. The relatively few property owners who wish or need to sell their homes will continue to find potential buyers hard to come by. Some will abandon their lots, which will remain vacant. If the owners have stopped paying the property taxes, the lots are effectively locked out of the market, either because the owners cannot be traced or because the lots await repossession or confiscation by the tax assessor. In a study of multiple colonias, approximately 22 percent of lots were vacant, and although the non-occupancy rate had dropped by around 8 percent between 2000 and 2010, it still remained high (Rojas 2012). Appropriate policies should focus on how to identify the current owners of vacant lots, and should create mechanisms and institutions that will bundle these lots into an institution's portfolio. In this way, they may eventually be brought back onto the market, either for prospective home buyers or for neighborhood services, utilities, green areas, and so on.

When owners are unwilling or unable to sell, another alternative is to hand over the lot or home to kin as a concession, or to rent it out. Our study for the Texas Department of Housing and Community Affairs found that approximately 22 percent of colonia residents were non-owners, and of these 79 percent were renters, invariably without a formal contract (Ward, Way, and Wood 2012).

## Policies for Upgrading

The ten-year study of colonias in Starr County revealed substantial home improvements and investment, yet much of the financing for improvements continues to be informal; homeowners eschew using their homesteads as collateral for loans (Durst and Ward 2013). Such informality should be respected, but in some areas microcredit support has been successfully utilized and could be expanded in the future. Tax rebates offer an important infusion of capital for many. Some potential recipients of grants are locked out of receiving improvement benefits because the dwelling unit is not at or cannot be readily brought up to code, even though the intervention might significantly improve conditions or reduce a particular hazard. Some flexibility and adoption of progressive compliance principles would help avoid these catch-22 situations.

## Targeting the Aged

Established colonias and IfHSs house gradually aging populations, many of whom have little mobility and have health problems. For them informality will continue to be a lifeline through which they can survive on small incomes, pensions, and Medicaid. Informality, however, presents many challenges, and policymaking is urgently required to target home improvements for these populations, such as ramps to front doors, shaded yard improvements, adequate ventilation, insulation, and bathroom modernization. Although many elderly do not have a need for private cars since they are no longer working, they often need transportation to enable them to go shopping or reach health care appointments. While neighbors and kin often oblige, policies to ensure adequate volunteerism and enhance access would be welcomed.

The cost of formal care in residential facilities and nursing homes is prohibitive for the low-income elderly, and IfHSs and colonias offer opportunities for informal care of aged parents. Informal care for the elderly is likely to become a growth area in the next twenty years as people live longer and a growing portion of the population cannot afford the costs of care. Colonias and IfHSs are one escape valve in this respect (Ward 2007).

## Infrastructure and Informality

Most infrastructure is provided privately and formally, but informality often exists alongside formal services. Many streets are unpaved, and while some streets may be eventually surfaced, they rarely carry formal or adequate storm water drainage systems. Informal disposal of garbage exists alongside formal and informal collection services. Septic systems break down for lack of maintenance or regular pumping. Policy approaches should promote greater awareness and support for recycling, as well as encourage rainwater capture and reuse of gray water wastes for spot yard irrigation. Counties could do more to promote periodic septic tank pumping—perhaps by paying for the service out of property tax revenues or, as in Bastrop County (Texas), making it mandatory, with the county adding the cost to the tax bill when residents do not comply.

However, formal policies sometimes have unanticipated consequences that can lead to new forms of informality. Developers, prevented by the model subdivision regulations from selling lots without infrastructure, are now sponsoring colonias with full services, but at greater cost and with aggressive titling that makes people feel vulnerable and allows for rapid foreclosure and flipping of properties. This also inhibits investment in home improvements, such that these subdivisions are becoming some of the poorest housing in Texas and comprise rudimentary shacks, campers, and dilapidated trailers (figures 3.3 and 3.4).

### Conclusion: Informality Is (Not) Dead; Long Live Informality!

This chapter has described one important dimension of informality in the United States today: self-help and self-build housing in low-income communities. I have shown how informality is a dynamic process that unfolds over time in response to new constraints, whether these are structurally determined or shaped by policy interventions from government or nongovernmental agents. Nor is this just a phenomenon related to housing. Other chapters in this volume explore informality in a range of situations, and other authors share my fascination with the dynamic nature of informality and the creative workarounds that people design to survive and move forward. Understanding these strategies and outlining sensitive policy responses is one of the principal tasks of the contemporary social scientist, architect, planner, or community activist.

Among the numerous dynamics that I have touched upon in this chapter, let me close with the one that I see as especially pressing for sociologists and legal scholars to consider: the transfer of informal housing assets to the next generation(s). Because the owners are poor and are perceived to have few or no assets, inheritance never figures as part of the conversation for low-income residents of colonias, as it does for many wealthy and middle-income households. And yet many low-income self-builders would claim two overriding reasons for undertaking the social costs and deprivation of living without adequate infrastructure, often in abysmal housing conditions: first and foremost, to have a place of one's own in which to live and raise a family; second, to create a patrimony (inheritance) for the children—an asset to leave to them that might one day help them into home ownership of their own.

In Latin America and in the United States the poor and working classes, through their own sweat equity and informal settlement development, have created an important housing asset that has ongoing use value, as well as potential exchange value (Ward 2012). In the Starr County, Texas, study described above, the average property values are just over $50,000—not a huge amount, but an asset nevertheless, and one that few are willing to gamble with by taking out loans against the home as collateral. In both Mexico and Texas, either the dwelling or the lot may allow for ongoing residential use and expansion for some adult members of the next generation and their families. Indeed, in some cases the latter already live on the lot in their parents' dwelling, or separately in another part of the lot that will, one day, become theirs. Or will it?

The lack of formal financing means that would-be sellers have to find workarounds: informal sales often at lower-than-market prices; or subletting or lending to kinsmen simply because the owners cannot sell but are unwilling to walk away. Some do abandon their properties, however, thus exacerbating informality since those lots remain unused and inaccessible, become overgrown, and often turn into informal dump sites. In the medium to long term, most owners will die intestate, and their beneficiaries may not be able to agree on how to share the inheritance. Some siblings will prioritize the use value, while others will want to sell their share of the inheritance. Maybe informal magnanimity will rule the day such that these beneficiaries will formally cede their shares to their less fortunate siblings, but my fieldwork and intensive case studies in Mexico often point in the opposite direction—toward tension and conflict. As is often the case, de facto occupation (of the dwelling or lot) will be nine-tenths of the law, but unless clean title is achieved, informality is compounded. Indeed, those who today have won their title deeds have moved from initial informality to formal full legal title, but if they do not leave a will, that patrimony will invariably lapse into informality and clouded title.

## Notes

1. By international standards this is a high level of ownership, but one caveat should be noted: the U.S. Census definition of home ownership includes those

who own (or are purchasing) a trailer or a mobile home without having any claim to ownership of the site.

2. Manufactured housing is defined as being built entirely in the factory under a federal building code administered by the U.S. Department of Housing and Urban Development. Homes may be single- or multi-section, are built upon a wheel base, and are transported to the site for installation.

3. The Office of the Attorney General (OAG) operates an online viewer containing information about 2,000 colonias. The US-Mexico Border Environmental Health Initiative (BEHI) offers information about 1,808 colonias; see http://borderhealth.cr.usgs.gov/datalayers.html. An advantage of the BEHI data set is that it has population estimates up to 2005.

4. These insights derive from various survey databases constructed by researchers at the University of Texas at Austin, several of which may be accessed at www.lahn.utexas.org (Texas Housing Database menu section).

5. The second study draws primarily on several border counties and forms part of a major survey commissioned by the Texas Department of Housing and Community Affairs in 2011–2012 (Ward, Way, and Wood 2012).

6. Texas Property Code, §5.079. The Texas Legislature, in its attempt to soften the harsh impacts of contracts for deed on consumers, adopted legislation barring a seller from enforcing a forfeiture clause after the buyer has paid 40 percent of the amount due under the contract, or after 48 monthly payments. Once a buyer has made the requisite payments, the seller must follow a nonjudicial foreclosure process similar to that used in foreclosures under a deed of trust and must refund the buyer whatever equity is left in the property after the foreclosure sale. Texas Property Code, §5.066.

## References

Davies, Christopher Shane, and Robert Holz. 1992. "Settlement Evolution of the '*Colonias*' along the US-Mexico Border: The Case of the Lower Rio Grande Valley of Texas." *Habitat International* 16 (4):119–142.

De Soto, Hernando. 2000. *The Mystery of Capital: Why Capitalism Triumphs in the West and Fails Everywhere Else*. New York: Basic Books.

Donelson, Angela, and Esperanza Holguin. 2002. "Homestead Subdivision/ Colonias and Land Market Dynamics in Arizona and New Mexico." Memoria of a research workshop, "Irregular Settlement and Self-Help Housing in the United States," 39–41. Lincoln Institute of Land Policy, September 21–22, Cambridge, MA.

Durst, Noah, and Peter Ward. 2013. "Measuring Self-Help Home Improvements in Texas Colonias: A Ten Year 'Snapshot' Study." *Urban Studies*. Sage, published online November 20. See also the unpublished report: http://www.lahn.utexas .org/Texas%20Colonias/TexasColonias4.html.

Grajeda, Erika, and Peter Ward. 2012. "Inheritance and Succession among Second and Third Generation Squatter Households in Mexico City." *Latin American Research Review*, special issue (December): 139–162.

Larson, Jane. 1995. "Free Markets in the Heart of Texas." *Georgetown Law Journal* 84 (December):179–260.

Larson, Jane. 2002. "Informality, Illegality, and Inequality." *Yale Law and Policy Review* 20:137–182.

Mukhija, Vinit, and Paavo Monkonnen. 2006. "Federal Colonias Policy in California: Too Broad and Too Narrow." *Housing Policy Debate* 17 (4):755–780.

Rojas, Danielle. 2012. "Documenting a Decade of Lot Occupation Change in 22 Texas County Colonias and Subdivisions: Satellite Image Analysis and Design and Results." From "Housing Sustainability, Self-Help and Upgrading in Texas Colonias: A Longitudinal Perspective—2002 plus 10," Lyndon B. Johnson School of Public Affairs, University of Texas. http://www.lahn.utexas.org/Texas%20 Colonias/TexasColonias4.html.

Ward, Peter M., ed. 1982. *Self-Help Housing: A Critique*. London: Mansell.

Ward, Peter M. 1999. *Colonias and Public Policy in Texas and Mexico: Urbanization by Stealth*. Austin: University of Texas Press.

Ward, Peter M. 2003. "Informality of Housing Production at the Urban-Rural Interface: The Not-So-Strange Case of the Texas Colonias." In Ananya Roy and Nezar AlSayyad, eds., *Urban Informality*, 243–270. Lanham, MD: Lexington Books.

Ward, Peter M. 2007. "Colonias, Informal Homestead Subdivisions and Self-Help Care for the Elderly among Mexican Populations in the USA." In Jacqueline L. Angel and Keith E. Whitfield, eds., *The Health of Aging Hispanics: The Mexican-Origin Population*, 141–162. New York: Springer.

Ward, Peter M. 2012. "'A Patrimony for the Children': Low-Income Homeownership and Housing (Im)Mobility in Latin American Cities." *Annals of the Association of American Geographers* 102 (6):1489–1510.

Ward, Peter M., Cecilia Giusti, and Flavio de Souza. 2004. "Colonia Land and Housing Market Performance and the Impact of Lot Title Regularization in Texas." *Urban Studies* (Edinburgh, Scotland) 41 (13):2621–2646.

Ward, Peter M., Jane Larson, Flavio de Souza, and Cecilia Giusti. 2011. "*Con el título en la mano*: The Meaning of Full Property Titles, and the Impact of Titling Programs upon Low Income Housing Improvements in Texas Colonias." *Law and Social Inquiry* 36 (1):1–82.

Ward, Peter M., and Paul Peters. 2007. "Self-Help Housing and Informal Homesteading in Peri-Urban America: Settlement Identification Using Digital Imagery and GIS." *Habitat International* 31 (2):205–218.

Ward, Peter, Heather Way, and Lucille Wood. 2012. "The Contract for Deed Prevalence Project: A Final Report Prepared by the authors at the University of Texas at Austin on Behalf of the Texas Department of Housing and Community Affairs." Lyndon B. Johnson School of Public Affairs, University of Texas. http:// www.lahn.utexas.org/Texas%20Colonias/TDHCA.html.

# 4

## Making and Supporting Community Gardens as Informal Urban Landscapes

Jeffrey Hou

Community gardening is enjoying a resurgence of interest in the United States as issues of health and urban food systems attract growing attention. In cities from coast to coast, a host of new initiatives also reflects interest in and awareness of community gardening's multiple benefits in food security, job training, community building, neighborhood revitalization, and activation of urban spaces. In New Orleans's City Park, for example, youth organizers and Tulane University's Tulane City Center created the Grow Dat Youth Farm to provide healthy food for local residents and develop youth leadership. In Oakland, California, urban food advocates are working in a variety of ways, including community gardening, to address food security and justice in the city's historically underserved neighborhoods (Prince 2013). In Seattle, where community gardens have enjoyed municipal support since the 1970s, new kinds of community gardens are being developed, from food forests to rooftop gardens, to meet the growing appetite for urban gardening.

Despite their popularity, however, community gardens remain one of the most poorly defined types of land use in North American cities. Spatially, garden sites exist in a wide variety of physical settings, including vacant lots, utility corridors, and public rights-of-way. They are sometimes mixed with or developed as part of housing complexes, schools, and health facilities. Institutionally, gardens are often considered as an interim use, eventually to be replaced by a higher-value development (Lawson 2004, 2005; Nordahl 2009). Only rarely, they are incorporated into a city's parks and open space system. But even in such formalized contexts, community gardens often exist through temporary agreements between different governmental agencies and jurisdictions, subject to political and institutional change. As a result, community gardens are often characterized by makeshift structures and fences, lacking permanence or formal design elements. The seasonally changing crops and plants also help reinforce the perception of community gardens as ephemeral spaces.

The informal dimension of community gardens has been both an asset and a challenge for community gardeners and supporters. On one hand, as informal open spaces, community gardens provide low-cost opportunities to turn underutilized urban spaces into productive landscapes. They have enabled communities to mobilize and undertake collective actions to address issues of neighborhood improvement, safety, food production, and the need for green amenities and social space. On the other hand, the perception of them as interim uses and the lack of institutional and legal support often put gardens at risk of displacement and relocation. The significant volunteer support that gardens require also puts a heavy burden on certain individuals in the community. As community gardening gains increasing interest and popularity in the United States, attempts to incorporate community gardens as informal spaces within a formal institutional framework present both challenges and opportunities for communities and municipalities.

This chapter examines issues and challenges facing community gardens as settings at the crossroad between informality and formalized planning. As one of very few cities in the United States with a municipal community gardening program, Seattle serves as a case study of how public policy and institutional actions supporting community gardening have been carried out without inhibiting the informal social arrangements that sustain community gardens. The study draws from previous fieldwork and recent interviews with key program staff and nonprofit leaders.[1] This chapter first gives a brief historic overview of urban gardening in the United States, followed by a discussion of community gardening in Seattle, in which I relate the successes, challenges, and lessons drawn from the city's community gardens movement. The chapter concludes by reflecting on the potential contributions of community gardens not only as landscapes and lived spaces of contemporary cities but also in the discourse and practice of city planning.

## A Historically Informal and Marginalized Urban Landscape

Community gardens in the United States usually consist of individual plots on urban sites of modest size. They are outcomes of collective efforts at the community and neighborhood level. In its various incarnations, community gardening has been around in the United States for over a century. In the early part of the twentieth century, urban gardening was promoted during wartime and during the economic depression to produce food and alleviate poverty (Lawson 2004, 2005). In the 1970s, as inner-city decline spread throughout the United States, community gardening became an urban revitalization strategy for many neighborhoods combating crime and vandalism (Lawson 2004, 2005; Warner 1987). During that time, groups such as the Green Guerrillas in New York City and Boston Urban Gardeners worked to reclaim and rebuild communities through gardening (Lawson 2004). In the context of the urban disinvestment of the 1970s, Sam Bass Warner (1987) argues that the community gardening movement reflected a politics of dignity and self-help. In both historical episodes, however, the support for community gardens was temporary. As wars ended and economic prosperity returned, governments stopped promoting gardening for food production and the alleviation of poverty (Lawson 2004, 2005). Similarly in private philanthropy, funding support shifted toward urban greening and beautification (Warner 1987).

During the 1970s, as community gardens became a strategy for combatting urban blight, public agencies had provided support for several thousand gardening projects (Jamison 1985). Some states and municipalities introduced supportive legislation, such as the Massachusetts Gardening and Farm Act of 1974 that enabled gardeners and farmers to use vacant public land at no cost (Warner 1987). Cities, including Oakland and New York City, have used Community Development Block Grants to fund community gardening efforts (Francis et al. 1984). However, lacking land tenure and official recognition, community gardens had only a precarious existence. In a 1996 survey conducted by the American Community Gardening Association, only 5.3 percent of 6,020 gardens tabulated were in ownership or trusts (ACGA 1998). In 1999, New York City was going to sell off more than 100 community gardens to developers. This came after twenty years of support for community gardening from the city's popular GreenThumb program (Kirschbaum 2000). More recently, gardeners and activists in Los Angeles fought but lost a widely publicized battle to save the South Central Farm, a 14-acre site located in an industrial area that supported hundreds of families of Mesoamerican descent (Mare and Peña 2010).

The precarious state of community gardens in U.S. cities partly reflects their ambiguous status in municipal planning and legal terms. Legal expert Jane Schukoske (2000) notes that community garden legislation has received little attention in the legal literature. According to her study,

codes of many U.S. municipalities use the term "gardens" only in reference to privately owned land, and rarely in the context of zoning provisions and other statues, while some municipal ordinances include them
within the definition of the broader term "park." This finding is echoed
by a survey of twenty-two U.S. city planning agencies by Kameshwari
Pothukuchi and Jerome Kaufman, who found community food system
issues to be low on the agenda of practicing planners, scholars, and
educators. One of the reasons was that "it's not our turf" (Pothukuchi
and Kaufman 2000: 116). And it was not until 2005 that the Annual
Conference of the American Planning Association started regular sessions
on the topic of food planning (APA 2007).

Laura Lawson (2004) notes that because community gardens are
perceived as opportunistic and temporary, they have been largely
ignored in long-range planning. Even in the 1960s and 1970s, with the
advent of advocacy planning, she states, "planners recognized community gardens as participatory assets without necessarily addressing the
implications for land use and open space planning" (Lawson 2004:
153). Three assumptions have shaped planning's general approach to
community gardens, according to Lawson: first, a fundamental mis-
match between desire for orderly urban planning and the incremental
gestures of gardens; second, the personal nature of gardening; and
third, the gardens' association with social actions rather than physical
entities. She adds, "The appropriate venue of this kind of activity . . .
was generally considered the realm of voluntary associations and civic
improvement societies and not of professionals" (Lawson 2004: 166).
Similarly, Warner (1987) observes that, unlike the northern European
model of government policies supporting urban gardening, public
response to community gardening in North America has been mixed:
"The idea of a city that would provide open spaces to those who
wished to garden was a concept quite beyond the American imagination" (Warner 1987: 16).

Over the years, community gardening has faced its share of criticism
from city staff and planning professionals. In a study that compared
community gardens with traditional urban parks, Mark Francis (1987:
106) found municipal staff likening the gardens to a "private club"
because they were typically fenced. He also noted that "the value of the
gardens as permanent open space was discounted by all officials who
were interviewed," and a common concern was that "they do not look
good" (Francis 1987: 107–108). Similarly, in examining issues of urban
food production, Darrin Nordahl (2009: 53) found that "most public

agencies discourage or downright prohibit the planting of edibles in public spaces, largely over concerns about maintenance and perceived mess."

To address the issue of impermanence, a variety of efforts have emerged in recent years to protect and bring stability to garden sites. Some of the techniques include use of park department stewardship, land trusts, conservation easements, and lease agreements (Kirschbaum 1998). Throughout the United States, many nonprofit organizations and private-public partnerships have developed to support community gardening in the face of limited municipal support. These include the Parkways Partners in New Orleans, a grant-funded nonprofit partnership that has built 142 gardens since 1992, mainly in low-income neighborhoods; NeighborSpace, a land trust in Chicago funded by the City, the Chicago Parks District, and the Cook County Forest Preserve District; and the Parks and People Foundation, an independent nonprofit in Baltimore that supports urban greening, restoration of natural resources, and a wide range of recreational and educational activities for youth (Kirschbaum 2000).

Among the growing number of organizational models, Seattle's remains an exemplary one that combines municipal support with an extensive network of nonprofit and community actors. Seattle's experience, therefore, offers a view into how planning and municipal institutions can collaborate with nongovernmental actors and partners to support community gardens as an integral part of the contemporary urban fabric in the United States.

## Community Gardening in Seattle

As in the rest of the country, urban gardening in Seattle has experienced multiple waves of growth, including efforts during the Great Depression such as the Airport farm (a 55-acre site in which food was grown and distributed to charitable agencies) as well as activities during the wars (Hou, Johnson, and Lawson 2009). After a lull in the 1950s and 1960s, a new wave of garden activism began in the 1970s that gradually led to the establishment of a municipal program and networks of supporters. The movement began with grassroots efforts to build garden plots at the Picardo Farm, which the city later leased from the Picardo family in 1973 as an experiment to support community gardening. The success of the ten-month experiment gave rise to the establishment of the P-Patch Community Gardening Program (Lawson 2005). Starting with ten garden sites in 1974, the number of P-Patch gardens (the name "P-Patch" honors the Picardo family; DON 2009) grew to 60 by 1993 under the oversight of the P-Patch Program (Alexander, n.d.; Hucka, n.d.). By 2010, the program was serving 4,400 gardeners in 75 sites scattered throughout the city, from dense downtown neighborhoods to suburbs, and on both private and public lands.[2] In addition to providing coordination and services for community gardens, the P-Patch Program supports market gardening, youth gardening, and community food security efforts. Today, the program is widely recognized as a model for other cities in the country (Kirschbaum 2000; Lawson 2005; Schukoske 2000).

While its leadership is important, the P-Patch Program is only part of an extensive web of support for community gardening in Seattle, rooted in a long history of civic activism (Hou, Johnson, and Lawson 2009), including such organizations as P-Patch Trust, Seattle Tilth, Solid Ground, and King County Master Gardeners. The P-Patch Trust, in particular, was formed as an advisory and support organization for P-Patch gardens. Formerly the Friends of P-Patch, the group was first formed in 1979 and incorporated as a nonprofit in 1994. Using its status as a nonprofit, the Trust partners with the P-Patch Program to acquire, build, preserve, and protect community gardens in Seattle's neighborhoods. In addition to fundraising and grant writing to support the gardens, it also carries blanket liability insurance for all P-Patch sites.[3]

The different organizations often collaborate, an important factor in supporting community gardening and related efforts. For example, the Lettuce Link program was conceived in 1998 to deliver excess produce to local food banks and encourage gardeners to grow food for the needy. The program was started through collaboration of the Fremont Public Association (now Solid Ground), the P-Patch Program, and Washington State University's Extension Food Garden Project (Borba 1994). Recently, to address the perennial shortage of garden plots and the persistent demand for them, an independent group started a website called Urban Garden Share that matches interested gardeners with available gardens in Seattle and a few other cities.

In addition to nonprofits and individual volunteers, the P-Patch Program also relies on support from city agencies. Specifically, the Seattle Department of Transportation (SDOT), Department of Parks and Recreation, Seattle Housing Authority, and Seattle Public Utilities have all collaborated with the P-Patch Program to provide sites for community gardens through leases or permits (Fisher and Roberts 2011). In 1995,

**Figure 4.1**
Bradner Gardens Park was developed through a collaborative effort between neighbors, a nonprofit organization, and city agencies. Photo credit: Vanessa Lee.

the Cultivating Communities program was started by the Friends of P-Patch and the Seattle Housing Authority to provide land, training, and technical support to families living in public housing, particularly immigrants, to grow food for consumption or for sale (Lawson 2005). More recently, a memorandum of agreement with SDOT was arranged to allow for long-term use of a public right-of-way by P-Patch through a "no-fee" annual street use permit (Fisher and Roberts 2011). Nonprofits and city agencies also work together on the development of specific sites. For example, the nine-acre Rainier Beach Urban Farm and Wetlands, currently under development, involves a partnership between the Department of Parks and Recreation, the Friends of Rainier Beach Urban Farm and Wetlands, and Seattle Tilth. The seven-acre Beacon Food Forest, located in the Beacon Hill neighborhood and adjacent to a park, is another collaborative effort between the P-Patch Program and Seattle Public Utilities.

Enabling legislation and supportive policies adopted by the city have been critical to community gardening efforts as well. In 1992, the Seattle

City Council passed resolution 28610 that declared general support for community gardening and specific support for making surplus land available for gardening (Lawson 2005). The city's 1994 comprehensive plan set the goal of one community garden per 2,500 households within the "urban villages"—areas in the city for planned, concentrated growth. Furthermore, the Urban Village Element of the city's current comprehensive plan (updated in 2009) includes a policy to promote interagency and intergovernmental cooperation to expand community gardening opportunities, and includes P-Patch community gardens among organizations given priority in using the city's surplus property. Additionally, "community garden" is listed as a type of open space acquisition and facility development that can be used to expand the open space network in an urban village. In 2008, in an effort to support urban food production, the City Council passed the Local Food Action Initiative that established goals and a policy framework for strengthening community and regional food systems, including community gardening. To support the initiative, a Food Systems Interdepartmental Team was established to coordinate actions among different city agencies. In 2010, in a new municipal ordinance adopted by the city, "community garden" became a primary use permitted in all zones (with restrictions only in designated manufacturing and industrial centers).

The operation of the P-Patch Program is supported by the city's general fund. In 2008, the program had a budget of $659,577, of which 9 percent covered operating costs (including water charges at most gardens, equipment and supplies, vehicle rental and fuel, professional services, and some miscellaneous costs), while 85 percent covered staff costs (DON 2009: 21). Nominal plot fees are also collected from gardeners to offset the cost of operation. In 2000 and 2008, with limited municipal resources yet strong demand for open space amenities, the city worked with civic organizations to launch two consecutive rounds of voter-approved tax levies to support acquisition, development, programming, and stewardship of parks and open spaces. The 2008 Parks and Green Spaces Levy, in particular, included a $2 million fund to support the development of additional community gardens. The levy also included $15 million of opportunity funds for projects that may include community gardens. As will be discussed later, since its inception in 1988, the city's Neighborhood Matching Fund Program has been a major source of regular support for the development of community gardens. In many gardens, volunteering and activities such as plant sales also help offset costs and raise funds for operation and maintenance.

## Informal Practices in a Formally Supported Process

From recent interviews with the P-Patch Program staff and P-Patch Trust leadership, as well as findings from an earlier study (Hou, Johnson, and Lawson 2009), it appears that informal practices in the development and everyday operation of the gardens have been no less important to their success than the institutional support. First, volunteerism and self-organization are a regular and important part of how community gardens are developed and managed on a daily basis. Although some P-Patch sites are managed directly by the P-Patch Program staff, other sites in the city are managed and run entirely by volunteers. Of the latter, some gardens are managed by voluntary site leaders, while others are managed collectively by a leadership team or a core group of volunteers. It is only in situations where there are no available site leaders or significant language barriers exist among the gardeners that the sites are managed directly by the P-Patch Program staff. For gardens with site leaders or leadership teams, garden operation is entirely self-organized. This allows their operation to correspond with the capacity and specific needs of the gardeners and the garden sites. The self-organizing aspect of the gardens also results in a great degree of flexibility that enables gardeners and communities to utilize the garden in different and sometimes unexpected ways. Unlike typical city parks that require permits and reservations for certain activities, decisions regarding events in community gardens are made solely by site leaders and volunteers.

With such flexibility, P-Patch sites have become settings for a wide range of activities, including not just food production but also social and educational events. In Picardo P-Patch, for example, a band approached the gardeners for permission to play in the garden and has since been performing during the garden's many work parties. Similarly, some gardens have incorporated yoga as part of the work party activities. P-Patch sites are also used as outdoor classrooms for gardening and composting as well as environmental education by groups such as the Urban Pollination Project (UPP), a citizen science project developed by a group of scientists at the University of Washington. The project encourages the participation of gardeners and citizens in research and learning activities concerning crops and bee pollination in urban areas. Over twenty sites now participate in the project. Similarly, another organization called City Fruit has been promoting the planting of fruit-bearing trees in the city. Starting with harvesting fruit trees, the group now holds classes on P-Patch sites for backyard gardeners and teaches techniques

**Figure 4.2**
Social events such as this one in the Danny Woo International Community Garden bring together and strengthen bonds between gardeners, residents, and volunteers. Photo credit: Leslie Gia Clark.

for growing fruit trees. On a regular and perhaps more mundane basis, the gardens have hosted a variety of activities that are important to local neighborhoods and the gardens themselves. These include community barbecues and potlucks, holiday parties, concerts, and plant sales. This growing array of activities has greatly expanded the social benefits of community gardens in the city. They demonstrate the gardens' potential and existing role as an amenity for the wider public and answer the common critique concerning community gardens as a "private club."[4]

With community building identified specifically as a goal of the P-Patch Program (DON 2009), the program staff are well aware of the wide range of social benefits of the gardens. Over the years, the program's philosophy has been well supported by the Department of Neighborhoods, which hosts the program. Originally part of the Department of Housing and Human Services, the P-Patch Program was reassigned to the Department of Neighborhoods in 1997 (Schukoske 2000). Founded in 1989 by former neighborhood organizer Jim Diers, who served as its director for fourteen years, the Department of Neighborhoods has been widely recognized nationally and internationally for its leading role as a municipal department supporting community development. Based on a model of community empowerment, its signature program, the Neighborhood Matching Fund, has served as a primary source of funding for the development of community gardens. Under the Neighborhood Matching Fund program, communities can apply for different categories of funding, including Small and Simple Projects (up to $20,000 per project) and Large Projects (up to $100,000 project) designed for different types of activities. To receive the match from the city, a community can either raise funds or mobilize volunteers and convert volunteer hours into a cash equivalent. By design, the grant encourages strong community mobilization, especially in communities with few financial resources.

In a way, the role of the P-Patch Program is not unlike that of the Neighborhood Matching Fund program. Rather than carrying out regulatory enforcement, the P-Patch Program has been more an enabler and liaison, as well as a matchmaker of resources for those in need. Although the P-Patch Program does provide guidelines and codes of conduct for garden sites concerning matters such as public access, plot assignments and renewal, types of fertilizers, requirement of volunteer hours, and overall city policy concerning race and social justice, much of the actual implementation is entrusted to site leaders and volunteers. According to program staff, when occasional conflicts within a garden or with neighbors occur, the resolution is usually worked out by the site leaders and immediate parties. Though the approach, in part, reflects the limited size and capacity of the program staff, it also reveals how the program sees itself less as an enforcement agency and more as a bridge between the municipal institution and the informal, community-based process. For example, when a group of garden supporters seek to utilize a city property as a garden site, the P-Patch Program helps coordinate with the city agency that manages the property. When high school students or programs look for opportunities for earning service-learning credits, they are directed by the P-Patch staff to gardens in need. When gardeners are in need of technical assistance, the staff directs them to local nonprofits that can provide such help.

## Persistent Struggles

While the P-Patch Program has been widely recognized as a national model, there have also been persistent struggles. First, land tenure continues to be a challenge as most sites, even those on city property, are arranged on the basis of temporary agreements. There have been recent episodes in which garden sites were relocated or threatened with other development even after decades in existence. In recent years, a growing number of P-Patches have been developed on park properties. But it was not until around 2000 that the city started considering P-Patches as a legitimate use of park space. And it was not until 2011 that a memorandum of agreement was signed with the Department of Parks and Recreation to formalize the arrangement. While there is now a better understanding of the public benefits of community gardens (as well as the financial advantage of self-maintenance), some Parks and Recreation staff still consider P-Patch gardens a private use of public property.

Successive municipal budget cuts have put the program under pressure to repeatedly justify its public benefits—a recurring challenge for advocates of community gardens. Over the years, the size of the program and its budget have remained small, despite the popularity of community gardening and its growing portfolio of sites and services. An evaluation of the program in 2009 reported that the program's ability to address the strong demand is complicated by the high cost and low availability of land, and its small staff size (DON 2009).

Additionally, to address the long waiting list for garden plots, the Department of Parks and Recreation recently proposed enforcing a three-year term limit for plot assignments. The proposal met with strong opposition from garden activists, who viewed it as counterproductive to the actual operation and management of the gardens that required the involvement of knowledgeable and experienced gardeners/volunteers. According to an estimate by the P-Patch Trust, the term limit would force two-thirds of the current gardeners to leave the gardens, resulting in many sites without seasoned gardeners and site leaders—a detriment to the long-term management of those sites.

In the face of these challenges, it appears that informal practices have again demonstrated their unique value. Specifically, the strong grassroots support and political capital cultivated through the community empowerment model has enabled the program and the movement to weather the storms and thrive. In the mid-1990s, when the city planned to sell the site of the Mount Baker P-Patch (a designated park site) for private development, garden activists organized and lobbied the city to stop the transaction. Eventually, a coalition of garden supporters put forward an initiative, called "Protect Our Parks," that required the city to replace park properties sold, traded, or converted to non-park uses with similar kinds of properties in the same neighborhood. The initiative was adopted by the City Council and became a city ordinance that saved the Mount Baker site as well as other park properties throughout the city. Garden supporters have also been instrumental in lobbying the city to protect the budget for the P-Patch Program. In 1993, the Friends of P-Patch promoted a joint City Council and mayoral resolution supporting community gardens, and in 2000 they launched a five-year plan with the P-Patch Program, which was also adopted by the ordinance (Macdonald, n.d.).

In a recent citywide budget cut, the P-Patch Program was able to have its budget restored by the City Council, thanks to strong backing from supporters of community gardens. The network of organizations also supported the ballot initiative for the 2008 levy, leading to funds for building more P-Patch gardens. Realizing the fiscal reality of the municipality and continued demand, the P-Patch Program is currently working with the P-Patch Trust to delegate some responsibilities to the Trust in order to alleviate the increasing workload on the limited staff and improve its services. Thanks to the strong opposition from gardeners, the Department of Parks and Recreation eventually backed away from the proposal to apply a term limit to the use of garden plots.[5] In all these instances, strong backing from individuals and organizations outside the municipal domain has been instrumental in supporting the program and the community gardening movement in the city.

### Coproduction of Urban Landscapes: Lessons from Seattle

Today, community gardens are some of the most creative and well-used open spaces in Seattle. In Bradner Gardens Park (formerly the Mount Baker P-Patch), neighborhood artists and students from local schools created colorful mosaics on benches, spigots, and restroom walls. Architecture students from the University of Washington worked with residents to create artful fences and shelters. These features not only help mediate the colocation of garden plots and other program elements in the park, but also transform the park into a delightful urban open space enjoyed by gardeners, neighbors, and visitors alike. In the Danny Woo International Community Garden, located in the International District and managed independently by a community organization, a large chicken coop was added recently as part of a new children's garden. The site now welcomes not only elderly immigrant gardeners but also younger children from the growing number of families in the neighborhood. Currently, a plan is being developed for a community kitchen with financial support from the Neighborhood Matching Fund. In the new UpGarden

**Figure 4.3**
The UpGarden P-Patch, one of the newest gardens in Seattle, turned the top of a multistory parking garage into a productive urban landscape. Photo credit: Jeffrey Hou.

P-Patch that sits on top of a multistory parking garage, designers and community members capitalized on the unique character of the site by incorporating a used vintage car filled in with soil and planted with vegetation. In addition, a used Airstream trailer serves as the tool shed. Currently in the planning process, the Beacon Food Forest in the Beacon Hill neighborhood is envisioned as a new type of forest garden that produces edible fruits and nuts. The implementation of the project is also supported by the Neighborhood Matching Fund.

While these gardens are all distinct from each other, they all straddle between institutional support and a significant grassroots process. On the one hand, informal, self-organized grassroots efforts have been critical to the strong community ownership of the garden sites. On the other hand, the P-Patch Program and the Neighborhood Matching Fund in particular provide the necessary institutional and financial support. Although conflicts between formal institutions and gardeners involved in informal garden activities do arise, as in the case of the Bradner Gardens Park or in the term limit debate, it is often the informal social processes that save the day in terms of mobilizing support for the gardens.

With the involvement of gardeners, neighbors, civic organizations, professionals, schools, and city staff, the gardens become a coproduced space.

The coproduction of community gardens as an informal yet socially engaged space holds significant implications for transforming not only the landscapes of today's city but also the long-standing discourse and practice of city planning. Specifically, the making and continued management of community gardens represents a collaborative model of placemaking in which citizen groups and city agencies have equally important roles. For citizen groups, the model presents opportunities to become more actively engaged in shaping and transforming the everyday landscapes of neighborhoods and districts, as well as assuming a greater role in the broader process of placemaking in the city. For city agencies and planners, it means a fundamental change in perspective and position: rather than maintaining full control of the process of city making, agencies and planners need to work with citizens and communities as partners.

As a normative practice, city planning has long focused on formal mechanisms at the expense of informal social processes and reciprocity. Even as participatory planning has become the norm in many municipalities, the form of participation has been limited to formalized venues such as public meetings, focus groups, workshops, and surveys that often stifle the creativity and spontaneity associated with informal social processes. The coproduction of community gardens in Seattle and the self-organized nature of developing and maintaining the garden sites suggest the ability of citizens and community groups to directly shape urban landscapes. Rather than competing modes of spatial production, the Seattle experience suggests that formal institutions and informal social mechanisms can coalesce and form effective partnerships that respond to the complexity of planning and placemaking in the contemporary city.

## Acknowledgment

The author wishes to thank Joyce Moty of the P-Patch Trust, Rich Macdonald, Kenya Fredie, and Laura Raymond of the P-Patch Program, and Michael Shiosaki of the Seattle Department of Parks and Recreation for being interviewed for this chapter. Their immense knowledge and input are invaluable to the findings presented here.

## Notes

1. The earlier study, completed in 2006, was supported by a grant from the Landscape Architecture Foundation through its Land and Community Design

case study series. My co-principal investigators were Julie Johnson and Laura Lawson. We conducted interviews with four P-Patch Program staff, fourteen site coordinators and program managers, twenty-two gardeners, and nine designers. For this chapter, I conducted in-depth, follow-up interviews with three P-Patch Program staff, one senior Parks staff, a senior garden activist, and a landscape architect.

2. Based on a survey conducted by the P-Patch Program in 2007, 55 percent of the P-Patch gardeners were low-income (defined as those earning less than 80 percent of the median income for the Seattle-Bellevue area, which was $75,600 in 2007). More than 75 percent of the gardeners earned less than the area median income; 48 percent lived in apartments; 77 percent had no gardening space where they lived; 20 percent were people of color. Program-wide, P-Patchers were 80 percent Caucasian, versus 70 percent for the city as a whole, 2.1 percent American Indian (1 percent for the city), and 15.2 percent Asian (13 percent for Seattle). The report recognizes areas for improvement, and notes that African Americans and Latinos are not well represented in P-Patches: 2.7 percent and 2.5 percent respectively (although growing from 2 percent and 1.5 percent in the 2004 survey), versus 8 percent and 5 percent for the city (DON, n.d.).

3. The insurance program was created as part of an effort to develop the Cultivating Communities program and serve low-income communities. The liability insurance covers only the gardeners.

4. In Seattle, the P-Patch sites are required to provide public access, and fences around garden plots are not allowed.

5. In response to the long waiting list, the P-Patch Program has taken actions including establishing a maximum square-foot limit for garden plots, limiting the number of sites that prospective gardeners can apply for at one time, and actively creating new garden sites. These measures have resulted in a shorter waiting list.

## References

ACGA (American Community Gardening Association). 1998. "National Community Gardening Survey: 1996." http://communitygarden.org/docs/learn/cgsurvey96part1.pdf (retrieved January 10, 2012).

Alexander, Gemma D. N.d. "Part 2: 1983–1993, Program's Second Decade a Time of Rebuilding." http://www.seattle.gov/neighborhoods/ppatch/aboutPpatch.htm#part2 (retrieved July 21, 2012).

APA (American Planning Association). 2007. "Policy Guide on Community and Regional Food Planning." http://www.planning.org/policy/guides/adopted/food.htm (retrieved July 26, 2012).

Borba, Holly. 1994. "City P-Patches Help Feed Low Income Residents." *Washington Free Press* 11. http://wafreepress.org/11/P_Patch.html (retrieved January 9, 2012).

DON (Department of Neighborhoods). 2009. "A Stroll in the Garden: An Evaluation of the P-Patch Program." http://www.seattle.gov/neighborhoods/ppatch/documents/PPatchEvaluation2009.pdf (retrieved July 22, 2012).

DON (Department of Neighborhoods). N.d. "Who are the P-Patch Gardeners? Results from the 2007 Survey." http://www.seattle.gov/neighborhoods/ppatch/aboutPpatch.htm#part4 (retrieved April 23, 2013).

Fisher, Andrew, and Susan Roberts. 2011. "Community Food Security Coalition Recommendations for Food Systems Policy in Seattle." Community Food Security Coalition, commissioned by the Seattle City Council.

Francis, Mark. 1987. "Some Different Meanings Attached to a City Park and Community Gardens." *Landscape Journal* 6 (2):101–112.

Francis, Mark, Lisa Cashdan, and Lynn Paxson. 1984. *Community Open Spaces: Greening Neighborhoods through Community Action and Land Conservation.* Washington, DC: Island Press.

Hou, Jeffrey, Julie M. Johnson, and Laura J. Lawson. 2009. *Greening Cities, Growing Communities: Learning from Seattle's Urban Community Gardens.* Seattle: University of Washington Press.

Hucka, Judy. N.d. "Part 1: 1973–1983, Picardo, Passion and People: 30 Years of P-Patching." http://www.seattle.gov/neighborhoods/ppatch/aboutPpatch.htm#part1 (retrieved July 21, 2012).

Jamison, Michael S. 1985. "The Joys of Gardening: Collectivist and Bureaucratic Cultures in Conflict." *Sociological Quarterly* 26 (4):473–490.

Kirschbaum, Pamela R. 1998. "Borrowed Land, Borrowed Time: Preserving Community Gardens." In *Community Greening Review 1998.* Columbus, OH: American Community Gardening Association.

Kirschbaum, Pamela R. 2000. "Making Policy in a Crowded World: Steps beyond the Physical Garden." In *Community Greening Review 2000.* Columbus, OH: American Community Gardening Association.

Lawson, Laura. 2004. "The Planner in the Garden: A Historical View into the Relationship between Planning and Community Gardens." *Journal of Planning History* 3 (2):151–176.

Lawson, Laura. 2005. *City Bountiful: A Century of Community Gardening in America.* Berkeley: University of California Press.

Macdonald, Rich. N.d. "Part 3: 1993–2003, Program Thrives in Third Decade, but Challenges Loom." http://www.seattle.gov/neighborhoods/ppatch/aboutPpatch.htm#part3 (retrieved July 21, 2012).

Mare, Teresa M., and Devon Peña. 2010. "Urban Agriculture in the Making of Insurgent Spaces in Los Angeles and Seattle." In Jeffrey Hou, ed., *Insurgent Public Space: Guerrilla Urbanism and the Remaking of Contemporary Cities.* London: Routledge.

Nordahl, Darrin. 2009. *Public Produce: The New Urban Agriculture.* Washington, DC: Island Press.

Pothukuchi, Kameshwari, and Jerome L. Kaufman. 2000. "The Food System: A Stranger to the Planning Field." *APA Journal* 66 (2):113–124.

Prince, Adams. 2013. "Urban Agriculture as 'Agricultural' Producer." In Jeffrey Hou, ed., *Transcultural Cities: Border Crossing and Placemaking*. London: Routledge.

Schukoske, Jane E. 2000. "Community Development through Gardening: State and Local Policies Transforming Urban Open Space." *New York University Journal of Legislation and Public Policy* 3 (2):351–392.

Warner, Sam Bass. 1987. *To Dwell Is to Garden: A History of Boston's Community Gardens*. Boston: Northeastern University Press.

# 5

## "This Is My Front Yard!" Claims and Informal Property Rights on Sidewalks

Anastasia Loukaitou-Sideris and Renia Ehrenfeucht

On February 26, 2012, neighborhood watch captain George Zimmerman spotted hooded teenager Trayvon Martin walking on the sidewalk of his gated neighborhood in Sanford, Florida. Details of their confrontation are muddy, but its outcome was tragic for Martin, who a short while later lay lifeless on the pavement. In the controversy and national soul-searching that followed, a number of claims and counterclaims were aired about racism, racial profiling, and the right of self-defense. What is relevant for this chapter is another claim: Zimmerman's claim on the public sidewalk of his neighborhood as a territory where he belonged and Martin did not. This perception of a right over public space that the "abutter" (Zimmerman) was supposed to have but the "outsider" (Martin) was not led Zimmerman to pursue and eventually gun down Martin. Indeed, Zimmerman did not wait for the police to exercise their formal authority but exerted his own informal means of control over the neighborhood sidewalk, with disastrous consequences.

Early twenty-first-century U.S. sidewalks are highly regulated spaces where ordinances govern virtually every activity but walking. Although formally regulated by municipalities, sidewalks are also informally controlled by the occupants of abutting properties.[1] We would argue that abutters exercise informal property rights on sidewalks that at times clash with the claims exercised on the same sidewalk by other social groups. We call these property rights informal as they are not reflected in deeds of trust or condoned by contracts or laws. Informal expressions of property interests and claims over public spaces may become at times potent enough to influence formal regulatory measures and enforcement practices. When this happens, these informal claims become formalized as rights through regulations that favor abutters over other sidewalk users.

The relationship of abutters to the sidewalks fronting their establishments is quite unique. The proximity and link between the sidewalk and the abutters' private property make abutters a special category of sidewalk users with identifiable interests and place-specific concerns. Such interests impact other users in both positive and negative ways, and at times bring abutters in conflict with other users and/or municipal authorities. Informal property claims lead abutters to exercise informal social control over sidewalks; claim the sidewalk for their own informal activities (e.g., garage sales, display of wares, apron parking, etc.); and develop synergies with other sidewalk users or enact resident-based grassroots initiatives with wider benefits.

This chapter examines the influence and impact of abutters' claims on sidewalks, and the municipal responses to them. A focused look at such claims—who makes them and how they are negotiated and exercised—helps to better explain the formal and informal controls on U.S. sidewalks as well as the differing property rights, responsibilities, and material conditions that shape their function as urban spaces. In the sections that follow, we first explain the special relationship between sidewalks and their abutting properties, as well as the role and responsibility of abutters as structured historically in U.S. cities. Abutters often take exclusionary measures but may also develop inclusionary and synergistic actions, and we discuss both situations. We also examine municipal reaction to competing sidewalk activities. We conclude by raising a number of questions for future research to better explain the formal and informal relationships between sidewalks as public space and sidewalks as an extension of adjoining properties. The chapter is informed by a survey of sidewalk ordinances and municipal interventions in California's four largest cities (Los Angeles, San Francisco, San Jose, and San Diego), interviews with city officials and enforcement agencies, and a review of media accounts of sidewalk conflicts and controversies in these cities.

## Interdependence of Sidewalks and the Abutting Properties

The notion that public spaces are "the people's property" (Staeheli and Mitchell 2008) and should be "relatively open to a range of people and behaviors" (Staeheli, Mitchell, and Nagel 2009: 634) has led many scholars to critique attempts to exert private interests over public spaces. In the last two decades, the relationship between property ownership and public space has generated considerable debate. Detailed accounts have shown how privatization of public space provision (Loukaitou-Sideris and Banerjee 1998; Sorkin 1992) and management through business improvement districts (BIDs) or public-private partnerships (Smith 1996; Zukin 1995) can make public spaces less open and accessible. A significant body of literature has examined the repercussions of the "enclosure of the commons" (Kohn 2004; Lee and Webster 2006) as manifested in gated communities (Blakely and Snyder 1999; Low 2003), shopping malls, corporate plazas (Frieden and Sagalyn 1989; Loukaitou-Sideris and Banerjee 1998), and entertainment districts (Banerjee et al. 1996).

The tendency to contrast this diminishing "publicness" with the perceived openness of traditional public spaces has created a dichotomy that considers public and private spaces as both discrete and distinct. To move beyond this binary, Margaret Kohn (2004) suggests that there is a conceptual continuum between public and private that takes into account ownership, access, and interaction with other people. In this view, sidewalks occupy one end of the continuum. They are publicly owned, can be accessed by all, and allow interaction among people. As parts of the public right-of-way, sidewalks remain open to travelers regardless of their personal characteristics or status. Neither the adjoining occupants nor any public body can legally curtail other people's movement along public streets and sidewalks.

But casting sidewalks at one end of the public-private spectrum is problematic. Sidewalks have a unique characteristic that affects their publicness, one that has been understudied by the literature on open space privatization. Unlike other public destinations—beaches, squares, or parks—sidewalks directly border abutters' front yards and businesses.[2] This proximity creates a functional, symbolic, and ongoing interdependence between the sidewalk and the private properties that abut them. Indeed, sidewalks function both as a front yard *and* a public space. To use Lyn Lofland's (1998) distinction,[3] sidewalks represent "parochial" spaces for abutters while they are perceived as public spaces by everyone else.

Sidewalks have daily impacts on adjoining properties. Some sidewalk activities may have negative impacts—noise, litter, congestion, or violence—that affect the abutters' sense of well-being. This proximity and interdependence between public and private property underlies the actions and interactions of abutters and other sidewalk users. It also leads abutters to make special claims on the sidewalks that front their property, use sidewalks for their own purposes (figure 5.1) and in different ways than other citizens (e.g., receiving deliveries or displaying wares), and exercise their own informal control that at times attempts to curtail, limit, or move elsewhere activities of other sidewalk users.

**Figure 5.1**
Private fence extending into sidewalk in New York City. Photo credit: Anastasia Loukaitou-Sideris.

However, control and intentional exclusion of other users and their activities captures only one dimension of the breadth and complexity of abutters' actions. City officials and planners also depend on abutters for their informal upkeep and care of sidewalks. While some maintenance—such as clearing snow and keeping sidewalks repaired—may be legally mandated in some cities, in other cities it only happens because of informal neighborhood norms (Garnett 2009). Some resident initiatives such as tree planting may have neighborhood and citywide benefits. Less tangibly, people know their neighbors and offer "eyes on the street" and helping hands, even though such actions may at times go terribly wrong (as the opening paragraph indicated). Indeed, abutters' actions and informal activities may influence sidewalk life for the better or the worse. This is not a new phenomenon.

**The Historical Context behind Abutters' Claims on Sidewalks**

The interdependence between urban sidewalks and the abutting properties goes as far back as the early nineteenth century, when the first sidewalks appeared in U.S. cities. Because nineteenth-century streets and sidewalks were assumed to benefit the abutters more than others, they were improved and paved at the abutters' request and expense, but administered through the municipal government. Municipal public works departments increasingly developed maintenance requirements and construction standards, but the costs and maintenance fell on abutting property owners. Abutters often maintained sidewalks adequately for their purposes but did not comply with municipal standards (Teaford 1984). Thus, sidewalks were intricately connected to the adjoining properties as much as or more than to the street.

In the late nineteenth and early twentieth century, construction costs and maintenance of the streets' travel lanes increasingly shifted to the public sector. Abutters, nevertheless, continued to be responsible for maintaining the sidewalks and paying for their construction. Despite this, municipal governments were held liable for trip-and-fall accidents, and a shared responsibility developed (Ehrenfeucht and Loukaitou-Sideris 2007).

Expanded municipal provision of streets and sidewalks in the nineteenth century led to increased municipal regulation of sidewalk activities (Novak 1996). Cities enacted dozens of ordinances to regulate public speaking, vending, and advertising as reformers and business leaders instigated efforts to domesticate the street (Baldwin 1999). The ordinances curtailed abutters' and other street users' rights to receive deliveries or display wares (Goheen 1994). These stricter municipal regulations were increasingly justified by the need for unimpeded pedestrian travel, and U.S. courts repeatedly upheld municipal regulations that favored unobstructed circulation (Ehrenfeucht and Loukaitou-Sideris 2007).

The shared responsibility for sidewalk provision and maintenance that was initiated in the early nineteenth century continues today. Many cities and states require that the abutting properties maintain the sidewalks and keep them clear of snow, ice, and debris as well as vegetation. The California Streets and Highways Code, Section 5611, for example, states that property owners have the responsibility to "maintain any sidewalk in such condition that the sidewalk will not endanger persons or property and maintain it in a condition which will not interfere with the public convenience." A survey of 82 cities in 45 states found that "[40] percent of the cities require property owners to pay the full cost of repairing sidewalks, 46 percent share the cost with property owners, and only 13 percent pay the full cost of repairing sidewalks" (Shoup 2010: 32). Public funds, in contrast, pay for the maintenance of travel lanes.

In our survey of policies, municipal codes, and ordinances of the four largest California cities, we found that all of them require abutting property owners to maintain the sidewalks and keep them clear of obstructions. Cities can require property owners to fix the sidewalks or they can make repairs and assess the cost to the property owners, and sidewalks are required with new construction.[4] Sidewalk regulation is under the auspices of the public sector, and a number of municipal departments have enacted different layers of formal control and authority over sidewalks. But in addition to municipal ordinances, codes, and police surveillance, abutters often also exercise a level of informal authority and social control that affects sidewalk uses.

In the following sections, we give examples to highlight how the informal property rights of abutters on sidewalks may lead to acts of sidewalk control, privatization, and exclusion of "outsiders," but also to resident-based initiatives with wider benefits. We draw examples from the four cities of our survey and discuss the pertinent sidewalk issues and municipal responses.

### Informal Control of Sidewalk Uses

In many neighborhoods and business improvement districts (BIDs), abutters' concerns about property crime lead them to install a layer of informal social control on the sidewalks through neighborhood watch programs or private security officers. While neighborhood watch groups and BIDs are citizen entities sanctioned by formal municipal authorities (police, city council), the decision to allocate resources and personnel to public-space security rests with the abutters.[5]

Starting in the mid-1960s and quickly spreading out to many neighborhoods around the country, neighborhood watch programs—often with the encouragement of local police departments—count on neighbors to be vigilant about their streets and act as the "eyes and ears" of the police (Duncan 1980). Through resident patrols, public watching, and community surveillance of neighborhood streets and sidewalks, residents look out for suspicious incidents and behavior. They are requested to report such behavior to the local police, though as the Florida case indicated, participants may be tempted to take action themselves when they perceive a problem.

Studies of neighborhood watch programs have found that wealthy homeowner-occupied neighborhoods are more likely to create them than low-income neighborhoods with more renters (Henig 1984; Lavrakas

1981). Neighborhood watch has been generally credited with augmenting traditional police preventive methods (Cirel et al. 1977) and achieving a degree of neighborhood cohesion. On the other hand, such programs run the risk of developing an insider-versus-outsider mentality if people visiting the neighborhood are perceived as suspicious and deemed undesirable by abutters because of their race, age, attire, or other personal characteristics.

In some commercial areas where merchants and property owners have established BIDs, informal control by private security officers seeks to eliminate sidewalk activities that are undesirable to abutting businesses. But critics have questioned the appropriateness of informal private control of public sidewalks and the right of abutters to decide what constitutes "unsuitable" behavior in public spaces (Loukaitou-Sideris, Blumenberg, and Ehrenfeucht 2005). Frequently, controversy has been generated by the efforts of BIDs to exclude street vendors from sidewalks in their areas. The fact that most BIDs operate in areas that street vendors find profitable for business (central business districts, suburban commercial and entertainment centers, transportation terminals, tourist attractions) generates spatial zones of conflict (Bromley 2000). Mostly immigrant vendors and their allies (immigrant rights groups, vending associations) advocate for vendors' rights to use the sidewalks for commercial exchanges, while abutting merchants and residents challenge and seek to deny this access. The power differential between abutters and street vendors leads authorities to be more attentive to the demands of abutters (Kim 2012).

The aforementioned attempts of neighborhood watch groups and BIDs to impose a layer of informal control over the streets and sidewalks of their neighborhoods leads at times to conflicts between abutters and other sidewalk users. These conflicts are multifaceted, stemming from fear of crime, direct competition between vendors and abutting shopkeepers, and conflicting perceptions of appropriate uses and order, as well as changing demographics and immigration.

### Property Claims, Privatization, and Exclusion

Some property claims on sidewalks may result in individual benefits but have detrimental effects on other users. Property claims can lead to exclusionary processes when property owners appropriate the sidewalk and/or street immediately adjacent to their property, making it unavailable to other users. Occupants of adjoining properties often use the sidewalks as a matter of course. Because it occurs regularly and in a way that is associated with their home, residents do not consider their use "exclusive" to others. In some cases, however, abutters actively try to restrict other people's activities, adopting a "Not in My Front Yard" response.

The linear zone of pavement that abuts private edifices and front yards provides at times a convenient space for the extension of the private realm into public space. In the late nineteenth and early twentieth centuries it was not uncommon for shopkeepers to display their merchandise or store deliveries and overstock on the sidewalks fronting their establishment. Indeed, as early as 1881, a *Los Angeles Times* article wondered, "Have the merchants who made a specialty of displaying their wares on the sidewalks secured special privileges in that respect, regardless of public convenience?" (in Loukaitou-Sideris and Ehrenfeucht 2009: 21). Ensuing municipal ordinances in Los Angeles and other U.S. cities prohibited the display of private wares on local sidewalks, upholding the rights of the general public to walk unobstructed on sidewalks.

Today, one rarely sees private wares on sidewalks in residential areas, other than the occasional sofa, left to be picked up by trash collectors (figure 5.2), and such "dumping" is considered illegal and is fined by

**Figure 5.2**
A sofa on the sidewalk. Photo credit: Melissa Johnson.

cities (Aldax 2009). However, in some residential areas, abutters' actions claim the sidewalk in front of their properties for private parking. This is particularly true in multifamily residential areas facing parking shortages, where residents park their cars illegally on driveway aprons and in front of driveways. As discussed by Donald Shoup in this volume, a survey of a neighborhood adjacent to the UCLA campus found 248 cars parked illegally on sidewalks and aprons, and landlords illegally renting public sidewalk space to their tenants for parking (Shoup, this volume).

Cars parked on sidewalks (figure 5.3) disrupt pedestrian movement and force pedestrians onto the streets. The situation affects all other users of sidewalks but is more severe for people in wheelchairs, who are forced to wheel on the roadway. Impassable sidewalks violate the Americans with Disabilities Act (ADA) of 1990 which, among other things, requires that physical access not be obstructed by discriminatory practices. In 2003, the U.S. Supreme Court rejected the city of Sacramento's appeal to overturn the Ninth Circuit Court's decision that the ADA applies to sidewalks. It ruled that city sidewalks were covered by the ADA, and therefore they must be accessible (*Barden v. City of Sacramento* 2002).

Under this federal mandate, cities must remove obstructing barriers along the sidewalks. Nevertheless, Los Angeles rarely enforces the municipal codes that prohibit parking on sidewalks and driveway aprons (Shoup 2006). Following the example of the nearby city of Long Beach, the Los Angeles city council is instead considering formalizing the informal practice of abutters with an amendment to its parking ordinance, which would allow residents to get permits to park in front of their driveways in the city's most densely populated neighborhoods (Eakins 2010).

In wealthy single-family neighborhoods, where residents own two- and three-car garages, parking on driveway aprons or on the street is rare. But as Shoup notes, "Many residents seem to think they own the parking spaces in front of their homes" (Shoup 2011: 434). They exert a layer of privatization on the public curb space in front of their properties by successfully petitioning municipalities to designate their streets for "resident parking only," thus exercising a not so subtle control of who can park in the neighborhood.

## Acts of Complementarity and Inclusion

So far, this account of abutters' claims to the sidewalks may give the impression that they are only motivated by narrow self-interest, and

**Figure 5.3**
Cars parked on the sidewalks of North Westwood Village, Los Angeles. Photo credit: Donald Shoup.

that their actions only result in exclusionary practices. While this may often be the case, the abutters' influence on the social life of sidewalks is more nuanced. As Jane Jacobs (1961) famously argued, many abutters make daily investments in time to maintain or improve the sidewalks, developing synergies with other local users and undertaking initiatives that enhance neighborhood quality, safety, and collective interests.

In some cases, sidewalks facilitate uses that may be mutually beneficial to a group of users and to the adjoining establishments. For example, the National Day Labor Survey found that 22 percent of day labor hiring sites exist in front of home improvement stores (Valenzuela et al. 2006). These stores informally accommodate such sites because it is convenient for contractors and homeowners or renters, who are the primary employers of day laborers, to buy materials and hire workers in the same place (Valenzuela et al. 2006). Recognizing such synergies, some Los Angeles County municipalities have requested that Home Depot provide resources for day labor centers (Associated Press 2007).

The responsibility that abutters feel for the sidewalks fronting their properties also leads to initiatives that beautify and green the streets and bring local and citywide benefits. Sidewalk improvements that abutters often undertake, such as tree planting and watering, benefit other sidewalk users and urban residents. Street trees are located in the ambiguous area between buildings and the street for which abutting property owners share responsibility with the city. Cities across the United States, including Los Angeles, San Diego, and San Francisco, are developing tree planting programs (Friends of the Urban Forest, n.d.; Million Trees LA, n.d.) and rely on residents' help to plant and maintain street trees. Maintaining an urban forest requires considerable investment (Krier 2008), and so even with significant political will behind the Los Angeles Million Trees Initiative, for example, the program depends on partnerships with corporations, nonprofit agencies, and city residents. Because ongoing tree care and maintenance are challenging, residents' involvement can offset funding shortfalls.

Such informal planting or watering of trees and keeping up of sidewalks are encouraged by municipal authorities because they are complementary to formal municipal interventions and improvements. On the other hand, as already noted, other claims or attempts at informal control by abutters may bring them into conflict with other sidewalk users. How do municipal actors intervene in such conflicts?

## Municipal Responses: Observations from Four California Cities

The four cities in our survey typically employ three strategies to address competing sidewalk claims.

### Formalizing the Informal: Ordinances and Permits

Ordinances and permits are the most common mechanism to formalize informal sidewalk activities (table 5.1). Historically, some abutters' actions have been sanctioned by municipal authorities, frequently resulting in sidewalk ordinances that privilege abutters over other city residents (Loukaitou-Sideris and Ehrenfeucht 2010). These include ordinances that completely prohibit certain sidewalk activities (e.g., street vending, littering, or loitering) on sidewalks and streets in front of private properties; allow them only for abutters (e.g., resident parking districts); or impose time and space sanctions that mainly protect abutting properties from nuisances (e.g., street performers allowed only for a maximum amount of time and at a minimum distance from private properties).

Ordinances have been issued in almost every U.S. city in response to abutters' complaints about street vendors. Such ordinances may ban street vending completely or limit the locations and types of products that can be legally sold by street vendors. Los Angeles has one of the strictest ordinances in the country, stipulating that "No person . . . shall on any sidewalk or street offer for sale, solicit sale of, announce by any means the availability of, or have in his or her possession, control or custody, whether upon his or her person or upon some other animate or inanimate object, any goods, wares, or merchandise which the public

Table 5.1
Selected Sidewalk Regulations in Four Cities

| Los Angeles | San Diego | San Jose | San Francisco |
|---|---|---|---|
| *Vending* | | | |
| Allows merchandise and food vending by permit only in special districts. Currently no active districts in the city. | Pushcarts permitted with neighborhood use permit in special zones. Solicitors and peddlers prohibited from certain areas. | Peddling permitted with license. Canvassers of periodicals need permit; fee required. | Allows peddling of goods for human consumption with permit subject to regulations. Regulates street artist and craftsperson sales. |

**Table 5.1**
(continued)

| Los Angeles | San Diego | San Jose | San Francisco |
|---|---|---|---|
| *Picketing* | | | |
| Prohibits picketing within 100 feet of a personal residence. | Prohibits picketing in a manner intended to incite a disturbance or a breach in the peace. | No picketing within 300 feet of targeted residential dwelling. | Groups of over 50 people require permit. Civic Center area is off-limits to actions. |
| *Loitering/Sleeping* | | | |
| Prohibits standing on sidewalks in a way that annoys or molests pedestrians or interferes with their free passage. | | Prohibits sitting or lying down on public sidewalks from 10:00–12:00 am. Prohibits loitering, standing or occupying sidewalks or willfully obstructing or interfering with pedestrians. | Prohibits sidewalk obstruction. Unlawful to stand on sidewalk in any business district, except as near as practicable to building line or curb line. Prohibits loitering beside ATMs. |
| *Panhandling* | | | |
| Prohibits annoying patrons of eating establishments by begging, soliciting, or loitering. | Prohibits aggressive solicitation of money or goods. Charitable solicitation requires permit. | | Prohibits aggressive solicitation. Unlawful to beg or practice begging in public streets or public places. |
| *Uses by Abutters* | | | |
| "Revocable permit" from Bureau of Engineering needed for sidewalk seating. Code regulates manner and location for gesturing, calling out, etc. relating to merchandise or services for sale. | Sidewalk cafes permitted with neighborhood use permit subject to provisions (not interfering with pedestrians; how it fits into an area). | Exhibiting wares on sidewalks not allowed, except with permits for special events. | Permit required for sidewalk café tables and chairs. Display stands for wares on sidewalks allowed with permit. |

Source: Municipal codes of Los Angeles, San Diego, San Jose, and San Francisco.

may purchase at any time" (City of Los Angeles, Ordinance 4.2.42.00 Regulation of Soliciting and Sales in Streets). In San Diego, city ordinances prohibit sidewalk sales of goods from carts. In recent years, the city's Neighborhood Code Compliance Department had stopped enforcing the ordinance, but recent complaints from abutting businesses have forced the Compliance and Police departments to take a more aggressive stance against unlicensed roving cart vendors (Kim, Nunez, and Montez interviews). Although San Francisco allows peddling on the sidewalks with permits, its vending requirements are hard to meet and expensive (Dugan 2009).[6] San Jose requires that stationary sidewalk vendors operate in designated and approved locations, and restricts hours of operation (Gathright 2002; San Jose Municipal Code 6.54.110).

Permits can allow an activity or a one-time event to take place after a formal request is made and certain criteria are met. Cities restrict the number of permits issued and impose controls on the type, manner, time, and location of informal activities such as street vending and street performing. Although cities can also institute such restrictions on picketing and demonstrations, they face more constraints because they must be mindful that participants have access to their intended audience. Permitting has disproportionately been required of sidewalk uses that are not affiliated with the adjoining property, and the ordinances are adopted in response to the concerns of local businesses and residents.

### Mediation among Conflicting Interests

On some occasions, public officials mediate among conflicting interests, not forbidding or allowing contested activities outright, but allowing them in ways that cause fewer nuisances to abutters. For example, San Francisco allows street musicians to perform on sidewalks only during certain times, and their sound "should not be unreasonably loud, raucous, jarring, or disturbing to persons of normal sensitiveness within the area of audibility" (quoted in Lookout News 2010). Cities also impose regulations regarding the minimum distance that performers should keep from building entrances. Similarly, because cities may not prohibit panhandling outright, they instead prohibit it within a given distance from ATMs, bank entrances, or other significant entries to private edifices.

### Offering Alternative Sites

At times, cities seek to provide alternative spaces for sidewalk activities and users that abutters wish to prohibit from sidewalks near their properties. For instance, the homeless are contained in skid row districts, and prostitution has historically been confined to red-light districts. Some cities seek to confine day laborers to day labor centers and skateboarders to skate parks. Street vendors are often removed from commercial streets and offered spaces in vending districts, swap meets, and markets. Although vending districts or markets, day labor centers, and skate parks are seen as alternatives, such strategies fail to acknowledge that different city areas are not interchangeable (Donovan 2008), and some sites are more useful to the vendors and day laborers or more appealing to skateboarders than others.

## Conclusion

Sidewalks integrate the street and abutting properties, and understanding them as complex public spaces requires a nuanced conceptualization of ownership and access, the nature of abutters' claims, the different impacts of spatial solutions, and formal and informal controls. Claims on sidewalks are constantly negotiated by three groups: people using sidewalks for transportation; the abutting property owners and tenants who use sidewalks for purposes related to their residence or business; and a variety of others who claim sidewalk space for economic or political purposes.

Municipal authorities respond to these claims by formally controlling and regulating sidewalks through ordinances and permits but have to balance three considerations. For one, as part of the urban infrastructure, sidewalks must remain accessible for the movement of all people. Second, the proximity of sidewalks to private properties means that abutters are more affected than other users by nuisances but also by improvements happening on the pavement fronting their properties. Lastly, concerns about equity, daily survival, and economic livelihoods represent additional considerations for municipal officials when they negotiate varying interests along the sidewalks. Policymakers may need to address the following questions to help them illuminate the balance of power and interplay of various interests and property claims on city sidewalks and to govern them equitably.

*How are property claims exercised and by whom, and how do they affect other groups?* Abutters are not homogeneous and have varied interests. For example, home improvement stores may benefit from day labor sites but neighborhood residents may complain. Since conflicts and complaints are often situation- and context-specific, policymakers need a more nuanced examination of who is impacted by a given action or activity, who exercises influence, and what affects outcomes.

*How, when, and where are ordinances enforced?* Research suggests that informal activities flourish when enforcement of regulatory ordinances is lax. This may allow flexibility but also leads to inconsistent enforcement and inequity, as more powerful groups may exercise more influence over the city council or police.

*How does provision of alternative sites or other spatial solutions impact different groups and areas?* Abutters' claims are context-specific, and negotiated agreements often result in moving people from a sidewalk to another space. Such actions may provide a solution satisfactory to everyone, if for example a day labor site can be conveniently located. In the case of street vending, however, moving street vendors to an enclosed market or a park may make street vending unprofitable.

*How can design help accommodate diverse sidewalk uses and users?* We need to better understand how arcades, curb extensions, and kiosks may be utilized to provide space for some sidewalk activities without disrupting others. Which design interventions create a better integration or a softer separation between sidewalks and adjacent properties? When are fences justified and when do they make bad neighbors?

*How do informal controls function and what are the impacts of more "eyes on the street"?* Jane Jacobs (1961) romanticized the benefits of informal control and natural sidewalk surveillance. As we have indicated, however, such control may also lead to exclusionary actions. We need a better understanding of how and when residents and businesses exercise control over others in spaces that adjoin their properties. In-depth analyses about how people's attention shapes others' street use can help explain the function of informal control as well as its positive and negative consequences.

*How do complementary activities and activity-rich neighborhoods function?* Most research in the area of property claims focuses on the conflicts and differences between property and business owners and other groups. We need more studies to understand the dynamics and the processes leading to neighborhoods that are well-integrated and feature a diverse mix of people and activities.

*How do sidewalks and sidewalk activities change when property claims disappear?* Property abandonment affects cities and neighborhoods in different ways, and a growing body of research examines shrinking cities (Oswalt 2006; Pallagast 2008). Some have considered innovative adaptations of abandoned properties, but few have examined the impact of property abandonment on sidewalk life or ways to reuse and reenergize abandoned public spaces.

In responding to such questions, planners and policymakers should strive to achieve three things:

- A more nuanced understanding of the differences among spatial contexts than what the ordinances can generally provide. This would reveal the different needs and conflicts at play in certain neighborhoods and lead to a negotiation of where and when activities can happen on particular sidewalk stretches, or whether alternative spaces should be provided.

- The creation of more "mixed-use sidewalks" (Kim 2012), where multiple uses and users can peacefully coexist, rather than "single-minded" spaces (Walzer 1986) exclusively occupied by one use. Here, the power of design should not be underestimated, as it can extend sidewalks, screen and separate conflicting uses, and provide appropriate and aesthetically pleasing settings to accommodate them.

- A clarification of the rights and privileges of abutters with an eye toward achieving wider social benefits. For example, Donald Shoup (1996, 2010) has written persuasively about ways for municipalities to "green" or repair sidewalks by initiating "point-of-sale strategies," planting street trees or fixing broken pavement and charging the property owner who sells his/her property. Municipalities can similarly privilege abutters with parking districts, where only residents can park cars at the curbs fronting their houses. Such privilege, however, should come with a fee, and this revenue should be allocated to benefit other sidewalk users.

In the end, the life that abuts the street influences sidewalks as public space. How diverse needs, interests, and competing claims are framed and negotiated on urban sidewalks tells us a lot about the type of democracy we live in.

## Notes

1. In our discussion of abutters, we do not distinguish between property owners and renters.

2. In the United States there is usually a public right-of-way that separates the public property of beaches, squares, or parks from private front yards or other private edifices.

3. According to Lofland (1998: 10), parochial spaces, in contrast to public or private spaces, are characterized by "a sense of commonality among acquaintances and neighbors who are involved in interpersonal networks that are located within communities."

4. Cities do not consistently enforce sidewalk maintenance regulations. In areas with limited incomes or a high percentage of rental property, sidewalks are less likely to be repaired. Enforcement is often less stringent because it is complaint-based, and tenants in lower-income neighborhoods are less inclined to register problems.

5. Participation in a neighborhood watch group is voluntary and ad hoc. BIDs are enacted by municipal governments after petitions from property owners (Houstoun 1997).

6. A permit for a food truck located on public property in San Francisco can cost a vendor $10,000.

## References

Aldax, Mike. 2009. "Dump Couch on Sidewalk, Face Fine." *San Francisco Examiner*, November 23. http://www.sfexaminer.com/blogs/under-dome/dump-couch-sidewalk-face-fine

Associated Press. 2007. "Home Depot Seeks Relief from Day-Labor Rules." Available at http://www.msnbc.msn.com/id/19453488/ (retrieved September 27, 2010).

Baldwin, Peter C. 1999. *Domesticating the Street: The Reform of Public Space in Hartford, 1850–1930.* Columbus: Ohio State University.

Banerjee, Tridib, Genevieve Giuliano, Greg Hines, and David C. Sloane. 1996. "Invented and Re-invented Streets: Designing the New Shopping Experience." *Lusk Review* 2 (1):18–30.

*Barden v. City of Sacramento.* 2002. "Class Action Settlement Agreement." http://www.dralegal.org/impact/cases/barden-v-sacramento (retrieved August 26, 2013).

Blakely, Edward, and Mary Gail Snyder. 1999. *Fortress America: Gated Communities in the United States.* Washington, DC: Brookings Institution.

Bromley, Ray. 2000. "Street Vending and Public Policy: A Global Review." *International Journal of Sociology and Social Policy* 20 (1/2):1–28.

Cirel, Paul, Patricia Evans, Daniel McGillis, and Debra Whitcomb. 1977. *Community Crime Prevention, Seattle, Washington: An Exemplary Project.* U.S. Department of Justice. Washington, DC: Government Printing Office.

Donovan, Michael D. 2008. "Informal Cities and the Contestation of Public Space: The Case of Bogota's Street Vendors, 1988–2003." *Urban Studies* (Edinburgh, Scotland) 45 (1):29–51.

Dugan, Tara. 2009. "Growing Crop of Vendors Hitting the Streets." *San Francisco Chronicle*, May 26, A1.

Duncan, J. T. Skip. 1980. *Citizen Crime Prevention Tactics: A Literature Review and Selected Bibliography.* National Institute of Law Enforcement and Criminal Justice, U.S. Department of Justice. Washington DC: Government Printing Office.

Eakins, Paul. 2010. "Long Beach Council Expected to Take Up Driveway Parking." *Press Telegram* (Long Beach), January 3. http://www.presstelegram. com/news/ci_14116183 (retrieved September 24, 2010).

Ehrenfeucht, Renia, and Anastasia Loukaitou-Sideris. 2007. "Constructing the Sidewalks: Municipal Government and the Production of Public Space in Los Angeles, California, 1880–1920." *Journal of Historical Geography* 33:104–124.

Frieden, Bernard, and Lynne Sagalyn. 1989. *Downtown Inc.: How America Rebuilds Cities.* Cambridge, MA: MIT Press.

Friends of the Urban Forest. N.d. "Help Us Create a Greener San Francisco." http://www.fuf.net/ (retrieved November 9, 2010).

Garnett, Nicole Stelle. 2009. "Private Norms and Public Spaces." *William and Mary Bill of Rights Journal* 18 (1):183–198.

Gathright, Alan. 2002. "San Jose Pins Hopes on Street Performers to Breathe Life into Dull Downtown." *San Francisco Chronicle*, February 3, A21.

Goheen, Peter G. 1994. "Negotiating Access to Public Space in Mid-Nineteenth Century Toronto." *Journal of Historical Geography* 20 (4):430–449.

Henig, Jeffrey. 1984. *Citizens against Crime: An Assessment of the Neighborhood Watch Program in Washington DC.* Washington, DC: George Washington University.

Houstoun, Lawrence. 1997. *BIDs: Business Improvement Districts.* Washington, DC: Urban Land Institute.

Jacobs, Jane. 1961. *The Death and Life of Great American Cities.* New York: Random House.

Kim, Annette. 2012. "The Mixed-Use Sidewalk: Vending and Property Rights in Public Space." *Journal of the American Planning Association* 78 (3):1–14.

Kohn, Margaret. 2004. *Brave New Neighborhoods: The Privatization of Public Space.* New York: Routledge.

Krier, Robert. 2008. "Tree-Planting Program Seeking New Source of Funding." *San Diego Union Tribune.* http://www.utsandiego.com/uniontrib/20080902/ news_1m2shade.html (retrieved August 26, 2013).

Lavrakas, Paul J. 1981. *Factors Related to Citizen Involvement in Personal, Household, and Neighborhood Anti-Crime Measures.* National Institute of Justice, U.S. Department of Justice. Washington, DC: Government Printing Office.

Lee, Shin, and Chris Webster. 2006. "Enclosure of the Urban Commons." *GeoJournal* 66 (1–2):27–42.

Lofland, Lyn H. 1998. *The Public Realm: Exploring the City's Quintessential Social Territory.* New York: Aldine de Gruyter.

Lookout News. 2010. "Council to Tackle Street Performance Noise Reduction and Related Issues." http://www.surfsantamonica.com/ssm_site/the_lookout/

news/News-2010/December-2010/12_06_2010_Council_to_Tackle_Street_Per formance_Noise_Reduction_and_Related_Issues.html (retrieved August 26, 2013).

Loukaitou-Sideris, Anastasia, and Tridib Banerjee. 1998. *Urban Design Downtown: Poetics and Politics of Form.* Berkeley: University of California Press.

Loukaitou-Sideris, Anastasia, Evelyn Blumenberg, and Renia Ehrenfeucht. 2005. "Sidewalk Democracy: Municipalities and the Regulation of Public Space." In Eran Ben-Joseph and Terry S. Szold, eds., *Regulating Place: Standards and the Shaping of Urban America,* 141–166. New York: Routledge.

Loukaitou-Sideris, Anastasia, and Renia Ehrenfeucht. 2009. *Sidewalks: Conflict and Negotiation over Public Space.* Cambridge, MA: MIT Press.

Loukaitou-Sideris, Anastasia, and Renia Ehrenfeucht. 2010. "Vibrant Sidewalks in the United States." *Access* 36:22–29.

Low, Setha. 2003. *Behind the Gates: Life, Security, and the Pursuit of Happiness in Fortress America.* New York: Routledge.

Million Trees LA. N.d. "About Million Trees LA." Available at http://www .milliontreesla.org/mtabout.htm (retrieved August 31, 2006).

Novak, William J. 1996. *The People's Welfare: Law and Regulation in Nineteenth-Century America.* Chapel Hill: University of North Carolina Press.

Oswalt, Philipp, ed. 2006. *Interventions.* Vol. 2 of *Shrinking Cities.* Ostfildern, Germany: Hatje Cantz Verlag.

Pallagast, Karina. 2008. "Shrinking Cities—Planning Challenges from an International Perspective." In Steve Rugare and Terry Schwarz, eds., *Cities Growing Smaller,* 6–16. Cleveland: Cleveland Urban Design Collaborative.

Shoup, Donald. 1996. "Regulating Land Use at Sale." *Journal of the American Planning Association* 62 (3):354–372.

Shoup, Donald. 2006. Letter to Los Angeles City Attorney Rocky Delgadillo, March 26.

Shoup, Donald. 2010. "Fixing Broken Sidewalks." *Access* 36:30–36.

Shoup, Donald. 2011. *The High Cost of Free Parking.* Washington, DC: American Planning Association Press.

Smith, Neil. 1996. *The New Urban Frontier: Gentrification and the Revanchist City.* London: Routledge.

Sorkin, Michael. 1992. *Variations on a Theme Park: The New American City and the End of Public Space.* New York: Hill and Wang.

Staeheli, Lynn A., and Don Mitchell. 2008. *The People's Property? Power, Politics, and the Public.* New York: Routledge.

Staeheli, Lynn A., Don Mitchell, and Caroline R. Nagel. 2009. "Making Publics: Immigrants, Regimes of Publicity and Entry to 'the Public.'" *Environment and Planning. D, Society and Space* 29:633–648.

Teaford, Jon C. 1984. *The Unheralded Triumph: City Government in America, 1870–1900.* Baltimore: Johns Hopkins University Press.

Valenzuela, Abel, Nik Theodore, Edwin Meléndez, and Ana Luz Gonzales. 2006. "On the Corner: Day Labor in the United States." http://www.sscnet.ucla.edu/issr/csup/uploaded_files/Natl_DayLabor-On_the_Corner1.pdf (retrieved September 27, 2010).

Walzer, Michael. 1986. "Public Space: Pleasures and Costs of Urbanity." *Dissent* 33 (4):470–475.

Zukin, Sharon. 1995. *The Cultures of Cities*. Cambridge, MA: Blackwell.

### Interviews

Bowie, Karen, Lt., City of Los Angeles Bureau of Street Services Investigation and Enforcement, December 2010.

Dangerfield, Troy, Lt., San Francisco Police Department Media Relations, December 2010.

Harris, Aaron, Los Angeles Police Department, December 2010.

Montez, Sandra, San Diego Police Department, Non-emergency issues, November 2010.

Nunez, Victor, Neighborhood Code Compliance, San Diego, November 2010.

Wallace, Kim, Neighborhood Code Compliance, San Diego, November 2010.

Two police officers in San Jose were also interviewed.

# 6

## Learning from the Margin: Placemaking Tactics

Nabil Kamel

Metropolitan Phoenix, like many other regions of the United States' Sunbelt, has experienced rapid growth in the postwar years and epitomizes a particular geography of urbanization (Gober 1984). This pattern of development presents two prominent characteristics: (1) the mass production of the built environment with large planned developments dominating the urban landscape; (2) leapfrogging outward expansion of real estate investments and simultaneous disinvestment in older suburbs.

This dislocated and uneven pattern of urbanization produces generic spaces that are devoid of a sense of place and undermines existing placemaking efforts. As new developments offer larger units with newer amenities, the more affluent middle- and upper-class homeowners move to these newer planned communities and are replaced by lower-income residents with different means and needs. However, the physical layout and formal regulations governing urban space remain those designed for communities of homeowners with stable employment, who own cars, shop at malls, and can spare time and means to participate in the various neighborhood activities and decisions. This environment is ill-suited to residents who depend on public transportation, work multiple jobs, and have limited disposable income and leisure time. As a result, the new residents moving into these neighborhoods have to invent their own placemaking tactics to resist a material and institutional reality that does not match their resources and aspirations (Diaz 2005). This chapter explores the production and meaning of these informal and improvised solutions in metropolitan Phoenix.

### Approach and Methodology

Scholars have examined informal practices from a cultural perspective (Arreola 2012; Rios 2010; Rojas 2010) and as a renegotiation of restrictive and often prejudiced regulation of urban space (Crawford 1995; Hou 2010; Loukaitou-Sideris and Ehrenfeucht 2009). In this chapter, I adapt the concepts of "strategies" and "tactics" conceptualized by de Certeau (1984) to connect the effects of planned development (strategies) and resident responses in maneuvering through them (tactics). Briefly stated, "strategies" are those formalized, codified, and external actions that aim at defining and regulating space. These include land use plans, zoning laws, building codes, and other formal regulatory tools. In contrast, "tactics" are opportunistic, calculated, and autonomous actions by local actors to redefine and renegotiate space outside the realm of legal use of the built environment—broadly defined. The purpose of this chapter is not the "discovery" of street play or a romanticizing of informal practices in the city. Rather, using de Certeau's framework, I seek to understand these practices of everyday life as situated in the context of resistance to a dominant sociospatial order. Scott's (1985) analysis of everyday forms of peasant resistance is here adapted to the urban context and is used to highlight the tacit struggle of marginalized social groups. In this context, tactics are seen as covert political actions that aim at redistributing control over property rights and, more broadly, over the right to the city. Owing to their practitioners' previous experiences with technologies of governance, surveillance, and reprisal, and due to the limited resources available, these hidden forms of struggle are designed to avoid detection and unnecessary attention. Focusing on nonsanctioned tactics, this chapter highlights the "double-jeopardy" condition of living in the margins of a region like metropolitan Phoenix: underserved and outlawed. Finally, these tactics are more than just a means of survival or a form of everyday (political) resistance to one-sided domination (Foucault 1979). Rather, they represent ways of reconstructing citizenship outside of, and in spite of, existing formal definitions of which rights to the city are granted or denied and to whom (Holston 2009; Hou 2010; Laguerre 1994).

The chapter distills evidence from tactics identified and documented in residential areas and representing a range of placemaking activities and purposes. First, a demographic analysis identified zip codes and census tracts with a median household income below the county median. This was complemented by a spatial analysis of historical aerial maps from the Maricopa County Flood Control District (FCD 2012). These maps cover the Phoenix region from 1930 to 2010 and were used to identify neighborhood changes and areas most affected by the freeway construction that has taken place since the 1950s. Google Earth and Google Maps were used to plot windshield survey itineraries in areas identified as low-income, disrupted by freeways, and with limited employment, retail, and entertainment opportunities. The purpose of the windshield survey was to identify nonsanctioned place-making activities in the areas identified above. The protocol for the windshield survey consisted of visual recording of the tactic with still images along with notations regarding the type of tactic, its location, time of day, day of the week, setup, activity, participants, and surrounding urban context. A brief interview was conducted, where applicable, to collect key information about the tactic, such as how it started, its frequency, and its purpose as well as participants' willingness to participate in extended interviews. Surveys were repeated in selected sites to identify changes in activity types and intensities at different times of the day and week. In-depth observation and informal interviews with participants were conducted for selected tactics. Where appropriate, participant observation methods were also used. A total of 108 instances of these tactics were documented and classified in 13 categories, as shown in table 6.1. Additional tactics not listed here included graffiti, political signs, roadside memorials, and day labor. Graffiti was excluded because we found it difficult to identify the participants. Political signs and roadside memorials were considered sanctioned implicitly or explicitly. Day labor was excluded since the tactics we examined focused primarily on residential areas.

The areas covered included neighborhoods in Phoenix, Mesa, Tempe, Chandler, and Glendale. As shown in table 6.1, tactics performed commercial functions as well as recreational and socializing ones. Spatially the tactics operated on participants' own property, public properties, and privately owned properties—vacant and occupied. Tactics included sidewalk vending, itinerant vending, regular yard sales, home businesses, guerrilla gardening, improvised playgrounds, and building additions and improvements. Only unsanctioned activities were considered. The following analysis synthesizes findings from the observations of these tactics and is divided into two sections. The first describes the constraints from which tactics emerge. The second presents three placemaking dimensions associated with these tactics. Due to the nature of these activities and to protect participants from possible persecution, all identities, locations, and distinguishing characteristics have been altered, concealed, or removed.

**Table 6.1**
Documented Tactics by Activity Type and Attributes.

| Tactic | Social Dimension | | Spatial Dimension | | |
|---|---|---|---|---|---|
| | Economic Generator | Recreational / Socializing / Networking | Occupy / Repurpose | | |
| | | | Public Space | Own Private Space | Other Private Space |
| Sidewalk vending | ● | | ● | | |
| Mobile vending | ● | ● | ● | | ● |
| Garage / yard sale | ● | ● | ● | ● | |
| Home business | ● | ● | | ● | |
| Home-based husbandry | ● | | | ● | |
| Guerrilla gardening | ● | ● | ● | ● | ● |
| Informal transportation | ● | | | | |
| Informal building addition | | | | ● | |
| Commercial spillover | ● | | ● | ● | |
| Informal signage | ● | | ● | ● | |
| Informal pathway / shortcut | | | ● | | ● |
| Informal playground | | ● | ● | ● | ● |
| Loitering / gathering | | ● | ● | | ● |

## Urbs Interrupta: Rigidities, Indeterminacies, and Spaces of Tactics

The urban form of the Phoenix metropolitan region reflects the several massive bursts of population growth that have taken place there. With each population surge, more housing units were built in anticipation of the next wave of newcomers. While the city of Phoenix grew rapidly in physical size from its incorporation in 1881, the city's total population remained small until the Second World War, when war industries expanded in the region. Aviation, electronics, and ammunition manufacturing became important employment sectors along with servicing the established "five Cs" economy: copper, cattle, citrus, cotton, and climate (Ross 2012). The war effort and the economic expansion that ensued added another C (construction) and solidified Phoenix's attachment to the freeway, the car, and mass production of housing. To a great extent, the Fordist mode of industrial production that characterized the U.S. economy during the postwar period extended to the production of the built environment. While Fordism as a political economic system in the United States eventually ran out of steam and was restructured along post-Fordist and neoliberal lines, the built environment in cities like Phoenix continued to be produced and organized according to the Fordist logic (Beauregard 2006; Hackworth 2007; Harvey 2005).

As in other parts of the United States, especially in Sunbelt cities, historic, cultural, regulatory, and political factors continued to favor investments in large-scale low-density single-family development in outlying areas over high-density small-scale infill development (Hirt 2012; McKenzie 1994; Talen 2012). As a result, the vast majority of housing construction in the Phoenix region continues to be associated with large-scale mass-produced development (Checkoway 1980; Ross 2012). This type of planned-community development is reproducible indefinitely, albeit with more variations in terms of size and theme than the earlier examples of the 1950s and 1960s. The urban pattern remains predominantly car-dependent, generic, standardized, and designed for a stable and predictable middle-class group of homeowners. In that respect, the urban form of a city like Phoenix is also an expression of the tension between a built environment produced and organized according to a Fordist logic of mass production for mass consumption and post-Fordist socioeconomic realities. This tension becomes more acute when economic, political, and cultural rigidities associated with a mass-produced urban environment designed for a homogeneous middle class are imposed on marginalized social groups.

For example, economically and financially the mass production of the built environment relies on large-scale investments targeting a predictable and stable consumer base. In order to sustain this mode of production, there is a constant need to find new spaces for investment and new consumers. Up to the great recession of 2007, finding new consumers was not a problem in Phoenix, where population growth far exceeded the national average (see figure 6.1). The city's population went from 48,000 people in 1930 to over 1,445,000 in 2010. Similarly, the political economy of urbanization in metropolitan Phoenix facilitated the horizontal expansion of development. In the period from 1950 to 2010, the land area of the city of Phoenix increased from 17.1 to 517.9 square miles—an increase of 2,922 percent (Rappaport 2003;

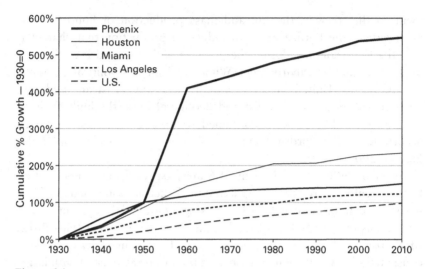

**Figure 6.1**
Phoenix population growth compared to other Sunbelt cities and United States, 1930–2010. Source: U.S. Bureau of the Census, various years.

U.S. Bureau of the Census 2012). Repeated cycles of real estate boom and speculation drove development and sustained the mass production of planned communities. However, this mode of production of urban space contrasts with rising socioeconomic uncertainties, rapid and intense cycles of boom and bust, changing household and lifestyle needs, and repeated bouts of fiscal austerity and cuts in social and physical infrastructure expenditures. Similarly, Fordist strategies underlying the current organization of the built environment embody political rigidities. The proclaimed communal values of planned unit development mask an obsession with property rights and property value that runs against inclusive civic participation and broader individual rights and social values (McKenzie 1994). Finally, the current production of urban space also embodies cultural rigidities. The one-size-fits-all development configuration, with its shallow, predictable, and sterile programming, reflects the tyranny of the lowest common denominator, homogeneity through compliance and assimilation, and an antiurban culture.

For less affluent residents, these various forms of rigidity create a mental and physical climate of isolation and incarceration. The oppressive nature of the Fordist organization of the built environment is resisted through local tactics of different types and scales, ranging from individual microtactics to collective ones with communal outcomes. In Phoenix, these tactics were observed to be more prevalent in older, culturally rich yet underserved neighborhoods. These neighborhoods, mostly of a suburban character, provide one of the few affordable housing choices for middle- and lower-income households. However, due to the centrifugal forces of development, these neighborhoods often have limited access to local retail, municipal services, stable employment, and public transportation. Moreover, the period of the 1960s and 1970s witnessed extensive freeway construction to connect ever more far-flung development. The unmitigated imposition of freeways, with their gargantuan scale and overpowering form, devastated several neighborhoods. The integrity and livability of these neighborhoods (or what was left of them) were further undermined as they lost a significant share of their residents, and homes were left abutting massive concrete structures and odd-shaped rights-of-way.

It is precisely in such indeterminate spaces of interrupted urbanization (both spatially and institutionally) that opportunities are seized and tactics emerge. For example, vacant lots are occupied by mobile markets. Incomplete development is encroached upon with building additions, garage sales, guerrilla gardening, and recreational uses. Exaggerated freeway rights-of-way are used for sidewalk vending, merchandise displays, playgrounds, and signage. Underutilized local access roads, culde-sacs, and sidewalks are activated as playgrounds, temporary markets, and regular garage sales. While the expression of these tactics varies according to site constraints and individual creativity in adapting features of the built environment, they share several characteristics in terms of the way they are socially constructed, which will be discussed in the next section.

## Dimensions of Tactics

Tactics unfold along multiple dimensions. In the face of a hostile material and institutional environment, residents adopt a "cloaked" setup for the deployment of their tactics. These tactics also perform other functions in countering mainstream and generic urbanization patterns of individuality, isolation, and erasure of memories. As seen below, the tactics presented here can reconnect fragmented urban spaces. Finally, tactics are functionally opportunistic by definition. Therefore, one of their main dimensions is a pragmatic activation of inert spaces and the adaptive reuse of urban elements.

## Hiding in Plain Site

"Hiding in plain site" is the characteristic of a tactic that is cloaked by sanctioned practices while performing a nonconforming function. This is achieved by adopting two or more opposing stances simultaneously: one that is of a sanctioned and legitimate practice and another that is unsanctioned. Only those in the know, or those who share the need for and knowledge of that tactic, would recognize this forbidden-permitted duplicity and operate accordingly, while others are likely to remain impervious to the signs, and the full extent of the tactic would elude their detection. The cloaking of a tactic is accomplished by shifting postures with respect to space and time in ways that blur the boundaries between public and private spaces, seriousness and play, and ephemerality and permanence. To do so, notions of legitimacy, public realm, and ownership are often delicately redefined to conceal unsanctioned activities. It is worth noting that the redefined notion of ownership is not about occupation and appropriation in the mutually exclusive sense typically associated with individual property rights. It is rather about the duplicity and simultaneity of being a space's owner and guest at the same time.

Regular yard sales are the quintessential example of hiding in plain site. Most cities in Arizona, including Phoenix, Tempe, Glendale, Mesa, and Chandler, regulate yard sales. Usually no more than three yard sales per address are allowed each year, and each sale can last no more than two or three days (City of Phoenix 2012). However, in marginalized neighborhoods, the interruption of urbanization described above extends to formal institutions. With no one really counting, a monthly or weekly yard sale is well cloaked in the guise of a sanctioned and wholesome "all-American" pastime (Crawford, this volume). Another example of stretching the limits of an innocuous activity is the front yard basketball game. In South Phoenix, kids between the ages of 7 and 14 set up a basketball court on their neighborhood street. In this case, instead of confining the game to the typical front yard (which can only accommodate a half court), they turn two basketball hoops to face each other on opposite sides of the street and use the entire width of the street as their court. This occupation of the street is temporarily relinquished when a car approaches and then is resumed after it passes. While the hoops are permanently turned to face the street and the basketball court is set all the time, the youths are obviously absent from the scene most of the time. It is only at known times that the game takes place and the street metamorphoses into a basketball court. The same inconspicuousness and temporality is present in an improvised skateboard park in Tempe. Here, too, there are no obvious traces of the temporary appropriation of a lot left vacant following the latest real estate bust. It is only when one considers the geometry that connects the placement of planks, boxes, and cement blocks that the empty lot reveals a skateboard obstacle course.

Shifting definitions of ownership are negotiated with equal ambiguity by a South Phoenix corn vendor. The vendor, a Latino man in his late thirties, his teenage son, and his white truck occupy an empty private lot every day from early morning to late afternoon when all the corn has been sold. Because the lot is on a major arterial, fenced from three sides, relatively well maintained, with parking for customers, and because the vendor has occupied it on a regular basis for several years with merchandise in full display from his truck, under an extending canopy, and with contact information in large lettering, he appears to be a rightful user of the site. Nothing betrays the fact that the vendor is occupying someone else's vacant site. Similarly, mixing seriousness and playfulness can provide another way to circumvent regulatory constraints. This is the tactic of "Al," a young Latino mobile vendor of sweet and salty snacks in the older Phoenix neighborhood of Maryvale. Complementing his treats with the cheerful colors and sounds of his tricycle and trumpet, Al also blends his work with the playful atmosphere of his young customers and adds a layer of harmlessness and innocence. Nevertheless, he carefully makes his way, choosing neighborhood streets and park paths in ways that minimize his risk of unwanted attention while maximizing his access to customers. Internal neighborhood streets are better than major arterials. The park's main entrance is better avoided. Good locations are where people congregate such as areas close to shading trees, gazebos, and other park structures. It is worth noting that, in the Phoenix region, the fees for a street vendor application and license are often equal to, if not higher than, the fees for a massage license, escort, or adult cabaret performer (City of Phoenix 2012).

Another form of hiding in plain site is found in "guerrilla gardening." We observed different forms of this tactic in various parts of the Phoenix region. In a West Phoenix apartment building, refugee families from Thailand and Myanmar transformed the poorly maintained barren landscape areas into microgardens that hold three to four plants each—mostly hot peppers, tomatoes, onions, and lettuces as well as some ornamental flowers. Typically, this kind of gardening is the work of female family members, especially that of mothers and grandmothers. In a Tempe neighborhood where the city still carries out flood irrigation, residents appropriated the adjacent right-of-way and made it into an

intensive vegetable garden. A more original example of guerrilla gardening was that of Mr. and Mrs. "William," who live in South Phoenix in
one of the many "arrested-development" subdivisions that have characterized the region's landscape since the housing bust. Of the 20 single-
family homes originally planned, only seven were completed, and instead
of retiring in a community surrounded by neighbors, the Williams found
themselves surrounded by dusty vacant lots. Since he likes gardening,
and his lot has limited space for gardening, Mr. William built a raised
garden bed out of used railroad ties in the vacant lot adjacent to his. A
garden hose extends from his property, over the separating wall, and into
the raised garden bed. No one seems to be bothered by this delicate act
of trespassing.

### Re-membering

The ever-incomplete urban form that results from the emphasis on perpetual horizontal expansion produces spaces that are cultural deserts,
where nature and history are reconstructed only in thematic ways as
extensions of development amenities. The banal and repetitive urban
forms reinforce isolation and exacerbate suspicion and fear of expressions of cultural difference (Low 2003). This cultural incarceration is
reinforced through the erasure of memories from the urban landscape
and from the daily experience of its dwellers. In response, placemaking
tactics reconnect places with hidden and erased memories, and communities with their distant members.

For example, regular yard sales are more than just an exchange of
goods. They are a mix of friendships and family reunions on one hand
and serious and industrious work by all members of an extended family,
and in many cases more than one family (Crawford, this volume), on the
other. The case of Mr. and Mrs. "Gonzales," in Central Phoenix, is a
typical example of such a small enterprise. A Latino couple in their late
forties to mid-fifties, the Gonzales start setting up their monthly yard
sale at 5:00 am. The merchandise, collected from other yard sales, back
alleys of more affluent neighborhoods, and from friends and relatives, is
moved out of the garage and neatly displayed on tables, in bins, and
hung on a large canopy. The display occupies their front yard, the dirt
stretch that was meant to be a sidewalk but was never completed, and
extends onto their portion of the cul-de-sac street. Their son drops off
more merchandise later in the day. Shopping at these regular yard sales
differs somewhat from the experience in a typical upper-middle-class
yard sale. Friends come by and help with a stubborn car problem and a

**Figure 6.2**
The Gonzales' yard sale: car repair, tire change, and friendly chat on a Sunday
morning before going to work. Photo credit: Rafael Fontes.

flat tire before Mr. Gonzales goes to his full-time job in a warehouse—on
Sunday (figure 6.2). Regular and accidental customers shop for bargains,
but there is virtually no bargaining taking place. Moreover, in marginalized communities, yard sales are the only suitable shopping option. "I
would shop at the mall too but it is too expensive . . . this yard sale
always has something I can buy," said "Miranda," a Latina bar waitress
in her early twenties, who was dropped off at the nearby bus station and
walked to the yard sale. She bought two $1 T-shirts that she will send
to her sisters across the border in Mexico: "they wanted something from
the U.S.," she added before leaving for work.

The corn vendor also carries a transnational connection. The *elote*
(white corn) he sells is used in *masa*, the dough for making tortillas,
tamales, and atole. The vendor's corn comes from a wholesaler in Phoenix
who ships it from Mexico. Because of his relatively long tenure in the
area and his connections with regular customers, the vendor also plays
a networking role in the community.

Different tactics create different types of connections. The street basketball court creates a space that connects the kids' play outdoors with
the nearby presence of adult family members indoors. The Williams'
guerilla garden is also a conversation piece that connects neighbors
through their complicity and shared sense of pride in this small act of
insurgence. The little produce yielded by this small garden is shared with
one of the families in the development. In return, the Williams get home-
made dishes and some help with gardening in Arizona's hot weather. In
all of these cases, placemaking involves more than just the physical
attributes of a space or even the practices inserted into it. It is also a
collective identification with a form of resistance embedded in practices

of everyday life on the margin: a shared—if not collective—consciousness of "otherness."

## Recycling Space

Contemporary urbanization in the Phoenix region, with its leapfrogging growth, generic planned development, and car-oriented infrastructure, creates obsolete spaces surrounded by incomplete urbanization, destroyed natural environment, and inadequate infrastructure and services. In underserved communities, placemaking tactics creatively find value in discarded urban spaces and elements. This is achieved through the revaluation of urban elements beyond their mere exchange value (i.e., market price as commodity) to lend to them also a use value (i.e., utility). Recycling space takes place in empty lots, vacant sidewalks, bland featureless walls, leftover spaces, spaces between spaces, as well as in underutilized streets, front yards, and residential spaces. Recycling space depends on individuals' skills and ability to reintroduce value into discarded urban elements. It requires ingenuity and creativity to identify possibilities and to repurpose existing elements without overtly transgressing their original (useless) state.

The regular yard sale is a clear example of recycling not only undervalued and often discarded household items but also urban space and elements. These yard sales repurpose the perpetually idle and hopelessly ornamental front yards, empty sidewalks, and exaggerated local streets into commercial spaces, communal areas for social gathering, and local reference points and landmarks. Similarly, the corn vendor reactivates a vacant lot and reuses elements from the site left by previous owners: the fence and gate legitimize and protect the enterprise, holes for signposts that have been removed are used to plant the shading canopy, parking spaces organize customers' circulation and parking, and so on. This repurposing shows the grace and subtlety with which recycling space is achieved. The same applies to the young adults who use construction debris to build a temporary and improvised skateboard park in a vacant lot in Tempe. The regular ritual of building their obstacle course is preceded by removing broken bottles, trash, and other hazardous debris. The activation of the neighborhood street in South Phoenix by turning it into a basketball court is another form of adaptive reuse of underutilized urban spaces. In Central Phoenix, highways left neighborhoods with odd-shaped swaths of land alongside on-ramps and overpasses. In one of these fragments, a group of six to eight sidewalk vendors have set up shop. The group consists mostly of women accompanied by young

**Figure 6.3**
Right-of-way vendors. Photo credit: Andrea Garfinkel-Castro.

children, but also includes a couple of adult men, who remain at a small distance from the main setup. Here, the bulky and featureless landscape is repurposed at a micro scale. A lonesome tree provides some respite from the relentless Arizona sun and is the focal point of this small urban node. The chain-link that fences off the neighborhood from the freeway is used to display clothes, rugs, blankets, mattresses, posters, and other large items. The recessed space of the right-of-way offers some extra width to an otherwise narrow sidewalk and is used to display other smaller items—from cosmetics to small electric appliances and toys (figure 6.3). This considerate setup avoids encroaching on pedestrian movement and possible complaints that may draw unwanted attention. Nearby, the neighborhood youth have set up a soccer field on a patch of land between the right-of-way of the same freeway and what is left of the neighborhood. The various types of guerrilla gardening mentioned above also represent forms of recycling spaces that were inert or under-utilized and turning them into valuable and productive spaces.

Another form of recycling space takes place on private property with building additions. Aside from the typical additions that expand livable space to accommodate larger households or multiple families, other

**Figure 6.4**
A building addition to fix a mobile home. Photo credit: Andrea Garfinkel-Castro.

additions serve other purposes. Mobile homes struggling to settle under Arizona's sun grow a second, more permanent, insulating skin (see figure 6.4). A notary public, bridal store, home-made food outlet, goat and sheep sales, and many other small home businesses maximize the utility of living rooms, kitchens, and front and backyards. Through these small acts of silent insurgence, the tenants of these dwellings have moved well beyond the much-lauded planning practice of mixed use. With minimal resources, they are devising socially and economically sustainable ways to implement "multiuse": each space serves more than one purpose in order to minimize down time. In the process of meeting basic needs through alternative sociospatial practices, they help to humanize a fragmented and sterile urban space, introducing cultural and material diversity in an otherwise homogeneous and generic landscape. Through an informal use of space and insurgent entrepreneurship, they implement their own vision of the right to the city.

## Conclusion

The Phoenix region, with its interrupted urbanization and discontinued urban form, represents a pattern of uneven urban development prevalent among rapidly growing cities of the Sunbelt. Marginalized residents are locked in a material and institutional environment designed for other times and other users. These constraints are renegotiated every day by a variety of placemaking tactics—despite the high risk, costs, and uncertainty associated with unsanctioned practices.

The cases reviewed here provide insights at several levels. For one, they reveal the intimate familiarity of residents with their built environment, and their creativity in generating opportunities for retrofitting unfavorable conditions. However, existing planning and decision-making mechanisms preclude them from formal participation in the production of urban space. In fact, placemaking tactics are an expression of the persisting conflict embedded in a pattern of uneven development that marginalizes communities by race, ethnicity, and class. In that sense, tactics are political statements of dissent and acts of resistance to archaic, arcane, and exclusionary forms of regulating urban space. Although covert and silent, this form of everyday resistance, when examined holistically, shows distinctive anarchist traits of shared values, mutual aid, freedom of initiative, and grassroots organization.

These placemaking tactics remain ad hoc, disjointed, and with limited linkages to other practices, making it difficult to perceive their production as a collective social movement in the conventional sense. However, in order to produce these tactics, a certain level of group cohesion and collective action must be present, whether in the form of tacit consent or complicitous participation (Scott 1985). While they have the potential to add up to deeper social and material changes, the limited organizational resources and skills in marginalized communities prevent these acts of dissidence from coalescing into a broad, large-scale, and overt movement to assert the right to define urban space.

Finally, the emergence and types of placemaking tactics in marginalized communities highlight the disparity between urban experiences in marginal communities and in mainstream ones. This is a function of a disconnection between formal regulatory visions and tools, on one hand, and the ability to address the range of social and material needs of diverse communities, on the other. The case is also compounded by ever more fiscally strapped municipal governments that have little appetite to intervene in regulating urban space in marginal communities, as long as local practices of dissent do not threaten the established order beyond the boundaries of these communities. This has led to divergent constructions of citizenship. In core communities, citizenship relies on legal rights provided and protected by formal institutions. Citizenship is defined and articulated by conforming to generic norms and practices. At the margin, citizenship is defined in terms of practices, not of rights. It is realized concretely in customized forms and norms of everyday practices that exist outside of and despite formal institutions (Holston 2009).

These findings carry significant implications for professionals involved in shaping urban space at the local level. It is well known that design clients—whether private investors or municipalities—are risk-averse and are not prone to deviate from successful development formulas. Nevertheless, urban planners, urban designers, and architects need to reconsider their position vis-à-vis the extent of control imposed on urban space and activities. Urban form should not be seen as an immutable constant to be rigidly controlled but rather as responsive to changing conditions and relations. Similarly, design should steer away from its emphasis on forms and products in favor of sociospatial practices. What practitioners can learn from tactics are the techniques of cloaking intentions, providing multipurpose solutions that address traditionally unmet needs, connecting with broader constitutions and stakeholders, and valuing space and maximizing its utility.

For research and pedagogy, the revolts witnessed in major cities around the world such as Cairo, Athens, Madrid, and London, as well as the various Occupy movements in U.S. cities, are expressions of a global (urban) malaise. They are manifestations of the limitations of incremental reformist approaches designed essentially to sustain a mode of production and its associated urban form, which inevitably generate uneven outcomes. Given the power differential among the various stakeholders involved in planning and design decisions, there is a need to shift the focus of research from control of space, with planning and design as predictive and prescriptive enterprises, to emancipation of space, with planning and design as enabling tools. Researchers can adapt the template provided by Marcuse (2009)—expose, propose, politicize—in order to increase their relevance in everyday processes of urban change. Cosmetic and purely form-based approaches have demonstrated their limitations. Urban research should address the root causes of uneven development and the reproduction of sociospatial informal practices. Similarly, and more than ever, the academic enterprise needs to proactively engage the practice and lead by example—by complementing conventional ex post facto academic research with interventionist experimental applications that are deeply immersed in local experiences and inputs. Finally, and in order to maximize their effectiveness, academic efforts need to maintain and mobilize functional ties with other agents of progressive change at various scales.

## Acknowledgment

This chapter is the product of a larger and ongoing research project supported by the Phoenix Urban Research Laboratory (PURL) at Arizona State University. I would like to thank Gabriel Diaz-Montemayor and Kristin Koptiuch for their insights and participation in the funded project, as well as research assistants Andrea Garfinkel-Castro and Margaret Diddams. This project would have not been possible without the participation of all the people who generously gave their time and shared their experiences.

## References

Arreola, Daniel. 2012. "Placemaking and Latino Urbanism in a Phoenix Mexican Immigrant Community." *Journal of Urbanism: International Research on Placemaking and Urban Sustainability* 5 (2–3):157–170.

Beauregard, Robert. 2006. *When America Became Suburban*. Minneapolis: University of Minnesota Press.

Checkoway, Barry. 1980. "Large Builders, Federal Housing Programmes, and Postwar Suburbanization." *International Journal of Urban and Regional Research* 4 (1):21–45.

City of Phoenix. 2012. "Fees & Payment Schedules." http://phoenix.gov/city clerk/services/licenseservices/licfees/index.html (retrieved July 15, 2012).

Crawford, Margaret. 1995. "Contesting the Public Realm: Struggles over Public Space in Los Angeles." *Journal of Architectural Education* 49 (1):4–9.

De Certeau, Michel. 1984. *The Practice of Everyday Life*. Berkeley: University of California Press.

Diaz, David. 2005. *Barrio Urbanism: Chicanos, Planning, and American Cities*. New York: Routledge.

FCD (Flood Control District of Maricopa County). 2012. GIS Aerial Photography Map. http://www.fcd.maricopa.gov/Maps/gismaps/apps/aerialsorder/appli cation/index.cfm (retrieved March 26, 2012).

Foucault, Michel. 1979. *Discipline and Punish: The Birth of the Prison*. Trans. Alan Sheridan. New York: Vintage Press.

Gober, Patricia. 1984. "Regional Convergence versus Uneven Development: Implications for Sunbelt SMSAs." *Urban Geography* 5 (2):130–145.

Hackworth, Jason. 2007. *The Neoliberal City*. Ithaca: Cornell University Press.

Harvey, David. 2005. *A Brief History of Neoliberalism*. New York: Oxford University Press.

Hirt, Sonia. 2012. "Form Follows Function? How America Zones." *Planning Practice and Research*. doi: 10.1080/02697459.2012.692982 (retrieved July 12, 2012).

Holston, James. 2009. "Insurgent Citizenship in an Era of Global Urban Peripheries." *City and Society* 21 (2):245–267.

Hou, Jeffrey. 2010. "(Not) Your Everyday Public Space." In Jeffrey Hou, ed., *Insurgent Public Space: Guerrilla Urbanism and the Remaking of Contemporary Cities*, 1–18. New York: Routledge.

Laguerre, Michel. 1994. *The Informal City*. New York: St. Martin's Press.

Loukaitou-Sideris, Anastasia, and Renia Ehrenfeucht. 2009. *Sidewalks: Conflict and Negotiation over Public Space*. Cambridge, MA: MIT Press.

Low, Setha. 2003. *Behind the Gates: Life, Security, and the Pursuit of Happiness in Fortress America*. New York: Taylor and Francis.

Marcuse, Peter. 2009. "From Critical Urban Theory to the Right to the City." *City* 13 (2–3):185–197.

McKenzie, Evan. 1994. *Privatopia: Homeowner Associations and the Rise of Residential Private Government*. New Haven: Yale University Press.

Rappaport, Jordan. 2003. "U.S. Urban Decline and Growth, 1950 to 2000." *Economic Review: Federal Reserve Bank of Kansas City* 88 (3): 15–44.

Rios, Michael. 2010. "Claiming Latino Space: Cultural Insurgency in the Public Realm." In Jeffrey Hou, ed., *Insurgent Public Space: Guerrilla Urbanism and the Remaking of Contemporary Cities*, 99–110. New York: Routledge.

Rojas, James. 2010. "Latino Urbanism in Los Angeles: A Model for Urban Improvisation and Reinvention." In Jeffrey Hou, ed., *Insurgent Public Space: Guerrilla Urbanism and the Remaking of Contemporary Cities*, 36–44. New York: Routledge.

Ross, Andrew. 2012. *Bird on Fire: Lessons from the World's Least Sustainable City*. New York: Oxford University Press.

Scott, James. 1985. *Weapons of the Weak: Everyday Forms of Peasant Resistance*. New Haven: Yale University Press.

Talen, Emily. 2012. "Zoning and Diversity in Historical Perspective." *Journal of Planning History*. doi: 10.1177/1538513212444566 (retrieved May 30, 2012).

U.S. Bureau of the Census. 2012. "Differential City Growth Patterns, 1950 to 2010." http://www.census.gov/dataviz/visualizations/016/508.php# (retrieved August 2, 2012).

# 7

## Surviving in America's Playground: Informal Sustenance Strategies among the Chronically Unhoused

Jacob Avery

Before it became an international entertainment destination, the land Atlantic City now occupies was a small windswept island off New Jersey's southern shore. Beginning in the early 1800s, entrepreneurial individuals believed that the island could be more: a seaside location where people could be offered experiences that differed dramatically from their daily lives. Though the city's founders could never have imagined what this place would become, Atlantic City is no longer a barren island. But while most people associate Atlantic City with gambling and well-to-do tourists, the unique entertainment landscape also provides opportunities for resource-poor people—the chronically unhoused—to maintain a minimal existence.[1]

Today, street beggars approach cars at traffic intersections, alcoholics pass out in alleyways, and proprietors of local businesses shoo them away from their storefronts. Visitors to the city physically and emotionally negotiate panhandlers' requests for spare change, often uncomfortably. Many locals and visitors interact with the unhoused population as an inconvenient though inescapable feature of the social fabric of this city. Atlantic City's unhoused population, who cling to the margins of conventional society, are sparsely integrated with the city that hosts them. Nevertheless, they find here the necessary ingredients that sustain their livelihoods—a "sustaining habitat" as sociologist Mitchell Duneier (1999) called it. Atlantic City offers a dense physical landscape with numerous pedestrians, the availability of cheap and free food, and several places to sleep throughout the city without fear of being harassed or cited by police. Viewed from a different angle, however, Atlantic City's entertainment landscape provides the necessary props that enable chemical addictions and disincentivize help-seeking behavior among resource-poor populations.

Beginning in 2005, I conducted observational fieldwork in Atlantic City's public spaces. I was interested in the survival strategies employed by the urban poor in contexts of diminished choice, and thus began volunteering at an emergency homeless shelter in Atlantic City in 2008. There I formed relationships with social service caseworkers, unhoused men and women, and other volunteers. Surprisingly, I did not encounter many people who had arrived at the shelter solely because they had lost everything in gambling. How the unhoused individuals I was meeting at the shelter and on the streets understand their relation to the urban context of Atlantic City was a question that animated my work. Through increased involvement, observations, and interviews with individuals at the shelter and on the street, I began to develop workable themes to write about. Of particular importance for this chapter was how Atlantic City provided a sustaining habitat for unhoused men and women. More specifically, though, I became interested in the informal economy and activities among Atlantic City's unhoused, both those who were staying at the shelter and those who remained outside (Avery 2012).

This chapter builds on prior ethnographic work on American homelessness.[2] I first discuss the geographic and social context of Atlantic City, then explain the concept of sustaining habitat and how it is demonstrated in the urban landscape of the city. Conveying how Atlantic City's entertainment ecology guides the daily activities of chronically unhoused individuals,[3] the chapter provides a detailed account of how the unhoused make money, locate sleeping spots, and survive in this peculiar urban landscape using a variety of informal sustenance activities. If social scientists and policymakers care about homelessness, we must turn our intellectual and interventionist gaze toward real homeless people doing the hard work of daily sustenance. While homelessness is the object of numerous academic investigations, an in-depth account of it in American communities remains a critical intellectual pursuit that can inform anti-poverty policies.

## Atlantic City: A Tale of Two Towns?

Atlantic City (hereafter AC) has always been a town geared around commercialized entertainment. From early on, AC provided its vacationers with diversions. In 1858, the city only registered 3,000 visitors. In 1939, sixteen million people traveled there (Federal Reserve Bank of Philadelphia 2009). The city owed its initial popularity to easy accessibility to large population centers (Philadelphia, New York, and Baltimore) of the

Northeast. Nelson Johnson, author of *Boardwalk Empire*, wrote of the city's dubious legacy: "If the people who came to town had wanted Bible readings, we'd have given 'em that. But nobody ever asked for Bible readings. They wanted booze, broads, and gambling, so that's what we gave them" (Johnson 2002: vii). Indeed, almost since its inception, AC's primary purpose has been to provide leisure activities for its visitors.

For nearly a hundred years, AC reigned as *the* entertainment capital of the United States. During a period of unprecedented economic prosperity following World War II, however, while many towns and cities flourished, AC struggled to maintain its prominence. The development of the Interstate Highway System, increased competition from places like Disney World, and cheaper airfares to vacation destinations across or out of the country all weakened the city's locational advantage. Tourism slowed and unemployment spiked. The city's loyal tourists abandoned the beach and boardwalk. AC epitomized the social and economic disinvestment taking place throughout U.S. inner cities during the 1960s. As one study has argued: "The city became a poster child for urban blight and decay. Journalists dubbed it 'Bronx by the Bay' and compared it to bombed-out Dresden and war-torn Beirut" (Simon 2004: 11–12).

Mindful of Las Vegas's continued success,[4] a coalition of local business leaders, casino executives, and state officials proposed casino gambling for AC as one way to reverse economic decline. They argued that legalized gambling would be a "unique tool" to facilitate the region's local economy, positioning the city on a trajectory for recovery (Sternlieb and Hughes 1983). The two key goals were revitalization of AC's lagging tourism and convention industry, and use of gambling as a mechanism to support the city's urban development. In 1974, a referendum that called for legalized casino gambling was placed on the state ballot but was defeated. During the 1976 general election, however, New Jersey voters passed a referendum that limited legalized casino gambling to AC. The first casino hotel—Resorts International—opened for business on May 26, 1978. By 2012, twelve casino resorts provided twenty-four-hour entertainment for patrons. The introduction of casinos significantly altered the economic, social, and spatial landscape of AC.

With few exceptions, any person over twenty-one years old may enter AC's casinos. They can walk the gaming floor and experience the cacophony of sounds, sights, and smells that characterize social interaction in that space. They can dance at nightclubs, drink alcohol at the bar, or place legal wagers on games of chance. Despite the self-marketing of casinos as fantasy zones where people "cut loose" from the constraints of daily life, casinos are highly controlled environments, where everybody's movements are monitored and tracked by armed security officers walking the gaming floor and by surveillance cameras placed throughout the building. Of course, this process of "bringing the casino public together," Bryant Simon asserts, "requires the deployment of updated confidence builders" (Simon 2004: 209). These confidence builders—the all-seeing security cameras and armed guards—ensure that people inside the casino have the illusion of protection from undesirable people who might threaten the casino patrons' good time (while also, of course, protecting the casinos' profits). One reason casinos craft these safe spaces may be to protect their customers from what lies just beyond their walls in AC.

Fear of the wider community may have worked to the casinos' advantage, keeping people on well-traveled paths and inside the casinos. Between inside and outside, the visual juxtaposition of poverty and wealth is dramatic. Away from the places where tourists typically congregate lies a community of concentrated poverty. Many houses are in disrepair. Whole tracts of land remain barren. Indeed, a curious feature of the AC landscape is that, despite hosting an industry that generates billions in revenue, the surrounding community has higher rates of poverty than New Jersey and the United States as a whole (Federal Reserve Bank of Philadelphia 2009).

To tourists, AC appears void of opportunity, save for the action that takes place within the casinos' walls: "A stark, vacant, poor city with a beach, the Boardwalk, and . . . inward-looking casino villages that leave only crumbs on the Monopoly streets around them" (Simon 2004: 11–12). To anyone who walks AC's streets, the stark juxtaposition between the casinos and the local community context is obvious. Not as obvious is how the tourism and casino industries provide a unique habitat where street-dwelling individuals develop ways to maintain a minimal existence by surviving day to day off "the crumbs" that Simon describes.

While there is a connection between the casinos and the numerous unhoused people walking AC's streets, that connection tends not to work in the direction one might expect, with individuals losing their money at the casinos and winding up stranded and without a place to stay. While this may be the case for some, many unhoused men and women arrived in AC through different channels. Some were released to the local shelter from county jails. Some came to the city looking for work at the casinos, others because of its unique entertainment context. No matter why they came, the urban context in AC provides a "sustaining habitat" (Duneier

1999) giving opportunities for marginal citizens to overcome material hardships. Owing to its unique landscape of opportunity, even the most resource-poor individuals have found novel ways to maintain a minimal existence within the sustaining habitat.

### Sustaining Habitat

While conducting ethnographic fieldwork among scavengers and sellers of written matter (magazines and books) on Sixth Avenue in New York City's Greenwich Village, Duneier made a discovery: individuals who scavenged and sold written matter on the street cultivated a basic subsistence (Duneier 1999). Most notably, these men were protected under a municipal ordinance permitting the resale of written matter. That point becomes significant when one considers the substantial pool of highly educated customers who lived in the neighborhood and were willing to purchase books and magazines sold on Sixth Avenue. For the several unhoused men Duneier encountered during his fieldwork, selling written matter provided a crucial way to make ends meet in a context of material deprivation. According to Duneier, the sustaining habitat's basic characteristics are (1) density of pedestrians, (2) availability of cheap or free food, and (3) numerous places to sleep without fear of being targeted by police or fear of violence.

Drawing on Jane Jacobs's (1961) claim that "eyes on the street" safeguard urban public spaces, Duneier asserts that high pedestrian density and continuous pedestrian presence in public space create environments where "respectable eyes dominate" the street scene, ensuring that strangers and outsiders do not disrupt the general peace. While Duneier contends that black unhoused men are generally regarded with fear and suspicion by the wider (white and middle-class) public, these sentiments do not always shape the emotional tenor of exchanges between unhoused men and pedestrians traversing the sidewalks. To the uncritical eye, the unhoused men may look like products of social disorder. But on the streets of Sixth Avenue, a proud bohemian neighborhood, they found a community context dense with people abiding by a "live and let live" attitude, as well as many sympathetic citizens willing to make charitable donations that sustain the unhoused men, both materially and physically.

The sustaining habitat's second basic characteristic, availability of cheap or free food, is crucial to the daily survival of resource-poor individuals. Soup kitchens that provide regular meals during the day offer nutritional sustenance to men, women, and children who have little money. In areas where food is relatively expensive, such as Sixth Street in Lower Manhattan, the provision of meals by churches and shelters frees up an otherwise significant expense of daily survival. Thus, money obtained through informal work on the streets can be put toward other expenses such as "feeding" drug and alcohol addictions. At other times, though, this money is used for more conventional expenses such as clothing, entertainment, and temporary housing. Because housing is expensive and emergency shelters are often crowded, finding temporary housing can be challenging. Thus, locating temporary spots for sleeping is a daily preoccupation among the unhoused.

The sustaining habitat has a third characteristic: an abundance of public places where unhoused individuals can sleep without harassment or legal citation. Magazine and book scavengers on Sixth Avenue, who did not have customary and regular access to permanent housing, secured spots throughout the city. One man on Sixth Avenue slept on the steps of a local church. Another slept inside the vestibule of a bank. Other individuals slept in chairs on the sidewalk or in the dark, dank subway tunnels. Finding and protecting sleeping spots was an important element in maintaining the sustaining habitat's lifeline.

Additional elements on Sixth Avenue—a neighborhood of residents sympathetic to marginalized black men, and who were willing to donate magazines and books to these men for resale on the street—coalesced to create a "working system," where unhoused men could sustain a minimal level of social, economic, and physical existence. Important to remember is that this sustaining habitat did not come together in a formal, planned manner. On the contrary, collective actions of numerous people and institutions—often working in informal, unplanned ways—shaped the Sixth Avenue habitat. The sustaining habitat is a useful concept for understanding why many unhoused individuals come to AC and stay there.

## AC as a Sustaining Habitat

With fewer than 40,000 residents, AC is small both by population and geography, compared to other U.S. cities where ethnographies of unhoused denizens have been documented (e.g., New York, Los Angeles, Austin, Philadelphia, San Francisco). Nevertheless, AC has the highest central-city rate of homelessness, as well as one of the densest homeless populations, in the United States (Lee and Price-Spratlen, 2004). The land base of AC is 11.4 square miles; counting water, the city limits encompass 17.4 square miles. The city rests on an island, just off the southern New Jersey shoreline on the Atlantic Ocean. In many ways, this sets the city apart from neighboring communities and cities. Absecon Island (which AC is built upon) is long, narrow, and surrounded by water. The Atlantic Ocean is a natural border on the northern, eastern, and southern points of the island, giving AC a distinct, self-contained character. As one travels south to cities like Ventnor (AC's neighbor on the island), one finds well-maintained houses, buildings, and city streets. While it is feasible to walk to neighboring cities from AC, the folk wisdom among AC's unhoused residents is that the housed residents and police officers would not tolerate this and would expeditiously usher them back to AC. Indeed, only somebody new to AC would make such a mistake. The public spaces of neighboring cities may be more inviting—with well-paved streets, well-maintained buildings, and lush yards and green spaces—but boundaries separating AC from neighboring cities are vigilantly maintained.

AC is easily navigable on foot (figure 7.1). There are copious sidewalks along long, narrow, and pedestrian-friendly streets. Two streets

Figure 7.1
Boardwalk in Atlantic City. Photo credit: Jacob Avery.

that run parallel to each other and to the casinos, boardwalk, beach, and ocean make for easy passage on foot from one end of the city to the other. To traverse even the longest distance from any one point in the city to another would take only an hour by foot, at a slow pace. To walk from the shelter to the boardwalk takes ten minutes. To walk from the southernmost to the northernmost casino on the boardwalk takes thirty minutes. To walk from the center of the boardwalk to the nearest liquor store takes ten minutes. Indeed, the transient poor new to town find a tight arrangement of social service institutions, public places, and commercial zones that are all easily accessible.

For unhoused individuals who have lived on the streets for many years, however, moving easily around some parts of the city is not possible. Many individuals have received both formal and informal bans from casino personnel. As one man told me, explaining that the casino gaming floor is off limits, "if you don't look like you're there to spend money, or if you look like you're from the street and you're not spending money, forget it. You'll definitely get fucked with." This tends to be true when one has "the [street] look" (multiple layers of dirty clothes, weathered and unshaved face) and is not spending money in the casino. Thus, for AC's unhoused residents, traveling to and from points in the city is never as easy as taking the shortest route. The easiest (and safest) passage is not always the most direct, and this differs from tourists' experiences of maneuvering around AC. Whereas tourists may find the easiest and safest passage by avoiding areas and walkways not connected to the casino, the unhoused have similar concerns but the opposite experience. (This does not mean the unhoused never cross into spaces occupied by tourists, or vice versa.) Maneuvering around menacing obstacles may take extra time and effort, but it is deemed worth it. In the main, though, for the unhoused denizens, travel time is minimal to any of their destinations within city limits, even with obstacles to avoid.

Since walking is the predominant mode of transportation for the street homeless, they are more visible and vulnerable when crossing neighborhood boundaries than an out-of-towner in a vehicle. To reach the local emergency shelter from the boardwalk, it is often faster to walk through the gaming floor to arrive on the city street on the other side of the casino. For the new arrival in town—one not carrying bags, suitcases, or sleeping bags on their person—this is a possibility. While security and video camera surveillance are heavy on casino gaming floors, an unhoused person who may "pass" as a visitor or patron can walk through the casinos.

The casinos and their patrons are especially important in sustaining life for AC's unhoused population. They provide opportunities to "hustle" and make money to sustain livelihoods. For the unhoused who consciously attempt to pass as casino patrons, AC's casinos offer opportunities to make small amounts of money. To do so, these men and women must maintain a clean, neat appearance so they do not attract attention from casino security or other casino patrons.

One method of making money is called the credit hustle. Once inside the casino, the credit hustle is simple to execute. To start, most credit hustlers secure a plastic drink cup (preferably with some liquid and ice still in it, and a casino logo) before entering the casino. These drink cups provide credit hustlers with a prop to help them pass as casino patrons. For the fullest effect, credit hustlers take little sips from the cup as they weave through the slot machine banks on the casino gaming floor. While they do this, they look for uncashed credits on slot machines. Since most slot machines have digital interfaces (as opposed to the antiquated coin slot) casino patrons insert dollar bills into the machine to buy credits for play. When cashing out from a slot machine, casino patrons receive a credit slip (similar to a receipt) that they redeem for cash at kiosks located on the casino floor. Many casino patrons either spend all their credits or cash out and retrieve their money from the kiosks after concluding play. Some patrons, however, leave credits on the machine when they conclude play, not bothering (or simply forgetting) to cash in small amounts of money. For instance, a casino patron playing a nickel machine will be required to play a minimum of five credits for each spin, costing them at least twenty-five cents per play. But with odd payouts and irregular wagers, a casino patron can play the slot machine to an odd number of credits below the minimum wager (i.e., four, three, two, or one credit). Instead of cashing out a receipt for fifteen or twenty cents or inserting more money, casino patrons leave these credits on the machine. This is precisely what credit hustlers want to spot. As they walk between slot machine banks, they keep an eye on each machine's credit readings. When they see a slot machine with credits remaining, they sit down at the machine, hit the cash out button, collect the receipt, and move on. For those who slide under the radar of casino security, credit hustling is an effective way of making $10–15 a day. The industry term for credit hustlers is "credit thieves," and casino employees refer to them as "credit critters." While credit hustling is not illegal, credit hustlers must remain vigilant to avoid trouble with casino personnel.

In addition to credit hustling, the physical structure and layout of the casinos are important in the lives of the chronically unhoused. Two features of the casinos' physical structure deserve mention. First, most casinos have a bus terminal connected to their hotel or gaming floor. Since casinos draw a significant portion of their patrons from areas close to AC, charter buses are a common mode of travel for visitors. On a daily basis, buses arrive from New York, Philadelphia, and other points in New Jersey, bringing thousands of visitors to the city and casinos. Consequently, the hotel casinos in AC have large passenger terminals where buses depart and arrive. These terminals, like the casinos themselves, are open twenty-four hours a day and seven days a week. They provide shelter from outside elements and are common places to sleep because they are heated and air-conditioned. One chronically unhoused man, "Jared," sleeps most nights in the bus terminals. Jared described his sleeping patterns in this way:

I try not to stay outside. They [i.e., the other chronically unhoused individuals] can sleep under the boardwalk if they want to. I'd rather go from one bus station to the next bus station to the next. I go from one bus station, and after they [casino security] tell me to leave from there, I go to the one next door. After they tell me to leave from there, I go to the one next door. Then, when they tell me to leave from there, I go back to the first one. So I'm like a basketball.

The practice that Jared describes is common among AC's unhoused population, particularly for those who do not sleep outside. As mentioned, the upside of sleeping in bus terminals is that they are climate-controlled, semipublic and protected spaces. Thus, while security guards are unlikely to let unhoused men and women sleep in a bus terminal for long periods of time, the terminals offer protection from violence and inclement weather. The downside to sleeping in bus terminals, though, is that one must sleep upright, and cannot typically stay in any bus terminal for more than a few hours before being asked to leave by casino security officers.

Since many street homeless who sleep in bus terminals also credit hustle, work the casino doors, or panhandle, one strategy employed to stave off security guards is to use money to purchase the cheapest bus ticket to the nearest town (typically these cost $3–5). The unhoused can purchase tickets and use them to validate their presence in the bus terminal. Then, before the tickets expire, they can sell them at reduced prices or barter them to another bus patron for coffee or food from vending machines.

While the newly unhoused can figure out the logistics of bus terminal sleeping, casino stairwell sleeping typically requires local knowledge derived from time and experience on the streets and befriending and learning from other individuals who know where such spots are located. The upside of sleeping in fire escape stairwells is that they are flat-surfaced, secluded, warm, and with exit doors leading outside from the ground floor. These exit doors become important since quick getaways are occasionally required—especially when the characteristic rumbling sound of somebody (typically casino security or personnel) descending the stairwell is heard. The downside of sleeping in casinos' fire escape stairwells is that, in order to reach the ground floor of the stairwell, one must first walk through the casino's gaming floor.

Throughout the city, numerous restaurants serve inexpensive or free food. Also, several soup kitchens operate throughout the city, where anyone who knows the location and time of food service can get a free meal; and there are several food stands along the boardwalk that sell hot dogs, funnel cakes, and pizza. Instead of "sparing change" to the unhoused who beg for change, many tourists offer to buy them food. The following excerpt, which details a conversation between myself and two unhoused men, G. and Fran, in AC, is illustrative:

Jacob:   What about food? How do you eat out here?
G.:   Um, here's the thing, Jake, you're never going to starve homeless in AC. You're never going to—it's never going to happen. There's places that feed every day . . . you're never going to starve here. You'd eat good, man! People give you club sandwiches and shit that they were going to bring home and give to their dog, I guess, I don't know.
Fran:   I was up here panhandling and I asked a person for money, a guy and his girl, and they said "no." And then the woman came back to me and said, "we're not going to give you any money, but we'll buy you breakfast." They bought me steak and eggs, coffee, and juice.
G.:   Yeah, you see, that happens. I remember one day, I asked a person for money and he said, "nah, but I'll buy you something. Let's go into Johnny Rockets" [a 50s-style restaurant that serves burgers, French fries, and milk-shakes]. And he said, "what do you want?" And I asked, "what can I get?" He said, "order whatever you want." He gave me twenty dollars, but he said I had to spend it there. And I have my friends out there, and I wasn't going to eat without them. And I brought 'em chili burgers and fries. And we all ate.

While AC's unhoused population can eat at the soup kitchens daily, these types of offerings from tourists are seen as special "treats." In general, the unhoused believe that food received from tourists, whether tourists buy them food or offer up leftovers as alms, is superior in quality to food served at soup kitchens, particularly food prepared in restaurants, even if someone else has already eaten part of it.

Owing to these features in the local landscape, AC's unhoused population face an ecological context that supports a minimal existence. At the same time, a large proportion of those dwelling outside, sleeping rough in the casino bus terminals, and begging for change on the boardwalk also manage severe chemical addictions. The extent to which AC provides a sustaining habitat for these individuals needs to be questioned, but where should social scientists and policymakers draw the line between sustaining and enabling?

## Conclusion

When unhoused people with few material resources find reliable ways to make money, eat, and sleep, the basic features of their livelihood are in place. This constitutes the essence of the sustaining habitat: where an ecological environment makes it possible for resource-poor individuals to maintain a minimal existence without formal housing arrangements and employment. The landscape of AC provides ample opportunities for newcomers and old-timers alike, particularly among the unhoused, to maintain a minimal existence, making money through panhandling, finding free or cheap meals as well as numerous niches to sleep, typically with impunity. Although this appears to approximate the sustaining habitat's features described by Duneier, AC's ecology differs from Sixth Avenue in New York.[5]

For unhoused people, AC could also be described as an *enabling*, rather than sustaining, habitat. As mentioned earlier, a large proportion of AC's unhoused population manages chemical addictions while piecing together the basics of food, shelter, and a social life. The chemical addiction component of their lives is a crucial point to understand because it organizes daily routines, where much time and effort goes toward alleviating chemical withdrawal symptoms. Money made from credit hustling within a casino or from panhandling need not go for food (for reasons described earlier), but instead can be put toward purchasing drugs or alcohol. Moreover, because AC is a twenty-four-hour town, tourists can be approached for money, casino gaming floors can be raided for small amounts of money or alcohol, and the bus terminals within casinos can be places of refuge at all times of day. Thus, the potential to enable one's addiction is at its height in AC. Every day, more unhoused men and women move into the area because they have few compelling alternatives, and in AC they find a small, quirky resort town where an individual's addictive behavior blends seamlessly into the city's ecological and social fabric.

What do we make of this? Since its inception, AC has been a site of destination and drift. Annually, millions of tourists come there to walk the famous boardwalk by the Atlantic Ocean, place legal wagers in the city's casinos, and engage in activities most American communities repress, such as drinking excessively and using illegal drugs. Here vices tamped down and tempered elsewhere meet an enabling habitat that encourages their fullest expression. Visitors receive near-constant encouragement from advertisements and billboards to "drink up," "try their luck," and stay up later than they are used to. The day-tripping tourist, who comes to AC to drink, gamble, and then go home, has long been the city's lifeblood. At the same time, AC has been a place where those with few compelling options elsewhere have discovered novel ways to survive off the entertainment landscape's crumbs. Such individuals, many of whom are chronically unhoused, survive without boarding at an emergency homeless shelter or enrolling in its behavioral health or work programs. While many suffer from severe drug and alcohol addictions, and though local social service facilities provide assistance for their unique troubles, they do not seek treatment in a committed way. Despite persistent efforts by outreach workers to bring them inside the treatment facility, they remain outside; and some individuals, after years of avoidances, die on AC's streets.

The situation in AC suggests that opportunities for survival by the marginal, addicted, and dispossessed abound. The fact that individuals who belong to the most resource-poor and health-challenged population in the United States have found ways to achieve minimal existence should not surprise us.[6] Evidence from a large body of social scientific and social welfare literature has shown poor people as active decision makers in their struggle to make ends meet.[7] What is important to stress here is how local context guides the behavior and informal activities of resource-poor individuals. In AC, we have seen how the formal tourist economy provides a context in which resource-poor individuals navigate an urban environment that facilitates their chemical addictions and disincentivizes help-seeking behavior by offering the basics of survival—food, shelter, and socialization—informally, with no strings attached. In the current economic context of widening social inequality in the United States, documenting *where* and *how* the extremely poor survive reveals how both scholars and policymakers can profitably seek new solutions to the old social problem of homelessness.

## Notes

1. Throughout this chapter, I use the neologism "unhoused" in place of "homeless." As many scholars have noted, definitional and conceptual problems abound when the term "homeless" is used to describe a group-based identity (Duneier 1999; Hopper 2003; Jencks 1995; Rossi 1991). Unhoused, I believe, is a more precise description of the social situation of people I came to know in Atlantic City. Their condition was characterized more by lack of a fixed, permanent residence than by social disaffiliation from wider society.

2. For leading examples of the past twenty years, see Bourgois and Schonberg (2009); Dordick (1997); Duneier (1999); Gowan (2010); and Snow and Anderson (1993).

3. According to the Department of Housing and Urban Development, individuals may fit the federal definition of chronic homelessness in one of two ways: as unaccompanied and disabled individuals who have been continuously homeless for one year or more; or as unaccompanied and disabled individuals who have at least four episodes of homelessness during the past three years.

4. On the surface, Las Vegas and Atlantic City seem similar, with casino gaming and tourism driving much local commerce; but as we dig further into their histories, analytical comparison becomes increasingly difficult. To risk oversimplification, Las Vegas's growth between 1930 and 1970 was largely tied to numerous federal spending projects (Rothman 2003), while casino gambling and the vice industry (e.g., prostitution) helped grow the city and create its distinctive economic niche. By contrast, regulated casino gambling did not arrive in Atlantic City until the late 1970s, and it was implemented as a unique tool for "urban redevelopment" for a decaying metropolitan area (Simon 2004; Sternlieb and Hughes 1983). The two cities are also quite different in size: in 2010, Las Vegas had 583,756 residents, a major U.S. city, whereas Atlantic City had 39,558, approximating a smaller town.

5. In Borchard's (2005) examination of homeless men in Las Vegas, he found that many of them came there for the same reasons that tourists did: they desired an environment where laws and norms about permissible behavior were relaxed. And, similar to my findings in Atlantic City, many men in Borchard's study resettled in Las Vegas because the city was deemed a good place to "get a fresh start" and secure a decent-paying job.

6. Homeless persons with serious mental illness and substance abuse problems constitute a large percentage of the chronically homeless (Burt 2001; Culhane, Metraux, and Hadley 2002). Research finds that more than half of the chronically homeless have co-occurring disorders of substance abuse and mental illness (Substance Abuse and Mental Health Services Administration 2007).

7. To reference just a few well-known examples of ethnographies that describe the decision-making processes of the urban poor, see Edin and Lein's (1997) *Making Ends Meet*; Liebow's (1967) *Tally's Corner*; and Stack's (1974) *All Our Kin*.

# References

Avery, Jacob. 2012. "Down and Out in Atlantic City." *Annals of the American Academy of Political and Social Science* 642 (1):139–151.

Borchard, Kurt. 2005. *The Word on the Street: Homeless Men in Las Vegas.* Reno: University of Nevada Press.

Bourgois, Philippe, and Jeffrey Schonberg. 2009. *Righteous Dopefiend.* Berkeley: University of California Press.

Burt, Martha. 2001. *What Will It Take to End Homelessness?* Washington, DC: Urban Institute Press.

Culhane, D., S. Metraux, and T. Hadley. 2002. "Public Service Reductions Associated with Placement of Homeless Persons with Severe Mental Illness in Supportive Housing." *Housing Policy Debate* 13 (1):107–163.

Dordick, Gwendolyn. 1997. *Something Left to Lose: Personal Relations and Survival among New York's Homeless.* Philadelphia: Temple University Press.

Duneier, Mitchell. 1999. *Sidewalk.* New York: Farrar, Straus and Giroux.

Edin, Kathryn, and Laura Lein. 1997. *Making Ends Meet: How Single Mothers Survive Welfare and Low-Wage Work.* New York: Russell Sage Foundation.

Federal Reserve Bank of Philadelphia. 2009. *Atlantic City: Past as Prologue. A Special Report by the Community Affairs Department.* Philadelphia: Federal Reserve Bank of Philadelphia.

Gowan, Teresa. 2010. *Hobos, Hustlers and Backsliders: Homeless in San Francisco.* Minneapolis: University of Minnesota Press.

Hopper, Kim. 2003. *Reckoning with Homelessness.* Ithaca: Cornell University Press.

Jacobs, Jane. [1961] 1992. *The Death and Life of Great American Cities.* New York: Vintage Books.

Jencks, Christopher. 1995. *The Homeless.* Cambridge: Harvard University Press.

Johnson, Nelson. 2002. *Boardwalk Empire.* Medford, NJ: Plexus Publishing.

Lee, Barret, and Townsand Price-Spratlen. 2004. "The Geography of Homelessness in American Communities: Concentration or Dispersion?" *City and Community* 3 (1):3–27.

Liebow, Elliot. 1967. *Tally's Corner: A Study of Negro Streetcorner Men.* Boston: Little, Brown.

Rossi, Peter. 1991. *Down and Out in America.* Chicago: University of Chicago Press.

Rothman, Hal. 2003. *Neon Metropolis: How Las Vegas Started the Twenty-First Century.* New York: Routledge.

Simon, Bryant. 2004. *Boardwalk of Dreams: Atlantic City and the Fate of Urban America.* New York: Oxford University Press.

Snow, David, and Leon Anderson. 1993. *Down on Their Luck: A Study of Homeless Street People.* Berkeley: University of California Press.

Stack, Carol. 1974. *All Our Kin: Strategies for Survival in a Black Community.* New York: Basic Books.

Sternlieb, George, and James W. Hughes. 1983. *The Atlantic City Gamble: A Twentieth Century Fund Report.* Cambridge: Harvard University Press.

Substance Abuse and Mental Health Services Administration. 2007. *Results from the 2006 National Survey on Drug Use and Health: National Findings.* Rockville, MD: Substance Abuse and Mental Health Services Administration.

# Part II

Responses

# 8

# The Irreconcilable Tension between Dwelling in Public and the Regulatory State

Renia Ehrenfeucht and Anastasia Loukaitou-Sideris

In 2012, a keyword search for "homelessness" in the newspaper database America's News resulted in over 74,000 articles written during the past five years. The articles told stories about the causes of homelessness and the impact of the recession, about shelter provision, the one-night (or point-in-time) counts, and the 10-year plans to end homelessness. Fewer articles referred to informal settlements such as colonias in Texas or the countless ways that people dwell in public under bridges and freeway overpasses or in other marginal urban spaces. The most notable articles for the purpose of this chapter discussed the frequency with which dwelling, working, or spending time in public elicited regulatory responses in cities across the United States.

The estimated 3.5 million people (or more than 1 percent of the U.S. population) who experience at least one night of homelessness in any given year get by in diverse ways (National Coalition for the Homeless 2009). Some live in cars or double up with friends or family. Others stay in shelters, sleep outside, squat in empty buildings, or establish camps on public or private land. Where people sleep influences how they contend with regular aspects of daily life including bathing, washing clothes, storing belongings, spending nonwork time, and planning for the future. People with no residence must do more in public spaces than domiciled denizens and have less certainty about how each day will unfold. Therefore they need to creatively strategize about how to dwell in public and how to adapt to changing circumstances.

People who have to spend much time in public, who cannot bathe or wash clothes frequently, and who carry their belongings become visible because these practices collide with societal norms. Public spaces are sites where housed urban residents and visitors come into contact with homelessness. Across the United States, city councils and mayors working with residents, businesses, and neighborhood associations have responded to homelessness by adopting restrictions on associated everyday activities including camping, loitering, and panhandling.

Regulation is not, however, a neutral mechanism to balance multiple interests in public spaces. Regulations standardize and formalize activities, thereby reducing the possibilities for street dwellers to autonomously adapt and use public spaces. When public space activities are adaptive, meaning that participants alter either their location or practices in response to personal needs or external circumstances, regulations can undermine street use *and* street users. Beginning with the 1991 report "Go Directly to Jail" that analyzed antihomeless ordinances in nine cities, the National Law Center on Homelessness and Poverty and the National Coalition for the Homeless have documented decades of efforts to criminalize public activities associated with homelessness (NLCHP 2011; NLCHP and National Coalition for the Homeless 2009; NLCHP 1991).

This chapter focuses on the tension created by regulating adaptive public space use. It draws from recent ethnographic literature about homelessness, a review of the ordinances of major U.S. cities targeting panhandling, loitering, and public sleeping and sitting, and reports about the regulatory trends targeting homelessness. First we give a brief historic overview of U.S. homelessness and the regulatory responses to it. We then draw from ethnographic literature that shows how people live in public and how regulations impact them. Two elements contribute to the irreconcilable tension between dwelling in public and the regulatory state: the diminishing urban commons and the influence of private property, which we next discuss. Finally, we offer examples of promising approaches to better accommodate life in public as well as strategies to achieve this. The assumption underlying this chapter is that cities need informal, flexible, and adaptive urban commons. Rebuilding the commons will require explicitly interrogating and reformulating the regulatory state.

### Visible Poverty and Regulatory Responses: A Brief Historic Overview

Visible poverty is a recurrent condition in cities. From colonial settlements to the cities of the early republic, towns established poorhouses and orphanages that were supported by taxpayer funds for "deserving" community members such as widows and orphaned children (DePastino 2003). Subsequent westward development, train travel, and urbanization led to large numbers of hobos or migratory workers in the late nineteenth and early twentieth centuries, who worked itinerantly and spent nonwork hours on the streets and in bars and flophouses. In response, social and private services such as shelters and soup kitchens developed for these men. The number of hobos waned by the 1920s, but the Great Depression led to widespread homelessness in the 1930s, a situation that only ended by an economy invigorated by the country's entry into World War II (DePastino 2003; Leginski 2007; Monkkonen 1984). During the relatively prosperous period following World War II, hypermobility gave way to increased urban settlement exemplified by suburban life (Jackson 1985; Wiese 2004).

Homelessness again increased dramatically in the 1970s and 1980s. As industrial cities lost their manufacturing base and suburbanization spread, inner-city neighborhoods lost both jobs and residents to the suburbs and the Sunbelt region, leading to what has been extensively characterized as the "urban crisis." Facing both housing discrimination and increasing unemployment, destitute urban denizens struggled to get by from day to day. They washed car windows and panhandled, among many other informal economic activities. The poorest among them squatted in empty buildings at night. But now, instead of the single white men who dominated skid row stereotypes during the first part of the century, African Americans were disproportionately represented, and more families and women were among those seeking shelter (Brunson 2011). Contrasting starkly with the suburban ideal, this phenomenon instigated a homelessness "crisis," and in response Congress adopted the McKinney Homeless Assistance Act (later the McKinney-Vento Act) on July 22, 1987 (NLCHP, n.d.).

Municipal regulation of visible poverty also has a long history. From the colonial era into the twentieth century, vagrancy ordinances were used by municipalities to target recurrent public space users. Vagrancy regulations classified people who begged or loitered repeatedly as "vagrants" and then fined, jailed, or expelled them (they were given a choice between jail and leaving town). Because the ordinances defined the offense as repeatedly acting unproductively—from loitering to being unwilling to work—they were used against itinerant workers as well as people who begged, women working in prostitution, and anyone whose actions could not easily be explained. Vagrancy ordinances were one among many regulatory tools. Pushed by reformers, business leaders, and municipal professionals, municipalities enacted hundreds of street ordinances regulating everything from displaying wares, to selling newspapers and flowers, to loitering and begging (Baldwin 1999; Ehrenfeucht and Loukaitou-Sideris 2007).

In 1972, in the landmark decision *Papachristou v. City of Jacksonville*, the U.S. Supreme Court held vagrancy ordinances to be unconstitutionally vague and limited municipal authority to criminalize a person because she or he was spending time unproductively. The decision found that vagrancy laws were an antiquated technique to tie people to the land. Ironically, *Papachristou v. City of Jacksonville* ushered in an active era of regulation in which more specific ordinances targeted begging, sitting, loitering, and rough sleeping under the guise of "quality of life campaigns" (Feldman 2004; Gibson 2004; Vitale 2008). Unwanted street activities symbolized urban decline and cities out of control, but rather than addressing conditions of poverty, these campaigns attacked the ways that people survived in public (Vitale 2008).

Cities had never proactively planned for street use. Instead, they regulated the street and proactively planned for travel along it (Ehrenfeucht 2012). When justifying street regulation, cities defined the pedestrian as "the public" and tried to eliminate street use by planning for unimpeded travel (Ehrenfeucht and Loukaitou-Sideris 2007). "Traffic logic"— reflecting the perspective of public works professionals and municipal engineers who view stationary people and objects as barriers to traffic flow—has continued to frame discussions about street planning into the twenty-first century (Blomley 2011).

## Dwelling in Public and the Regulatory State

When homelessness became newly visible in the 1980s, it was defined as a distinct condition that was subject to analysis and policy intervention. Scholars investigated the relative importance of a range of individual and structural factors, and found that deindustrialization, unemployment, and unaffordable housing were primary drivers (Baxter and Hopper 1981; Hopper 2003; Jencks 1994). Among people living in poverty, 10 percent experience homelessness for at least one night annually (Brunson 2011). Sociologists and anthropologists also used ethnographic methods to understand how people live while homeless (Avery, this volume; Baxter and Hopper 1981; Borchard 2005; Duneier and Carter 1999; Glasser and Bridgman 1999; Gowan 2010; Wasserman and Clair 2010). These accounts show that people regularly must adapt in order to face the daily challenges brought about by the lack of permanent residence.

From the perspectives of the diverse people dwelling in public, there is no typical day. They make different decisions about where and when to sleep, how to work and earn money, where to get food, where to bathe, and how to store belongings, as well as how to maintain relationships with family members including children, acquire health care, and myriad other tasks. All sleeping options have tradeoffs. Some urban shelters allow for long-term residence and have lockers and shower facilities, but others offer only nighttime accommodation. Even the best shelters offer no privacy, and few spaces are available for adults to rest during the day. When shelters are full, as they often are, those who cannot secure a space might sleep in the near vicinity, extending a shelter's street presence into the neighborhood (Borchard 2005; Wasserman and Clair 2010).

The stereotypical dirty, down-and-out homeless person panhandling on a street corner represents a very visible condition that many homeless people seek to avoid. Finding the districts that house homeless services and the worst-off depressing, they seek shelter elsewhere, in abandoned buildings, parks, and empty lots (Borchard 2005). Others establish camps where they set up tents or build temporary shelters under freeways and other spaces that offer protection from the rain and relative privacy (Wasserman and Clair 2010).

Homeless residents develop countless additional strategies for sleeping, such as living in cars or buying bus passes, giving themselves a temporary space that is relatively safe from violence and bad weather (Gowan 2010; Avery, this volume). Libraries provide access to bathrooms and sinks for washing (often in violation of posted regulations) and, if someone pretends to be reading, a space where he or she can sleep for a couple of hours (Borchard 2005). Some walk all night, fearing sleeping outdoors or getting cold, and finding relative safety and warmth sleeping during the day (Borchard 2005; Hopper 2003; Lyon-Callo 2004; Wasserman and Clair 2010).

Being homeless creates unending challenges. People live under the constant threat of their belongings being stolen as well as being harassed, looked down upon, and even at times assaulted by housed residents. When women live outside, in addition to all the same difficulties as men, they face the danger of sexual assault. Women appear in outdoor situations less frequently than men (Baxter and Hopper 1981; Borchard 2005; Glasser and Bridgman 1999).

Many people experiencing homelessness earn money in some way. Only a small percentage of all homeless people panhandle, and not all panhandlers are homeless. Many homeless people see panhandling as a way to make money when one hits rock bottom. They find it humiliating and would rather work (Gowan 2010; Wasserman and Clair 2010). Panhandling is a controversial activity that brings homeless people to business districts and other areas with pedestrian traffic. Panhandling reportedly can bring 10 dollars or more an hour, but it is irregular, and over the course of a day people make on average a few dollars per hour. For those with few options—either because they are discouraged or injured and unable to work—it might be the only way to obtain much-needed money.

Work strategies take people on and off the street. Day labor is the most common way for men to find work. Indeed, estimates from Chicago suggest that half of day laborers are homeless (Theodore 2003). Numerous day labor agencies facilitate placing workers, but some people prefer labor pick-up sites on street corners or warehouse parking lots because they provide more autonomy, even if they also are more likely to result in wage theft. Many also engage in a bricolage of formal and informal economic activities (Snow, Anderson, Quist, and Cress 1996) that include day labor, dumpster diving and selling found goods, collecting recyclables and selling scrap metal, selling plasma, and at times selling drugs and stealing (Borchard 2005; Duneier and Carter 1999; Snow, Anderson, Quist, and Cress 1996; Wasserman and Clair 2010). In San Francisco, some "pro" recyclers (who collect cans and bottles that can be returned for rebate) engage solely in this activity, seeing it as a full-time occupation and developing regular routes and work practices (Gowan 2009). Disrupted sleep, lack of bathing and clothes-washing facilities, and arrests all interfere with work. Additionally, work itself can lead to direct violations of numerous ordinances including "loitering" at day labor spots, resting in public spaces with shopping carts, and unauthorized street vending.

When day laborers do not land a job or when bad weather prevents vending and scavenging, people have time to spend, and most nonworking hours are spent outside. Like all people, those who are homeless need downtime and leisure, but many have more downtime than they really desire (Wasserman and Clair 2010). Outdoor recreation may include alcohol and drug use, which public officials and business owners find disruptive, although much time is spent in other ways. Some chronically homeless people suffer from addiction and mental health conditions, but point-in-time counts have determined that they reflect the minority of people who experience homelessness (NLCHP 2011: 26).

The excess time, nevertheless, leads to the stereotype that homeless residents do nothing but hang around, and to the more visible conflicts about homelessness in neighborhoods. After selling plasma, for example, men might stay nearby, as is attested by the "no loitering" signs posted

**Figure 8.1**
"No Loitering" sign on the wall of the New Orleans Mission. Photo credit: Renia
Ehrenfeucht.

outside a Las Vegas clinic (Borchard 2005). Other services for people
who are homeless affect surrounding businesses and neighborhoods
because of the accompanying time spent there, and Dallas and Charlotte,
among other cities, have increasingly prohibited sharing food in public
spaces or in locations where nearby businesses complain (NLCHP and
National Coalition for the Homeless 2009).

The police, as enforcers of the regulatory state, become a source of
trouble for homeless people trying to get by from day to day. The police
instigate street sweeps to clear them from a given area, disrupting their
sleep and daily routines (Garnett 2005; NLCHP and National Coalition
for the Homeless 2009). During sweeps, people lose belongings including
identification cards, medicine, sleeping materials, and warm clothes.
Enforcing no-loitering provisions (figure 8.1) can lead to the loss of work
or make a tired or sick individual keep moving. Public space regulation
can even prolong periods of homelessness, and there are documented
accounts of people missing work or housing appointments because they
have been jailed for camping or urinating in public (NLCHP 2011;
NLCHP and National Coalition for the Homeless 2009). Ordinance
enforcement can make a difficult daily life impossible.

## The Inherent Tensions in Formalizing Street Life

A web of municipal public space ordinances defines how urbanites can use the streets and sidewalks in U.S. cities. The regulations—the formalization of informal street life—define when, where, and how people can act, thereby lessening individuals' opportunities to adapt to local circumstances without running into legal problems. Although regulations can also have the benefit of offering more predictability, the regulatory approach has failed as a proactive way to accommodate public space use for two interrelated reasons. First, extensive regulation has reduced the capacity of urban public spaces to function as a commons that allows urbanites to engage in activities consistent with their needs. Second, the dominant property regime in the United States privileges private property interests in public spaces at the expense of common use, and people with stronger property claims influence public space controls more than those with weaker property claims.

### The Diminishing Commons

Eyes across the nation turned to Seattle when the city strived to eliminate all visible poverty from its downtown neighborhoods (Gibson 2004; NLCHP 1993). Using the rise of violent crime as justification, the city began to crack down on homeless residents. In 1987, it enacted antibegging legislation in the form of an ordinance against interfering with pedestrians (Seattle City Ordinance 113697). The ordinance prohibited a range of activities including sitting and lying in any way that would interfere with the passage of pedestrians or automobiles. While few people were arrested, the police used the ordinance to clear downtown streets of homeless individuals (NLCHP 1993). In 1993, Seattle strengthened its antibegging legislation, prohibiting any sitting or lying in downtown or neighborhood business districts between 7 am and 9 pm and restricting access to parks from 11 pm to 6 am. The city's Parks Department also sought to reduce the number of benches in parks used by people appearing to be homeless (NLCHP 1993).

Seattle was not unique in its efforts to crack down on visible homelessness. In the 1990s, cities across the United States took similar actions, including these examples:

- Reno Administrative Code §8.12.015(b) prohibited sitting or lying on sidewalks in the downtown redevelopment district.

- Philadelphia Municipal Code §10-611(1)(b)-(c), (2)(g)-(h) prohibited sitting for more than one hour in any two-hour time period, or lying on sidewalks in designated districts.

- Austin Municipal Code §9-14-4 prohibited sitting or lying on public sidewalks in the downtown business area.

- Denver Municipal Code §38-86.1 made it unlawful for any person to knowingly sit or lie down on the public right-of-way in the downtown Denver Business Improvement District between the hours of 7 am and 9 pm.

Since the 1990s, cities have continued to adopt ordinances as well as amend enacted ordinances in the face of legal challenges and changing circumstances. A survey of 235 cities conducted by the National Law Center on Homelessness and Poverty found that 33 percent of cities prohibited camping in parts of the city, while 17 percent had citywide camping prohibitions. Thirty percent prohibited sitting or lying in at least some areas; 47 percent prohibited loitering in particular public spaces, and 19 percent prohibited loitering citywide. Bans on camping and on loitering in public spaces had increased by 7 and 11 percent, respectively, in the three years since the previous survey (NLCHP and National Coalition for the Homeless 2009).

As Jeremy Waldron (1991) has famously argued, daily life is inherently spatial. A person is not free to do something, to sleep or sit for example, unless he or she has somewhere to do it. Because of this, advocates have had some success in arguing that restrictions against sleeping, sitting, or begging *anywhere* are too onerous, and such ordinances have faced repeated court challenges. In response, cities have modified ordinances to avoid First Amendment challenges (relating to the communicative functions of panhandling), Fourth Amendment challenges (relating to unreasonable searches and seizure of people's belongings), and Eighth Amendment challenges (relating to cruel and unusual punishment in denying people a place to sleep).

In response to these challenges, ordinances are regularly amended, but city officials have continued to use regulation as the primary way to address street use. The ordinances have ongoing impact on how thousands of urban residents sleep, find employment, work, eat, relax, sit, rest, and panhandle. Because ordinary activities other than travel are restricted, and many necessary daily life functions are prohibited, homelessness "naturally entails the violation of all sorts of 'quality of life' ordinances" (Wasserman and Clair 2010: 86). Regulatory policy toward street homelessness, however, has not reduced the presence of people who are homeless, or decreased the incidences of storing belongings, begging, or sitting and sleeping in public (Garnett 2005). People continue to turn to public spaces to dwell because they must dwell somewhere.

## The Influence of Private Property

Proponents of quality-of-life campaigns were often attempting to facilitate downtown revitalization. By the 1990s, gentrification became an observable trend in many U.S. cities as middle-income residents returned to city centers seeking historic architecture, urban amenities, and diverse neighbors (Brown-Saracino 2009; Freeman 2006; Gibson 2004; Vitale 2008). New property owners and investors had a keen interest in what occurred on the streets (Atkinson and Bridge 2005; Freeman 2006; Gibson 2004). Few gentrifiers wanted to live with the grittiness resulting from deep societal inequality, and cities stepped up their enforcement of regulations targeting homeless people, producing a "consumptive public sphere and its preoccupation with aesthetic appearance" (Feldman 2004: 29). Gentrification processes and the emphasis on private property values facilitated displacement and eviction. As Nicholas Blomley (2009: 577) has argued, homelessness is "produced, regulated and legitimized through property." Gentrification can result in more people becoming homeless as housing becomes unaffordable. Local gentrification processes also displace homeless residents from gentrifying areas (Blomley 2009; Gowan 2010; Snow and Mulcahy 2001).

Private property interests influence street activities in distinct ways. Business owners, residents, and other property owners want urban streets to attract residents and businesses, and work with public officials and municipal professionals to set the tone of the street, shaping what is or is not permissible. Adopted ordinances orient the hours of activities and character of the spaces to reflect the rhythm of the abutting properties. Because sidewalks abutting buildings are also viewed as an extension of the adjacent property, property owners and tenants attempt to control their thresholds and sidewalks (Loukaitou-Sideris and Ehrenfeucht, this volume). In Seattle during a period of heightened regulatory activity, property owners would often call the police to enforce a state law against trespassing when homeless people took shelter in their buildings' thresholds, even if this happened after business hours (NLCHP 1993).

Jane Baron (2004) has argued that the situation of homelessness can be understood as a problem of "no property," which results in a series of other disadvantages: no right to cleanliness; no right to put belongings anywhere, and therefore no right to keep what you cannot carry; and oftentimes, no right to stay put. Indeed, the right to rest, store, or be clean is dependent on access to private property. Additionally, participation in commercial activities is limited to those with the ability to pay who also conform to middle-class conduct and appearance (Low 2006). As a result, the condition of no property also denies people access to commercial services.

The problem of no property, however, is not easily remedied. With no right to housing, people fight for their right to use public spaces to live or beg, which many have noted are meager successes (Baron 2004; Mitchell 2003). The ongoing attempts to eliminate the "crisis" of visible poverty are entrenched in a property regime that associates respectability with private property, separates private and public functions, and assigns each to different spaces, thereby denying people who are homeless legitimacy in discussions about neighborhood use.

## A New Approach to a Recurrent Condition

A significant body of scholarship has critiqued public space controls as unjust and undemocratic because the efforts to eliminate people who are homeless make life harder for these individuals and privilege private property interests in public spaces at the expense of common use (Blomley 2009; Loukaitou-Sideris and Ehrenfeucht 2009; Mitchell 2003). Planners must also consider another important observation. Quality-of-life campaigns have lessened neither homelessness nor its impacts on areas where people dwell. In other words, they have been ineffective. But how can cities rebuild an urban commons that makes public spaces available to all residents while still reenchanting city spaces as sites of pleasure and possibility?

An extreme proposal has advocated controlling "chronic misconduct" in public spaces by making some areas available for activities associated with homelessness in order to keep other areas clear. This would recreate skid rows, creating spaces for homeless people to be, while limiting their use of other districts (Ellickson 1996). The objective is to make public spaces more comfortable for more people by eliminating those who make some people uncomfortable. We suggest another alternative. Cities can plan proactively to accommodate street activities rather than banish or confine them. Although this has yet to occur, many cities have taken positive steps to build an urban commons that accommodates more people, helps those dwelling in public to live decently, and mitigates the controversial impacts that occur when people dwell in public. These goals can provide the basis for planning an inclusive urban commons.

The provision of service centers such as Seattle's Urban Rest Stop can address some of the problems of living in a state of no property. The Urban Rest Stop, a program of the Low Income Housing Institute that received funds from both the city and the Downtown Seattle Association, provides restrooms, showers, and laundry, and opens early on weekdays so that people can come to get ready for work. In 2006, the Urban Rest Stop provided 55,000 showers and 19,000 loads of laundry (Urban Rest Stop, n.d.). The city of Portland has provided 24-hour free public restrooms called the Portland Loo (City of Portland, n.d.). Melbourne, Australia, has a Living Room in its central business district that provides a full range of health services in addition to phones, Internet, laundry, showers, some storage, food, and a place to spend time (Living Room, n.d.). When people are homeless, they make a great effort to wash using library or fast food restaurant restrooms, despite the prohibitions and negative responses they receive (Borchard 2005; Gowan 2010). When people have access to washing facilities and can store their belongings, they live more comfortably, become indistinguishable from people who are housed, and have an easier time finding and keeping work.

Well-maintained street spaces that accommodate diverse people and activities make an area vibrant. New York City has placed movable chairs in some underutilized and residual street spaces, and in San Francisco the city supports resident efforts to create pocket parks but also ensures they remain open to everyone. This provides more areas available for people to sit. Public space users—both homeless and housed—can be expected to keep public places clean and well-maintained, but this also requires that the city provide basic services such as garbage collection.

Few cities have actively planned for dwelling in public because, instead of being community stakeholders, homeless residents are defined as outsiders who are invading a neighborhood or a business district (Wasserman and Clair 2011). Some cities have begun to reverse this trend. Puyallup, Washington, reversed a municipal ordinance against camping in order to allow religious organizations to host temporary encampments. Seattle has also explored providing a tent city (Seattle Channel 2010).

In a few instances, cities have removed regulations or decided against establishing a regulation when a new situation came to their attention.

Seattle, for example, repealed a law that had enabled law enforcement officials to remove individuals from establishments open to the public (such as stores or coffeehouses) even if they were not violating business codes. New Orleans decided not to prosecute informal street vendors when it realized that existing regulations could not accommodate many patterns of existing vending activity. Such decisions actively allow use of public spaces and are the building blocks of an urban commons.

Ethnographic research has repeatedly shown that homeless denizens make rational decisions when facing severe constraints (Baxter and Hopper 1981; Borchard 2005; Duneier and Carter 1999; Gowan 2010; Wasserman and Clair 2010, 2011). These decisions can include eschewing shelters, even if space is available (which often is not), seeking work in public, or panhandling in addition to or instead of finding a free meal. All urban residents must be able to make autonomous decisions about their survival and participate in decisions about common spaces, and that is the ultimate objective of planning for more rather than less public space use.

## Conclusion: The Streets as Commons

Public space ordinances compose a formal regulatory framework that eliminates adaptive uses of public space. Although ordinances appear neutral, they respond to middle-class concerns and result in public spaces that become inhospitable to those who are homeless. They are, nevertheless, also ineffective because people continue to use spaces that they need. Attempts to sanitize public spaces also result in predictable and less interesting public environments for everyone (Zukin 2009). Viewing the streets as an urban commons and envisioning ways to accommodate as many public space activities as possible is a more productive approach. Based upon efforts occurring in different cities, the following four strategies can facilitate more flexible urban public spaces.

*Invest in the commons.* To accommodate more activities, public entities must provide needed infrastructure from seating to public water fountains, from shade to public toilets, instead of leaving them to be provided by private businesses only for their clients. The availability of public amenities can help reduce conflicts. Public toilets would lessen the need and embarrassment of public urination; enough public seating will provide space for short- and longer-term occupancy; and public trash receptacles can take care of the garbage generated by street vending or outdoor meals. Street users can help maintain public spaces, but public facilities and services are necessary for that to be possible.

*Value public space users and building occupants equally.* A better balance can be found between the interests of abutting residences and businesses and those of public space users. Instead of creating processes in which representatives for people who are homeless and other public space users (e.g., street vendors) must defend their street use, the objective should be to develop strategies to accommodate more varied activities.

*Mitigate the impacts of "no property."* Some impacts of activities associated with homelessness are directly related to the condition of no property. These can be partially mitigated by developing accessible storage facilities, showers, and laundry facilities. Many of these facilities are currently provided in conjunction with shelters or other services, but more are needed. Additionally, public facilities and institutions can make existing services readily available to more users.

*Reconsider regulations.* Regulating public space use has become the most common municipal strategy to address public space controversies. Cities, however, must reconsider whether, when, and where regulations are necessary. In some cases, by regulating less and instead focusing on creating a shared public commons, cities can do more to resolve problems without fueling the irreconcilable tension embodied in regulatory actions that harm street dwellers.

Urban residents value the public realm and want to be enchanted by the city. These four strategies can help revitalize an urban commons that makes public spaces available for visitors and residents alike, for both regular and ephemeral activities. Cities have addressed street and park use with regulation rather than proactive planning for over a century. This has neither reduced controversy nor created the type of cities that urbanites are envisioning in the twenty-first century. The new century needs a new approach, one that recognizes the need for both formal and informal activities and favors allowing rather than restricting urban life in public.

### References

Atkinson, Rowland, and Gary Bridge. 2005. *Gentrification in a Global Context: The New Urban Colonialism*. London: Routledge.

Baldwin, Peter C. 1999. *Domesticating the Street: The Reform of Public Space in Hartford, 1850–1930*. Columbus: Ohio State University Press.

Baron, Jane. 2004. "Homelessness as a Property Problem." *Urban Lawyer* 36 (2):273–288.

Baxter, Ellen, and Kim Hopper. 1981. *Private Lives/Public Spaces: Homeless Adults on the Streets of New York City.* New York: Community Service Society of New York, Institute for Social Welfare Research.

Blomley, Nicholas K. 2009. "Homelessness, Rights and the Delusions of Property." *Urban Geography* 30 (6):577–590.

Blomley, Nicholas K. 2011. *Rights of Passage: Sidewalks and the Regulation of Public Flow.* Abingdon, U.K.: Routledge.

Borchard, Kurt. 2005. *The Word on the Street: Homeless Men in Las Vegas.* Reno: University of Nevada Press.

Brown-Saracino, Japonica. 2009. *A Neighborhood That Never Changes: Gentrification, Social Preservation, and the Search for Authenticity.* Chicago: University of Chicago Press.

Brunson, Susan. 2011. "Guest Editor's Introduction." *Cityscape* (Washington, DC) 13 (1):1–5.

City of Portland. N.d. "The Portland Loo." Available at http://www.portland oregon.gov/bes/59293 (retrieved July 20, 2012).

DePastino, Todd. 2003. *Citizen Hobo: How a Century of Homelessness Shaped America.* Chicago: University of Chicago Press.

Duneier, Mitchell, and Ovie Carter. 1999. *Sidewalk.* New York: Farrar, Straus and Giroux.

Ehrenfeucht, Renia. 2012. "Precursors to Planning: Regulating the Streets of Los Angeles, California, c 1880–1920." *Journal of Planning History* 11 (2): 107–123.

Ehrenfeucht, Renia, and Anastasia Loukaitou-Sideris. 2007. "Constructing the Sidewalks: Municipal Government and the Production of Public Space in Los Angeles, California, 1880–1920." *Journal of Historical Geography* 33 (1):104.

Ellickson, Robert C. 1996. "Controlling Chronic Misconduct in City Spaces: Of Panhandlers, Skid Rows, and Public-Space Zoning." *Yale Law Journal* 105 (5):1165–1248.

Feldman, Leonard C. 2004. *Citizens without Shelter: Homelessness, Democracy, and Political Exclusion.* Ithaca: Cornell University Press.

Freeman, Lance. 2006. *There Goes the 'Hood: Views of Gentrification from the Ground Up.* Philadelphia: Temple University Press.

Garnett, Nicole Stelle. 2005. "Relocating Disorder." *Virginia Law Review* 91 (5):1076–1134.

Gibson, Timothy A. 2004. *Securing the Spectacular City: The Politics of Revitalization and Homelessness in Downtown Seattle.* Lanham, MD: Lexington Books.

Glasser, Irene, and Rae Bridgman. 1999. *Braving the Street: The Anthropology of Homelessness.* New York: Berghahn Books.

Gowan, Teresa. 2009. "New Hobos or Neo-Romantic Fantasy? Urban Ethnography beyond the Neoliberal Disconnect." *Qualitative Sociology* 32 (3):231–257.

Gowan, Teresa. 2010. *Hobos, Hustlers, and Backsliders: Homeless in San Francisco*. Minneapolis: University of Minnesota Press.

Hopper, Kim. 2003. *Reckoning with Homelessness*. Ithaca: Cornell University Press.

Jackson, Kenneth T. 1985. *Crabgrass Frontier: The Suburbanization of the United States*. New York: Oxford University Press.

Jencks, Christopher. 1994. *The Homeless*. Cambridge: Harvard University Press.

Leginski, Walter. 2007. "Historical and Contextual Influences on the U.S. Response to Contemporary Homelessness." The 2007 Symposium on Homelessness Research. Available at http://aspe.hhs.gov/hsp/homelessness/symposium07/leginski/ (retrieved July 20, 2012).

Living Room. N.d. "The Living Room." http://www.youthprojccts.org.au/health/programs/living-room (retrieved Spetember 20, 2012).

Loukaitou-Sideris, Anastasia, and Renia Ehrenfeucht. 2009. *Sidewalks: Conflict and Negotiation over Public Space*. Cambridge: MIT Press.

Low, Setha M. 2006. "How Private Interests Take Over Public Space: Zoning, Taxes, and Incorporation of Gated Communities." In Setha M. Low and Neil Smith, eds., *The Politics of Public Space*, 81–103. New York: Routledge.

Lyon-Callo, Vincent. 2004. *Inequality, Poverty, and Neoliberal Governance: Activist Ethnography in the Homeless Sheltering Industry*. Peterborough, Ont.: Broadview Press.

Mitchell, Don. 2003. *The Right to the City: Social Justice and the Fight for Public Space*. New York: Guilford Press.

Monkkonen, Eric H. 1984. *Walking to Work: Tramps in America, 1790–1935*. Lincoln: University of Nebraska Press.

National Coalition for the Homeless. 2009. "How Many People Experience Homelessness?" Available at http://www.nationalhomeless.org/factsheets/How_Many.html (retrieved June 1, 2012).

NLCHP (National Law Center on Homelessness and Poverty). 1991. "Go Directly to Jail: A Report Analyzing Local Anti-Homeless Ordinances." National Law Center on Homelessness and Poverty, Washington, DC.

NLCHP. 1993. "The Right to Remain Nowhere." Report. National Law Center on Homelessness and Poverty, Washington, DC.

NLCHP. 2011. "Criminalizing Crisis: The Criminalization of Homelessness in U.S. Cities." Report. National Law Center for Homelessness and Poverty, Washington, DC.

NLCHP. N.d. "Homelessness and Poverty in America." Available at http://www.nlchp.org/hapia.cfm (retrieved July 21, 2012).

NLCHP and National Coalition for the Homeless. 2009. "Homes Not Handcuffs: The Criminalization of Homelessness in U.S. Cities." Report. National Coalition for the Homeless, Washington, DC.

Seattle Channel. 2010. "Community Meeting on Homeless Encampment 11/18/2010." Available at http://www.seattlechannel.org/videos/video.asp?ID =1031044 (retrieved May 4, 2012).

Snow, David A., Leon Anderson, Theron Quist, and Daniel Cress. 1996. "Material Survival Strategies on the Street: Homeless People as *Bricoleurs.*" In Jim Baumohl, ed., *Homelessness in America,* 86–96. Phoenix: Oryx Press.

Snow, David A., and Michael Mulcahy. 2001. "Space, Politics, and the Survival Strategies of the Homeless." *American Behavioral Scientist* 45:149–169.

Theodore, Nik. 2003. "Political Economies of Day Labour: Regulation and Restructuring of Chicago's Contingent Labour Markets." *Urban Studies* (Edinburgh, Scotland) 40 (9):1811–1828.

Urban Rest Stop. N.d. "History." http://www.urbanreststop.org/urban-rest-stop-history02.html (retrieved September 20, 2012).

Vitale, Alex S. 2008. *City of Disorder: How the Quality of Life Campaign Transformed New York Politics.* New York: New York University Press.

Waldron, Jeremy. 1991. "Homelessness and the Issue of Freedom." *UCLA Law Review* 39:295–324.

Wasserman, Jason, and Jeffrey Clair. 2010. *At Home on the Street: People, Poverty, and a Hidden Culture of Homelessness.* Boulder: Lynne Rienner Publishers.

Wasserman, Jason, and Jeffrey Clair. 2011. "Housing Patterns of Homeless People: The Ecology of the Street in the Era of Urban Renewal." *Journal of Contemporary Ethnography* 40 (1):71–101.

Wiese, Andrew. 2004. *Places of Their Own: African American Suburbanization in the Twentieth Century.* Chicago: University of Chicago Press.

Zukin, Sharon. 2009. *Naked City: The Death and Life of Authentic Urban Places.* New York: Oxford University Press.

# 9

## Learning from Informal Practices: Implications for Urban Design

Michael Rios

Many low-income communities present a conception of urban space that does not fit easily into regulatory frameworks and municipal ordinances. Some of its manifestations in the built environment include the appropriation of public and private land for a range of purposes and informal activities that defy land use norms, zoning requirements, and the law. These same places are often targeted by a planning agenda that views them as sites of gentrification and test beds for the latest sustainability idea. Consequently, punitive policies and practices are used to criminalize informal activities as a strategy of "urban cleansing." These range from fines for building code violations and banning of public assembly to neighborhood preservation and day labor ordinances. There is increasing evidence, from Florida to California, that planning practices have been used to enforce policies aimed at suppressing the informal economy, in many instances forcing individuals to flee in fear (Harwood 2012; Polakit and Schomberg 2012).

At first glance, transgressive practices of spatial appropriation would seem to mirror what has elsewhere been labeled "informal" urbanism, although a punitive policy and policing environment in U.S. cities may suggest differences. In African and Indian cities, urban informality has been discussed as rules and norms that differ from formal institutions (Assaad 1996); as a series of encounters and transactions that connect myriad economies, spaces, and processes that are governed by different logics (Hansen and Vaa 2004; Roy 2005); and as an expression of sovereignty, territorialization of state power, and mode of production of space defined by deregulation (Roy 2005, 2009a, 2009b). Despite a focus on cities of the global South, a number of theoretical insights from this literature are relevant to the conditions found in U.S. cities and raise critical questions for the future trajectory of urban design. For example, what can be learned from the spatial practices and material conditions of urban informality? How can we respond to informality positively through planning or policy, and how can urban design be employed to envision informal settings differently? Following Roy (2011), I view informality as a heuristic device to describe the entanglements and shifting relationships between urban livelihood, policy, and planning.[1] However, given this chapter's focus on urban design, I am interested in how informality is implicated in discursive representations of place—in zoning codes, maps, and plans—and its relationship to spatial practices found on the ground—in neighborhoods, streets, and individual sites. I analyze the spatial manifestations and aesthetics of informality with an understanding that places are sites of "world making"—social imaginations of space that are produced as individuals and groups negotiate material and social relations to secure the necessities of life. This acknowledges that residents, developers, professionals, institutions, the state, and other actors simultaneously assess and intervene in the same spaces of everyday life.[2] To highlight how informality can inform urban design practice, the chapter describes an experimental studio with undergraduate students at the University of California, Davis. The studio documented spatial practices found in Sacramento's most racially and ethnically diverse district, proposed a series of interventions that circumvent the expected use of urban space, and problematized existing planning policies and practices. I conclude by identifying some implications for urban design that engage in the spatial practices found in marginalized places, and explore the relationship between urban livelihood and material thinking.

## The Spatialities of Urban Informality: A Brief Overview

The relationship between urban informality and spatial practices hinges on what is considered legitimate, whether sanctioned by law or fitting within the norm of a hegemonic order. Postcolonial critiques of development have been a dominant theme in the literature on urban informality (Miraftab 2009; Roy 2011; Roy and AlSayyad 2004; Yiftachel 2009).[3] Equally relevant are transnational perspectives that highlight how different citizen rights are conferred with respect to informal practices (Holston 2008; Roy 2003). Relevant to American urbanism, a pointed observation is that "'First World' urban and metropolitan theory is curiously silent on the issue of informality as a mode of the production of space" (Roy 2009c: 826). While this may be true from the vantage point of the global South, an important question is to what extent transnational perspectives apply to the conditions of urban informality in U.S. cities, where planning and urban design are practiced in a highly restrictive legal environment.

Of postcolonial urbanists, Ananya Roy has offered the most piercing critiques of Western planning (2005, 2009a, 2009b, 2009c, 2011). Roy (2009c) offers a number of key insights relevant to the spatiality of urban informality. These include how:

- The state is implicated in the very nature of informality and often operates in informal ways to assure territorial flexibility through extralegal, social and discursive forms of regulation;

- Different forms of spatial value produce uneven geographies and the splintering of urbanism through the informal production of space;

- Urban informality is a "mode of subjectivity" and provides a different reading of mobilization, resistance, and agency in urban politics.

In empirical studies, others have demonstrated the ways in which urban informality reveals the unintended consequences of the law and provides openings to challenge and change planning policies for practical and political purposes. One example from Bangalore illustrates how squatters consented to paying for water pipes imposed by a regional government in order to bargain for legitimate land tenure (Ranganathan, forthcoming). Another case, in Mumbai, shows how infrastructure improvement is not only the focus of planners but also the creative domain of the most affected (Appadurai 2001). This example highlights how planning is a venue for negotiation and change of policies and also community designs. Parallel to this literature, within the United States, there has been an increased focus on microscale tactics of spatial appropriation (Kamel, this volume). Discourses of "everyday," "tactical," and "guerrilla" urbanism emphasize the creative and often temporary transgressions of public and private space by individuals and small collectives for a range of purposes (Chase, Crawford, and Kaliski 1999; Hou 2010; Lydon 2012). Within architectural circles, there also has been a reengagement with informal spatial practices and their ecoaesthetic possibilities (Bell and Wakeford 2008).

The turn to informal urbanism has been described by some as "active humanism feeding on poverty eradication programs" and the "poaching activities of contemporary architecture practice . . . into an ever-hungry culture industry" (del Real 2010: 150–151). Another critique of such architectural interventions accuses them of holding a romanticized view of poverty. It argues that this "aestheticization of poverty" and fetishization of the everyday may have the effect of diverting attention from and depoliticizing deep-rooted structural problems (Roy 2004). Some have also been critical of postcolonial theory that overemphasizes political resistance "at the expense of a more prosaic assessment of the material constraints facing the urban poor and the resources they use to address those constraints" (Varley 2013: 16).

## Invisibility, Aesthetics, and the Informal City

While the aestheticization of poverty, politics, and agency is problematic, the issue of aesthetics should not be overlooked. In urban design, the topic of aesthetics has centered on the formal and scenographic qualities of the built environment (Nasar 1994; Taylor 2009). However, aesthetics also has a political purpose. In planning, it is often used to reinforce dominant views and normative beliefs of order and legitimacy, concealing the sensibilities of multiple publics and rendering invisible the everyday practices and livelihoods of the marginalized. Alternatively, aesthetics can have an affective quality—triggering emotional responses and revealing sensory possibilities and understandings that activate novel forms of subjectivity (Guattari 1995).

With respect to urban informality, an engagement with aesthetics and the uncanny spaces of marginality draws attention to which things are visible in the city and which are not, and problematizes existing social boundaries. Marginalized spaces of the city disrupt notions of core/ periphery and nation/citizen, and open up a space for politics through cultural practices (Vidler 1992). This is the supplementarity that cultural theorist Homi Bhabha (1994) speaks of—a liminal space between dominant narratives of identity and the hauntings of violence associated with the memories of the marginalized. Bhabha illuminates how histories and cultures constantly encroach on the present, demand new ways of understanding social relations, and require negotiations between marginalized groups and powerful interests. At stake are the political outcomes of the production of competing images of the informal city. Indeed, marginality draws attention to the spatial contradictions found in many informal settings, but also provides openings for aesthetic engagement and an emplaced practice that involves material thinking and collaborative human action. This "aesthetics of marginality" can disrupt normative and a priori views of urban informality and, by extension, allow for new rights to be imagined, claimed, and enacted.

This alternative view of aesthetics draws attention to the issue of ethics. If place is an assemblage of ideas and practices that are discursively constructed and have affective qualities, then planning and urban design are in a position either of cooperation with or opposition to the social reproduction of marginality. If, as some argue, space and politics should be more central to planning theory (Roy 2009a), then the role of aesthetics in space and politics is self-evident. As cultural geographer Jane M. Jacobs (1998: 275) has noted, "If the visual regimes of contemporary cities are thought about as activated spheres of practice in which various vectors of power and difference are meaningfully negotiated, then the story of aestheticization of the city will unfold in ways that will defy the expected."

This staging of difference points to a supplemental image of, and trajectory for, the city. The relevance for practice is coming to terms with difference not as an urban anxiety but as a form of grounding *in* place. This raises questions about the way planners and urban designers think about place and the fixity of boundaries between the visible and the invisible, the formal and the informal. The ethical imperative, then, is not the avoidance of aesthetics. Rather, what I call an aesthetics of marginality renders the invisible visible, produces new social imaginaries of space and place, and visualizes different spheres of decision making and institutional arrangements.

### Experiments in Placemaking: The South Sacramento Studio

In what ways does informality materialize in specific times and places? How can urban design respond to these spatial practices and material conditions? What are the implications for urban design practice? These were some of the questions addressed by an undergraduate urban design studio during the spring of 2011. The main goal was to use urban informality as a lens to critically analyze planning policies and discursive representations of place, and explore the possibilities and limits of urban design in response to urban informality.

### South Sacramento as Periurban Landscape

South Sacramento is not a coherently defined district of the city, but is characterized by different jurisdictions, overlapping neighborhoods, and a multiplicity of foreign-born populations. The area can be called "periurban," a space in between the core city to the north and the agricultural fields and sprawling suburbs to the south. South Sacramento has a concentration of multiethnic neighborhoods comprised primarily of immigrant and refugee populations that live in a mix of low-rise apartment complexes and single-story houses. Many of these groups settled into the area after World War II as a result of a number of events. One was the urban renewal of the city's West End, which forced the southward migration of a significant number of these communities. Another was the construction of Highway 99 in 1963, which bypassed major commercial corridors in the area such as Stockton Boulevard. White flight, the availability of cheap commercial and residential land, and racially restrictive neighborhoods to the north further fueled migration into South Sacramento. A further wave of migration came after the fall of Saigon in 1975, when a number of South Vietnamese refugees settled in the area. Initially about 3,000 Vietnamese and Chinese from South Vietnam settled here, followed by Hmong, Mien, and Lao refugees. The concentration of Asian immigrants and the existence of mutual assistance and volunteer associations and religious and nonprofit organizations facilitated the latter migration. More recently, and especially after the dot-com bust in Silicon Valley, the area has experienced an influx of Vietnamese and Chinese Americans from San Jose.

With a population of over 40,000, South Sacramento includes both incorporated and unincorporated sections of Sacramento County. The nonresidential areas are organized along two major north/south commercial corridors, Franklin and Stockton Boulevards, and a series of east/west corridors that connect Interstate 5 to the west and Route 99 to the east (figure 9.1). South Sacramento's commercial corridors are comprised primarily of low-rise strip malls, auto repair shops, and apartment complexes. A number of factories and agriculture-related industries also dominate the landscape, mostly to the south. Over half of Sacramento County's 1.4 million residents live in unincorporated areas, where it is difficult to impose zoning and slow-growth policies that can be used for exclusionary purposes. Combined with the affordability of housing, this has facilitated a multiethnic settlement (Dingemans and Datel 1995). The difference between incorporated and unincorporated areas is distinguished by the type and quality of services provided by the city or county. For example, crime is significantly higher in the county's unincorporated areas, given the lack of police presence compared to in the city. Boundaries between incorporated and unincorporated areas are also evident in the presence or absence of activities such as outdoor vending and food trucks, due to differences between the city and county codes as well as the varying levels of code enforcement.

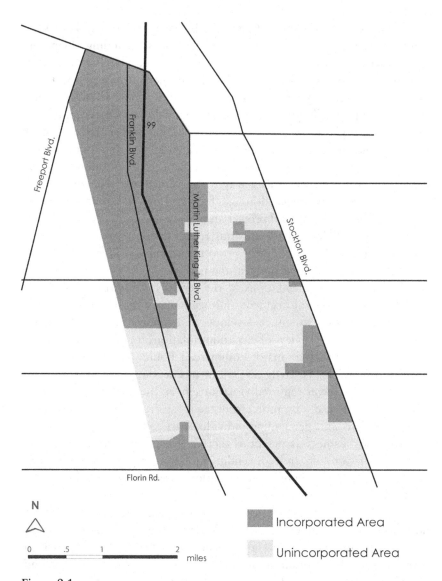

**Figure 9.1**
South Sacramento's core area between Franklin and Stockton boulevards. Image credit: Michael Rios.

South Sacramento, especially the area between Franklin and Stockton boulevards, faces a number of acute challenges, including dwindling government resources to support redevelopment, scarcity of private investment capital, lack of jobs, and higher crime and poverty rates than surrounding areas. Given these conditions and the concentration of multiethnic and primarily low-income neighborhoods, the area is commonly viewed as the ghetto of Sacramento. The dominant discursive frame is one of crime and gangs, abandonment and risk. The de facto planning strategy has been to attract new development as an antidote to these commonly held views and as a way to fundamentally reimagine South Sacramento. For example, although forecasts are less than optimistic about economic growth and project an incremental recovery in ten years or more, a 2009 Urban Land Institute report envisions growth solely in terms of large-scale development projects and expects interest by developers as a game-changing event in the near term.

One of the recommendations of the report is "enactment of design guidelines and code enforcement and beginning a more proactive code enforcement process to reduce developer and investor risk" (Urban Land Institute 2009: 9). A review of city code violations for South Sacramento indicates that along the major commercial boulevards enforcement is uneven at best. This is partly a result of business improvement districts, where there are fewer reported violations given the presence of business associations that use soft-enforcement tactics such as district-wide education campaigns and persuading individuals to comply. However, where there are no business associations there are numerous code violations, especially for vending. Indeed, vending violations represented sixteen of the twenty-six documented code violation cases along Franklin Boulevard between 2005 and 2012.

But code enforcement and design guidelines seem to be in conflict with how urban spaces are often used in South Sacramento. The reliance on proscriptive and prescriptive approaches to policy and design, which reveal cultural assumptions about how land is to be used, for whom, and for what purpose, is at odds with the existing spatial practices in South Sacramento. In the UC Davis studio, students were asked to test assumptions about land, property, and zoning by beginning with, but expanding upon, the spatial circumstances found on the ground. Studio briefs drew attention to struggles over public space, matters of livelihood, and rights of inhabitation. The pedagogical exercise also raised a thorny question with respect to the paradoxical nature of informality and its relationship to planning and urban design practice: when is it best to intervene and when not? The decision hinges on the specificity of time and place: weighing the benefits and risks of action and inaction, anticipating consequences, but also recognizing unintended effects.

### Engaging the Uncanny Spaces of Marginality

In the initial phase of the studio, students were asked to identify sites of spatial appropriation, use, and adaptation that were unfamiliar to them but elicited emotional responses. For many, this was antithetical to how they were taught to conduct analysis. Rather than assuming project boundaries or poring over land use and zoning maps, students spent several days in South Sacramento observing how sites were used for unintended purposes. They visually documented activities using photographs, video clips, and other media and supplemented these with a narrative (e.g., a journal or poetry) to capture the embodied qualities of the site. The aim was to use both analytical and aesthetic forms of representation to expose social and material conditions that were in conflict with norms of zoning and land use. This included the use of streets and sidewalks as spaces of economic exchange, as well as the appropriation of strip mall parking lots and private property for a range of purposes.

For some students, these and other sites would later serve as the basis for specific design interventions. In many ways, the student designs were conventional and drew from skills typically acquired in studio settings. More important than the designs, however, was the process that guided the students' work. This included interviewing individuals encountered at different sites and collecting oral histories from different immigrant and refugee communities. As a result, student proposals were a sincere response to the spatial appropriations and material conditions of site as well as the local knowledge shared by individuals. Overall, the proposals sought to create spaces between formal and informal structures, public and private land, and among different social groups. The student ideas were then assembled into a booklet to stimulate dialogue about future strategies that build on existing spatial practices. The result was "The Citizen's Guide to South Sacramento," which is intended for public agencies, nonprofit organizations, and community groups to assess existing policies and inform ongoing planning activities.

One site of focus was the parking lot of an auto parts store that also serves as the location for a recycling center operating out of a shipping container, a taco truck, and a chopped fruit cart. Research revealed that the site has a mix of formal and informal uses. The recycling center is one of over twenty-five in South Sacramento and, as part of the state's

CalRecycle program, provides a convenient location for residents to receive money for recycled beverage containers. A directory of recycling centers for the region reveals that most are found in low-income neighborhoods. The taco truck parks in the private lot in part to avoid ordinances that require food trucks to move every half hour (in the city of Sacramento) or every two hours (in unincorporated areas).

The fruit cart at the site illustrates how vendors take advantage of other discrepancies in regulation. Most vendors do not have a county permit sticker to sell fruit, nor are they allowed to operate in the public right-of-way without an event permit from the city. However, when cited for violations, vendors do not present identification, given that many are undocumented. Because of this, even documented individuals do not carry identification cards. This creates a problem as code enforcement officers cannot mail citations that would require a court appearance to a residential address. In addition, the city does not have the authority to confiscate fruit carts, so they rely on the county's Environmental Health Division that has the power to do so. It takes considerable time to coordinate intergovernmental resources, so the city and county have relied on infrequent sweeps to confiscate fruit stands. For every fruit cart that is confiscated, far more fill the void.

Legal matters aside, the auto parts store's parking lot supports the livelihood of entrepreneurs, workers, and residents alike. Its highly visible location, ample parking, and complementary uses create a "public" space in the privately owned parking lot. For example, El Sinaloense, the taco truck, has a loyal following and relies on a stable customer base each day. The ability to park the truck for long periods of time makes El Sinaloense a permanent feature. Similarly, EH Recycling draws residents who seek a source of supplemental income. Less permanent, but frequently present, is the fruit cart situated on the sidewalk at the edge of the site. This strategic location ensures visibility from the street so that vendors can sell fruit to automobiles that stop on the road, those that park in the lot, as well as residents walking by. However, there is a constant vendor turnover due to the often undocumented status of vendors and the occasional sweeps that confiscate carts.

A student proposal responded to the site's activities by installing a number of shade structures with built-in counters that can be easily taken down and stored. Consideration of the type and temporal nature of existing uses and circulation determined the location of these structures (figure 9.2). The proposal envisioned the site as a hybrid space of public and private functions, and included areas for other vendors and non-

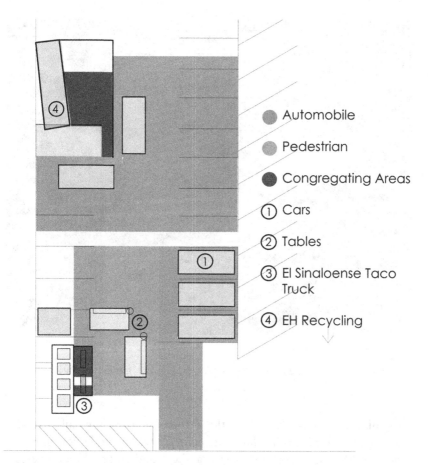

**Figure 9.2**
Student proposal. Credit: Janelle Imaoka. Image credit: Michael Rios.

profit organizations providing services to area residents. Because of the high concentration of money transfer establishments in the neighborhood, an informational area for the distribution of financial literacy material was also proposed.

Another example of a spatial practice in South Sacramento is the cultivation of land by Hmong refugees, who find it difficult to assimilate into American culture and seek the familiarity of a life they left behind in parts of Laos, Cambodia, and Vietnam. Their gardens, often found on vacant or underutilized plots, represent formal and informal arrangements with property owners and nonprofit organizations. The gardens are a source of food for many low-income Hmong families and in

**Figure 9.3**
Aerial photograph of gardens cultivated by Hmong families. Source: Google
Earth™.

particular the elderly, who view the gardens as a site for daily exercise
and socializing with other Hmong seniors. One of the largest gardens,
nine acres that serves forty families, can be found on Franklin Boulevard
and was created through an informal arrangement between Hmong
gardeners and an adjacent Catholic elementary school that owns the land
(figure 9.3). Gardeners pay the priest for water usage, but are not charged
for garden plots.

The garden is located across the street from a Hmong grocery store
and a nonprofit organization that provides social services to South Sacramento's Southeast Asian refugee communities. Given this context,
another student proposed the creation of a facility that would serve as
a Hmong cultural hub, which is currently lacking in Sacramento. In
discussions with Hmong elders, the student discovered a need for a facility to store cultural artifacts, offer language classes, as well as be an event
space for Hmong weddings. The proposal called for strategically positioning the facility next to the garden and making a physical connection
to the Hmong-serving uses across Franklin Boulevard. The facility would

also address the need for a permanent venue for the annual Hmong New Year celebration that draws thousands of Hmong from Sacramento and other points in the Central Valley. Currently, this multiday cultural event takes place at the California Exposition and State Fair, but the Hmong leadership would prefer to find a less costly location. The proposed cultural facility would also allow for a weekend farmers' market for produce grown at the garden and provide space for established Hmong farmers, who currently participate in Sacramento, Stockton, Modesto, and Fairfield markets.

Another student proposed reusing a portion of an existing strip mall parking lot for a night market to serve the larger pan-Asian population. Over the past thirty years, an Asian business enclave has developed along Stockton Boulevard, thanks to a concentration of Southeast Asians, especially Vietnamese, who settled in the area in the late 1970s and early 1980s. In 2010, at the behest of a number of Vietnamese business owners, the city officially designated the area as "Little Saigon." Today, there are over seven Asian supermarkets that anchor strip malls filled with Vietnamese and Chinese restaurants along a two-mile stretch of Stockton Boulevard. One of the larger supermarkets, Shun Fat Market, is flanked by a series of Asian businesses that face onto a large parking lot which is difficult for pedestrians to navigate. People are seen hanging out near their cars while eating food and socializing with family and friends. These site conditions and lack of an outdoor meeting space provided the impetus for the proposed night market, which is a feature common in many Vietnamese and Chinese cities. The market would be a flexible and shared-use space that accommodates parking for the strip mall during the day but transforms into a lively marketplace in the evening. Architectural elements and lighting features would break down the scale of the large supermarket to create a pedestrian feel, but also a visible landmark in an automobile-dominated landscape.

Collectively, the student work documented the different spatial practices and range of site conditions found in South Sacramento that were situated within a larger context of historical, political, and economic forces. Other interventions differed in scale and scope, from a modest proposal for temporary structures to the introduction of flexible programming and permanent buildings. These examples reflect a continuum from informal to more formalized uses as well as levels of coordination between individuals and various institutions.

The student proposals raise a number of issues concerning informality. In the first example, is the proposal for shade structures warranted? It can be argued that the site's existing uses function well and there is little need for further improvement. In the second example, there is a rationale for site upgrade given the surrounding circumstances and the desire of Hmong leaders for a much-needed community facility. The highly prescribed nature of the proposed night market draws attention to the use of formal aesthetics in urban design. It can be argued that a themed night market has little to do with the spatial practices of informality and begins to threaten the possibilities for informal street vending in the surrounding area. Another concern is the commodification of identity—in this case through the use of pan-Asian imagery. However, the proposal anticipates the desire for a marketplace, as the county's building permit database indicates that two farmers' market proposals are in the preapplication phase for sites within a quarter mile of the strip mall site. Perhaps more important than the specific details of the proposals is the fundamental issue they raise regarding the tension between formal planning interventions and urban informality. If there is a role for design, then it is critical to determine when interventions are warranted, and to what extent. However, some of these issues are not easily resolved by urban design alone.

Despite the concerns raised here, the studio served a valuable purpose in revealing a number of spatial practices often overlooked by planners and urban designers. The result was a collection of counterrepresentations that challenge norms of sight and site. Some examples included spaces situated between public and private domains, as well as different readings of what constitutes mixed use. In response, some design interventions transgressed property boundaries, while others capitalized on localized social ecologies. Rather than following existing zoning and codes, the proposals privileged the livelihood of urban inhabitants and speculated about alternative material and social relations. In some cases, the proposals went further by considering new institutional designs resulting from negotiations between individuals and groups, nonprofit organizations and government agencies. In sum, the studio experience drew attention to the relationship between urban design and informality, which has both practical and theoretical implications for practice.

## Implications for Recovering Place

Although modest in scope, experiments in placemaking in informal and often marginal landscapes, such as the ones described here, prompt a reconsideration of urban design practice in response to the questions posed at the outset. Concerning matters of place, current preoccupations of planning and urban design tend to ignore or minimize issues of urban livelihood. At best, there is an emphasis on localized decision-making processes in the form of citizen engagement. This typically takes the form of public meetings, community charrettes, and other tools of planning that can create illusions of democracy. However, such processes leave little room for questioning how and why the boundaries between public/private and formal/informal are constituted. In addition to discouraging dialogue outside of narrowly defined problems, these processes fail to acknowledge that some of the people most negatively affected by planning decisions are the least visible. This includes undocumented individuals as well as those who do not participate in planning decisions for fear of reprisal.

One remedy is to stage difference through an aesthetics that has revelatory, imaginative, and negotiatory purposes. Staging difference acknowledges how the planning and design of cities often masks everyday urban livelihoods—through official maps, GIS databases, and other technologies of the profession. By contrast, an *aesthetics of revelation* creates a fissure in representation by recognizing the informal, the unfamiliar, the local that are often absent in official planning discourses. Urban designers should learn from the ingenuity of such spatial practices and be equally creative in the use of laws, their discrepancies, and the creation of regulations that allow for flexibility and multiple interpretations. In practice, an aesthetics of revelation documents the spatiality of informality as a form of counterconduct by the dispossessed and a countermapping to official representations of space. At a minimum, this includes problematizing land use categorizations and zoning classifications such as "mixed use" and "single-family," "public" and "private."

While aesthetics has a cognitive role in matters of visibility and legibility, other effects have social and material consequences. An *aesthetics of imagination* sketches new sensory dimensions of places and informs how sociomaterial relations are constituted. Speculations that challenge the present order of things also move beyond the constraints of existing building codes, policies, and zoning regulations. In practical terms, this does not entail a complete rupture from existing regulations, but rather focuses on the unintended consequences of policy and exploiting loopholes in the law to reconfigure sociospatial relations. An aesthetics of imagination also builds on the social ecology of the local by enabling spatial practices to flourish from below rather than constraining these activities from above. Spatial imaginations of place raise critical questions about what is by proposing what might be. This seemingly retrograde, but ultimately reflexive, perspective considers how struggles over space, the necessities of life, and claims of recognition and ownership can begin in the future.

An important task in urban design is to envision sociomaterial assemblages that create openings for new political subjectivities. Consequently, an *aesthetics of negotiation* visualizes new forms of governance and citizenship, both formal and informal. These spheres do not necessarily focus on the official public realm, but rather on the space where differences are recognized, negotiated, and mediated. This requires the formation of coalitions that can reimagine the production of space toward social ends with economic and legal benefits. A challenging but important task for the planning field is to reveal knowledge, and to link, bridge, and mobilize multiple imaginations toward a supplemental image of the city. Here, a role for urban designers and planners is brokering between marginalized groups and others (including the state) to facilitate the materialization of both spatial and social rights.

In conclusion and in regard to placemaking, an aesthetics of marginality cannot be divorced from the social, institutional, economic, and political conditions found in particular locations. Documenting the spatialities of urban informality and its material conditions begins to shed light on what is often meant to remain hidden. Validation of these practices highlights the constraints and limits of laws that prevent important economic and social activities from flourishing. Contextualizing marginality and emplacing informality also tempers universal responses to issues of urban livelihood. Going beyond representation will require a deeper engagement with the marginalized themselves, on their own terms, and in the many places they call home. Shifting the scale of focus to place as a site of livelihood and reimagining professional practice as an expression of everyday citizenship is a starting point.

New social arrangements in the city have revealed unconventional, novel forms of spatial appropriation and inhabitation. Cases in the United States and in the global South demonstrate creative responses to the unintended consequences of laws, and how individuals and groups exploit regulatory contradictions and loopholes. These comportments prompt a reconsideration of how space is produced and places are assembled, and the possibilities therein. Urban informality draws attention to issues of livelihood and rights of inhabitation that are easily neglected, especially in U.S. planning and urban design discourse. A focus on an aesthetics of marginality is one way to draw attention to the shadows of the discipline and the need for a deeper ethical engagement.

## Acknowledgment

This research was supported by a grant from the USDA Cooperative State Research, Education and Extension Service (Hatch project #CA-D*-END-7717-H).

## Notes

1. Elsewhere, I have employed a heuristic framework of spatial claims to raise questions about the relationship between urban design practice and marginalized groups (Rios 2010).

2. In social ecological terms, places can be viewed as assemblages of different ideas and practices that involve negotiations between groups and their environments. This definition draws from Manuel DeLanda's (2006) engagement with assemblage theory to highlight the sociomaterial nature of places and the utility of site as both urban analytic and potential. See also McFarlane (2011), who argues the importance of assemblage thinking in critical urbanism.

3. Although the topic of informality has roots in Latin America, Latin American scholars have taken a different approach to urban informality than their counterparts elsewhere in the global South, employing a poststructural reading for the most part (Varley 2013).

## References

Appadurai, Arjun. 2001. "Deep Democracy: Urban Governmentality and the Horizon of Politics." *Environment and Urbanization* 13 (2):23–43.

Assaad, Ragui. 1996. "Formalizing the Informal? The Transformation of Cairo's Refuse Collection System." *Journal of Planning Education and Research* 16:115–126.

Bell, Bryan, and Katie Wakeford, eds. 2008. *Expanding Architecture: Design and Activism*. New York: Metropolis Books.

Bhabha, Homi. 1994. *The Location of Culture*. London: Routledge.

Chase, John, Margaret Crawford, and John Kaliski, eds. 1999. *Everyday Urbanism*. New York: Monacelli Press.

De Landa, Manuel. 2006. *A New Philosophy of Society: Assemblage Theory and Social Complexity*. London: Continuum.

Del Real, Patricio. 2010. "Review Essay." *Journal of Architectural Education* 64 (1):149–151.

Dingemans, Dennis, and Robin Datel. 1995. "Urban Multiethnicity." *Geographical Review* 85 (4):458–477.

Guattari, Félix. 1995. *Chaosophy*. New York: Semiotext[e].

Hansen, Karen, and Mariken Vaa, eds. 2004. *Reconsidering Informality*. Uppsala: Nordiska Afrikainstitutet.

Harwood, Stacy Anne. 2012. "Planning in the Face of Anti-immigrant Sentiment: Latino Immigrants and Land Use Conflicts in Orange County, California." In Michael Rios and Leonardo Vazquez, eds., *Diálogos: Placemaking in Latino Communities*, 36–49. London: Routledge.

Holston, James. 2008. *Insurgent Citizenship: Disjunctions of Democracy and Modernity in Brazil*. Princeton: Princeton University Press.

Hou, Jeff, ed. 2010. *Insurgent Public Space: Guerrilla Urbanism and the Remaking of Contemporary Cities*. Oxford: Routledge.

Jacobs, Jane M. 1998. "Staging Difference: Aestheticization and the Politics of Difference in Contemporary Cities." In Ruth Fincher and Jane M. Jacobs, eds., *Cities of Difference*, 252–278. New York: Guilford Press.

Lydon, Mike, ed. 2012. *Tactical Urbanism II*. Miami: Street Plans.

McFarlane, Colin. 2011. "Assemblage and Critical Urbanism." *City: Analysis of Urban Trends, Culture, Theory, Policy, Action* 15 (2):204–224.

Miraftab, Faranak. 2009. "Insurgent Planning: Situating Radical Planning in the Global South." *Planning Theory* 8 (1):32–50.

Nasar, Jack L. 1994. "Urban Design Aesthetics: The Evaluative Qualities of Building Exteriors." *Environment and Behavior* 26 (3):377–401.

Polakit, Kasama, and Yexsy Schomberg. 2012. "Finding a Place Called 'Home': Homemaking as Placemaking for Guatemalan Immigrants in South Florida." In Michael Rios and Leonardo Vazquez, eds., *Diálogos: Placemaking in Latino Communities*, 141–154. London: Routledge.

Ranganathan, Malini. Forthcoming. "Paying for Pipes, Claiming Citizenship: Political Agency and Water Reforms at the Urban Periphery." *International Journal of Urban and Regional Research*.

Rios, Michael. 2010. "Claiming Latino Space." In Hou 2010: 99–110.

Roy, Ananya. 2003. "Paradigms of Propertied Citizenship: Transnational Techniques of Analysis." *Urban Affairs Review* 38 (4):463–491.

Roy, Ananya. 2004. "Transnational Trespassings: The Geopolitics of Urban Informality." In Roy and AlSayyad 2004: 289–318.

Roy, Ananya. 2005. "Urban Informality: Toward an Epistemology of Planning." *Journal of the American Planning Association* 71 (2):147–158.

Roy, Ananya. 2009a. "Strangely Familiar: Planning and the World of Insurgence and Informality." *Planning Theory* 8 (1):7–11.

Roy, Ananya. 2009b. "Why India Cannot Plan Its Cities: Informality, Insurgence and the Idiom of Urbanization." *Planning Theory* 8 (1):76–87.

Roy, Ananya. 2009c. "The 21st-Century Metropolis: New Geographies of Theory." *Regional Studies* 43 (6):819–830.

Roy, Ananya. 2011. "Slumdog Cities: Rethinking Subaltern Urbanism." *International Journal of Urban and Regional Research* 35 (2):223–238.

Roy, Ananya, and Nezar AlSayyad, eds. 2004. *Urban Informality: Transnational Perspectives from the Middle East, Latin America, and South Asia*. Lanham, MD: Lexington Books.

Taylor, Nigel. 2009. "Legibility and Aesthetics in Urban Design." *Journal of Urban Design* 14 (2):189–202.

Urban Land Institute. 2009. *Stockton Boulevard Imagined: An Advisory Services Panel Report*. Washington, DC: Urban Land Institute.

Varley, Ann. 2013. "Postcolonising Informality?" *Environment and Planning. D, Society and Space* 31:4–22

Vidler, Anthony. 1992. *The Architectural Uncanny: Essays in the Modern Unhomely*. Cambridge, MA: MIT Press.

Yiftachel, Oren. 2009. "Theoretical Notes on 'Gray Cities': The Coming of Urban Apartheid." *Planning Theory* 8 (1):88–100.

# 10

## Formalizing City Farms: Conflict and Conciliation

Matt Covert and Alfonso Morales

Food has always entwined politics and economics (Murray 2007). Today, urban agriculture (UA), the growing and processing of food within or at the developing fringes of urban areas,[1] draws both conflict and cooperation. Some UA practices take place outside the official regulatory system, and as such they are deemed informal or even illegal. Nevertheless, metropolitan areas in the United States account for a significant amount of the food produced in the country (Jackson-Smith and Sharp 2008). UA's recent resurgence in the United States owes much to changing public attitudes regarding the social, economic, and environmental consequences of the industrial food system. However, its regulation is still evolving, and the practice is largely informal. The transformation from unregulated and informal urban food production practices to systemic integration of UA into local and state laws and ordinances is fraught with conflict among those with different views about the urban landscape and acceptable urban food cultivation.

Nonetheless, it is not surprising that the unregulated may seek formalization or regulation for its political legitimacy (Oswald 1997; Wade and Bunting 2007). Our primary objective in this chapter is to better comprehend informality through a case study of formalization. As food production attitudes and practices evolve, they inevitably conflict with habitual modern attitudes and behaviors. This chapter focuses on a particular conflict around UA in Kansas City, Missouri, that eventually led to formalization of an informal activity. In June 2010, the Kansas City city council passed an urban agriculture zoning ordinance in response to a land use policy conflict between advocates of UA and realtors, neighborhood associations, and an ever-shifting set of local political actors. This chapter focuses on that process—particularly the strategies, coalitions, and messages—and outcomes associated with the successful social mobilization and organizing that accomplished this political outcome.

The chapter concludes by discussing how proponents of UA achieved symbolic legitimacy by transforming themselves from "others" to vital elements of the pluralistic polity.

The chapter begins with a brief discussion of urban food systems, specifically as they involve land use regulation. We then turn to the Kansas City case. Ours was an applied research project, initiated as a community-university partnership to understand and support regulatory change affecting UA. The community's question was: How can we change our ordinances, and how can the University of Wisconsin support us? Additionally, we asked: What are the (regulatory) problems faced by urban agriculturists, and how can we advance supportive ordinances? Our methods included content analysis of communication memos and local media accounts. We reviewed relevant municipal ordinances, and conducted open-ended interviews with stakeholders involved in the conflict and supporters and opponents of the urban agriculture ordinance. Additionally, the first-listed author participated in a private Google group supporting the community organizations described below. As advisor to the mobilization, he had access to email communications between important actors.

## Urban Agriculture: Conflict and Regulation

Martin Bailkey and Joe Nasr (2000: 6) define UA as "the growing, processing, and distributing of food and other products through intensive plant cultivation and animal husbandry in and around cities." Food and land are intimately connected, and land is a unique resource. It is fixed in space and subject to seasonal changes, though emerging techniques (e.g., vertical farming, season-extending techniques) may alter its relative quantity and usefulness. Over the last century, land use policy separated agricultural practices from urbanizing and modernizing cities. Doing so informalized urban food production. Despite the importance of urban food production (Lawson 2005), regulation and discretion have rendered many UA practices informal and served to marginalize food producers and construct them as unwelcome, or at best peculiar, practitioners of antiquated activities.

Urban agriculture has two typical sources of conflict, NIMBYism and regulations. Raquel Maria Dillon (2010: 1) illustrates the typical NIMBY ("not in my back yard") conflict: "The challenge for cities is to balance the potential to grow green businesses with the concerns of neighbors who don't want a thriving, for-profit enterprise next door, never mind the noise and smells that come from compost and small livestock." In terms of regulation, Kubi Ackerman (2011: 3) argues that "bureaucratic challenges are a major barrier to the expansion of urban farming." Progressive ordinances and codes, nonetheless, can provide a pathway for formally sanctioned UA (Mukherji 2009).

Nina Mukherji and Alfonso Morales (2010) reviewed progressive UA ordinances in several cities. They found noteworthy examples in Portland and Vancouver, where land inventories are used to integrate UA into planning and policymaking (Mendes et al. 2008). Cleveland and Denver recently enacted beekeeping ordinances that tightly regulate that activity, while also protecting it from a land use perspective (City of Cleveland 2010; City of Denver 2008). Denver also began a process of developing a citywide vision, called Denver Seeds, for UA as an engine of job creation and food access (www.heirloomgardens.org). In Albuquerque, New Mexico, the city's Climate Action Task Force (2009) produced a Climate Action Plan that, among other recommendations, put food production within city limits at the forefront of its sustainability efforts by encouraging it in municipal codes. These examples demonstrate how cities are beginning to view UA as deserving of formalization through regulation.

Notwithstanding these recent examples, we know little about the process that produces the formal regulation of UA, particularly the ways in which stakeholders engage each other in designing, opposing, modifying, and passing or rejecting regulations. Nor do we comprehend the consequences—individual, political, and social—of such changes. This chapter examines one such instance of regulatory change, in Kansas City, Missouri, which recently passed a UA ordinance after a brief but contentious public battle. This case shows how conflict and coalition building shapes collective action; how customary practices are formalized and become subject to regulation; and how these policy processes help legitimate emergent social identities.

## Urban Agriculture in Kansas City

Kansas City, Missouri, is the largest city in the state of Missouri and the core of its second largest metropolitan statistical area. An important agricultural and transportation center, Kansas City has more freeway lane miles per capita than any other major U.S. city (Public Purpose 2002). Additionally, the city experienced suburban sprawl similar to that of other U.S. cities in the mid-twentieth century that left a deteriorating urban core and wealthy, outlying suburbs linked to amenities by freeways (Gottstein interview). Like other large cities, Kansas City, and the surrounding region in general, have had difficult race relations, which have been especially evident in the region's struggles with education integration following the *Brown v. Board of Education* decision (Davis 2004). Today, the city deals with segregation and concentration of poverty, both of which have deleterious effects on the community as a whole.

Kansas City has a strong-mayoral form of municipal government. The mayor acts as the thirteenth member of the city council. The city council is responsible for overall governance and budgeting, while the mayor is responsible for signing ordinances and setting an overall policy direction. Kansas City also has relatively strong neighborhood associations. The city has over 200 neighborhood groups, which vary in spatial scale from small groups representing one block to associations representing sprawling neighborhoods (City of Kansas City 2009). Outside of these groups, local governmental jurisdictions are often difficult to identify because the metropolitan area spans the Missouri-Kansas state line, county boundaries cut through the urban area, and the area spans many local water districts. These multiple jurisdictions pose regulatory challenges for those interested in engaging in UA (Gottstein interview).

In Kansas City's former zoning code (the city now has a unified development code), sections 88.110 through 88.140 described the permitted, conditional, and prohibited uses in each base zoning district. These sections of the code protected people's right to garden in their backyards, but as in most municipalities the land use provisions failed to comprehend the emerging realities of UA, particularly regarding animals and on-site sales. In effect, many agriculturists were producing food informally, outside the law. These practices burst into the public consciousness in the summer of 2009. In a relatively affluent neighborhood, composed largely of single-family homes on the south side of Kansas City, Brooke Salvaggio and her husband, Dan Heryer, worked on their urban farm, Badseed Farms, where they operated a small community-supported agriculture (CSA) operation (figure 10.1).[2] A neighbor, irritated at the presence of goats on the farm, called the city to complain. Salvaggio and Heryer had more goats than the city code allowed, and they received three citations in the mail. Besides fighting the citations, they saw an opportunity to challenge the zoning regulations on their land. Needing an ally with organizational capacity, they contacted Katherine Kelly of the Kansas City Center for Urban Agriculture (now Cultivate Kansas

**Figure 10.1**
Dan Heryer holding sweet potatoes from Badseed Farm. Photo credit: Brooke Salvaggio.

City). Together they worked to convince Councilman John Sharp, council member for their district, to support a zoning variance for their urban farm.

Meanwhile, city and state officials and neighborhood leaders were also becoming increasingly interested in food policy issues. There was a successful effort in the Missouri House of Representatives to create a statewide Urban Agriculture Task Force, and an effort to address the issue at the city level. Jason Holsman, a state representative from Kansas City, introduced HB 1848, which directed the establishment of this task force, in January 2010, and the bill passed unanimously through the Committee on Agricultural Policy (house.mo.gov). On May 16, 2010, the state senate passed unanimously the final (slightly amended) version of Bill 1848 (www.cityfarmer.info). Most advocates believed that this issue would engender little, if any, controversy. However, the composition of the task force reflected the interests of government and agriculturists but not of stakeholders with potentially contrasting views, like realtors, developers, and neighborhood associations.

**Figure 10.2**
View of Badseed Farm. Photo credit: Brooke Salvaggio.

## Conflict over the Ordinance and Outcomes of the Political Process

On April 8, 2010, two simultaneous events ignited a broader conflict in the city. First, Badseed Farms received a zoning variance for 13.5 acres of land, settling its specific case and allowing for the raising and selling of food on that property (figure 10.2). Second, Councilman Sharp introduced a zoning ordinance amendment regarding UA, which was supported by the mayor and several other council members. This proposed amendment, which eventually became Ordinance 100299, was crafted over several months with the input of city planning officials, UA advocates, and other community members. It concentrated on UA as an economic activity in residential zones. Their attention to formalizing UA was important, but they did not recognize potentially competing interests with a wholly different vision for what their neighborhoods should and should not include. The inaccuracy of the supporters' assumptions about how easy it would be to gain support for the amendment soon became apparent.

On April 20, 2010, the city council took public testimony on Ordinance 100299, and proponents were surprised at the intense opposition.

According to Kelly, the level of opposition and the arguments deployed were "disproportionate to the potential impact of the ordinance," including arguments that the inevitable pesticide application would poison neighbors, that the streets would become unsafe for children, and that property values would plummet while crime would soar (Kelly interview). While Kelly advanced the proposed ordinance, realtor Stacey Johnson-Cosby spoke for the opposition. The opponents included homeowners' associations, neighborhood associations, realtors, and their allies in city government. Supporters comprised a diverse coalition, including the Kansas City Center for Urban Agriculture, KC Healthy Kids, Health Care Foundation of Greater Kansas City, Kansas City Food Circle, some neighborhood associations, and allies in city government. Mayor Mark Funkhouser's administration had been interested in setting up an Urban Agriculture Task Force, and some council members, including Beth Gottstein, sought to integrate UA into the city's new unified development code, which was being developed at the time.

### The Political Mobilization

The timing of the development code review, interest on the part of many council members, and the media prominence of the Badseed Farms conflict framed the larger debate over land use policy for UA. Over the spring and summer of 2010, a battle of ideas and subsequent mobilization occurred. These included vigorous debate between city council officials, planners, and the public at three public hearings, vociferous media coverage for and against the ordinance, and the mobilization of supporters on both sides.

This mobilization had at its heart a core of activists and supporters who used online tools to discuss issues, strategy, examples from elsewhere in the country, and framing/messaging alternatives. Both supporters and opponents tried to use online communication to their advantage. The Kansas City Center for Urban Agriculture actively used a listserv to send quick updates to supporters and to notify them of impending hearings, volunteer opportunities, and the like. In early May, an unknown opponent of the measure became a member of the supporters' online group and began feeding internal group emails to other opponents, forcing Kelly, who managed the listserv, to start over and rebuild the group. Again, Kelly was taken aback by what she viewed as the heavy-handed tactics of the opposition (Kelly interview). In retrospect, the opposition to the UA ordinance in Kansas City is not altogether unexpected considering post-World War II land use policy and suburbanization—particularly the early emphasis on strictly segregating land uses and the use of zoning to exclude unwanted groups—and the importance of home ownership as the primary source of personal wealth for many families (Babcock 1966; Mui 2011).

Media coverage also played a role in the process. Coverage was not uniform. Two area television stations had coverage on the issue that Patty Noll, of the city planning office, described as "sensationalistic" (Noll interview). KCUR, a local public radio station, ran a segment that Kelly saw as heavy on the "Not in My Back Yard" sentiment but that struck Noll and Gottstein as "evenhanded" (Noll and Gottstein interviews). Both agreed that the endorsement of the ordinance by the *Kansas City Star*, the city's primary print newspaper, helped the case of supporters.

Endorsements by chief executives of local government can help publicize and provide crucial momentum for changes in municipal policy. However, the endorsement by Kansas City Mayor Mark Funkhouser was seen by some UA supporters as a slight negative. The embattled mayor faced a recall effort in 2009 over accusations of nepotism involving his wife and perceived failures of leadership (Martin 2009). Even though the recall effort was ultimately unsuccessful, and Kelly and Gottstein were grateful to have his support, they also saw his involvement as something of a political liability. While the mayor's endorsement of the ordinance did not negatively affect the final outcome in this instance, the fact that it was an issue before the public speaks to the need to understand more fully the idiosyncrasies of local political dynamics.

### The New Ordinance and Its Outcomes

The end of this process saw Kelly's coalition winning the day. Nevertheless, the final Ordinance 100299 represents an amalgamation born of the competing interests, actors, and ideas. Most importantly, the ordinance legitimizes many activities, formalizing practices as well as providing support for people to learn new roles and practice new identities as urban farmers.

First, the final ordinance allows on-site economic activity but limits it to the period of May through October, during the Kansas City growing season; it also lays out specific guidelines for how on-site sales can occur. For example, in addition to making on-site sales legal during the growing season, urban farmers cannot plant row crops (like corn and wheat) in front yards, and home gardens must be treated as an accessory to the residence itself.

Second, the ordinance separates UA in residential areas into three categories: home gardens, community gardens, and community-supported agriculture (CSA). Councilman Sharp proposed the ordinance, but he is perceived by some UA advocates as favoring home and community gardens over community-supported agriculture. Despite more participation in the process from advocates of CSA, it is subject to the most scrutiny in the ordinance. For instance, CSA farms must apply for a special permit for on-site sales. Despite additional scrutiny, CSA practitioners acknowledge that their businesses are now secure in ways they were not before. This indicates that legitimizing processes rarely proceed uniformly, but are instead nuanced. Though UA is now formalized, its formalization bears distinct consequences for practitioners of different types of agriculture. Might these distinctions become pernicious and produce conflict between those identifying themselves with different types of UA? While not within the scope of our chapter, this and related questions merit further scrutiny.

City officials and supporters of the measure are optimistic about the potential effects of the ordinance. Planner Noll believes that the ordinance is likely to let neighbors better share their bounty with each other, while also encouraging a wide variety of positive economic activity by church groups, youth organizations, and other community garden groups, which will result in improved food access. Related UA activities in food processing and distribution are expected, which will afford individuals new experiences and opportunities for self-definition. Kelly, a tireless advocate for UA as director of Cultivate Kansas City, is particularly excited about the prospects for immigrants and youth involved in UA. In short, proponents hope for a richer civil society, deeper and more nuanced social experiences, and a more robust and resilient local economy, all as the result of the formalization of previously informal activities.

### Lessons Learned

Our case study illustrates one type of urban agriculture ordinance, but UA manifests itself in many ways (vertical farming, hydroponics, etc.), and so we should expect additional ordinances to follow—especially in resource-constrained environments (Covert 2012). The Kansas City case helps us articulate conceptual lessons with respect to the notion of informality, as well as practical advice for proponents of UA. Conceptually, when dealing with issues of land use planning in the United States, a century of experience has demonstrated the shortcomings of planning approaches predicated on static "if-then" deployment of relatively inflexible categories. In contrast, UA demands thinking that recognizes the various perspectives held by the participants and the multiple goals achievable in any one space. By understanding their possible interactions, even dualistic theoretical constructs like formal/informal can be negotiated (Morales 2001).

The other conceptual lesson about informality is how it is used to frame the debate about UA. On the one hand, opponents of the Kansas City ordinance cast urban farmers as "the other" at the opening salvo of the conflict during a city council meeting. They suggested that selling food harvested in residential areas would create a carnival atmosphere that would ignore law and social norms. This depiction and claims of the lawless behavior that could result from the ordinance reflected a fear of the unknown combined with a NIMBY sentiment. Those opposed to the ordinance cast themselves as formal and legitimate, and the urban farmer "other" as informal and illegitimate. On the other hand, public officials and the public came to believe that urban farmers and gardeners had the best interests of their neighborhoods at heart and were genuinely willing to make concessions to enshrine their businesses in law. This position had the advantage of casting opponents as rigid, uncompromising, and resistant to change. In a sense, advocates for the ordinance were seen as wanting to enlarge the sphere of possible economic activity, while opponents' concerns appeared too limiting and old-fashioned.

A notable observation was that some opponents of the ordinance, particularly some residents from the affluent sixth district, were the children of farmers. Kelly hypothesized that their opposition to the ordinance as it existed was not about the language of the bill, but rather about their view of the legitimate scale of "agriculture" as represented by the conventional food system with its large farms and feedlots, large trucks, chemicals, tractors, feed bins, and the associated noises and smells (Kelly interview). Obviously, this explanation for some people's views cannot be generalized to large groups. Even so, it highlights the importance of talking about UA in ways that tap into and reframe preconceived notions, and, importantly, it illustrates the struggle for identity and legitimacy in (re)emergent practices like UA. Such perceptions serve as starting points for ongoing discussions in which parties learn to substitute habitual beliefs with concrete understanding of each other and their activities. This move is central to overcoming pernicious uses of the formal/informal distinction and to substitute for it a dialectic approach to policy formation, implementation, and regulation.

Our case study also has a number of lessons for practitioners and students of UA and its (re)emergent activities. First, reconstructing urban food production requires reconstructing perceptions of what it is. This is as much experiential as a matter of framing and recovering earlier rationales for UA, and of discovering new reasons for it (Lawson 2005). This case shows how UA blurs the line between gardening and commercial agriculture. The consequence was the divergent perceptions of UA held by farmers and city council members, perceptions that produced ambiguous communication and a confusion of priorities that made crafting the ordinance more difficult. Practically speaking, communicating around UA demands special attention to relationship building and clear communication.

An additional lesson of the Kansas City case concerns the important role city planners can play in UA. The Badseed Farms conflict coincided with a growing interest in food issues at the state and municipal levels. City planners delivered high-level responses to the proposed ordinance change. They helped build important bridging relationships between the various parties, and they developed an ordinance that both sides could accept. In a follow-up interview Noll noted the importance of the new regulatory structure to organizations and individuals in identifying and advancing their goals:

I have heard that some community gardens groups have been selling produce at gardens with no problems whatsoever. That's what the ordinance was designed to do, and there have been no complaints. In one particular garden, youth take the produce and sell it in their neighborhood. People are generally happy with [the ordinance]. The food policy coalition group has moved on and is talking about creating a food hub. Accomplished what they set out to do with zoning! (Noll interview, 2012)

While Noll's concluding comment belies the occasionally paradoxical attitude of planners toward their regulatory tools, her observations confirm the importance of the new regulations to UA in Kansas City as well as the social consequences of UA. Perhaps most important is how the new ordinance is releasing the energy of organizations in advancing new goals. In short, Kelly and Gottstein both spoke highly of the professional and dedicated work by Noll and others in the planning department to help navigate the process of changing the city's zoning ordinance. The dynamics of every city are different, making it difficult to generalize these experiences, but it is safe to say that planning personnel can make an important difference. In this case, professional discretion made a contentious process easier.

Another lesson speaks to how UA is framed by opponents, proponents, and policymakers. Gottstein, Noll, and Kelly all emphasized the potential benefits of on-site urban agricultural sales in alleviating food deserts, providing economic development, and contributing positively to environmental and public health issues. Many inner-city neighborhoods in Kansas City have significant amounts of unused land. Kelly believes that this process highlighted for city officials and for residents the potential for sustainable economic development by taking advantage of such land. She described this in the context of broad-based and collaborative strategies:

It's clear to me, when I see what others are doing, how they're doing it and what they are accomplishing, that there are economic realities that we're slowly changing. But we know this is such hard work, and to know we're able to do it, legitimately, and get better doing it, and to do it with other people to achieve their economic goals and other things they desire . . . I'm glad of the support we get from the City, from universities, and I'm sure we'll work with others. It's fantastic that people are working towards so many goals, [goals] that help people and neighborhoods, and that involve people and organizations of all different kinds. (Kelly interview)

Kelly's remarks raise a few important points. First is her observation of growing diversity in UA activities, what Morales (2009, 2012) calls "speciation." In short, this means that, as in any robust ecology, there are a number of different ways to achieve the many broadly similar goals people are pursuing. Still, Kelly is interested in the parallel economic, social, health, and other opportunities now made possible by this ordinance. Furthermore, Kelly suggests the long-held belief that appropriate regulation provides an impetus for action among the public, the growth of individual business, and public participation in economic and political life. The ordinance as a whole; particularly the concession regarding CSA operations that appeared in the final version, demonstrates the economic opportunities that result from the process and the success of advocates' framing of UA as an economic development tool.

## Conclusion

One approach to informality casts it as an innovative response to failures of the market economy and polity. In our case we found a more nuanced situation—inclusive and clear regulations were demanded and assisted in fostering UA practices as inventive responses to economic challenges. The great legal historian J. Willard Hurst found it was stable regulatory regimes and expectations that fostered the "release of energy" in economic activity (Hurst 1956). It is that sort of legal stability that supports innovation in UA. Such legal change was demanded by agriculturists holding new values, and their mobilization produced this novel regulatory environment enabling UA and its associated activities. We learned that many supporters of the new urban agriculture ordinance were initially surprised by the intensity of the opposition, but such opposition should come as no surprise. Conflicts over land use, particularly when they involve conflicting visions of the use of the land in people's neighborhoods, are fraught with strong emotions. However, the spirit of compromise found in this case is heartening.

Speaking more generally, various types of UA—aquaponics, vertical farming, greenhouses, and the like—should signal (especially to shrinking cities) that rich economic, social, and political activities are still possible, even if population is in decline. Concern over the future of large urban areas should eventually trump narrow interests, but we acknowledge that such changes in local political economy will not be without conflict. Indeed, Detroit provides numerous examples of conflict over UA as a land use (Mogk, Kwiatkowski, and Weindorf 2012). However, we find fascinating and important the scholarly projects about the clashing identities that stimulate such conflict, and we call for further research, historical and comparative, into how scale (community or corporate) and purpose (community and/or economic or organizational) interact with identities (gardener versus farmer), and how these variables change over time and with what implications (see for instance Morales 2011b). Most generally, we learn again that parties to negotiated conflict should remember the shared fate at the heart of this conflict and the importance of maintaining or renewing a dialogue. It is interaction and shared purposes that enrich who we are and who we can become.

## Acknowledgments

The authors, listed in alphabetical order, acknowledge careful comments from John Peck, Sara Randle, and Kelliann Blazek; and the support of the United States Department of Agriculture, National Institute of Food and Agriculture (USDA Award 2011-68004-30044).

## Notes

1. Urban agriculture can also include distributing, selling, consumption, and disposal of food. For research on distribution, particularly farmers' markets and street vendors, see Morales, Balkin, and Persky (1995), Morales and Kettles (2009), Mukherji and Morales (2010), Morales (2011a), Day-Farnsworth and Morales (2012), Pfantz and Morales (2013), and Pfantz and Morales (forthcoming).

2. Community-supported agriculture (CSA) consists of "a community of individuals or families who make financial pledges to a farm (typically small or mid-sized) up front. In turn, each receives a share of produce throughout the growing season" (http://foodglossary.pbworks.com/w/page/31253712/FrontPage).

## References

Ackerman, Kubi. 2011. *The Potential for Urban Agriculture in New York City: Growing Capacity, Food Security and Green Infrastructure*. New York: Urban Design Lab, Earth Institute, Columbia University.

Babcock, Richard F. 1966. *The Zoning Game: Municipal Policy and Practice*. Madison: University of Wisconsin Press.

Bailkey, Martin, and Joe Nasr. 2000. "From Brownfields to Greenfields: Producing Food in North American Cities." *Community Food Security News* (Fall 1999/Winter 2000): 6.

City of Cleveland. 2010. "Restrictions on the Keeping of Farm Animals and Bees." City of Cleveland Codified Ordinances 347.02.

City of Denver. 2008. "For an Ordinance Relating to Chapter 59 (Zoning), Denver Revised Municipal Code, Amending Allowed Accessory Uses in Residential Zone Districts to Permit Keeping of Domestic Honey bees." Denver Revised Municipal Code Council Bill 548.

City of Kansas City. 2009. "Know Your City Government: Mayor and Council." Available at www.kcmo.org (retrieved November 18, 2011).

Climate Action Task Force. 2009. "City of Albuquerque Climate Action Plan: Climate Action Task Force Recommendations to Mayor Martin J. Chavez." http://cabq.gov/cap/cap-presentation/CATFPowerPointREV09.pdf (retrieved February 6, 2012).

Covert, Matt. 2012. "Growing the Desert: Urban Agriculture Land Use Policy in the American West." Master's thesis, Nelson Institute for Environmental Studies, University of Wisconsin-Madison.

Davis, Donna M. 2004. "50 Years beyond Brown: Separate and Unequal in Kansas City, Missouri." *American Educational History* 31 (1):7–12.

Day-Farnsworth, Lindsey, and Alfonso Morales. 2012. "Satiating the Demand: Planning for Alternative Models of Regional Food Distribution." *Journal of Agriculture, Food Systems and Community Development* 2 (1):227–248.

Dillon, Raquel Maria. 2010. "Urban Gardeners versus Zoning Laws." *Christian Science Monitor*, February 16.

Hurst, Willard. 1956. *Law and the Conditions of Freedom in the Nineteenth-Century United States*. Madison: University of Wisconsin Press.

Jackson-Smith, Douglas, and Jeff Sharp. 2008. "Farming in the Urban Shadow: Supporting Agriculture at the Rural-Urban Interface." *Rural Realities* 2 (4): 1–12.

Lawson, Laura J. 2005. *City Bountiful: A Century of Community Gardening in America*. Berkeley: University of California Press.

Martin, David. 2009. "Funkhouser Recall Papers Filed." *The Pitch*. www.the pitch.com (posted April 6).

Mendes, Wendy, Kevin Balmer, Terra Kaethler, and Amanda Rhoads. 2008. "Using Land Inventories to Plan for Urban Agriculture: Experiences from Portland and Vancouver." *Journal of the American Planning Association* 74 (4): 435–449.

Mogk, John E., Sarah Kwiatkowski, and Mary Jo Weindorf. 2012. "Promoting Urban Agriculture as an Alternative Land Use for Vacant Properties in the City of Detroit: Benefits, Problems and Proposals for a Regulatory Framework for Successful Land Use Integration." *Wayne Law Review* 56 (4):1521–1580.

Morales, Alfonso. 2001. "Policy from Theory: A Critical Reconstruction of Theory on the 'Informal' Economy." *Sociological Imagination* 38 (3): 190–203.

Morales, Alfonso. 2009. "A Woman's Place Is on the Street: Purposes and Problems of Mexican American Women Entrepreneurs." In John S. Butler, Alfonso Morales, and David Torres, eds., *Wealth Creation and Business Formation Among Mexican-Americans: History, Circumstances and Prospects*, 99–125. West Lafayette, IN: Purdue University Press.

Morales, Alfonso. 2011a. "Public Markets: Prospects for Social, Economic, and Political Development." *Journal of Planning Literature* 26 (3):3–17.

Morales, Alfonso. 2011b. "Growing Food AND Justice: Dismantling Racism through Sustainable Food Systems." In Allison Alkon and Julian Agyeman, eds., *Cultivating Food Justice: Race, Class and Sustainability*, 149–176. Cambridge, MA: MIT Press.

Morales, Alfonso. 2012. "Cultivating Montreal: Community Agriculture and Urban Renewal." Lecture delivered to a special consultation on urban agriculture invited by the City of Montreal and the Department of Public Health of the Province of Quebec, Montreal, April 24.

Morales, Alfonso, Steve Balkin, and Joe Persky. 1995. "The Value of Benefits of a Public Street Market: The Case of Maxwell Street." *Economic Development Quarterly* 9 (4):304–320.

Morales, Alfonso, and Gregg Kettles. 2009. "Healthy Food Outside: Farmers' Markets, Taco Trucks, and Sidewalk Fruit Vendors." *Journal of Contemporary Health Law and Policy* 26 (1):20–48.

Mui, Ylan Q. 2011. "Americans Saw Wealth Plummet 40 Percent from 2007 to 2010, Federal Reserve Says." *Washington Post*, June 11.

Mukherji, Nina. 2009. "The Promise and the Pitfalls of Municipal Policy for Urban Agriculture." Master's thesis, University of Wisconsin-Madison.

Mukherji, Nina, and Alfonso Morales. 2010. "Zoning for Urban Agriculture." *Zoning Practice* 26 (3):1–8.

Murray, Sarah. 2007. *Moveable Feasts: From Ancient Rome to the 21st Century, the Incredible Journeys of the Food We Eat.* New York: St. Martin's Press.

Oswald, L. 1997. "The Role of the 'Harm/Benefit' and 'Average Reciprocity of Advantage' Rules in a Comprehensive Takings Analysis." *Vanderbilt Law Review* 50 (6):1450.

Pfantz, Megan, and Alfonso Morales. 2013. "Starting a Supplemental Nutrition Assistance Program: Information for Starting This Program at a Farmers Markets." *Journal of Extension* 51 (1): 1–5.

Pfantz, Megan, and Alfonso Morales. Forthcoming. "Increasing the Healthiness of Consumers through Farmers Markets." *Journal of Extension*.

Public Purpose, The. 2002. *Highway and Motorway Fact Book*. http://www.publicpurpose.com/hwy-tti99ratio.htm (retrieved November 16, 2011).

Wade, William, and Robert Bunting. 2007. "Average Reciprocity of Advantage: 'Magic Words' or Economic Realities—Lessons from Palazzolo." *Urban Lawyer* 39:319–370.

### Interviews

Gottstein, Beth, City Councilwoman, City of Kansas City, April 2010.

Kelly, Katherine, Co-Founder and Executive Director, Cultivate Kansas City, March, April, and June 2010, November 2011, and August 2012.

Noll, Patty, Project Manager, Zoning and Development Code at City Planning and Development Department, City of Kansas City, Missouri, April and May 2010 and August 2012.

# 11

## A More Delicious City: How to Legalize Street Food

Mark Vallianatos

Over the past several years, Los Angeles has been praised for its informal food scene. According to food writers and urbanists, the city and region seems to be constantly spinning off not just innovative cuisines but also different ways and places to sell and enjoy food. In 2010, *Food & Wine* magazine named Roy Choi one of its ten best new chefs (Brion 2010). Choi is the chef of the Kogi BBQ Truck, a popular taco truck that sells Korean-Latin fusion food. Choi, along with Kogi cofounders Alice Shin and Mark Manguera, helped launch the national and now international trend for gourmet food trucks that announce their stops on Twitter (Arellano 2012: 266–269). A week after the launch of the Kogi Truck in late 2008 (before its success made him famous), Choi defined its signature Korean BBQ taco as Los Angeles in a meal:

Everything you get in that taco is what we live in LA. It's the 720 bus on Wilshire, it's the 3rd street Juanita's Tacos, the Korean supermarket and all those things that we live everyday in one bite. That was our goal. To take everything about LA and put it into one bite. (Behrens 2008)

Gourmet food trucks, as well as traditional taco trucks and trailers, serve the streets of Los Angeles. If you need groceries, look for produce trucks that take routes through immigrant neighborhoods. Street food is even more diverse on the sidewalks. Vendors push carts designed for mobile vending. Others sell food and drinks out of strollers or grocery carts jury-rigged for vending with an assortment of coolers, grill tops, propane tanks, tinfoil or sheet metal walls/heat shields, utensils, and condiments. Street food does not always move around and come to you. Sometimes it waits on metal grills, tables, and tarps temporarily placed on the sidewalk. At its most basic, street food "stands and walks" in Los Angeles, held by vendors on street medians or by the side of the road. They sell bags of oranges or carry ready-to-drink coconuts into traffic to hand through car windows.

This street food helps make Los Angeles a more casual city by blurring formal categories of time and space, cuisine and culture, commerce and law. From tacos or bacon-wrapped hot dogs after a night out to a stop at a cut fruit cart on a hot afternoon, carts and trucks extend the hours and places that people buy, sell, and eat food. These mobile meals create hot spots of social interaction in a city that too often lacks an active public life. The blending of ingredients and recipes, in what food critic Jonathan Gold calls "dripping plates of food drawn straight from the city's recombinant DNA" (Gold 2012: 1st par.), lends an air of cultural solidarity, at least in the shallow form of epicurean appreciation, to a region where immigration has transformed demographics without always integrating society.

Street food is also a significant element of the informal economy, with many vendors operating outside of the law. Despite its reputation as a hotbed of street food, Los Angeles is the only one of the ten most populous cities in the United States that does not allow sidewalk vending of food (National Policy and Legal Analysis Network to Prevent Childhood Obesity and Public Health Law and Policy 2010). (While sidewalk vending is illegal in the City of Los Angeles, vending food from trucks is allowed under state law.)[1]

In this chapter, I explore why sidewalk vending is illegal in Los Angeles, and why and how it should be legalized. The chapter is organized into five sections. The first provides a brief history of street food in Los Angeles. The second describes the regulation of mobile food vending in the city. The next characterizes the nature of mobile vending, based on a survey of vendors in South Los Angeles. The fourth discusses why sidewalk vending of food in Los Angeles should be legalized, and how a legal scheme for vending should be set up. The chapter concludes on a hopeful note with mention of a new campaign under way to legalize sidewalk vending in Los Angeles.

### History: "Respect the Architects"

Tweeting taco trucks do indeed represent innovation, but they also draw on the city's history as a magnet for immigrants and an epicenter of car culture and eating at the speed of driving. The region birthed the modern fast food industry (Schlosser 2001). Taco Bell, the first fast food chain serving Mexican food, loosely modeled its tacos on those founder Glen Bell had eaten at Mexican restaurants in San Bernardino, a city east of Los Angeles (Arellano 2012: 59–64).

Roy Choi's reference to Juanita's Tacos, a traditional taco trailer that parks at 3rd and Western in Koreatown, reminds us that there have been taco trucks in Los Angeles since at least the early 1970s. Originating mainly in East Los Angeles, these catering trucks are known as *loncheras*. They traditionally parked during the day in industrial areas without many food options to sell to factory workers, and then at night sold on streets in neighborhoods with large Latino populations (Chee et al. 2009).

These trucks pioneered motorized street food in the Los Angeles region. Sociologist Oliver Wang, who mapped the stops of the first wave of Twitter trucks, commented:

I don't care if your truck is mashing up Vietnamese banh mi with Philly cheesesteak or serving Filipino chicken adobo wrapped in lavash bread; if you're a catering truck serving cheap food off the street, you're still following the lead of the old fashioned taco trucks that have been a part of this city's food fare for 30+ years. Respect the architects. (Wang 2009: 8th par.)

Taco trucks are themselves heirs to earlier forms of street food that, like present-day trucks and carts, sometimes drew the ire of competing merchants and the attention of regulators and inspectors. In the late nineteenth and early twentieth century, wandering "tamale men" in San Francisco, Chicago, New York, and other large cities sold tamales, often from buckets heated by steaming water. Gustavo Arellano relates in *Taco USA* that local tamale vendors were vehicular from the start:

Given Los Angeles' spread-out geography even in those embryonic days, wandering tamale men didn't take hold in L.A. as they did in the rest of the United States; a cart or wagon was necessary, not only to travel from home to downtown but also the better to procure a spot on the bustling streets. . . . As dusk fell, a cavalry of two-by-four pushcarts and eight-foot-long wagons with walls that opened up to reveal cooks inside wheeled their way towards the Plaza [de Los Angeles] and its vicinity, setting up shop until last call and beyond. (Arellano 2012: 55)

By the turn of the twentieth century, downtown restaurants began urging the Los Angeles City Council to restrict tamale sellers. In 1910, to defend their livelihood, tamale wagon owners organized a counterpetition with the signatures of more than 500 customers. A century before a similar saveourtacotrucks.org petition was organized (Winters Keegan 2008), they argued that "the lunch wagons are catering to an appreciative public, and to deprive the people of these convenient eating places would prove to be a great loss to the many local merchants who sell the wagon proprietors various supplies" (Arellano 2012: 56). Vending on sidewalks was, however, banned by the 1930s.

In addition to the hostility of some brick-and-mortar businesses, another reason sidewalk vending is illegal in Los Angeles has to do with the changing perceptions of streets and sidewalks. As Anastasia Loukaitou-Sideris and Renia Ehrenfeucht explain, early sidewalks were hosts to diverse activities:

[S]hopkeepers displayed fruit and vegetables. . . . Street peddlers also made a living on the street. Public orators could highlight the ravages of capitalism or preach salvation. Children played around building stoops, and dandies strolled along the pavement. (Loukaitou-Sideris and Ehrenfeucht 2009: 20–21)

Local political and opinion leaders, supported by engineers who designed the transportation infrastructure, began to impose order on sidewalks and remove obstructions like display cases of adjacent businesses. Laws and street design pushed pedestrians off the streets and onto the sidewalks and redoubled efforts to keep sidewalks clear as unobstructed routes for pedestrians rather than as places to gather (Loukaitou-Sideris and Ehrenfeucht 2009: 20–26).

Sidewalk vending did not reemerge as a significant activity in Los Angeles until the 1970s and 1980s, when immigration from Latin America and Asia coincided with a loss of industrial jobs caused by deindustrialization and the end of the Cold War. Many new arrivals turned to the informal economy, including sidewalk vending, for work. The association of sidewalk vending with immigrant workers and immigrant communities helps explain the third reason why sidewalk vending is illegal in Los Angeles. From restrictions on Chinese laundries in the late nineteenth century to racially restrictive property covenants in the mid-twentieth, land use controls in the city have long been tinged by racist assumptions (Kolnick 2008). Although attitudes are changing, sidewalk vending has been viewed as a foreign and chaotic activity, a Third World occupation, rather than as an opportunity to encourage business formation and provision of food in low-income areas.

**Law: "No Person . . . Shall on Any Sidewalk or Street Offer for Sale"**

Street food vendors in the city of Los Angeles are subject to municipal, county, and state regulations that govern whether, what, where, and how they may sell food on the public right of way: streets and sidewalks. The City of Los Angeles Municipal Code (LAMC) section 42(b) prohibits sale of any products, including food, on sidewalks. "No person, except as otherwise permitted by this section, shall on any sidewalk or street offer for sale, solicit the sale of, announce by any means the availability of, or have in his or her possession, control or custody, whether upon his or her person or upon some other animate or inanimate object, any goods, wares or merchandise which the public may purchase at any time" (LAMC IV 42(b)). Violations of this ban are considered misdemeanors, and violators face up to six months in jail and a $1,000 fine.

In 1994, this ban on sidewalk vending was amended to allow the establishment of up to eight "Special Sidewalk Vending Districts" (LAMC IV 42(m)). Vending districts were meant to be pilot areas. Complicated regulations, including a requirement that 20 percent of surrounding landowners and residents sign the application in favor of a new district (LAMC IV 42(m) 2.b), and assignment of vendors to specified, fixed locations (LAMC IV 42(m) 22.c), made it difficult to establish vending districts. Only one vending zone, in MacArthur Park, was ever created. According to those who participated in, regulated, or observed this district, it failed due to restrictions placed on participating vendors and competition from illegal vendors operating nearby (Harris interview; Kettles 2004).

With no vending district currently existing, food vending is illegal on all sidewalks in the city of Los Angeles. Enforcement of this regulation falls to the city's Bureau of Street Services. The bureau's thirty-five inspectors enforce over a hundred provisions of local and state law, including vending issues and illegal dumping. Gary Harris of the bureau's Investigation and Enforcement Division explained that his staff tends to focus enforcement actions on vending violations that include additional offenses beyond simply selling on the sidewalks. For example, selling pirated DVDs can be a felony in California, so enforcement might target sidewalk vendors believed to have counterfeit or bootlegged items for sale. The bureau does, however, make arrests for simply vending when they receive complaints or when they have already issued a warning to an illegal vendor (Harris interview). In the almost eleven months between July 1, 2011, and May 23, 2012, they arrested 284 vendors for violating LAMC section 42(b).[2]

While sidewalks are subject to municipal regulations, sale of food from vehicles in the adjacent roadways throughout California is regulated by section 22455 of the California Vehicle Code (CVC). This code states that a "commercial vehicle engaged in vending upon a street may vend products" upon "bringing the vehicle to a complete stop and lawfully parking adjacent to the curb" (CVC 22455 (a)). Local jurisdictions can "adopt additional requirements for the public safety regulating the type of vending and the time, place, and manner of vending from vehicles upon any street" (CVC 22455 (b)). The latter clause gives localities the power to regulate food trucks. Courts have interpreted the law with a stress on "public safety." Ordinances banning catering trucks from doing business near restaurants or from parking in residential neighborhoods, or requiring trucks to move frequently, have been struck down as conflicting with the state code, as restraints of trade, as vague, or as not really enhancing safety (Eagly 2012).

All establishments that sell food to the public, including mobile vendors, are subject to the California Retail Food Code (CRFC). The Los Angeles Department of Public Health enforces the code in Los Angeles County. Health requirements vary by the type of food to be sold, by whether any food is prepared on the vehicle, and by the type of vehicle (which health rules refer to as a "mobile food facility"). Some rules apply to all mobile vendors, such as the requirement to park vehicles within 200 feet of a bathroom that vendors are authorized to use, and to store vehicles at commissaries every day while not in use (CRFC 114315 and 114295). Commissaries are places where trucks or carts can be cleaned, and where waste products like dirty water and used cooking oil can be removed and replenished. It is never permissible for vendors to keep a cart or truck at their homes. If vendors handle food, their vehicle should have a hand-washing cart, with plumbing capable of heating water. If vendors cut or otherwise prepare food, they need an additional sink, ideally with three chambers, to clean utensils that have touched food (CRFC 114313; Powell interview).

With so many unlicensed mobile vendors, County Department of Public Health enforcers are kept busy inspecting, citing, and seizing illegal vehicles. Every forty-five days the department fills its 20,000-square-foot warehouse with confiscated food carts and equipment. Because most cited vendors do not appear in court to contest the seizure of their carts, most vehicles taken off the sidewalks are eventually sold for scrap metal (Powell interview).

### Data: "Usted no es un inspector y no compartirá la información con la policía o los inspectores de salud"[3]

Los Angeles is a big city located in a large county and sprawling region. Food vending in the area is a complex industry, operating partly in the formal economy and partly in its shadows. Studies have found that sidewalk vending is a source of income for many immigrant families in the city, with many adults but also their teenagers and younger children vending on sidewalks (Estrada and Hondagneu-Sotelo 2011). While it is impossible to capture the totality of mobile and sidewalk vending, I will try to provide an overview of the scale of vending activities as well as a snapshot of vendors' operations and attitudes drawn from surveys of vendors in South Los Angeles.

According to a count of permits from the Bureau of Specialized Surveillance and Enforcement, Environmental Health Division, Los Angeles County Department of Public Health, in May 2012 there were 6,280 mobile vendors in the county with valid health permits to sell food. Of these mobile vendors, a little over two thousand operated carts, while the rest used trucks. To be precise, there were 1,159 carts with permits to sell prepackaged foods and beverages, 644 carts licensed to steam hot dogs, and 144 carts licensed to sell unpackaged foods or beverages such as pretzels, churros, coffee, and snow cones.[4] Terrance Powell, Director of the Enforcement Bureau of the County's Department of Public Health, estimates that there are approximately twelve thousand additional mobile and sidewalk vendors active in the county without health permits (Powell interview). This makes for approximately eighteen thousand vendors operating in Los Angeles County. Figure 11.1 shows one of these vendors.

Between 2010 and 2011, to get a better idea of how vendors operate and whether mobile vending holds potential as a source of healthy food, Occidental College's Urban and Environmental Policy Institute partnered with the Community Redevelopment Agency of Los Angeles (CRA) and Esperanza Community Housing Corporation, a nonprofit organization, to survey vendors operating in parts of South Los Angeles. I was part of Occidental College's research team. The project grew out of a community food assessment that we had worked on in three neighborhoods in South and Central Los Angeles (Azuma et al. 2010). In our discussions with residents about the challenges of accessing a healthy meal and ideas to improve the food environment in their neighborhoods, one of the themes that they emphasized repeatedly was transportation. Mothers described the difficulty of taking public transit to reach stores with better selection, such as transferring lines while carrying bags and managing children on crowded buses. Because of the difficulties of getting around to shop, many people who do not own a car end up walking to the closest store, which probably does not have a great selection of healthy food, including fruits, vegetables, and lean meats.

Responding to this resident input, we looked for opportunities and links between transportation, food, and health. Our partnership with the

**Figure 11.1**
A Los Angeles street vendor. Photo credit: Rudy Espinoza.

CRA and Esperanza researched ways to get good food to people and take people to good food in Southeast Los Angeles. Mobile and sidewalk vendors selling healthy food appeared to be a possible response to the lack of access to healthy and affordable food that many area residents face. To learn more about vendors selling food on streets and sidewalks, we interviewed forty-five vendors operating in the project area, asking them about the type of vehicles used, types of food offered, type of food preparation, and revenue from sales. We also inquired about the vendors' awareness of vending laws and gauged their interest in a permitting system (Vallianatos et al. 2011). To overcome the concerns of vendors, some of whom were operating without permits and may have feared that inquiries were connected to law enforcement, surveys were conducted by

Spanish-speaking health promoters from Esperanza, who, as neighbor-hood residents, found it easier to interact with vendors in a supportive, nonintimidating manner.

Of the mobile vendors surveyed, the majority (80 percent) owned their own vehicle, 17.8 percent were employees of the vehicle owner, while only one rented their vehicle. Twelve vendors were operating out of pushed or pulled improvised vehicles such as shopping carts. Eight vendors operated small carts, six operated small motorized food trucks, while another six operated large motorized food trucks. The remaining thirteen vendors stated that they had no vehicle, were nonmobile (operat-ing from a grill or table), or were selling out of a car trunk.

Table 11.1 lists the different categories of food being sold by these vendors. The most common items were beverages and two food catego-ries that have low nutritional value: fried foods and snack foods. A quarter of the vendors surveyed, however, sold healthy foods—whole or cut fruit or vegetables. Of the forty-five vendors surveyed, only five advertised healthy food and five showed health grades or permits. None of the vendors displayed nutritional information.[5]

Vendors get their food and supplies from a variety of sources, often purchasing from more than one source. Three-quarters reported buying supplies from retail sellers; twenty vendors (44 percent) cooked the food they sold at home; fifteen (33 percent) bought supplies from wholesale markets in downtown Los Angeles; five bought from mobile vendor commissaries; and only two bought from farmers' markets. Sale revenues

**Table 11.1**
Categories of Food Sold by 45 Surveyed Street Vendors

| Type of Food | Number of Vendors |
| --- | --- |
| Beverages, bottled | 19 |
| Fried foods | 18 |
| Snack foods (e.g., chips) | 15 |
| Cooked meals (e.g., tacos) | 12 |
| Fruit/vegetables, whole | 11 |
| Fruit/vegetables, cut | 11 |
| Beverages, poured (e.g., horchata) | 7 |
| Ice cream/frozen snacks | 6 |
| Hot dogs | 4 |
| Prepackaged meals (e.g., sandwiches) | 2 |

Source: Author's survey (2011).

ranged considerably, from $40 to $500 per day, with an average of $162.50.

Fewer than one third (30.2 percent) of those interviewed reported being aware of laws governing sidewalk or mobile vending. Twenty-one vendors reported having had encounters with law enforcement in the past. Of those, five reported encounters with the police, three with the county's health department officials, and the rest with both, or with the City of Los Angeles Bureau of Street Services' Investigation and Enforcement Division. Seven vendors reported that they were let off with only a warning, but another five were fined between $35 and $160.

If a legal permit were available, half of the vendors surveyed said they would pay up to $100 for it, seven would pay for a permit "no matter its cost," and only two vendors would not pay for a permit.

### Policy Recommendations: "Legalize and Incentivize"

The desire for a permit by most surveyed vendors is notable. Allowing vendors to transition to legal sales would help relieve them of the stress of facing inspectors, confiscation of their vehicles, and fines. Legal sidewalk and mobile vending could also potentially help improve access to healthy food in areas without enough full-service grocery stores, farmers' markets, or sit-down restaurants. Produce trucks and carts, in particular, can expand the number of places where fruits and vegetables are easily available (figures 11.2 and 11.3). Although much of the food currently sold by vendors is high in fat, salt, and sugar, policymakers have little influence over what they sell. Legalization would provide an opportunity to regulate and influence what street vendors sell.

Legal sidewalk vending can also improve the vitality and walkability of cities by giving people a reason to walk and be outside. Increasing the number of people on city sidewalks can also make neighborhoods safer by ensuring more eyes on the street, and may have a positive spillover effect on local stores as more people are out strolling and shopping.

With these objectives in mind, the city of Los Angeles should allow permitted sale of food on city sidewalks. A legal permitting process would recognize the value of street and mobile vending, create opportunities for entrepreneurship in the formal economy, and allow the city to regulate and influence street food. However, policymakers would need to address a number of questions.

- *How many?* There should not be a cap on the number of permits available or the number of sidewalk vendors allowed to operate. In

**Figure 11.2**
A fruit truck on the street. Photo credit: Rudy Espinoza.

New York City, where the number of traditional food vending permits has been capped at 3,000 since 1979, there is a twenty-year waiting period to get a permit. Vendors lucky enough to have a permit often illegally "rent out" their permit for $12,000 to $20,000 per year (Wolan 2010).

- *Where?* Sidewalk vending should be allowed in all areas of the city where there is sufficient space on sidewalks, and where vendors can abide by health requirements. The city should not assign specific spaces to sidewalk vendors but should establish spaces where they can station their carts so they do not block pedestrians, doorways, ramps, etc., as is done by regulation in cities such as Portland, Oregon (City of Portland Office of Transportation 2009).

**Figure 11.3**
A fruit cart. Photo credit: Rudy Espinoza.

- *What are the requirements to operate legally?* The city should require vendors to have a vending permit and business license, and to carry liability insurance. Vendors will need to follow the County's health regulations and be responsible for the removal of their trash.
- *Who can vend?* Many vendors are undocumented workers. The city should set up the permitting process so that forms of identification and data available to undocumented residents are also accepted for obtaining permits.
- *Who can veto?* Sidewalk and mobile vending should not require permission from adjacent restaurants or food stores, even if the mobile vendors are selling similar products. The city can encourage vendors to partner with stores and sell their food or produce on the street. Stores or restaurants with appropriate facilities can become commissaries for vending carts (Los Angeles County Department of Public Health 2011: 1–2).
- *What must carts and vehicles look like?* The city should not mandate the aesthetics of the carts. Nevertheless, the city, with input from the

Los Angeles County Health and Human Services and cart manufacturers, can develop and promote standardized cart and vehicle designs that are easy to construct and operate, and also meet food handling and storage regulations

- *How to help vendors?* The city should create a "one-stop shop" where vendors can apply for all necessary permits, and should conduct outreach and training to encourage vendors to apply for permits while instructing them about their rights and responsibilities. Workshops with information about New York City's Green Cart program are offered in multiple languages, for example (New York City 2011). Additionally, the city could help vendors link with micro-finance programs as was done through the Michigan's Neighborhood Food Movers program (State of Michigan 2010: 6).

In neighborhoods where there are not enough stores selling a wide selection of fruits and vegetables or restaurants with healthy meals, mobile and sidewalk vending can be a source of affordable, healthy food. Los Angeles should use financial and locational incentives to encourage more vending of healthy items by produce trucks, food carts, and other mobile vendors. The following represent a series of policy recommendations for healthier street food.

- *Cheaper permits for healthy food vendors.* The city can consider offering a reduced-price permit for vendors who sell only, or mainly, healthy food items. The city would need to define "healthy items" by establishing nutrition criteria, as Kansas City has done for vendors in parks (Kansas City Parks and Recreation 2006) or—what is probably easier to enforce—by issuing lower-cost healthy vending permits to vendors of fruits and vegetables, as New York City has done with its Green Cart program (New York City 2011).

- *Access to more areas.* The city should allow healthy food vendors to sell in areas that are off-limits to other mobile vendors. For example, only healthy food vendors could sell near parks or transit stations.[6]

- *Priority access to public/private financing.* The city should prioritize vendors of healthy items for public financing or low-cost loans.

- *Links to sources of local, healthy food.* The city should help vendors identify sources of healthy local produce and prepared food.

- *Waiver of commissary requirement or support for community commissaries.* The city could work with Los Angeles County to explore whether vendors of fruits and vegetables can be exempted from having to store carts and trucks in a commissary, as is done in San Antonio (National Policy and Legal Analysis Network to Prevent Childhood Obesity and Public Health Law and Policy 2010). They should also support vendors and community organizations that want to run vending commissaries for healthy vending. An Oakland zoning variance allows a restaurant and commissary for fruit vendors to operate in a low-income neighborhood (Oakland City Planning Commission 2008).

### Conclusion: "You Can Still Smell the Food, but See Nothing . . ."

In 2009, Los Angeles Mayor Antonio Villaraigosa created a Food Policy Council Task Force to mark the thirtieth anniversary of farmers' markets in LA. The task force produced a report on strategies to ensure good food for Los Angeles and recommended the establishment of a permanent Food Policy Council (Los Angeles Food Policy Task Force 2010). The council was established in January 2011 and instituted a number of working groups, including a street food group. The street food working group brought together community-based organizations that work with sidewalk vendors; health and environmental advocates; gourmet and lunch truck operators; and staff from the City and County of Los Angeles.

Some participants were primarily interested in public health and in encouraging the vending of fresh produce in low-income neighborhoods. Others were concerned with vendors' rights and legalization. The working group reached consensus that doing one required doing both. That is, the goal of healthy vending provides a strong argument for legalizing sidewalk vending; and making vending legal increases the incentives and disincentives available to promote the sale of healthy food. In 2012, the working group launched a campaign to legalize sidewalk vending (Fine 2012). In November 2013, two Los Angeles City Council members representing heavily vended East and South Los Angeles districts, José Huizar and Curren Price, introduced a motion calling for "recommendations on possible regulation that could effectively permit and regulate *food street vending* on City sidewalks and parkways" (Los Angeles City Council 2013). The motion also requested recommendations on legalizing the vending of nonfood merchandise.

This emerging campaign is an exciting development, but it faces a number of challenges. First, can it generate broader support, win over champions in the Los Angeles City Council, and overcome the political and business establishment's traditional hostility to street food? Second, can the campaign strike a balance between its goals, the interests of regulators, and the constraints of health codes? The campaign wants to legalize sidewalk vending in a way that allows many existing vendors to become legal (which suggests inexpensive permits and flexibility as to what, where, and how vendors can sell). The Bureau of Street Services would like a higher permit fee that can pay for the stepped-up enforcement that they believe is essential to a successful permit system. And, as I have discussed, health codes have specific requirements for food handling and preparation, which make carts expensive and harder to transport and price many vendors out of the system. Third, can incentives for vending of healthy food successfully encourage more vendors to offer fruits, vegetables, and healthy meals for sale?

According to Terrance Powell, "lookouts" operate in some heavily vended areas to warn vendors of approaching inspectors. County enforcement teams might arrive on a street just in time to "still smell the food, but see nothing" (Powell interview). Scattered enforcement of municipal and county regulations, low entry costs for sidewalk food vendors, and the demand for street food creates an odd juxtaposition in which street food is forbidden but ubiquitous. Do we want these mainstays of Los Angeles's streets and informal economy to continue to play their cat-and-mouse game with inspectors? To fade away like ghosts—the scent of delicious food lingering on a street corner from which the vendors have vanished? Or can we allow vendors, through policy change and legalization, to take on a more central and legitimate role in shaping the future of food and urban life?

## Acknowledgments

I acknowledge colleagues and partners who surveyed vendors and helped lay the groundwork for a campaign to legalize street vending in Los Angeles: Giulia Pasciuto, Melinda Swanson, Robert Gottlieb, Amanda Shaffer, Jesus Garcia, Jason Neville, Jessica Gudmundson, Heng Lam Foong, Jenny Scanlin, Matt Mason, Ana Nolan, Beth Weinstein, Michael Davies, Matthew Dodson, Yelena Zeltser, Antonia Ezparza, Gina Padilla, Jorge Barron, David Mendez, Jessica Mejia, Ana Vallianatos, Michael Sin, Anne Farrell-Sheffer, Gwendolyn Flynn, Gregg Kettles, Rudy Espinosa, Clare Fox, Paige Dow, Albert Lowe, Sandra McNeil, Faisal Roble, James Rojas, Nathan Baird, Julian Leon, Katherine Hulting, Kristin Jensvold-Rumage, Janet Favela, Erin Glenn, Carlos Ardon, Crystal

Crawford, Lauren Dunning, Michele Grant, Mike Dennis, Jessica Durrum, Alexandra Agajanian, Claudia Martinez Mansell, Alexa Delwiche, Paula Daniels, Maria Cabildo, Gary Harris, Terrance Powell.

## Notes

1. Food truck operators should have a business license from the city where the truck operates, and should also comply with requirements of the California Retail Food Code and numerous regulations in regard to their vehicle's parking, commuting, and maintenance.

2. Data from Investigation and Enforcement Division, City of Los Angeles Bureau of Street Services, June 20, 2012.

3. Text from instructions to a Spanish-language survey instrument. It translates as: "You are not an inspector and will not share information with police or health inspectors."

4. Data from Bureau of Specialized Surveillance and Enforcement, Environmental Health Division, Los Angeles County Department of Public Health, provided by Lauren Dunning, Division of Chronic Disease and Injury Prevention, Los Angeles County Department of Public Health, May 31, 2012.

5. The surveys were completed before Los Angeles County required food carts to display health grades that have for years been visible in the windows of restaurants in the county (Lin 2010).

6. The Los Angeles County Metropolitan Transportation Authority has a small program with food carts outside of ten to fifteen public transit stations. As of May 2010, most participating vendors sold hot dogs (Metro Operations Committee 2010).

## References

Arellano, Gustavo. 2012. *Taco USA: How Mexican Food Conquered America.* New York: Scribner.

Azuma, Andrea Misako, Susan Gilliland, Mark Vallianatos, and Robert Gottlieb. 2010. "Food Access, Availability, and Affordability in 3 Los Angeles Communities, Project CAFE, 2004–2006." *Preventing Chronic Disease* 7 (2):A27. http://www.cdc.gov/pcd/issues/2010/mar/08_0232.htm?s_cid=pcd72a27_e.

Behrens, Zach. 2008. "Eat This: Korean BBQ with the Edge of a Street Taco." LAist, December 4. http://laist.com/2008/12/04/kogi_bbq.php#photo-1.

Brion, Raphael. 2010. "Food & Wine Magazine's Best New Chefs Announced." April 6. http://eater.com/archives/2010/04/06/food-wine-magazines-best-new-chefs-2010-announced.php.

Chee, Morgan, Jésus Hermosillo, and Lawrence Joe. 2009. "A Sectoral Analysis of the 'Loncheras' Sub-Sector in Los Angeles County." UCLA Department of Public Affairs / School of Urban Planning.

City of Portland Office of Transportation. 2009. "Sidewalk Vending Cart Permit Application Packet." http://www.portlandoregon.gov/transportation/article/ 275061.

Eagly, Ingrid V. 2012. "Criminal Clinics in the Pursuit of Immigrant Rights: Lessons from the *Loncheros*." *UC Irvine Law Review* 2:91–124.

Estrada, Emir, and Pierrette Hondagneu-Sotelo. 2011. "Intersectional Dignities: Latino Immigrant Street Vendor Youth in Los Angeles." *Journal of Contemporary Ethnography* 40 (1):102–131.

Fine, Howard. 2012. "Street Vendors Cook Up Challenge to Sidewalk Sales Ban." *Los Angeles Business Journal*, October 8.

Gold, Jonathan. 2012. "How America Became a Food Truck Nation." *Smithsonian Magazine*, March 2012. http://www.smithsonianmag.com/travel/How-America-Became-a-Food-Truck-Nation.html.

Kansas City Parks and Recreation. 2006. "Vending Policy." http://www.kcmo .org/idc/groups/parksandrec/documents/parksrecreation/012710.pdf.

Kettles, Gregg W. 2004. "Regulating Vending in the Sidewalk Commons." *Temple Law Review* 77 (1):1–45. http://papers.ssrn.com/sol3/papers.cfm?abstract_id =897498.

Kolnick, Kathy A. 2008. "Order Before Zoning: Land Use Regulation in Los Angeles, 1880–1915." Ph.D. diss., University of Southern California, 2008.

Lin, Rong-Gong, II. 2010. "L.A. County Gives Initial OK for Food Truck Grading Plan." *Los Angeles Times*, October 13.

Los Angeles City Council. 2013. Council File 13-1493. November 6, 2013. http:// cityclerk.lacity.org/lacityclerkconnect/index.cfm?fa=ccfi.viewrecord&cfnumber =13-1493.

Los Angeles County Department of Public Health. 2011. "Plan Check Facilities for Mobile Food Facilities and Mobile Support Unit." http://search.lapubli chealth.org/eh/docs/vip/PLAN_CHECK_GUIDELINES_1.pdf.

Los Angeles Food Policy Task Force. 2010. "Good Food for All: Creating a New Regional Food System for Los Angeles." http://goodfoodlosangeles.files.word press.com/2010/07/good-food-full_report_single_072010.pdf.

Loukaitou-Sideris, Anastasia, and Renia Ehrenfeucht. 2009. *Sidewalks: Conflict and Negotiation over Public Space*. Cambridge, MA: MIT Press.

Metro Operations Committee. 2010. *Status of Food Vendor Programs*. Los Angeles: Los Angeles County Metropolitan Transportation Authority.

National Policy and Legal Analysis Network to Prevent Childhood Obesity and Public Health Law and Policy. 2010. "Mobile Vending Laws in the 10 Most Populous U.S. Cities." http://changelabsolutions.org/sites/changelabsolutions .org/files/MobileVending_chart_FINAL_2010.02.17.pdf.

New York City. 2011. "Green Cart Program." http://www.nyc.gov/html/doh/ downloads/pdf/cdp/green-cart-workshop.pdf.

Oakland City Planning Commission. 2008. Staff report, July 16, 2008. http:// www.oaklandnet.com/government/ceda/revised/planningzoning/Commission/ CM08-162-1_staff_report.pdf.

Schlosser, Eric. 2001. *Fast Food Nation: The Dark Side of the American Meal.* New York: Houghton Mifflin.

State of Michigan. 2010. "MI Neighborhood Food Movers Fresh Food Delivery Program." http://web.archive.org/web/20100528054835/http://michigan.gov/documents/foodmovers/MNFM_Manual_290427_7.pdf.

Vallianatos, Mark, Giulia Pasciuto, Melissa Swanson, and Amanda Shaffer. 2011. "Bringing People to Good Food and Good Food to People: Enhancing Food Access through Transportation and Land Use Policies." Urban and Environmental Policy Institute, March 2011.

Wang, Oliver. 2009. "Ode to the Taco Truck." *Atlantic*, August 11. http://www.theatlantic.com/national/archive/2010/08/ode-to-the-taco-truck/61292/#.

Winters Keegan, Rebecca. 2008. "The Great Taco Truck War." *Time*, April 25. http://www.time.com/time/nation/article/0,8599,1735104,00.html.

Wolan, Christian. 2010. "Vendor Rules Promise Less Art, More Cupcakes in City Parks." *Gotham Gazette*, April 2010. http://www.gothamgazette.com/index.php/topics/102-parks/497-vendor-rules-promise-less-art-more-cupcakes-in-city-parks.

### Interviews

Harris, Garry, Investigation and Enforcement Division, City of Los Angeles Bureau of Street Services, June 2012.

Powell, Terrance, Bureau of Specialized Surveillance, Los Angeles County Department of Public Health, July 2012.

# 12

## Crystals, Mud, and Space: Street Vending Informality

Gregg Kettles

Informality is enjoying renewed attention now, particularly within the United States, as the economic downturn has forced many to make ends meet outside the traditional, formal economy. Some rent out a room in their home illegally. Others scavenge and run perpetual garage sales on their front lawn. Still others turn to selling things on the street. Street vending is generally assumed to be one of the most visible of these examples of informality (Epstein 1994: 2164; Priest 1994: 2269; Venkatesh 2006: 156, 187). This is so even though there is no single definition of informality or understanding of what constitutes an informal activity.

Some commentators view informality in terms of social or business relationships that allow an activity to take place outside government regulation. In this view, it is not that the activities themselves break any law, but that they have been structured legally to avoid certain legal requirements or interventions that otherwise would have applied (Dickerson 2011; Larson 2002; Light 2004; Sassen 2009). This view of informality may be labeled "law avoiding." Street vending fits well within this definition because it is typically not regulated as stringently as storefront establishments. A competing branch of commentary defines informality not in terms of "law avoiding" but rather of "law breaking." For De Soto (1989), Priest (1994), and Venkatesh (2006), informality refers to activities that are illegal from the start and pursued by participants who are tempted to break the law. Street vending also fits this definition well, because vendors often operate in defiance of municipal ordinances. Street vendors are mobile, enjoy lower rates of capital investment than their storefront counterparts, and trade in goods cheap enough for cash to be the common, if not exclusive, means of exchange. These qualities tempt some vendors to ignore rules regarding where and how they may conduct their business, as well as to avoid reporting their income to tax authorities.

Whether informality is viewed as law avoiding or law breaking, law is an indispensable aspect of it. De Soto (1989) and Venkatesh (2006) have argued that informality is the result of laws that are overburdensome. Larson (2002) contends that informality, at least in the context of U.S. colonias, is the product of a regulatory vacuum. She argues that the law should be extended gradually so that what are now informal activities are gradually made formal.

Law, however, is not a monolith. Different laws may be categorized in at least two ways, based on their structure or on their subject. In terms of structure, a law may be "crystal" or "mud." Crystal laws are applied objectively: "Speed limit: 55 miles per hour." By contrast, mud laws are applied subjectively: "Drivers should exercise reasonable care." What constitutes "reasonable care" is in the eye of the beholder. Laws may also be categorized according to their subject. Laws are aimed at activities, and a given activity may be described in a number of ways, which we might summarize by the questions who, what, where, why, when, and how. Imagine that a homeowner put on a rock concert in her backyard, with music so loud that it blew out the windows of her neighbor's home. This activity may be in violation of at least two laws. One may restrict *where* rock concerts may be held, barring such commercial activities from residential neighborhoods altogether. A second law may limit *how* rock concerts may be held, limiting how loudly the music may be played. Though they apply to a single activity, each of these laws has a different subject. The subject of the first law, regarding *where* the concert may be held, is intrinsically spatial. The subject of the second law, regarding *how*, is nonspatial.

These alternative structures and subjects—is a law crystal or mud? is it spatial or nonspatial?—give rise to questions about the nature of informality. Does the structure of a given law make a difference in determining what is informal and what is not? Stated differently, to what extent is informality the result of laws that are either crystal or mud? What about the laws' subject? To what extent is informality the outcome of laws that are spatial as opposed to nonspatial? These questions cannot be robustly answered just by looking at the letter of the law. As law moves from theory to reality through its enforcement, analysis of the enforcement of laws can help reveal their impact on informal activities.

Despite the substantial commentary that views informality in terms of law, limited empirical work has been done on how informality may be shaped by these alternative structures and subjects of laws. Street vending in New York City presents an excellent opportunity to fill this gap in the literature. There are thousands of street vendors in the city, and municipal laws on street vending are voluminous and varied in their structure and subject. Some are crystal, others mud. Some are spatial, others nonspatial. Moreover, the city issues thousands of citations to street vendors each year. The richness of New York City's experience with street vending offers an opportunity to develop a deeper understanding of the nature of informality.

Following this introductory section, I set out a theoretical framework, arguing that informality cannot be understood apart from law and law enforcement. I also contend that aggressive enforcement of crystal rules gives rise to complaints that compliance with the law is "impossible," while enforcement of mud rules leads to claims that the law is confusing and subject to abuse and arbitrary application by law enforcement officials. Next, I apply these theories to the street, discussing empirical work based on analysis of more than 127,000 citations, or notices of violation, issued by New York City law enforcement officials to street vendors over a five-year period. The final section draws some conclusions for policymakers. For those wishing to reduce informality by easing the burdens on street vending, a good place to start would be to relax or roll back crystal and spatial rules.

## Informality as the Product of Spatial, Nonspatial, Crystal, and Mud Laws

Informality cannot be understood apart from law. Law cannot be understood apart from law enforcement. As Jane Larson observed in her examination of informal housing in the Texas borderlands, to enact a law for purely symbolic purposes is not an accepted use of the law. "Within our legal tradition, where the law does not demand compliance, the rule of law symbolically and publicly falters. From the perspective of a rule of law regime characteristic of a liberal democracy, law's effectiveness depends on its enforcement" (Larson 2002: 176). To learn how informality is shaped by law, one must study the means and levels of enforcement of the various laws that make certain activities informal.

The difference between crystal and mud laws ties into broader questions of law and law enforcement (Rose 1988), and demands a more detailed explanation. Consider the following two laws:

No general vendor shall vend . . . within ten feet from entrances or exits to buildings which are exclusively residential at the street level. (New York Administrative Code §20-465(q)(3))

**Figure 12.1**
Moustapha Thioune, vendor of hats, New York, 2012. Photo credit: Street Vendor Project.

[A vending cart's] umbrella shall be safely secured to the . . . cart and maintained in good condition and repair. (24 Rules of the City of New York §601(m)(2))

The first is an example of a law that may be applied objectively. Armed with a tape measure, a law enforcement official may quickly determine on the street whether the rule has been violated. In fact, there should be no need to call on law enforcement. Anyone could determine for herself whether the activity is in violation of the law, and do so with relative ease. One can imagine quibbles, of course. Does the act of merely laying out goods on the sidewalk constitute "vending"? Where does "ten feet" get measured, to the door or to the steps leading to it? From where the goods are laid out, or from where the vendor was seen standing? But these kinds of uncertainties seem minor compared to the general certainty of the rule. Disagreements over its application are likely to be rare and quickly resolved. The objective nature of this law and those like it has given rise to such labels as "bright line rule," "crystal rule," or simply "crystal" (Rose 1988).

The second rule quoted above is an example of a law that may not be applied objectively. What is the meaning of "safely secured" or "in good condition and repair"? A law enforcement official does not have the luxury of using a tape measure to decide. Application of the rule is subjective and requires an exercise of judgment. One person may judge that an umbrella is "safely secured" and maintained in "good condition and repair," while another finds that the same umbrella fails to satisfy the law. There may of course be unanimity at the extremes: consider a new umbrella triple-bolted to the cart on the one hand, and a cart without any umbrella on the other. But in the vast middle between the narrow extremes, disagreement and uncertainty are likely to predominate. What about a vending umbrella that is somewhat faded and attached to the cart with baling wire? Dispute resolution will be complicated. Confusion will reign. The subjective nature of a law like this has given rise to such labels as "flexible standard," "muddy standard," or simply "mud" (Rose 1988).

Whether the laws to be enforced are predominantly crystal or mud has important consequences. Aggressive, repeated enforcement of crystal rules leads to claims that it is impossible to comply with the law. Where activities are made informal by crystal rules, there can be no dispute about the law. The actor engaged in an informal activity knows full well whether she is breaking the law. She may be surprised at being caught, but she cannot be surprised that her conduct is illegal. Crystal rules are violated with eyes wide open.

When the law is knowingly violated on a widespread and repeated basis, those activities come to have an air of inevitability about them. It is impossible for informal actors not to find themselves either outside the law or in violation of it. There is anecdotal evidence of this in the scholarly literature. Residents of colonias studied by Larson are perfectly aware that their homes do not comply with building codes. As one local community leader put it, "People here want good houses . . . but the truth is that [I] can't [buy a good house]. . . . So I am going to build whatever I can" (Larson 2002: 175). The urban poor in a Chicago neighborhood studied by Sudhir Venkatesh (2006) are drawn to informal activity, or "hustling," for the same reason. The homeless there provide security services and perform other odd jobs for storefront merchants in order to survive.

By contrast, enforcement of mud rules leads to claims that the law is confusing and maybe even enforced arbitrarily. Because of the uncertainty surrounding the meaning of mud laws, actors cannot reasonably anticipate how those rules will be applied to them. Consider, for example, the law that a vendor's cart "umbrella shall be safely secured to the . . . cart and maintained in good condition and repair." A vendor may have an umbrella that is sagging because of bent and broken tines. Were a police officer to cite or arrest the vendor for violating the rule regarding umbrella safety, the vendor might be surprised. There is a good chance that the vendor honestly believes she is in fact in compliance with the law. Mud rules are violated with eyes open, but blinded by a fog of confusion.

The risk that mud rules will be viewed as confusing draws our attention to those with the power to interpret the law and enforce it: judges and police officers. Though unexplored in the context of informality, the power that mud laws put in the hands of police officers has drawn a great deal of attention from legal academics, civil rights attorneys, and the courts. Laws proscribing vagrancy or loitering and other rules designed to maintain order in public spaces have a long history in the Western legal tradition (Garnett 2009: 9–10; Ehrenfeucht and Loukaitou-Sideris, this volume). But by the middle of the last century, they increasingly came to be seen as a tool by which law enforcement denied civil rights to racial minorities and others. This view reached its highwater mark in 1972, in the case of *Papachristou v. City of Jacksonville*, when the U.S. Supreme Court overturned the vagrancy convictions of eight individuals, whose allegedly illegal conduct consisted of nothing more than riding in a car or walking down a sidewalk late at night. The Court held that the vagrancy ordinance, which prohibited, for example, "wandering or strolling around from place to place without any lawful purpose or object" (*Papachristou v. City of Jacksonville* 1972: 158 n.1), was unconstitutional because it was too vague. The court explained that the ordinance failed "to give a person of ordinary intelligence fair notice that his contemplated conduct is prohibited by statute" (ibid.: 162). It also encouraged "arbitrary and erratic arrests and convictions" (ibid.).

Though an extreme case, *Papachristou* demonstrates the consequences of mud laws. Actors cannot know with certainty whether their actions are legal or not. Mud rules lead to complaints that the law is confusing and enforced arbitrarily.

### Street Vending Informality in New York City

Few places offer a better opportunity to test how informality is impacted by alternate structures and subjects of law—crystal versus mud, spatial versus nonspatial—than New York City. The city has a rich history of street vending and street vending regulation (Loukaitou-Sideris and Ehrenfeucht 2009). Today, New York City has an estimated 13,000 street vendors (Brown et al. 2011). The practice of street vending is the subject of numerous regulations. All the rules governing general vendors are found in, or issued pursuant to, the city's Administrative Code (Rules of the City of New York §3-109). Food vendors are subject not only to Administrative Code rules but to those of the New York City Health Code (Rules of the City of New York §§3-107, 3-110).

Spatial and nonspatial rules are both well represented. Vendors of items other than food—"general vendors"—are subject to at least forty-five separate rules. These cover everything from maintaining records of legal compliance to when and where vending may take place. Spatial rules are numerous, and sidewalks on many city blocks are off-limits for street vending. Even for those blocks that are open, vendors are required to keep minimum distances from building entrances, bus stops, curbs, etc. (Rules of the City of New York §3-109). Regulation of food vendors is also robust. They are subject to nearly fifty separate rules. In addition to spatial rules similar to those that apply to general vendors, food vendors are subject to nonspatial rules, many of which are designed to promote good nutrition and protect the public from food-borne illnesses. Requirements address such things as hand-washing facilities, food holding temperatures, and disclosure of calorie content (Rules of the City of New York §§3-107, 3-110).

Both general vendors and food vendors are subject to some crystal rules and some mud rules. Of the nearly one hundred rules that apply to street vending, two-thirds are crystal and one-third are mud.

Pursuant to New York's Freedom of Information Law, the Street Vendor Project, a vendor advocacy organization, requested and received information about all notices of violation (NoVs) issued to street vendors in New York City over the five-year period from 2006 to 2010. For each NoV this information included: the section number of the law listed as the reason for its issuance, the result of the administrative hearing (if any), the penalty amount imposed (if any), and the amount paid (if any). The following analysis is based on this data.

### The Data

New York City provided information for 127,758 NoVs. For purposes of this study, each NoV was coded as either "crystal" or "mud." (Approximately 3 percent of the NoVs state only that the violation was of the

**Figure 12.2**
Mohammed Omran, vendor of prepared foods and drinks, New York, 2012.
Photo credit: Street Vendor Project.

Health Code and fail to identify the specific section of the law, which
prevented these NoVs from being coded as crystal or mud.) Each NoV
was also coded as either "Administrative" or "Health." From our data,
there is no strong correlation between crystal and mud on the one hand
and Administrative and Health on the other. Among Health Code rules,
there are nearly equal numbers of crystal and mud. Among Administrative Code rules, crystal rules outnumber mud by a ratio of two to one.
The picture changes, however, when the rules are enforced, as shown in
table 12.1. NoVs for Administrative Code rules that are crystal outnumber those for mud rules by a ratio of more than forty-five to one.

A number of rules in the Administrative Code are nonspatial. For
example, a food vendor may be cited for vending without a license,
vending from an unpermitted cart, or vending non-food products (New
York City Administrative Code §§17-307(a), 17-307(b), and 17-307(b)
(1)). But the Administrative Code's spatial rules are the most frequently
enforced. More than half the citations were for violations of fifteen sections of the Administrative Code. Of these, two-thirds were for violations

**Table 12.1**
New York City Street Vending Notices of Violation, 2006–2010: Crystal and
Mud by Administrative and Health

|         | Administrative | Health  |
| ------- | -------------- | ------- |
| Crystal | 94,058         | 15,025  |
| Mud     | 1,943          | 13,285  |

**Table 12.2**
New York City Street Vending Notices of Violation, 2006–2010: Crystal versus
Mud and Administrative versus Health

|            | Crystal  | Mud     | Administrative | Health  |
| ---------- | -------- | ------- | -------------- | ------- |
| Number     | 109,083  | 15,228  | 96,001         | 31,757  |
| Proportion | 0.85     | 0.12    | 0.75           | 0.25    |

of spatial rules. Because most of the Administrative Code rules that are
the subject of enforcement are spatial, I use "Administrative" as a proxy
for "spatial." Likewise, I use "Health" as a proxy for "nonspatial." The
number of NoVs falling into each category, crystal versus mud and
Administrative (spatial) versus Health (nonspatial), is shown in table
12.2.

Each NoV was also coded for whether it was dismissed at an administrative hearing.[1] If a fine was imposed, each NoV was also coded for
whether that fine was paid. Regression models were developed to measure
the impact of the structure and subject of the law cited in an NoV on
the probability of dismissal at an administrative hearing and payment of
fine imposed. One logistic regression model was used to relate the variables crystal versus mud and administrative versus health to the probability that an NoV will be dismissed. The results of this model are set out
in table 12.3. Another regression model was used to relate these same
variables to the probability that a fine imposed pursuant to an NoV
would be paid. The results of this model are set out in table 12.4. Both
models have small *p*-values, of 0 and 0.013 respectively, suggesting that
the results of each are statistically significant.

**Crystal and Mud Laws**
As shown in table 12.2, at least 85 percent of the NoVs were for violations of crystal laws. That is, New York City law enforcement officials

**Table 12.3**
Predicted Probability of Dismissal

|  | Administrative | Health |
| --- | --- | --- |
| Crystal | 0.24 | 0.17 |
| Mud | 0.25 | 0.18 |

were five times more likely to cite a vendor for violating a crystal law than a mud one. The predominance of crystal laws is not diminished when NoVs are followed through the judicial process. As indicated in table 12.3, for a vendor challenging an NoV at a hearing, it matters very little whether the law is crystal or mud.

This is surprising. Crystal laws are supposed to be so clear that there is no need to go to court to resolve disputes. Any NoVs for a crystal law should, so the theory goes, be uniformly upheld. One possible explanation is that even the most crystal-seeming rules are occasionally uncertain in application. In other words, the quibbles imagined previously, over what constitutes "vending" and where "ten feet" gets measured, are not uncommon. It is also possible that, where the law at issue is mud, law enforcement officials will avoid writing an NoV in marginal cases. Instead, they will issue an NoV only when the violation of a mud rule is especially egregious, and law enforcement officials are reasonably confident that the NoV will be upheld when adjudicated. The predominance of crystal rules in enforcement is similarly undiminished when one examines the payment experience for fines. As shown in table 12.4, for a vendor considering paying a fine, whether the law violated was crystal or mud makes very little difference.

Thus, street vending informality in New York City is less about dealing with confusing mud rules and more about enforcement of crystal rules that are impossible to obey. "Impossible" seems especially apt when one takes into account enforcement levels. Since there are approximately 13,000 vendors in the city, and 127,000 citations were given over the course of five years, each vendor received on average two citations per year. Since many vendors only vend occasionally, this figure likely understates the average number of citations received by full-time vendors. In one recent year, vendors surveyed by New York's Street Vendor Project reported receiving an average of 6.7 citations (Street Vendor Project 2006: 14). That street vending laws in New York City are predominantly about impossible crystal rules rather than confusing mud rules is further supported by the statements of vendors themselves. After interviewing 100 vendors, a Columbia University urban planning graduate student project concluded: "[A]s complicated as the rules and restrictions seem to be, vendors understand them. Instead, it is not possible for vendors to follow every single rule and regulations and still run a successful business. Thus, the vending industry is forced to break the rules in order to exist" (Brown et al. 2011: 47).

The data for crystal and mud laws bear lessons for law writing and law enforcement. The *Papachristou* case warns against mud rules. Their ambiguity puts them at risk of becoming traps not only for the unwary, but also for those who know the law and believe they are in compliance with it. Thus, there might seem to be a danger that law enforcement officials will misuse their discretion and write more citations for violations of mud rules. But this expectation is not supported by the facts in New York City. Law enforcement officials on the street overwhelmingly issue NoVs for crystal rules. Moreover, NoVs issued for mud rules are accepted by the administrative courts of New York City at about the same rate as NoVs for crystal rules (table 12.3). Thus in spite of the *Papachristou* warning, the courts do not perceive the enforcement of mud rules as more capricious than that of crystal rules.

The fairness of mud rules might be undercut if fines issued for their violation were less likely to be paid than fines for violation of crystal rules. But the case for this is not strong. The probability that a payment will be made on a fine is only marginally higher for a violation of a crystal rule than for that of a mud rule (table 12.4). NoVs for mud rules enjoy nearly equal acceptance by courts and offenders alike. Mud rules and their enforcement appear fair, or at least not much less fair than crystal rules. Stated differently, if street vending rules are unfair, it is not because some of them are mud. Their unfairness is due to something else.

### Spatial and Nonspatial Laws

What about the subject of the rules enforced: Are they primarily spatial—rules about *where* vending may take place—or primarily nonspatial—rules about *how* vending may be conducted?

As shown in table 12.2, three-quarters of the NoVs were given for violation of the Administrative Code, and only a quarter were for violation of the Health Code. Given the correlation of these two categories with spatial and nonspatial rules, this suggests that spatial rules are more likely than nonspatial to be enforced through the issuance of an NoV. The predominance of spatial rules in the issuance of NoVs is somewhat

**Figure 12.3**
Md Akhand, vendor of fresh produce, New York, 2012. Photo credit: Street
Vendor Project.

**Table 12.4**
Predicted Probability of Payment

|         | Administrative | Health |
| ------- | -------------- | ------ |
| Crystal | 0.18           | 0.35   |
| Mud     | 0.17           | 0.34   |

undercut when one follows the citations to court. As table 12.3 indicates,
NoVs for Health (nonspatial) rules are less likely to be dismissed than
NoVs for Administrative (spatial) rules

The predominance of spatial rules in street vending law enforcement
is further undercut when NoVs are followed from the courthouse to the
treasury. As shown in table 12.4, the city is more likely to collect on a
fine for violations of nonspatial, predominantly Health, rules. Nonetheless, most citations, whether viewed when issued, when adjudicated in
court, or when paid, are for violations of spatial rules. The burden of
street vending informality in New York City is predominantly spatial.

There is evidence that the unfairness in the enforcement of spatial rules is recognized by the stakeholders. Although law enforcement officials issue three times as many NoVs for spatial (Administrative) as for nonspatial (Health) rules (table 12.2), an NoV for a nonspatial rule is more likely to survive a court hearing. As illustrated by table 12.3, the probability that an NoV for a spatial (Administrative) rule will be dismissed in court is 40 percent higher than that for an NoV for a nonspatial (Health) rule. Additionally, table 12.4 demonstrates that offenders are *twice as likely* to pay a fine issued for violation of a nonspatial rule. The probability that a fine imposed pursuant to an NoV for a spatial rule will be paid is less than 20 percent. Thus, both judges and street vendors are pushing back against enforcement of spatial rules.

Pushback could be explained in at least two ways. One is the identity of the agency writing the NoV. NoVs for nonspatial (Health) rules are generally issued by the city health department, while those for spatial (Administrative) rules are generally issued by the police (Basinski interview). Members of the health department may simply do a better job than the police of documenting violations and presenting them at hearing. This hypothesis might explain why NoVs for health rules are more likely to be upheld at a hearing, but not why fines for health violations are more likely to be paid.

Another possible explanation is that spatial rules are perceived as unfair. A number of studies have demonstrated the ability of vendors to develop informal rules to order themselves, including their use of space (Kettles 2006; Morales 2010). The practical effect of New York City's spatial rules in excluding vending from large parts of the sidewalk and the city as a whole is also well documented (Brown et al. 2011). Since they dismiss NoVs for spatial rules more often, hearing officers also seem to view spatial rules as unfair.

The perceived unfairness of spatial rules may also explain why vendors are less likely to pay fines for their violation. New York City vendors are required to renew their licenses periodically. The city will not renew a vendor's license if he or she has failed to pay a fine for a violation of the law deemed by the city to be "critical" (Basinski interview). It may be that the city, perhaps under pressure from vendors and their advocates, has designated as "critical" few spatial rules but lots of health rules. The city may have determined that violation of a spatial rule is less serious, and may deem it unfair to refuse to renew a vending license solely on the ground that a vendor has failed to pay a fine for violating a spatial rule. Testing these hypotheses, however, is beyond the scope of this chapter.

## Conclusion

These findings suggest some opportunities for policymakers. For those seeking to make informal activities formal, they should approach the law with care. Their time would be better spent on finding ways to make the law less burdensome, not on trying to make it more certain. Crystal rules do enjoy low costs of dispute resolution. But if they are so burdensome as to render compliance impossible, those savings risk being swamped by missed opportunities for trade. If crystal rules cannot be trusted to yield good results, perhaps more use should be made of mud rules. The data suggest that law enforcement officials and the courts, in New York City anyway, may be trusted not to abuse their discretion.

Policymakers seeking to make vending less informal should also consider how to bring about greater opportunities to vend. The citation data from New York City suggest a problem in the restrictiveness of spatial rules. The amount of space that has been set aside for legal vending is inadequate. The rules governing where vending carts may be placed, both with respect to other uses on or adjacent to the sidewalk and within the larger fabric of the city, should be examined. Relaxing these restrictions would likely help bring street vendors out of informality. It would also bring about greater respect for the law. The treatment of notices of violation for spatial rules by courts reviewing them, and vendors called upon to pay fines imposed pursuant to them, indicates that the spatial rules as they stand now are on shaky ground. This may be because many people, including hearing officers and city licensing authorities, view them as unfair.

## Acknowledgments

I would like to thank the following individuals: Sean Basinski of the Street Vendor Project and Professor Alfonso Morales of the University of Wisconsin, who shared data and resources to analyze it; and John Davis and Brittany Schwefel of the University of Wisconsin, who performed excellent statistical analyses. Any errors are mine.

## Note

1. While some NoVs are processed in a criminal court, the vast majority are adjudicated by a city administrative agency, the Environmental Control Board (ECB). The ECB has 13 members, consisting of the heads of seven city departments and six other persons appointed by the mayor and confirmed by the city

council (Charter of the City of New York §1049-a). The process of challenging any NoV starts with an administrative hearing. It is presided over by a hearing officer, an attorney who has been appointed to that position by the ECB (Basinski interview). Unlike criminal court proceedings, ECB hearings are nonjudicial affairs. The rules of evidence are more relaxed, and defendants are not provided with court-appointed attorneys to represent them.

# References

Brown, Rembert, Doneliza Joaquin, Jackie Keliiaa, Kyle Kirschling, Devin McDowall, Sara Ben Rosenberg, and Michael Snidal. 2011. "New York City Street Vendors." Street Vendor Studio final report, Spring 2011. Columbia University, Graduate School of Architecture, Planning and Preservation.

Charter of the City of New York. 2012. Available at http://72.0.151.116/nyc/charter/entered.htm.

De Soto, Hernando. 1989. *The Other Path: The Invisible Revolution in the Third World*. New York: Harper and Row.

Dickerson, Claire Moore. 2011. "Informal-Sector Entrepreneurs, Development and Formal Law: A Functional Understanding of Business Law." *American Journal of Comparative Law* 59 (1):179–226.

Epstein, Richard A. 1994. "The Moral and Practical Dilemmas of an Underground Economy." *Yale Law Journal* 103 (8):2157–2177.

Garnett, Nicole Stelle. 2009. *Ordering the City: Land Use, Policing and the Restoration of Urban America*. New Haven: Yale University Press.

Kettles, Gregg. 2006. "Formal versus Informal Allocation of Land in a Commons: The Case of the MacArthur Park Sidewalk Vendors." *Southern California Interdisciplinary Law Journal* 16:49–96.

Larson, Jane E. 2002. "Informality, Illegality, and the Law." *Yale Law and Policy Review* 20:137–182.

Light, Donald W. 2004. "From Migrant Enclaves to Mainstream: Reconceptualizing Informal Economic Behavior." *Theory and Society* 33 (6):705–737.

Loukaitou-Sideris, Anastasia, and Renia Ehrenfeucht. 2009. *Sidewalks: Conflict and Negotiation over Public Space*. Cambridge, MA: MIT Press.

Morales, Alfonso. 2010. "Planning and the Self-Organization of Marketplaces." *Journal of Planning Education and Research* 30 (2):182–197.

New York City Administrative Code. 2012. Available at http://72.0.151.116/nyc/AdCode/entered.htm.

*Papachristou v. City of Jacksonville*. 1972. 405 U.S. 156.

Priest, George. 1994. "The Ambiguous Moral Foundations of the Underground Economy." *Yale Law Journal* 103 (8):2259–2288.

Rose, Carol. 1988. "Crystals and Mud in Property Law." *Stanford Law Review* 40 (3):577–610.

Rules of the City of New York. 2012. Available at http://72.0.151.116/nyc/rcny/ entered.htm.

Sassen, Saskia. 2009. "Cities Today: A New Frontier for Major Developments." *Annals of the American Academy of Political and Social Science* 626 (1):53–71.

Street Vendor Project. 2006. *Peddling Uphill: A Report on the Conditions of Street Vendors in New York City.* New York: Urban Justice Center.

Venkatesh, Sudhir Alladi. 2006. *Off the Books: The Underground Economy of the Urban Poor.* Cambridge, MA: Harvard University Press.

**Interview**

Basinski, Sean, Director of Street Vendor Project at the Urban Justice Center, New York, September 23, 2012.

# 13

## "Keep Your Wheels On": Mediating Informality in the Food Cart Industry

Ginny Browne, Will Dominie, and Kate Mayerson

While the image of the street vendor in the United States has changed many times over the last century, the occupation remains a staple in the popular imagination of urban life. From the pickle peddlers of New York's Lower East Side to the *paleteros*[1] of Los Angeles's MacArthur Park, the endurance of street vending in major U.S. cities at the turn of the twenty-first century underscores its vital importance as a source of economic opportunity for low-income and immigrant communities. For people traditionally excluded from access to capital and decent-paying work in the mainstream economy, self-employment through informal vending has historically provided better income and greater independence than other available work (Morales 2000; Valenzuela 2006).

At various times municipal governments in the United States have both encouraged and outlawed informal vending in their jurisdictions. As early as the 1910s, city governments publicly attested to the importance of street vending as a source of jobs and income for city residents. In 1914, for example, a commission created to study pushcart vendors in Chicago issued a report to the Chicago City Council that declared street vending a solution to the problems of unemployment, poverty, and the rising cost of living in cities (Morales 2000). In order to formalize what they saw as a critical source of economic activity in Chicago, city administrators created a vending district around the Maxwell Street Market, which still exists today. As further evidence of its historic role in both labor markets and local economies, street vending was a category of employment listed in the U.S. census until 1940 (Morales and Kettles 2009).

Over the last 30 years, the transformation of the global economy has driven a resurgence of street vending both globally and nationally. In the United States, this rise in vending has been followed, more recently, by a renewed interest among a variety of sectors—from farmers to planners to immigrant rights advocates—in its potential community and economic development benefits. The American Planning Association has devoted an issue of the *Planning Advisory Service* to the role street vending can play in revitalizing urban neighborhoods, while the Ford Foundation is funding an ongoing project to promote public markets as key economic development tools for low-income and immigrant communities (Ball 2002; Project for Public Spaces and Partners for Livable Communities 2006). At the federal level, the Office of Community Services at the U.S. Department of Health and Human Services Administration for Children and Families has increased funding for the creation and expansion of public markets in low-income neighborhoods through their Community Economic Development Program (Office of Community Services 2012).

Despite this renewed interest, most large city governments in the United States have been less supportive, often citing concerns over public health and unfair competition for brick and mortar businesses. Some, like Los Angeles, have banned certain types of vending entirely, relying on policing as a management strategy. Others, such as New York, have created complex regulatory environments, indecipherable to some vendors and nearly impossible to follow (Kettles, this volume). These attempts to manage vending have been largely unsuccessful, imposing high costs on those incorporated into formal structures and criminalizing those who are not.

By contrast, Portland, Oregon, has adopted a tolerant and supportive attitude toward vending. Since the beginning of the Great Recession in 2008, the city has seen the arrival of hundreds of food vending carts, which now serve every possible type of food and enjoy wide popularity. Proponents of the carts argue that they have generated new economic and pedestrian activity in the city's downtown, and have infused the built environment with newly vibrant and colorful street facades. Yet, both literally and figuratively, the carts exist in the city's interstitial spaces. Often clustered on temporarily vacant private land, Portland's food carts are only marginally regulated by the city and county. Here the boundaries of formality have been continually tested and renegotiated as Portland adapts to the growth of the food cart industry.

This chapter presents a case study of the recent emergence of food vending carts in Portland, focusing on the role of city planners in mediating informality. We draw lessons for planning practice that we hope will be useful to others charged with responding to informal activities. Our research relied on a series of interviews conducted from May 2011 to July 2012. We spoke with many of those whose work has shaped the food cart industry in Portland, including city planners, staff at Multnomah County Environmental Health Services and the Community Capacitation Center, food cart landlords and promoters, business associations, and community-based organizations. We also reviewed existing and historic planning codes, policies, and permitting processes, and conducted a scan of relevant news sources.

We contend that Portland's vending industry is an important source of economic opportunity, particularly for immigrants and those without ready access to capital or well-paying jobs. Although there are many reasons for this success, we argue that it is at least partly due to the city's unique regulatory approach. While the planning profession has traditionally focused on plans, codes, laws, and maps, we believe planners in Portland have been particularly successful in managing vending because they have not relied exclusively on these regulatory methods. Instead, they have utilized other forms of regulation such as administrative actions and enforcement, public opinion, private actors, and market forces. In doing so, they have helped to expand vending's regulatory container—maximizing both vendors' opportunities and public priorities such as health and safety. Portland's innovative approach provides a model for planners seeking to address informal activities. It also yields lessons for theory, supporting efforts to understand the fluidity of informality and the ways in which states and societies shape its bounds.

## Informality in Theory: From Duality to Exception

While street vending is one of the paradigmatic examples of informality, Portland's food carts defy definition as clearly formal or informal. This section places Portland's food carts in a broader discussion of informality, illustrating their position within a quasi-formal regulatory container bounded by legal, administrative, and extralegal forces.

Since the early 1970s, informality has been largely understood by contrast to its inverse. Early studies, such as those of Hart (1973) and the International Labour Organization (1972), sought to differentiate regulated, highly capitalized wage labor from the informal, unregulated income-generating activities of those without access to proletarian work (Hart 1973). Many subsequent studies have sought to clarify the borders of informality, exploring the political, economic, and social criteria by which it may be distinguished from formality (summarized in Gerxhani 2004).

However, as early as 1978 scholars challenged the "clumsiness" of this duality (Bromley 1978), and examined the interdependence of, and linkages between, formal and informal activities (AlSayyad 2004). As studies of informality have multiplied, other scholars have also critiqued the traditionally narrow focus on purely legal regulation, arguing that all activities are socially produced and regulated in some manner (Morales 2000). While regulation may be formalized in law, it also functions through discretionary administrative actions and enforcement and through "informal institutions" like social norms and public opinion (North 1990).

Borrowing from Giorgio Agamben's concept of "states of exception," or gaps within the rule of law created by state power, Roy (2005: 149) takes the insight of extralegal regulation one step further. She contends that "the planning and legal apparatus of the state has the power to determine when to enact this suspension [of order], to determine what is informal and what is not, and to determine which forms of informality will thrive and which will disappear." Although Agamben (1998) finds these exceptions in the practices of war, siege, and security—in what Yiftachel (2009) terms the "gray spaces" of colonialism, the Guantánamos and occupied territories of the world—Roy expands the idea to encompass exception more broadly. Like AlSayyad and several contributors to their jointly edited book, she argues that states are increasingly cultivating exception and informal practices to backfill the intensifying material insecurity created by the neoliberal restructuring (Roy 2005; Roy and AlSayyad 2004).

The "states of exception" formulation is useful because it illustrates that while informality may transgress or skirt legal regulation, it nonetheless operates on a terrain that is actively managed by the state and other actors. This is clearly shown in the case of Portland's vendors. They are working in many ways that can be characterized as informal, within the interstices of zoning, health and safety, and motor vehicle codes. At the same time, street vending takes place within bounds constructed and managed by legal regulation and administrative actions, as well as informal norms and institutions. While some of these forces are beyond the control of the state, many are within its purview. As we shall see, planners in Portland have effectively engaged with these forces to shape the opportunities available to vendors. In the next section, we discuss the current and historical context of Portland's food

**Figure 13.1**
A cluster or "pod" of carts in downtown Portland. Photo credit: Ben Palmquist.

carts, then turn to the process by which their regulatory container has been constructed.

## Food Carts: A New Street Vending Paradigm in Portland

In the last five years, Portland has seen the birth and astronomic growth of a new industry: food carts. These carts are a phenomenon unique to Portland. They are small (under 16 feet long), serve countless varieties of food, and cluster like tiny buildings on parking lots and vacant land throughout the city, as illustrated in figure 13.1. While in 2007 there were only 35 registered carts in Portland's Multnomah County (Cutno, Adriaenssens, and Douangchia 2010), Multnomah County Mobile Food Unit staff now report that the number has grown to nearly 700. Indeed, the food cart industry has become a defining element in Portland's urban fabric and culture.

Although Portland's vendors bear some similarity to vendors in other cities, they are unique in many ways. While other cities are known for sidewalk pushcarts (like New York) and food trucks (like Los Angeles), the vast majority of street vendors in Portland operate out of food carts located on private, rather than public, property. These food carts are stationary, semipermanent trailers. Yet because they are small, have wheels, and can theoretically be moved, they are considered motor vehicles in city code and therefore operate outside the typical regulations facing other stationary, brick-and-mortar businesses in Portland.

Due in large part to these loopholes, food carts dominate vending in Portland. There are also a small number of pushcart vendors licensed to operate on public property, but these represent less than 5 percent of the city's vendors and are subject to far more detailed and restrictive regulations than are carts on private land (Flores interview). Pushcart vendors must secure city approval for cart design, siting, hours of operation, graphics, and signage. Conversely, Portland also has a number of vendors that operate completely unregulated, selling goods from unlicensed vessels such as coolers and trucks. While no concrete estimates of these informal operators were available at the time of our study, in comparison with food carts they are few, small-scale, and often overlooked—at times, intentionally—by city government (Robinson interview).

The majority of Portland's food carts on private property are grouped in what are known as "pods," or clusters of carts on a single piece of land. Many pods are on private lots that are temporarily vacant and await development (Urban Vitality Group 2008). These pods appear to offer both the advantage of shared facilities—such as seating, bathrooms, and waste disposal—and a shared customer base that makes them vibrant and viable destinations (Urban Vitality Group 2008). As these pods overwhelmingly serve pedestrians, they both benefit from and fuel pedestrian activity in their surrounding areas (Seltzer interview; Urban Vitality Group 2008: 7). Figures 13.2 and 13.3 illustrate how pods turned a relatively empty space in downtown Portland into a bustling activity center along the edge of a parking lot. While planners typically create active, pedestrian-oriented street fronts using tools like maximum setbacks, height and bulk manipulation, and design guidelines, the food carts have accomplished the same result with an unplanned "tactile urbanism" (Kamel, this volume).

Food cart vending in Portland has also proven to be a successful economic development tool, providing jobs and entrepreneurial opportunities to those with limited resources. While exact data are difficult to obtain, planners estimate that each cart produces between one and four jobs (Flores 2010). Assuming those job generation rates, today's

**Figure 13.2**
An empty lot in downtown Portland on SW 4th Avenue, between Hall Street and
College Street, in July 2005. Source: Google Earth™.

669 carts currently provide somewhere from 669 to 2,700 jobs. Furthermore, food carts appear to produce reasonably sustainable employment and financial independence for vendors. Estimates suggest that
cart owners staffing their carts alone can net $20,000–40,000 a year,
though this figure declines significantly if a cart owner hires employees
(Flores 2010; Urban Vitality Group 2008: 35). While startup costs
are often beyond the reach of those with the fewest resources, carts
have a relatively low capital cost ($6,000 to $30,000), making them
significantly easier to finance and less risky than a brick-and-mortar
restaurant.

## The Rise of the Food Cart
It is our contention that the dramatic proliferation of food carts on
private property was made possible by three factors: a history of support

**Figure 13.3**
The same lot occupied by pods in August 2010. Source: Google Earth™.

and a tolerant attitude from the city, gaps in formal regulation, and innovation by private actors. This section details the ways in which these factors have converged to produce Portland's food cart boom.

Portland has a long history of tolerance toward vending, as table 13.1 illustrates. As early as 1888, a new city ordinance established a licensing process for vendors of "fruit, candy, cakes, nuts, or other sweet meats from stands or wagons, on any of the streets of the City of Portland" (Auditor, City of Portland 2012). For almost a century the code remained unchanged. In the mid-1970s the city added Chapter 17.26 to the city code, a modernized ordinance that allowed for sidewalk vending in commercial zones (Auditor, City of Portland 2012). Although the city code does not address vending on private property, the zoning code allows it in commercial zones. While gaps remain in the available history of Portland's zoning code, it appears that vending in commercial zones has always been a legal land use.

Table 13.1
Street Vending Legislation in Portland

| Year | Code | Milestone |
| --- | --- | --- |
| 1888 | 5619 | Original ordinance to provide for licensing vendors of "fruit, candy, cakes, nuts or other sweet meats from stands or wagons, on any of the streets of the City of Portland." |
| 1976 | City Code Chapter 17.26 | Modernized regulation to allow vendors of food products and fresh cut flowers to conduct business on sidewalks within commercial zones subject to the issuance of a permit, the payment of a fee, and the meeting of certain conditions. (Presumably, private-property vending carts legalized as well.) |
| 1993 | Council Resolutions 35225 | Task force developed to recommend revised procedures for street vending. |
| 2003 | Administrative Rule TRN-10.05 | Updated, streamlined sidewalk vending regulations compiled in a single packet available through the Bureau of Transportation. |
| 2008 | | City Center Parking begins leasing parking spaces, becoming the first large-scale private property owner providing space for vending carts. |
| 2011 | | Over 600 vending carts operate in Portland. |

Source: All data collected via City of Portland Auditor's Office EFILES website: http://efiles.portlandoregon.gov/.

In recent years, this tolerant regulatory environment has turned to active support for vending. As Mayor Sam Adams explained in an interview:

[We set] the bar of entry into the street food industry low. The regulations in other cities make it difficult for street food vendors to start. We try to stay the heck out of the way. Food safety is the most important to us, but otherwise we try to keep start-up costs low for the vendor and the licensing process under ten days. We want to do everything we can to help grow and foster our street food scene. As you know, we're very focused on buying local and being local. So while we don't subsidize these start-ups, we try to keep it free of red tape while keeping it safe. (Delaney 2010)

Having political champions on their side has softened enforcement. The city's history of tolerance, and its active support for the carts, created a political atmosphere in which the industry could grow.

Gaps in formal regulation afford vendors a level of flexibility that eases operational burdens. As outlined earlier, a gap in city code designates food carts as motor vehicles, which gives vendors the ability to operate stationary carts without being subject to the building code. A gap in the tax code also benefits smaller vendors: while vendors are required to obtain a business license within sixty days of starting operation, the city code does not require operators to pay business taxes unless gross receipts total more than $50,000 per year, further reducing operating costs for vendors, and tempering the common tax evasion argument against street vendors. While all vendors are subject to formal business regulations, insurance requirements, and approval and inspection from the Multnomah County Health Department, they nonetheless operate within multiple regulatory gaps that allow them to be considered motor vehicles—eliminating many of the barriers to entry faced by brick-and-mortar restaurants.

While public-sector support was essential, and gaps in regulations fostered the boom, it was actually private actors who enabled and led the carts' growth. The food cart boom began in 2008 when City Center Parking, owned by the Goodman family, the city's largest private landowner, started leasing vending spaces in their surface parking lots in downtown Portland. Prior to the company's decision to lease parking spaces, there were only a few vendors on private property in the city. A downtown location in the Goodman lots guaranteed vendors a steady customer base, a base that was multiplied because the carts were now grouped together. For the Goodmans, vending made obvious economic sense. Food carts typically pay somewhere between $500 and $600 each month in rent (Flores 2010), far exceeding the market rate for monthly parking spaces, even downtown, where rates vary between $150 and just over $200 per month.

As the phenomenon grew, other clusters, or pods, formed across the city. Sometimes they occupied parking lots, but they have increasingly formed on vacant land awaiting development. Whether on parking lots or vacant land, the economics of food carts have created strong incentives to convert temporarily vacant land, or land reserved for cars, to serve new, pedestrian-oriented land uses—in this case, vending.

Notwithstanding the myriad economic benefits of Portland's bustling new industry, it is important to note that food carts emerged in Portland in the middle of a recession. When the economy rebounds, and as empty storefronts develop into new businesses, demand for parking and land for development will increase. Moreover, leases for vending cart spaces are typically for one year, much shorter than the five- to ten-year leases common for brick-and-mortar restaurants. Thus food carts face the threat of displacement as other land uses become more profitable.

## Contested Boundaries

Over time, the regulatory container in which vendors operate has been renegotiated as various actors have sought to expand or limit its bounds. This section explores this process, paying particular attention to the role of planners in managing vending's regulatory environment.

As already noted, activities like vending may be regulated by formal laws and codes but also by administrative actions, enforcement, and the informal institutions of public opinion and social norms. Most cities have traditionally relied on laws and their enforcement to regulate vending. In some ways Portland has done the same. Planners have, for instance, made multiple revisions to existing codes regulating vending. Pushcarts on private, and especially public, property must comply with some formal regulation. For both types of carts, the Multnomah County Health Department has been quite active in regulating health and safety. Just as brick-and-mortar restaurants receive annual inspections, so do food carts, and fire, water, and electric regulations remain rigid. However, the general trend has been toward streamlining and simplifying city codes rather than adding additional requirements (Auditor, City of Portland 2012).

In keeping with its permissive rather than restrictive approach to vending, the city has not relied on policing or enforcement to regulate informal vending. Unlike New York for instance, which issues tens of thousands of citations a year, or Los Angeles, whose Department of Building and Safety operates the Pro-Active Code Enforcement task force explicitly charged with citing illegal vendors, Portland issues very few citations (Duncan interview). Rather, county officials try to create pathways toward formality and encourage vendors to become licensed.

While Portland has tended not to rely on enforcement against unregulated vendors, as the quasi-formal food cart industry has grown some city leaders have increasingly sought ways to regulate the carts through enforcement. Technically, food carts remain carts only insofar as they are self-contained structures. City code requires that any extra amenities on the exterior of the cart must attach to the vehicle itself, not the ground beneath it. However, vendors often place temporary street furniture, such as plastic tables and chairs (as illustrated in figure 13.4) in the public right-of-way, sometimes constructing elaborate patios under large awnings. Legally, these amenities require building or sidewalk café

**Figure 13.4**
Unlicensed seating on the public right-of-way. Photo credit: Eric Fredericks.

permits, which depend on insurance, site drawings, and other kinds of formal documentation. In the past several years, there have been a few high-profile confrontations with city administrators as vendors test the limits of these regulations.

As violations have become more conspicuous, City Commissioner Randy Leonard, who oversees departments issuing water, fire, and electrical permits, has cracked down on carts.[2] In 2010, his departments cited vendors for structural and electrical violations and sought to shut down the carts entirely. Due to media and public outcry, as well as a lack of personnel to regulate and enforce, Leonard relented, at least for the time being. Still, the conflicts surrounding illegal structures, trash pickup, and sidewalk seating have not disappeared. Occasional crackdowns serve as a reminder that there are boundaries to the Portland vending system, and when vendors push them, the city may choose to push back.

While private landowners were central to creating the regulatory container within which food carts flourished, the bounds of that container were challenged fervently by other private-sector forces. The food carts' primary opponent, the Portland Business Alliance (PBA), which represents restaurant owners, has attempted to sway public opinion against vending. They claim that vending carts represent a lack of commitment to the business cycle by the owners (with gaps in regulation giving vendors an ability to bypass building code and business taxes), and that their recession-era success has been detrimental to brick-and-mortar businesses (Frisch interview). They have called the carts "jalopies" that make downtown Portland "look like a shantytown" and cause blight rather than vibrancy. Blaming food carts for clogging sidewalks and parking lots, the PBA points to land use regulation to support their argument that "parking lots are zoned for parking, not for businesses" (Frisch interview). However, the zoning code does allow for food carts in parking lots. Despite the PBA's desire to tighten the boundaries of regulation, food carts have continued to expand.

Planners have responded to this situation in unique ways. While in some cases they have turned to the traditional tools of legal regulation and enforcement, they have mostly perceived their role far more broadly. As Benjamin Duncan, program development specialist at Multnomah County, summarizes: "My sense is that our work can . . . reflect a model for how government can best engage and navigate the tricky world of regulation, promotion of micro-enterprise, and communication and relationship building with communities that have barriers or trust issues with regulatory agencies" (Duncan interview).

This approach is exemplified by Alma Flores, economic development planner at the City of Portland until October 2010, who was particularly instrumental in supporting the vending industry and pushing planners beyond their traditional roles. When complaints about food carts reached the Bureau of Planning or the Bureau of Development Services, Flores reached out to vendors on her own time to "educate, not regulate" (Flores interview). For example, she created a PowerPoint presentation to share with vendors called "Keep Your Wheels On," which outlined the limits on cart vending created by existing regulation and strategies to avoid violations.

In addition to education, planners have also conducted substantial outreach—particularly to those often excluded from formal opportunities. Flores, for instance, is on the board of directors of the Hacienda Community Development Corporation, where she worked on the Micro-mercantes program, encouraging the development of female-owned tamale operations among the vending cart businesses (Flores interview). The county's Community Capacitation Center, in partnership with the Health Department, has also conducted a series of focus groups for tamale vendors, designed to educate informal vendors about food safety and to solicit input on microenterprise. While staff reported significant challenges in establishing trust, it is nonetheless a far cry from the punitive approaches taken by many other cities.

By providing outreach and education to vendors and engaging critically with their needs as well as public health and safety concerns, Portland's planners have been able to maximize the benefits of vending while minimizing its potential dangers. To be sure, the Portland approach is a new one, and experiments in planning, however promising, often involve multiple iterations of success and failure before they produce a reliable, replicable result. Still, planners and policymakers can draw lessons from the Portland case study, which we explore further in the following section.

### Lessons Learned

Our examination of the rise of Portland's food carts holds important implications for planning practice and theory. In Portland, the regulatory regime that has allowed vending to thrive is shaped by formal regulation, discretionary enforcement, public opinion, and societal norms. The borders of this regime are continually renegotiated by a range of political and economic forces. Planners have played a key role in this process, working to expand vending's regulatory container while also ensuring the health and safety of Portland residents. An overarching lesson is that innovative and successful planning mediations of informality are possible, and perhaps necessary, in the spaces between and outside traditional regulation.

By all accounts, planners' engagement of nontraditional tools and strategies has been a key to Portland's successful mediation of informal vending. Although there might have been pressure to increase regulations or even prohibit food cart vending when it started, planners and policymakers found a different path. Planners became at once mediators, educators, and outreach workers, promoting shared goals of economic development and opportunity in Portland. The relative consensus around these goals inside and outside city government was also critical in allowing planners to reimagine their role in responding to informality. In the absence of such a consensus, planners' interventions might well have been unsuccessful. While some carts push the boundaries of formal regulation, traditional methods of responding to code violations have become unpopular in a city that now prides itself on street vending.

The Portland story also has implications for the relationship between the public and private sectors in pursuing social purposes. We have highlighted the importance of private-sector actors, especially the Goodman family, in creating the conditions in which vending could expand and flourish. At the same time, we must underscore the contingency of private-sector contributions in the broader economic context that shapes urban markets today. While innovations in the private sector can and do help solve planning problems, as demonstrated in the Portland case study, we maintain that it is *never* the role of market forces alone to determine whether and how informal activity happens. Rather, as is also demonstrated in the Portland study, planners must play a central and active role in negotiating a successful regulatory regime amid multiple interests and forces. Planners interested in mediating informality must be aware of, and willing to engage with, the shifting nature of public opinion, administrative activity, and the market. In particular, they should reflect on the ways in which state power can be used to make new resources available, provide protection against predatory forces, or bring together those with common interests to advocate collectively.

The respective roles of the public and private sectors in the success of Portland food carts raises additional questions for planning practice, which we discuss next.

### Ongoing Questions

Despite the success to date of Portland's approach to food carts, the industry remains quite precarious, and a number of questions remain about its effectiveness in meeting the material needs of vendors, especially low-income people and immigrants. While a relative lack of legal regulation has helped food carts to flourish, the consequent importance of other modes of regulation may make the industry more susceptible to changes in the market, enforcement, or public opinion.

Whereas vending in most U.S. cities occurs in public or semipublic spaces—sidewalks, streets, plazas, and transit stations—Portland's food carts have thrived on private land. In particular, they temporarily occupy spaces intended for other uses such as parking and real estate development. These locations allow vendors to operate with fewer regulations than their peers on public land. However, they also expose vendors to the precariousness of the market. As the economy rebounds, it is likely that both vacant lots and parking spaces will command higher values, potentially displacing food cart pods. Portland's vendors have benefited also from a supportive public and a tolerant approach to enforcement. However, these soft forms of regulation, not codified in law, are subject to change with the whims of the public and administrators, and could easily shift to constrain rather than support food carts.

This case also poses questions about who wins and who loses when the bounds of informality shift. As regulatory borders move, they restructure the rules governing participation. For example, the extent to which vendors must interface with public agencies in order to operate has direct consequences for the participation of immigrant vendors, especially those without documentation. Other consequences take place as the economic and social contexts of vending change. While financial necessity led many low-income vendors to open food carts a few years ago, today the popularity of the carts and the city's relative tolerance is attracting a new—often younger and wealthier—demographic to the industry, making it harder for less-capitalized vendors to compete. Some advocates feel that, due to their success, food carts may be nearing a point of market saturation, as land for carts in populated areas has become scarce and variety in new foods is reaching a limit. On both ends of the spectrum are parties that could be squeezed out by these well-capitalized vendors operating low-cost food carts: low-income vendors and brick-and-mortar restaurant owners. Planners need to be aware of these dynamics as they mediate informality, paying careful attention to those who may lose out.

As the political terrain surrounding informality shifts in Portland, there are indications that the city's embrace of food carts is opening doors for other, even less formal street vendors. As we write, the state of Oregon has just approved the creation of a new licensing category for pushcart vendors (Teske interview). In the spring of 2012, Multnomah County Health Department staff, including many of those who have championed the rise of food carts, spearheaded an effort to formalize vendors who sell homemade food, often tamales, from coolers. These immigrant vendors are among the most precarious in the city and lack the resources needed to operate a food cart. In partnership with two community-based organizations, the Health Department is designing new bicycle-drawn coolers that comply with health code and will be implementing a new outreach and training program to help these vendors become licensed.

Although still in its inception, we believe this program, in the context of the Portland story more broadly, holds enormous potential as a model for larger cities whose planning agencies have been either unwilling or unable to carve out a safe and healthy regulatory space for street vending. At a time when states have renounced full employment and social safety nets, pursuing instead economic policies that actively produce inequity, poverty and precariousness, informal activities like vending serve as essential livelihood for millions worldwide. While we do not see informality as a substitute for a just and inclusive political economic system, we believe interventions such as those taking place in Portland can and do fuel change.

## Notes

1. *Paleteros* are vendors who sell *paletas*, or ice pops, out of pushcarts.

2. Portland has a commission form of government: the mayor, four commissioners, and the auditor comprise the city's six elected officials. The mayor and the commissioners make up the City Council (Auditor, City of Portland 2012).

## References

Agamben, Giorgio. 1998. *Homo Sacer: Sovereign Power and Bare Life*. Palo Alto: Stanford University Press.

AlSayyad, Nezar. 2004. "Urban Informality as a 'New' Way of Life." In Roy and AlSayyad 2004: 7–32.

Auditor, City of Portland. 2012. "City Charter, City Code and Portland Policy Documents." http://www.portlandonline.com/auditor/index.cfm?c=26653 (retrieved August 24, 2012).

Ball, Jennifer. 2002. "Street Vending: A Survey of Ideas and Lessons for Planners." Planning Advisory Service Report No. 509. American Planning Association, Chicago.

Bromley, Ray. 1978. "Introduction: The Urban Informal Sector: Why Is It Worth Discussing?" *World Development* 6 (9/10):1034–1035.

Cutno, Mike, Zachary Adriaenssens, and Vanhvilai Douangchia. 2010. "Atlanta Street Food Feasibility Study." School of City and Regional Planning, Georgia Institute of Technology.

Delaney, Daniel. 2010. "The Mayor of Mobile Eats." *VendrTV Blog*, May 25. http://vendr.tv/blog/cartivores/mayor-sam-adams.

Flores, Alma. 2010. "Portland Food Carts." Presentation at La Cocina Street Food Conference, San Francisco, August 22–23.

Gerxhani, Klarita. 2004. "The Informal Sector in Developed and Less Developed Countries: A Literature Survey." *Public Choice* 120:267–300.

Hart, Keith. 1973. "Informal Income Opportunities and Urban Employment in Ghana." *Journal of Modern African Studies* 11 (1):61–89.

International Labour Organization. 1972. *Employment, Income and Equality: A Strategy for Increasing Productive Employment in Kenya*. Geneva: International Labour Organization.

Morales, Alfonso. 2000. "Peddling Policy: Street Vending in Historical and Contemporary Context." *International Journal of Sociology and Social Policy* 20 (3/4):76–98.

Morales, Alfonso, and Gregg Kettles. 2009. "Healthy Food Outside: Farmer's Markets, Taco Trucks, and Sidewalk Fruit Vendors." *Journal of Contemporary Health Law and Policy* 26:120–148.

North, Douglass. 1990. *Institutions, Institutional Change, and Economic Performance.* New York: Cambridge University Press.

Office of Community Services. 2012. Website. http://www.acf.hhs.gov/programs/ocs/ (retrieved August 24, 2012).

Project for Public Spaces and Partners for Livable Communities. 2003. *Public Markets as a Vehicle for Social Integration and Upward Mobility: Phase I Report: An Overview of Existing Programs and Assessment of Opportunities.* Washington, DC: Project for Public Spaces. http://www.pps.org/pdf/Ford_Report.pdf.

Roy, Ananya. 2005. "Urban Informality: Toward an Epistemology of Planning." *Journal of the American Planning Association* 71 (2):147–158.

Roy, Ananya, and Nezar AlSayyad, eds. 2004. *Urban Informality: Transnational Perspectives from the Middle East, Latin America, and South Asia.* Oxford: Lexington Books.

Urban Vitality Group. 2008. *Food Cartology Report.* Portland: Portland State University.

Valenzuela, Abel, Jr. 2006. "Economic Development in Latino Communities: Incorporating Marginal and Immigrant Workers." In Paul Ong and Anastasia Loukaitou-Sideris, eds., *Jobs and Economic Development in Minority Communities,* 141–158. Philadelphia: Temple University Press.

Yiftachel, Oren. 2009. "Theoretical Notes on 'Gray Cities': The Coming of Urban Apartheid?" *Planning Theory* 8 (1):87–99.

## Interviews

Duncan, Ben, Multnomah County Health Department, January 2012.

Flores, Alma, City of Portland, May 2011.

Frisch, Lisa, Portland Business Alliance, May 2011.

Robinson, Jamaica, Multnomah County Community Capacitation Center, February 2012.

Seltzer, Ethan, Portland State University, May 2011.

Teske, Nathan, Hacienda Community Development Corporation, July 2012.

# 14

# Regulating Day Labor: Worker Centers and Organizing in the Informal Economy

Abel Valenzuela Jr.

Throughout the United States and elsewhere, men by the thousands and their employers gather daily, usually in public spaces during the early morning, to negotiate an exchange of cash wages for a job. If you were to drive or walk by one of these hiring sites, you would notice small groups of mostly men, dressed in scruffy, unkempt attire well suited for construction work or the other manual, difficult and dirty work that is often undertaken by day laborers. You might ask whether this economic exchange is legal, whether the financial transaction is in cash, and what if any regulations or laws exist to monitor or curb this economic exchange. You might also wonder whether the workers and employers pay taxes, whether they contribute to worker compensation insurance, whether they abide by occupational safety and health laws, what the legal status of the workers is, whether abuses occur, and why employers would seek out workers through this market.

This chapter examines day labor to shed light on informality in the United States, paying particular attention to some of the key character-istics that define informality and work. I focus on worker centers, a key intermediary in the day labor market, as an institutional response to protect workers in this informal market. In addition, I argue that a robust and burgeoning civil society infrastructure for migrants, day labor orga-nizing strategies, and a broader migrant effort at reclaiming the city help buffer some deleterious impacts of day labor work. These factors are moving day labor toward a more formal market with increased protec-tions, labor standards, and other regulations that make it less vulnerable and exploitative.

## Informality at Work: Day Labor

Scholars of work and informality broadly agree that informal prac-tices are an integral component of modern capitalism, a universal and irreversible feature of globalized economies (Castells and Portes 1989; Kruijt and Koonings 2009; Sassen 2001; Tabak 2000). A key characteristic of informality is the downgrading of workers, who receive fewer or no benefits and lower wages while facing higher rates of occupational hazards and worse conditions than those prevailing in the formal economy. Saskia Sassen (2001: 294) describes informality as "the production and sale of goods and services that are licit but produced and/or sold outside the regulatory apparatus covering zoning, taxes, health and safety, minimum wage laws, and other standards." She notes that the state plays a defining role in realigning employment relations, and in the United States this has led to a significant growth of informal work. For example, the dismantling of manufacturing-based unions and construction trades has played a key role in the rise of the service sector and informality.

Manuel Castells and Alejandro Portes (1989) emphasize the local nature of informal work, offering as examples the informal work activities that take place in very small establishments (VSEs). VSEs such as landscaping or small construction firms have low visibility and use casual hiring practices, often involving day labor or domestic work. These local informal work activities typically take place in communities with large concentrations of immigrants, who provide the labor, but also involve other residents, employers, and community stakeholders. Castells and Portes also note the rise and role of intermediaries as a result of informal work in formal industries such as construction or moving. These intermediaries range from street-level brokers to worker center hiring halls to temporary staffing and job placement agencies. The local nature of informal work and the importance of intermediaries are apparent in day labor work.

In previous research, I have detailed the characteristics of day labor work (Valenzuela 2003). Two types of day labor industries exist: informal and formal. Informal day labor is characterized by men who solicit temporary daily employment by searching in the "open air," i.e., in curbside or visible markets such as empty lots, street corners, parking areas, or in front of home improvement establishments. Soliciting work in this manner is a visible part of the urban landscape in the United States (Valenzuela 1999; Valenzuela and Melendez 2002; Valenzuela et al. 2006) and globally, including in Mexico (Vanackere 1988), South America (Townsend 1997), Japan (Fowler 1996; Giamo 1994; Gill 1994; Gill 2001; Marr 1997; Marr et al. 2000), and South Africa (Blaauw and Krugell 2012; Harmse, Blaauw, and Schenck 2009; Schenck and Blaauw

**Figure 14.1**
Day laborers soliciting work. Photo credit: Abel Valenzuela.

2011). In contrast, formal day labor is provided by temporary staffing agencies or "hiring halls" visible in storefront establishments that place on-call workers in job assignments at or slightly above the minimum wage. Temporary staffing agencies are less visible than informal sites, and are primarily located in neighborhoods with large concentrations of low-skilled, unemployed, minority and immigrant residents (Peck and Theodore 2001).

A key characteristic of day labor is its spatial ubiquity. The search for day labor work is highly visible, encompassing large and small hiring sites spread across urban and suburban areas. Hiring sites vary. They can be in front of stores, along a park's periphery, where vehicles and construction trucks pass, at gas stations, church parking lots, community centers, empty lots, and along elevated rail and metro lines in gritty urban neighborhoods. The spatial dimensions of the day labor market are fluid. New workers enter this market daily, while others leave it. Hiring sites diminish, grow in size, or disappear, while new ones emerge in different neighborhoods.

The men who search for work this way often refer to themselves as *jornaleros* (Valenzuela 1999) or *esquineros* (Malpica 1996), Spanish words derived from "work" and "corner" respectively. In New York and other cities in the Northeast, the location of men gathering to informally

**Figure 14.2**
Day laborers seeking work. Photo credit: Abel Valenzuela.

search for work is often called a "shape-up" (Leonard and O'Shea 1997), in reference to the stevedores that once lined up daily at docks and ports in hope of getting hired for the day. In today's vernacular, men "shaping up" are undertaking day labor or *jornalero* work (Valenzuela and Melendez 2002).

Most day laborers are male, foreign-born (mostly from Mexico and Central America), recently arrived (less than three years), and undocumented. They have low levels of education and a poor command of English. This suggests that day laborers are likely to have difficulty communicating with employers and understanding the legal, cultural, social, and economic nuances of the United States. The National Day Labor Survey[1] finds that the day labor workforce in the United States is predominantly immigrant and Latino; fewer than one in ten are born in the United States, while three-quarters are undocumented (Valenzuela et al. 2006). This precarious undocumented status helps explain the day laborers' participation in this and other exploitative and informal labor market activities. It also highlights the need for comprehensive immigration reform.

Earnings for day labor are poor. The median hourly wage of day labor assignments is $10. However, this figure masks wages at the low and high ends of the wage distribution. At the low end, slightly more than 6 percent of assignments pay between the minimum wage and $7 an hour, and 22 percent of assignments pay between $7 and $9.99 an hour. At the upper end of the wage distribution, 46 percent of day labor jobs pay between $10 and $11.99 an hour, while one-quarter of the jobs pay more than $12. Although the majority of assignments pay $10 per hour or more, the monthly and yearly earnings of most day laborers place them among the working poor (Valenzuela et al. 2006). Because wages are paid in cash and rarely taxed, these figures mask a wage premium for workers and significant tax and worker compensation savings for employers.

Jobs are labor-intensive and dangerous. Because most day labor jobs are concentrated in the construction industry, various and frequent hazards exist. The National Day Labor Survey found that one in five day laborers had suffered a work-related injury, and more than half of those injured did not receive medical care (Valenzuela et al. 2006). Day laborers regularly suffered employer abuse and violence. Almost half of those surveyed had experienced wage theft (nonpayment or underpayment), while 44 percent were denied food, water, or breaks while on the job (Valenzuela et al. 2006).

The search for day labor work takes place outside of the formal economy and shares some of the most harmful characteristics of informality. However, a confluence of three key developments—emergent worker centers, migrant civil society, and a burgeoning right-to-the-city movement—are helping to create a more humane and less exploitative day labor market. Anchoring these developments is the worker center movement, a constellation of place-based (usually local or citywide) centers or organizations that advocate on behalf of workers in occupational sectors that are difficult to organize, such as domestic workers, taxi drivers, day laborers, and restaurant workers (Fine 2006). Day labor worker centers offer an example of one type of organizing strategy outside the traditional labor union model, one that is coupled with a burgeoning civil society responding to sociocultural and economic concerns affecting immigrant neighborhoods.

## Regulating Informality: Day Labor Worker Centers

Worker centers serve as an important first defense against unscrupulous employers and poor working conditions, and they provide a space where day laborers can congregate and employers can find them (Valenzuela et al. 2006). These spaces provide a safe, hassle-free, supportive, and

**Figure 14.3**
A day labor worker center. Photo credit: Abel Valenzuela.

friendly environment for workers. In some cases, these sites are simply enclosed, open-air venues with seats or benches. In their more developed form, they are hiring halls operated by full-service community organizations that protect workers' rights, provide services, and sponsor community events.

In these centers, the workers obtain a safe public space that allows for economic exchanges without the pressure of having to compete with other workers, automobile traffic, and passersby. They also provide recent arrivals with an opportunity to become better integrated into local communities. They serve as a staging area for workers to participate in civil society by coming into contact with other organizations striving for immigrant integration and human and civil rights. When developed innovatively, worker centers can also be very rewarding for local communities. For example, worker centers provide space to bring together residents, merchants, patrol officers, employers, elected officials, workers, and other community stakeholders to discuss and resolve the tensions that sometimes arise between day laborers and local residents.

The creation of day labor worker centers is a relatively recent phenomenon, with most (57 percent) having been established since 2000 (Valenzuela et al. 2006). The centers are typically located near informal day labor hiring sites, offering both workers and contractors an alternative to the unregulated sites found on street corners and in parking lots. Location can be a crucial determinant of a center's success. As a result, they tend to be established in areas where workers and employers have ready access to each other. Worker centers are created through partnerships with migrant civil society, sometimes in collaboration with local governments, faith-based organizations, law enforcement agencies, and other community partners such as local businesses and labor unions. According to the National Day Labor Study, the overwhelming majority (68 percent) of worker centers are operated by community-based organizations (Valenzuela et al. 2006).

The primary purpose of day labor worker centers is to regulate the day labor market by intervening in the market and establishing rules governing the search for work and the hiring of workers. Fundamental to their value is the ability of worker centers to intervene on both the demand and supply sides of the day labor market. On the demand side, worker centers monitor the actions of employers, increase the transparency of the hiring process, and provide an institutional foundation for holding employers accountable for workplace abuses. On the supply side, they organize and normalize the hiring of day laborers, monitor worker quality, and provide opportunities for workers' incorporation into the formal economy through employment assistance and, in some cases, skills training.

Worker centers regulate the day labor market through three principal activities: wage setting, job allocation, and wage claims, including grievance resolution and worker education. All three are important for curtailing abuses and improving the working conditions of day laborers. The setting of a minimum wage is enforced through wage floors or strict guidelines that both workers and employers are expected to follow. Setting a minimum wage defuses competition between desperate workers and prevents employers from fostering competition between different groups of workers, thus effectively taking low-wage bidders out of the hiring equation. Some worker centers apply wage-setting strategies such as setting different minimum wage rates according to occupation or the role that the worker will undertake, such as assistant or skilled worker (Theodore, Valenzuela, and Melendez 2009).

The allocation of jobs is also a crucial regulatory strategy and follows principles of fairness in distributing work opportunities. Left to the vagaries of the market, instances of abuse, competition, and wage depression by employers pitting workers against each other are likely. Most worker centers put in place a distribution system that allocates jobs randomly, with special provisions that provide for employers' preferences and a requisite skill set to complete the job. Job allocation is important because the imbalance between the number of workers and jobs means that on any given day a significant number of workers will not secure employment. Demand fluctuations by the day, week, and month make day labor work unstable. To distribute the available jobs, most worker centers have developed different lottery systems and hiring lists to allocate jobs.

Almost all worker centers assist day laborers in making and filing wage claims, contacting current and former employers, filing claims with wage enforcement authorities, and providing legal advice or referral (Theodore, Valenzuela, and Melendez 2009). The more creative worker centers partner with local law schools or legal aid clinics to assist day laborers with grievances and the filing of wage claims. In addition, the centers also help to integrate workers in civic life, provide workshops on labor, human, and immigrant rights, demystify the legal contours of immigration status, and provide training and education to develop skills.

It is noteworthy that worker centers also work with day laborers who are not involved in the center but choose to search for work nearby at an informal site. The logic for doing this is that abuses and wage theft decrease pay and worsen work conditions across a local and regional context. Intervention is required so that nearby hiring sites are not left vulnerable to the exploitation of unscrupulous employers, who may exert downward wage pressure, undermining the minimum wages set at the formal worker centers.

Thus, worker centers have emerged as an innovative institutional response to the workplace abuses that day laborers endure in the informal economy. Worker centers, however, are just one strategy in a broader organizing campaign and partnership with civil society to change the day labor market, improve the working lives of immigrant day workers, normalize their labor market participation, and broaden their integration into society. I describe this growing social movement next.

### Curbing Informality: Migrant Civil Society and the Right to the City

Los Angeles and other parts of the United States are witnessing emerging coalitions of migrant, female, minority, and low-skill workers partnering with community-based organizations, labor groups, and umbrella alliances to act collectively. These coalitions are also partnering with clergy, university researchers, elected and appointed officials, organized labor, and environmental groups that make up a broader civil society. Their collective objectives are to make cities and their institutions, such as those of work, health, and education, function more effectively and justly for immigrants, women, people of color, and other urban residents. Key to this social movement, which has been called the migrant civil society (Theodore and Martin 2007), is a resurgence of organized labor and other worker and student labor organizing campaigns.

In many cities throughout the United States, a network of day laborers, advocates, and community-based organizations has come together to form the National Day Labor Organizing Network (NDLON). The network is the major catalyst in the rise of day labor worker centers. NDLON has also become part of a wider national campaign to protect immigrant rights by advocating for the federal passage of comprehensive immigration reform. NDLON supports the fair treatment and incorporation of undocumented immigrants in all segments of society. In particular, the network advocates for a pathway to eventual citizenship through immigration reform. Its national scope is evident in its affiliations with the AFL-CIO and Change to Win, the two largest labor federations in the United States. The partnership with the mainstream labor movement is an example of its strategy to develop greater regulation and legitimacy for informal day labor work.

NDLON's strategies are unique, long-term, and supportive of immigrant normalization. While much of the migrant civil society is focused on broader movement building and developing political influence, the network focuses its efforts on the rights and livelihoods of immigrants, especially undocumented workers who are often victims of unsafe work conditions, abuses, and wage theft (Milkman, Gonzalez, and Narro 2010). It addresses individuals and their families through hundreds of different programs, activities, social gatherings, fundraisers, hometown associations, and political events that help incorporate newcomers into U.S. society, civic culture, political processes, and other institutions. The integration and normalization of undocumented immigrants is a very important strategy in improving the working lives of day laborers and giving them a right to the city (Lefebvre 1968).

Through the efforts of NDLON, the day labor market and the workers it employs are changing (Cummings 2011; Dziembowska 2010; Valenzuela 2007). Its success comes from organizing into a strong national network, establishing key collaborations with the labor movement, exerting influence on public policy at the federal and local levels, and undertaking legal and popular media battles to fight anti-day labor legislation and anti-immigrant images that dominate the public discourse (Dziembowska 2010). As a national network, NDLON's member organizations come together to collectively develop strategy and plan national actions, share best practices, and create community-based, regional, and national alliances to improve working conditions for day laborers and migrant workers. NDLON's activities have included the opening of and management training of worker centers in many neighborhoods throughout the country, organizing and educational campaigns for workers on street corners, leadership development through popular education, and organizing and providing services, including legal clinics and workshops that promote and defend the labor and civil rights of immigrant workers, particularly day laborers.

The underlying catalyst for improving immigrant workers' rights is the moving of the day labor market from the shadows of informality into more regulated arrangements with safeguards for workers. Worker centers represent only a very small portion of all informal hiring sites available to day laborers. A large share of the day labor workforce still needs to be organized for a truly transformative shift from informal to formal, or quasi-formal, work. But where worker centers exist, they provide a promising and innovative approach to augmenting workers' rights in the contingent day labor market (Beard and Edwards 1995; Kalleberg 2002; Smith 1997). Although conventional wisdom suggests that organizing or unionizing informal workers is impossible, the worker centers demonstrate the possibility of collective action and bargaining in unregulated labor markets.

### Conclusion: Informality and Regulation in Day Labor Work

Despite the real and impressive gains in improving and regularizing day labor work, large segments of this market remain untouched by any type of collective organizing effort. As a result, most day laborers lack adequate workplace protection. Several factors, such as the vast geography of the day labor market, its national breadth, the high cost of organizing, and the large number of workers with undocumented status, make a more complete shift from informal to formal work difficult. Metropolitan regions such as Los Angeles, San Francisco, New York, and Houston have stronger intracity networks among day labor advocates and organizers, workers' rights organizations, a strong labor movement, and other components of migrant civil society that make organizing there significantly easier. But many other regions have a weak migrant civil society infrastructure or, worse, a native population so hostile toward unauthorized immigration that migrants "self-deport," or move to another state. Even under favorable conditions, many hiring sites and day laborers shun collective efforts or simply do not know of them because of the fluid, unstable, and independent characteristics of this market.

Organizing is labor-intensive and expensive. Many hiring sites, regions, and municipalities with significant numbers of day laborers remain outside of NDLON's influence, and do not benefit from the advantages of a robust migrant civil society. Sustained efforts to organize and advocate on behalf of day laborers, to collaborate with education and jobs training programs, and to partner with organizations that seek to improve worker human capital would serve to transition day laborers into formal and more stable employment. Nonetheless, some parts of the day labor market are unlikely to move toward regulation in the short term, and the federal government is partly responsible. Different federal agencies and their data collection efforts have shown little interest in categorizing, tracking, documenting, identifying, or regulating day labor work in any meaningful way. To illustrate, the ongoing Current Population Survey Contingent Worker Supplement that collects important data on day labor has not disaggregated the day labor definition. As a result, analysis of this data is limited to a broader, more expansive definition of day labor, rendering any assessment of open-air day labor markets impossible. In 2002, the General Accounting Office published a report on day labor that called for increased data accuracy and research investment (U.S. General Accounting Office 2002). Efforts to coordinate government data collection, with public agencies working in collaboration with researchers, day labor advocates, and the legal community, would result in greater government oversight and regulation of this market.

Similarly, efforts to bring together the migrant civil society, city officials, and the federal government, particularly planners and policymakers, would be an important strategy for the short and long term. Planners should encourage mixed-use sidewalks through zoning and planning processes that enable a more sensitive and thoughtful approach to regulating the search for work in public spaces (Kim 2012; Loukaitou-Sideris and Ehrenfeucht 2009). Planners should also be involved as partners with the migrant civil society and its efforts to reclaim the city for the millions of residents, including those without documents, who experience great hardships. This is particularly important given the shift in responsibility for service provision from the federal to local governments, diminished municipal coffers, and the fewer benefits, resources, and services available to the poor. Despite diminished resources and services, planners should be encouraging city programs and departments to work with existing worker centers and support the creation of new centers. Finally, because hazards and injuries in day labor are so commonplace, planners and policymakers should work more closely with federal officials to monitor and enforce existing Occupational Safety and Health Administration rules. Sustained advocacy for comprehensive immigration reform, including a path to citizenship, is also necessary.

Of course, some informal components of the market are unlikely to disappear, such as the cash exchange for completing a work assignment or the informal negotiation of wages. Negotiating one's wage is not necessarily bad, particularly if a worker is able to secure higher wages or is empowered to walk away from a job if underpaid. At the same time, increased regulation and formalization of the day labor market will help shift other components of this market, such as the risk of not getting paid, toward less exploitation and greater protection for workers.

Increased regulation is likely to be positive not only for workers but also for municipalities. While it is not clear whether taxing day labor will produce any public revenue, since workers earn so little that their meager earnings would likely qualify them (if they have documents) for government subsidies and tax breaks, there are benefits to the government that are not tax-related. Equally important are the quasi-regulatory activities, many under the broad rubric of organizing, advocacy, and outreach efforts, of worker member organizations like NDLON. The success of many of NDLON's policies, campaigns, and legal battles are well documented (Cummings 2011; Dziembowska 2010; Valenzuela 2007), but less noticed are the many local activities that serve to educate and politicize day laborers. These include the use of social and family gatherings, such as soccer tournaments between different hiring sites, in which families communicate with each other (and eat, rest, and play together) and advocates relay key information regarding immigrant and worker rights. Students at different college campuses, including my own university, partner with local worker centers to provide volunteer work such as English as a second language (ESL) classes and related workshops on civics, hygiene, health, and immigrant and civil rights. Other examples of local organizing efforts include popular education, street theater, and other creative ways to communicate to day laborers their rights as workers. These efforts are part of a larger strategy of immigrant incorporation and normalization, and a direct outcome of a strong migrant civil society. Combined, these activities complement and support efforts toward increased regulation of day labor work.

Worker centers and an active migrant civil society have striven to formalize and regulate day labor work with some marked success. Their efforts can be appreciated if we consider that the alternative would be to leave this market to the dictates of bad employers and mean-spirited and racially tinged municipal policies advocated by extreme anti-immigrant groups, with a likely spike in workplace abuses, wage theft, and injuries among day laborers. Efforts to regularize day labor are bringing tangible results, leading to important local policies, improvements in labor market outcomes, and the creation of best-practice strategies and innovations that ensure continued shifts away from informality and toward increased protections, wages, and employment prospects for day laborers.

## Note

1. The National Day Labor Study (I was co-principal investigator with Edwin Melendez and Nik Theodore) is comprised of two data collection projects. The first was a random sample of day laborers drawn from 264 hiring sites in 139 municipalities in 20 states and the District of Columbia. A total of 2,660 day laborers were surveyed during July and August 2004. They were asked a series of questions regarding their work experiences, demographic characteristics, and issues related to day labor work. The second component was a survey of worker center executive directors and senior staff. The survey focused on the ways in which centers maintain or improve wage rates, allocate jobs, and redress grievances. It involved interviews with the directors and staff of 60 of the 61 day labor worker centers that were operating at the time of the survey (2004–2005). Some of the interviews were completed face to face, others by telephone. Each worker center was mailed a copy of the survey protocol and an explanation of the study. No incentive was offered to encourage participation. Interviews lasted approximately one hour.

## References

Beard, Kathy M., and Jeffrey R. Edwards. 1995. "Employees at Risk: Contingent Work and the Psychological Experience of Contingent Workers." *Trends in Organizational Behavior* 2:109–126.

Blaauw, Phillip F., and Waldo F. Krugell. 2012. "Micro-evidence on Day Labourers and Thickness of Labour Markets in South Africa." Economic Research Southern Africa, Working Paper 282.

Castells, Manuel, and Alejandro Portes. 1989. "World Underneath: The Origins, Dynamics, and Effects of the Informal Economy." In Alejandro Portes, Manuel Castells, and Lauren A. Benton, eds., *The Informal Economy in Advanced and Less Developed Countries*, 11–37. Baltimore: Johns Hopkins University Press.

Cummings, Scott. 2011. "Litigation at Work: Defending Day Labor in Los Angeles." *UCLA Law Review* 58 (6):1617–1703.

Dziembowska, Maria. 2010. "NDLON and the History of Day Labor Organizing in Los Angeles." In Ruth Milkman, Joshua Bloom, and Victor Narro, eds., *Working for Justice: The L.A. Model of Organizing and Advocacy*, 141–153. Ithaca: ILR Press, Cornell University.

Fine, Janice. 2006. *Worker Centers: Organizing Communities at the Edge of the Dream*. Ithaca: Cornell University Press and the Economic Policy Institute.

Fowler, Edward. 1996. *San'ya Blues: Laboring Life in Contemporary Tokyo*. Ithaca: Cornell University Press.

Giamo, Benedict. 1994. "Order, Disorder and the Homeless in the United States and Japan." *Doshisha Amerika Kenkyu* 31:1–19.

Gill, Tom. 1994. "Sanya Street Life under the Heisei Recession." *Japan Quarterly (Asahi Shinbunsha)* 41:270–286.

Gill, Tom. 2001. *Men of Uncertainty: The Social Organization of Day Laborers in Contemporary Japan*. Albany: State University of New York Press.

Harmse, Alet, Phillip Blaauw, and Rinie Schenck. 2009. "Day Labourers, Unemployment and Socio-economic Development in South Africa." *Urban Forum* 20(4): 363–377.

Kalleberg, Arne L. 2002. "Nonstandard Employment Relations: Part-Time, Temporary and Contract Work." *Annual Review of Sociology* 26 (1): 341–365.

Kim, Annette. 2012. "The Mixed-Use Sidewalk: Vending and Property Rights in Public Space." *Journal of the American Planning Association* 78 (3):1–14.

Kruijt, Dirk, and Kees Koonings. 2009. "The Rise of Megacities and the Urbanization of Informality, Exclusion, and Violence." In Kees Koonings and Dirk Kruijt, eds., *Megacities: The Politics of Urban Exclusion and Violence in the Global South*, 8–28. New York: Palgrave-Macmillan.

Lefebvre, Henri. 1968. *Le Droit à la ville*. Paris: Anthropos.

Leonard, Warren J., and John J. O'Shea. 1997. "A Quantitative Analysis of 'Shape-ups' on Long Island: A Report Prepared for the Workplace Project." Hofstra University.

Loukaitou-Sideris, Anastasia, and Renia Ehrenfeucht. 2009. *Sidewalks: Conflict and Negotiation over Public Space*. Cambridge, MA: MIT Press.

Malpica, Daniel M. 1996. "The Social Organization of Day-Laborers in Los Angeles." In Refugio I. Rochin, ed., *Immigration and Ethnic Communities: A Focus on Latinos*, 81–92. East Lansing, MI: Julian Samora Research Institute.

Marr, Matthew D. 1997. "Maintaining Autonomy: The Plight of the American Skidrow and Japanese *Yoseba*." *Journal of Social Distress and the Homeless* 6 (3):229–250.

Marr, Matthew D., Abel Valenzuela, Jannette Kawachi, and Takao Koike. 2000. "Day Laborers in Tokyo, Japan: Preliminary Findings from the San'ya Day Labor Survey." Working Paper (Technical Report) 00-01. Center for the Study of Urban Poverty, Institute for Social Science Research, University of California, Los Angeles.

Milkman, Ruth, Ana Luz Gonzalez, and Victor Narro. 2010. "Wage Theft and Workplace Violations in Los Angeles: The Failure of Employment and Labor Law for Low-Wage Workers." Institute for Research on Labor and Employment, University of California, Los Angeles.

Peck, Jamie, and Nik Theodore. 2001. "Contingent Chicago: Restructuring the Spaces of Temporary Labor." *International Journal of Urban and Regional Research* 25 (3):471–496.

Sassen, Saskia. 2001. *The Global City: New York, Tokyo, London.* Princeton: Princeton University Press.

Schenck, Rinie, and Phillip F. Blaauw. 2011. "The Work and Lives of Street Waste Pickers in Pretoria: A Case Study of Recycling in South Africa's Urban Informal Economy." *Urban Forum* 22(4): 411–430.

Smith, Vicki. 1997. "New Forms of Work Organization." *Annual Review of Sociology* 23:315–339.

Tabak, Faruk. 2000. "Introduction: Informalization and the Long Term." In Faruk Tabak and Michaeline A. Crichlow, eds., *Informalization: Process and Structure*, 1–22. Baltimore: Johns Hopkins University Press.

Theodore, Nik, and Nina Martin. 2007. "Migrant Civil Society: New Voices in the Struggle over Community Development." *Journal of Urban Affairs* 29 (3):269–287.

Theodore, Nik, Abel Valenzuela, Jr., and Edwin Melendez. 2009. "Worker Centers: Defending Labor Standards for Migrant Workers in the Informal Economy." *International Journal of Manpower* 30 (5):422–436.

Townsend, Camilla. 1997. "Story without Words: Women and the Creation of a Mestizo People in Guayaquil, 1820–1835." *Latin American Perspectives* 24 (4):50–68.

U.S. General Accounting Office. 2002. "Worker Protection: Labor's Efforts to Enforce Protections for Day Laborers Could Benefit from Better Data and Guidance." GAO-02-925. General Accounting Office.

Valenzuela, Abel. 1999. "Day Laborers in Southern California: Preliminary Findings from the Day Labor Survey." Working Paper (Technical Report) 99-04. Center for the Study of Urban Poverty, Institute for Social Science Research, University of California, Los Angeles.

Valenzuela, Abel. 2003. Day Labor Work. *Annual Review of Sociology* 29:307–333.

Valenzuela, Abel, Jr. 2007. Immigrant Day Laborers: Myths and Realities. *NACLA Report on the Americas* 40 (3): 25–29.

Valenzuela, Abel, and Edwin Melendez. 2002. "Day Labor in New York." Working Paper 02-03. Center for the Study of Urban Poverty, Institute for Social Science Research, University of California, Los Angeles.

Valenzuela, Abel, Nik Theodore, Edwin Melendez, and Ana L. Gonzalez. 2006. "On the Corner: Day Labor in the United States." Center for the Study of Urban Poverty, University of California, Los Angeles.

Vanackere, Martine. 1988. "Conditions of Agriculture Day-Labourers in Mexico." *International Labour Review* 127 (1):91–110.

# 15

## Informal Parking Markets: Turning Problems into Solutions

Donald Shoup

Cities regulate every aspect of parking, using everything from time limits for on-street parking to zoning requirements for off-street parking. Cities also employ legions of parking enforcement officers to ensure that drivers obey these regulations, and tickets for parking violations are a major revenue source. Los Angeles, for example, earned $134 million from parking tickets in 2011 (City of Los Angeles 2012: 307). If so much parking is formal, regulated, and policed, what then is informal parking? And what can we learn from the informal parking market that might improve public policies for the formal parking market?

Informal parking markets operate outside the regulated system, and they can fill a market niche hard to serve in any formal way. Residents near sports stadiums, for example, often rent their driveways and yards to spectators on game days. This informal market serves venues featuring infrequent peaks in parking demand that are hard to handle using formal methods.

But informal parking can also create problems, as when drivers illegally park on the sidewalks in older neighborhoods that lack ample off-street parking. Cars parked on sidewalks make a neighborhood less walkable and make life more difficult for people with disabilities, especially those who use wheelchairs.

Where informal parking works well, it makes better use of land. Where informal parking works badly, however, it can make neighborhoods less walkable and livable. I will first discuss informal markets for off-street and on-street parking, and will then present a case study of informal parking that suggests a promising reform of the formal parking market.

**Figure 15.1**
Informal parking near the Coliseum, Los Angeles Olympics, 1984. Photo credit:
Tom Zimmerman, Collection of the Los Angeles Public Library.

## Informal Off-Street Parking Markets

Informal parking markets operate in many older neighborhoods near
sites that generate short, sharp, infrequent increases in parking demand.
They often appear near the Los Angeles Coliseum, for example, where
residents charge nonresidents to park in their driveways on game days
(figure 15.1). Drivers may have to walk a few blocks to the stadium, but
after the game they can leave from a residential driveway much faster
than from a congested stadium lot where everyone is trying to exit at
the same time. Drivers may think that paying for parking is un-American,
but residents who receive the revenue know that paying for what you
use is a traditional American value.

The demand for game day parking is so strong that some cities have
begun to regularize informal markets. For example, the University of
Michigan stadium in Ann Arbor is the largest in the United States. With
seats for 110,000 fans, it has drawn crowds of over 100,000 for every
home game since 1975 (University of Michigan, n.d.). Like most cities,

Ann Arbor prohibits parking on lawns, but its ordinance also states, "This subsection shall not be applicable on those days when football games are played in The University of Michigan stadium" (Ann Arbor Municipal Code 5:166 (1)).

This ordinance and the large peak crowds at Michigan Stadium have created an informal market in off-street parking. Residents park their own cars for free on the streets before the games to create as many off-street spaces as possible on their lawns, driveways, and back yards. These paid off-street parking spaces can accommodate many more cars than the free curb spaces do, so the informal market significantly increases the total parking supply. The city could charge $25 for on-street parking on game days, but since the city leaves parking free, entrepreneurs take advantage of it.

Residents post signs that show their price of parking (typically around $25) and advertise the "EZ Out" aspect of parking on the lawns: drivers can simply drive over the curb to exit, instead of waiting in a long line to exit from a regular parking lot after a game. The many dispersed lots thus reduce the severe congestion caused by peak entry and exit queues.

Like formal markets, the informal markets for parking are now shifting onto the Internet, and several start-ups have tapped the market for parking in driveways. ParkatmyHouse, which began in Britain, is one of the most successful of these peer-to-peer operations, and it is expanding into the United States (www.parkatmyhouse.com/us/). Parking Panda is another peer-to-peer Internet market that operates in Baltimore, Philadelphia, San Francisco, and Washington, D.C. The website shows the location, price, and even a photo of each available parking space. Parking Panda accepts the driver's reservation and payment for the space, and sends the proceeds (less a 20 percent transaction fee) to the parking space owner once a month.

When Parking Panda started, it matched drivers who want to park with people who have a parking space to offer—a model of bartering and trading known as collaborative consumption. But Parking Panda also works with commercial garage owners who practice a yield management strategy. When a garage has many empty spaces, it can offer discounts on Parking Panda to fill them without reducing regular prices for the general public. As the garage fills, the online prices rise but prices posted at the entrance to the garage remain fixed. Different drivers can thus pay different prices for parking in the garage at the same time, just as different airline passengers can pay different prices for adjacent seats on a flight.

Websites like Parking Panda are part of the new "sharing economy" that uses the Internet to let households and companies share otherwise idle resources. The major market for these websites may turn out to be garages that vary their prices in real time to optimize occupancy and maximize revenue. What started as informal off-street parking markets around athletic events may eventually become sophisticated formal parking markets with dynamic pricing.

## Informal On-Street Parking Markets

Payments for on-street parking are rent for the temporary use of land. If parking is scarce but free, competition for the free spaces can induce "rent-seeking" behavior: using resources to obtain a larger slice of the existing pie rather than to make the pie bigger. In her analysis of competitive rent-seeking behavior, Anne Krueger (1974: 291) explains how scarce resources are squandered in rent-seeking situations:

Rent seeking results in a divergence between the private and social costs of certain activities . . . rent seeking activities are often competitive and resources are devoted to competing for rents.

Informal markets can be quite profitable where on-street parking is greatly underpriced. Doormen for apartment buildings in expensive neighborhoods in New York and San Francisco have become successful parking entrepreneurs. At posh apartment buildings on Russian Hill in San Francisco, some doormen use the buildings' taxi zones to park cars for visitors, and drivers usually tip them $20 for the service. When a curb space opens up near the building, the doorman parks the visitor's car in it. If a resident who parks on the street then comes home and cannot find a curb space, the doorman moves the visitor's car back to the taxi zone to create a curb vacancy and receives another $20 tip from the resident.[1]

To allow for street cleaning, New York City prohibits parking for a 90-minute period on one side of the street on Mondays, Wednesdays, and Fridays, and on the other side on Tuesdays, Thursdays, and Saturdays. During the 90 minutes each day when parking is prohibited on the side being cleaned, many residents double-park their cars on the other side where parking is permitted.[2] This alternate-side requirement also creates an informal market controlled by doormen. Residents who park on the street give keys to their cars to their doormen, whom they pay a monthly fee to move their cars from one side of the street to the other.

When drivers want to use their cars, they ask the doormen where their car is. O'Neill (2012) reports that some doormen try to leave gaps of curb space in front and behind each vehicle they park on the street, to prohibit other drivers from using the space. When the doorman needs to park another car, he simply moves the first car forward to create a second parking space out of the two gaps.

Teachers also take advantage of informal parking markets for free curb parking. A study in Alexandria, Virginia, found that school custodians regularly moved teachers' cars to a new curb space every three hours to evade time limits (Olsson and Miller 1979). The school district thus spent the public's money to defeat the city's on-street parking regulations.

Some informal parking markets have a work requirement. Residents of Boston and Chicago traditionally use old lawn furniture to claim curb parking spaces they have shoveled out after a snowstorm. Boston city council member Bill Linehan explained, "It's a cultural thing. When people work hard to clean a spot, you want people to respect that. It's part of living in a dense community" (Viser 2007).[3]

Using a lawn chair (often called a parking chair) to claim a shoveled-out parking space after a snowstorm is an informal part of the culture, but claim jumpers can dispute the ownership. For example, for how long after a snowstorm is the parking chair valid? Boston residents expect between two and four days, but the period is hard to enforce. What happens if someone moves a parking chair and takes the shoveled-and-claimed space? This claim jumping creates many disputes, with slashed tires and broken windows as the price for trespassing. If someone removes a parking chair and another driver innocently parks in the shoveled space, the aggrieved shoveler may attack the wrong car.

Opponents of the shoveling-for-parking rule argue that claiming public space as private property is unfair. But McChesney (2001) counters that earning the informal, temporary reward of a guaranteed parking space provides a valuable economic incentive to shovel the snow:

Some find it unfair to exclude others from using a resource. But the ability to exclude provides the incentives to create more resources, reducing scarcity over time. Popular writers focus on perceived unfairness. But economists observing the controversy will see the wealth-increasing invisible hand at work again—this time hoisting a snow shovel.

These examples of rent-seeking behavior in the competition for on-street parking suggest that cities can seek some rent of their own.

Elsewhere I have argued that cities should charge fair market prices for curb spaces and spend the revenue for local public investments (Shoup 2011). An on-street parking space is land; like all other land, its value depends on its location. Underpriced curb parking encourages many forms of wasteful rent-seeking behavior. Cities that set parking meter rates to yield one or two open spaces on every block will eliminate all this waste and will earn the full rental value of scarce public land.

## A Case Study of Illegal Informal Parking

Illegal informal parking is common in many countries, and it often does great harm. Where on-street parking is underpriced and overcrowded, many drivers feel they have no alternative to illegal parking. The *Los Angeles Times* describes the chaotic informal parking in Mexico City: "Cars dominate nearly every square inch of Mexico City's public space. Vehicle owners double- and triple-park on the streets, to say nothing of curbs, sidewalks, gardens, alleys, boulevards and bike paths" (Dickerson 2004: 26).

This anything-goes informal parking is more common in developing countries, but drivers also park on sidewalks in some California cities, although it is clearly illegal:

No person shall stop, park, or leave standing any vehicle whether attended or unattended . . . on any portion of a sidewalk, or with the body of the vehicle extending over any portion of a sidewalk (California Vehicle Code §22500).

Despite this legal prohibition, Los Angeles and a few other cities have adopted a policy of "relaxed enforcement" of the law against parking on sidewalks.[4] The informal custom of parking on the sidewalk has evolved in some neighborhoods in response to a shortage of free parking spaces on the streets and the city's failure to enforce the law.

## Informal Parking in North Westwood Village

I began to study informal parking on sidewalks in 2005 when teaching a course on urban transportation economics at UCLA. Many of the students lived in North Westwood Village, a neighborhood next to campus, and they mentioned that drivers often park on the aprons of driveways (the paved area between the sidewalk and the street), with part of the car extending over the sidewalk (figure 15.2). Parking enforcement officers ignored this violation because the North Village is a student area and its city council member had requested relaxed enforcement.

**Figure 15.2**
Cars parked on the sidewalk in North Westwood Village. Photo credit: Donald Shoup.

Most cars are too long to park entirely on the apron, and many drivers park with the front of the car extending over the sidewalk. Some also park on the driveway with the back of the car extending over the sidewalk (and no part of the car on the apron). No matter how far the cars extend over the sidewalk from either the apron or the driveway, drivers call it apron parking.

Unfettered parking over the sidewalk is a good example of what George Kelling and James Wilson referred to as the "broken windows" theory of urban disorder:

Social psychologists and police officers tend to agree that if a window in a building is broken and is left unrepaired, all the rest of the windows will soon be broken. . . . One unrepaired broken window is a signal that no one cares, and so breaking more windows costs nothing. (Kelling and Wilson 1982)

If we substitute cars parked on sidewalks for broken windows, North Westwood Village illustrates this theory. Where enforcement officers do not ticket the first cars parked on the sidewalk, more drivers will park on the sidewalk. Eventually, drivers will park on sidewalks throughout the neighborhood. Because the city has relaxed parking enforcement, an informal parking market has taken over the sidewalks.

North Village residents have developed informal protocols for dealing with apron parking. For example, if cars are parked on the apron, how do residents who park in the garage of an apartment building get out? To solve this problem, some apron parkers exchange car keys and can move apron-parked cars blocking the driveway.

On days when parking is prohibited on one side of the street for the weekly street cleaning, every car illegally parked on the side of the street being cleaned usually gets a ticket. Cars illegally parked over the sidewalk on the other side of the street, however, rarely receive a ticket. The parking enforcement officers selectively ticket street-cleaning violations and ignore parking on the sidewalks. If an apron-parked car extends into the street on the side being cleaned, however, it *always* receives a street-cleaning ticket. The failure to enforce laws against parking on the sidewalks suggests that parked cars are more important than pedestrians.

My students began to study informal parking in the North Village. They counted parking spaces and parked cars, analyzed census data, interviewed residents and property owners, and documented the situation with many photographs. Table 15.1 summarizes their findings about parking on the streets and aprons in North Westwood Village.[5]

The students counted 205 cars parked on the driveway aprons, and the 2000 census showed that 11,021 residents live in the North Village. This suggests that only 2 percent of the residents park their cars on an apron (205 ÷ 11,021), but their cars extend over the sidewalks on almost every block.

If only 205 residents without cars replace residents who park on the aprons, the reduction in parking demand will be enough to clear the sidewalks of parked cars. A population shift toward residents who do not own a car can happen quickly: the 2000 census found that almost half the residents in the North Village had lived there less than one year (which is understandable because student apartments have a high turnover rate). Living in the North Village without a car is manageable because it is across the street from the UCLA campus.

Since there are not enough apron parking spots for all tenants who want one, landlords either charge tenants for parking on the aprons (usually about $50 a month) or give them permission to apron-park when they lease an apartment (and presumably charge higher rent for the privilege). If landlords could no longer rent apron parking spaces to

**Table 15.1**
Curb Parking Occupancy Rates in North Westwood Village

| Street | Curb Parking Spaces | Legally Parked Cars | Cars Parked in Aprons | Others Ilegally Parked Cars | Total Illegally Parked Cars | Total Occupancy (%) |
|--------|------|------|------|------|------|------|
| | (1) | (2) | (3) | (4) | (5) = (3)+(4) | (6) = [(5)+(2)]/ (1) |
| Landfair | 118 | 112 | 54 | 24 | 78 | 161 |
| Roebling | 25 | 21 | 16 | 0 | 16 | 148 |
| Glenrock | 46 | 46 | 15 | 1 | 16 | 135 |
| Midvale | 89 | 84 | 26 | 1 | 27 | 125 |
| Levering | 97 | 90 | 26 | 3 | 29 | 123 |
| Gayley | 79 | 77 | 15 | 3 | 18 | 120 |
| Kelton | 129 | 125 | 23 | 5 | 28 | 119 |
| Ophir | 61 | 59 | 9 | 1 | 10 | 113 |
| Strathmore | 136 | 129 | 17 | 2 | 19 | 109 |
| Veteran | 70 | 68 | 4 | 3 | 7 | 107 |
| Le Conte | 7 | 6 | 0 | 0 | 0 | 86 |
| Total | 857 | 817 | 205 | 43 | 248 | 124 |

tenants, students who own cars would find apartments without off-street parking less desirable and might decide that another part of town with more off-street parking would be a better place to live. As a result, more apartments would become available at lower rents to students without cars. Clearing cars off the sidewalks would also make the North Village more walkable.

### Political Support for Apron Parking

Michael Dukakis, former governor of Massachusetts and Democratic candidate for president in 1988, lives in the North Village when he teaches in the Luskin School of Public Affairs at UCLA during the winter. He walks to campus, and was appalled to see the chaos on every block as he threaded his way between cars on the sidewalks. He contacted city officials to seek remedies but was ignored, much to his dismay. Nevertheless, due to his celebrity, Dukakis became notorious for protesting apron parking in the North Village.

Political uproar followed, at least in the blogosphere. Apron parkers in the North Village vilified Dukakis (and occasionally me) in blog posts, many scatological but a few amusing. I learned how difficult it is to reform a practice once it has been established. As Oliver Wendell Holmes said, "A thing which you enjoyed and used as your own for a long time, whether property or an opinion, takes root in your being and cannot be torn away without your resenting the act and trying to defend yourself, however you came by it" (Holmes 1897). When it comes to parking, informal does not mean easily changed.

Many people have a stake in apron parking and do not want it to end. Landlords who now rent apron parking privileges to their tenants would lose revenue to which they have no legitimate claim. Residents have also come to depend on apron parking, even if they realize they are blocking the sidewalks.

### The Americans with Disabilities Act

Informal parking on the sidewalks may seem solely a local issue, but in 2003 the U.S. Supreme Court ruled that the Americans with Disabilities Act (ADA) applies to sidewalks. The decision in *Barden v. Sacramento* requires cities to make public sidewalks accessible to people with disabilities. Because of this ruling, cities must remove barriers that block access to sidewalks.[6] This decision has created a serious liability for Los Angeles because the city has informally allowed drivers to park their cars on the sidewalks in North Westwood Village, although it violates both California and Los Angeles law.

Two ADA lawsuits against the city have spurred reform. Both lawsuits deal with broken sidewalks and cars parked on the sidewalks. The lead plaintiff in one was a UCLA student who uses a wheelchair and had to make a long detour on the way to campus because cars parked on the sidewalks prevented him from taking the shortest route through the North Village (Pesce 2007). The lawsuit alleges:

Due to his mobility disability, Named Plaintiff Victor Pineda uses a motorized wheelchair. Plaintiff Pineda is a graduate student at UCLA and lives in residential North Westwood Village. . . . Plaintiff Pineda has consistently experienced apron parking on a number of sidewalks. . . . The narrow spaces between the vehicles on the sidewalk prevent Plaintiff Pineda from traveling along the sidewalk. As a result, Plaintiff Pineda often must travel on the street to reach his destination, literally risking his life.[7]

After years of neglect, lawsuits have forced the city to reconsider the informal policy of relaxed enforcement for apron parking violations, and to decide exactly what should be legal and what should not.[8]

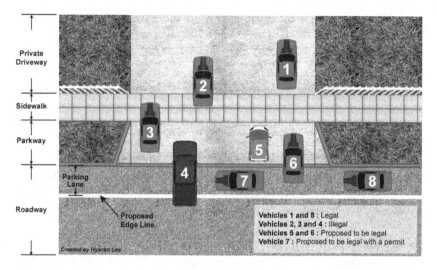

**Figure 15.3**
Proposal for legal apron parking in Los Angeles. Graphic: Hyeran Lee.

### Regularizing Apron Parking

Because of the ADA lawsuits, city staff proposed allowing apron parking that does not extend over the sidewalk or too far into the street. Figure 15.3 illustrates the proposal.[9] Cars parked on the aprons could extend onto the street as far as the width of the parking lane, and cars could also parallel park on the street in front of the apron if they have a permit. Parking with part of the car extending over the sidewalk or into the street beyond the parking lane would remain illegal.

Vehicle 7 in this proposal illustrates the easiest reform: parallel parking in front of one's own driveway, which some cities already allow. Although parallel parking on the street in front of a driveway does not accommodate as many cars as perpendicular apron parking does, the parked cars do not extend over the sidewalk or into the street beyond the parking lane. Residents can use these block-your-own-driveway permits to provide guaranteed parking for guests, home help, and service vehicles.[10]

Parallel parking in front of a driveway is illegal in Los Angeles, but enforcement officers do not issue citations in front of single-family houses unless someone complains. Parallel parking in front of an apartment building's driveway poses difficulties, however, because it can block access for all the residents who park off-street. Nevertheless, it may work if residents cooperate by sharing keys to the parallel-parked cars that block the driveway.

Formal rules for apron parking can cure the problem of informal parking on the sidewalks only if the city enforces these rules consistently, but Los Angeles's proposed apron-parking rules would be hard to enforce. The city must first establish criteria for citing cars that extend too far over the sidewalk (from the apron or the driveway) or too far into the street. How far is too far? If vehicles 5 and 6 in figure 15.3 are legally parked in the apron, parking enforcement officers cannot see from their patrol cars whether any other vehicles illegally extend over the sidewalk. In this scenario, they have to get out of their cars to examine each vehicle.

### Easing the Path to Formality

Given the threat of ADA lawsuits over inaccessible sidewalks, all cities that informally allow illegal parking on sidewalks will need to find ways to mitigate the withdrawal pains caused by enforcing the law. Fortunately, Los Angeles has already established one program that promises to ease the path to formality: dedicated curb parking spaces for shared cars.[11]

Car sharing's greatest benefit is to divide the fixed costs of automobile ownership (including parking) among a group of potential users. Because all residents have access to the shared cars, the neighborhood becomes more attractive to everyone who does not own a car.

Shared cars in the North Village can serve the approximately half of all residents who do not own a car, attract even more residents who do not own a car, and thereby reduce the demand for curb parking. In public meetings, however, some residents who park on the street vehemently opposed car sharing because of the loss of curb parking. Despite this opposition, the city contracted with Zipcar, a car sharing company, to place its cars on the streets.

The city has dedicated seven on-street spaces in the North Village to Zipcar, and the company has obtained four more off-street spaces. My students' survey of on-street parking found 857 legal curb spaces in the North Village (see table 15.1). While the shared cars remove seven curb spaces from the parking supply (0.8 percent of the total curb spaces), they probably reduce parking demand by many more spaces by reducing the demand for private cars. Several studies have estimated that each shared car replaces between 9 and 13 private cars (Osgood 2010; Martin and Shaheen 2011). The 11 shared cars in the North Village may therefore have reduced the demand for parking by between 99 and 143 spaces. The shared cars can reduce, rather than increase, the competition for curb parking.

Similar opposition to car sharing arose in 2010 when Hoboken, New Jersey, reserved curb spaces at corners throughout the city for 42 shared cars, so that 90 percent of the population lives within a five-minute walk of a shared car. The city estimated that each "Corner Car" would replace 17 private cars, but car owners strongly opposed the loss of curb parking:

At the beginning of the program, 42 of the city's roughly 9,000 on-street spaces were sacrificed to a city car-sharing program, known as Corner Cars, leading many residents to decry the arrival of new vehicles on their blocks, where claims to curbside space have long been regarded as sacrosanct. . . . As of July 2012, nearly a quarter of the program's roughly 3,000 members said they had given up their cars or decided against buying one because of the car share. Since 2009, the number of people with residential parking permits has decreased by about 1,000, to 16,000 total parking permits (Flegenheimer 2012).

We can use the Hoboken data to estimate how dedicating 42 curb spaces to shared cars reduced the demand for parking. If a quarter of the 3,000 car share members shed one car, each shared car replaces about 18 private cars (750 ÷ 42). From another angle, if car sharing explains the 1,000 fewer residential parking permits, each shared car reduces the demand for curb parking by about 24 spaces (1,000 ÷ 42). Allocating a few curb spaces exclusively to shared cars can thus improve parking availability even for residents who park their own cars on the street.

Like peer-to-peer parking reservations, car sharing is an example of collaborative consumption based on sharing rather than owning resources. Because sharing a car also means sharing a parking space, it can greatly reduce the demand for parking. As the Internet is key to easily finding and reserving the shared cars, the growing ubiquity of smartphones helps to explain the growing popularity of car sharing. The web-based formal market for car sharing may thus eventually help to resolve the problems caused by informal parking on sidewalks.

### A Formal Market for Curb Parking

The loss of apron parking in the North Village will increase the already high demand for curb parking. To address these problems, Los Angeles can allow the residents of any block in North Westwood Village to adopt an overnight parking permit district that prohibits overnight parking on the street except by permit holders. Enforcement officers need to make only one visit during a night to cite all cars parked without permits. Los Angeles charges residents $15 per year (less than half a cent per day) for each permit in an overnight parking permit district. Residents can also buy guest permits for $1 per night.

Given the high residential demand for on-street parking in North Westwood Village, the demand for overnight permits will greatly exceed the supply of on-street parking spaces. The city can keep the permit price low and limit the number of permits in some way, such as by a lottery. Alternatively, the city can charge a fair market price for the permits, so that the number of permits demanded will equal the supply of on-street parking spaces.

Suppose Los Angeles charges North Village residents the same price for a parking permit that UCLA charges students for a parking permit in the nearby campus residence halls—$89 a month. If the city charges $89 a month (about $3 a day) for 857 overnight permits (equal to the number of on-street parking spaces in the North Village), the new revenue will amount to about $76,000 a month (857 × $89). If the demand for permits priced at $89 a month is more or less than the 857 curb parking spaces, the city can nudge the price up or down. The right price for the overnight permits is the lowest price that will prevent a shortage of curb parking.

Paying for curb parking will never be politically popular, but it will make it possible for residents to find a curb space more easily. To increase the acceptability of this market-based solution, the city can spend all the new parking revenue to improve public services in the North Village: to repair broken sidewalks, plant street trees, and fill potholes—all of which the North Village needs. These public improvements will greatly increase the livability of the North Village and can satisfy the city's impending obligation to make the sidewalks accessible for the disabled.

Overnight parking permits may not solve all the curb parking problems in the North Village. Commuters to UCLA, for example, may try to park free in the North Village during the day. In this case, the city can add a daytime permit district on blocks that request it. If the residents agree, the city can also allow nonresidents to pay for parking on blocks that have daytime vacancies, and the revenue will pay for even better public services.

Dedicating parking revenue to the neighborhood that generates it has built political support for paid parking in other cities (Kolozsvari and Shoup 2003; Shoup 2011). The 857 motorists who park on the streets overnight will pay a fair market price for their permits, and in return they will find it much easier to find a curb space. Everyone else will pay nothing and will benefit from the new public services financed by the permits.

### The Sound of Change

A solution to the problems created by apron parking in North Village will have long-term economic and environmental benefits but also short-term political costs. As Niccolò Machiavelli wrote in *The Prince* in 1532, "There is nothing more difficult to plan or more uncertain of success or more dangerous to carry out than an attempt to introduce new institutions, because the introducer has as his enemies all those who profit from the old institutions, and has as lukewarm defenders all those who will profit from the new institutions" (Machiavelli 1965: 26). Or as Woodrow Wilson (1918: 286) said almost 400 years later, "If you want to make enemies, try to change something."

Most people want sustainable cities, great public transportation, less traffic, and more walkable neighborhoods. But they also want free parking, which conflicts with all these other goals. Fortunately, few people will have to give up a car if the city enforces the law against parking on the sidewalks in the North Village. Instead, a few car owners will decide that the North Village is not the best place to rent an apartment, and people who cannot afford a car will take their place. During the transition, the whining will be the sound of change.

### Turning Problems into Opportunities

Informal parking markets often respond to the failure of cities to create formal markets for on-street parking. Even on some of the most valuable land on Earth, cities offer free curb parking on a first-come-first-served basis. In dense neighborhoods, how could informal markets for this free parking not emerge?

If curb parking is free, entrepreneurs will find ways to create informal markets that serve drivers who are willing to pay for convenience. These informal markets respond to the problems caused almost entirely by free curb parking. The shortage of free curb parking is not merely a problem, however. It is also an opportunity to create a formal market with fair prices that allocate land for parking efficiently: *parking reform is land reform*. A fair, formal market for on-street parking will reduce traffic congestion, air pollution, and greenhouse gas emissions, and will generate ample public revenue.

Fair market prices can end the Hundred Years' War over free curb parking, and the new parking revenue will provide a peace dividend to rebuild our neglected public infrastructure. Livable, walkable cities are worth far more than free parking on the streets and sidewalks.

## Acknowledgments

I am grateful to Eric Agar, Spencer Graham-Thille, Heather Jones, Anastasia Loukaitou-Sideris, Vinit Mukhija, Gregory Pierce, Chirag Rabari, Justin Resnick, Alex Schaffer, Patricia Shoup, and Doreen Zhao for their excellent editorial advice. I am also grateful to Eric Agar and Hyeran Lee for assistance with the graphic art. The University of California Transportation Center provided financial support for this research.

## Notes

1. I am grateful to Howard Strassner of San Francisco for explaining this arrangement to me.

2. Gonzalez (2008) explores the ethics of double parking during street-cleaning hours; a local police official explained to him that the police "tolerate double parking as a 'courtesy' when alternate side regulations are in effect."

3. Rheault (2001) presents a photographic exploration of shoveling for parking in Boston. Sibley (forthcoming) provides a cultural and legal analysis of shoveling for parking.

4. For example, San Francisco has an informal policy of not citing cars parked on the sidewalk if the cars leave some room for pedestrian access: http://shoup.bol.ucla.edu/ParkingOnSidewalksInSanFrancisco.pdf.

5. The students' research is available online at www.its.ucla.edu/shoup/North WestwoodVillageDatav3.pdf.

6. Shoup (2010) explains ADA requirements for sidewalk accessibility.

7. Pages 8–11 in the lawsuit *Pineda v. City of Los Angeles*: www.its.ucla.edu/ shoup/PinedaVsCityOfLosAngeles.pdf. The second lawsuit that involves apron parking on sidewalks is *Willits v. City of Los Angeles*: http://shoup.bol.ucla.edu/ WillitsVsLosAngeles.pdf.

8. When I first learned that the ADA requires accessible sidewalks, I wrote to the Los Angeles city attorney to explain the informal parking problems in North Westwood Village, and asked him if the city would begin to enforce the law against parking on sidewalks. Perhaps naively, I expected an answer. When I received no answer, I wrote to city council members, the mayor, and the deputy mayor for transportation (who was a former student), but never received a single reply to any of my 30 letters and email messages. This correspondence is avail-

able online at www.its.ucla.edu/shoup/ParkingOnSidewalksInNorthWestwood Village.pdf.

9. Memo from the Los Angeles Department of Transportation to the City Council, "Apron Parking/Parking in Front of Driveways," November 7, 2011: http://shoup.bol.ucla.edu/ApronParkingReform.pdf.

10. Hermosa Beach, for example, issues permits for drivers to block their own driveways: http://shoup.bol.ucla.edu/HermosaBeachDrivewayParkingPer mit.pdf.

11. See Osgood (2010) for an explanation of how cities allocate on-street parking to shared cars.

## References

City of Los Angeles. 2012. Budget for the Fiscal Year 2012–13. http://cao.lacity .org/budget12-13/2012-13Proposed_Budget.pdf (retrieved October 18, 2012).

Dickerson, Marla. 2004. "Mexico's Economy Is Vrooming." *Los Angeles Times*, December 26.

Flegenheimer, Matt. 2012. "Data Show a City's Car Sharing May Be Working, but Doubts Persist." *New York Times*, September 2.

Gonzalez, David. 2008. "Don't Box Me In, Double-Parker." *New York Times*, September 10. http://cityroom.blogs.nytimes.com/2008/09/10/the-moral-theolo gy-of-double-parking/.

Holmes, Oliver Wendell Jr. 1897. "The Path of the Law." *Harvard Law Review* 10:457.

Kelling, George, and James Q. Wilson. 1982. "Broken Windows." *Atlantic*, March. www.theatlantic.com/magazine/archive/1982/03/broken-windows/ 304465/ (retrieved May 7, 2013).

Kolozsvari, Douglas, and Donald Shoup. 2003. "Turning Small Change into Big Changes." *Access* 23:2–7.

Krueger, Anne. 1974. "The Political Economy of the Rent-Seeking Society." *American Economic Review* 64 (3):291–303.

Machiavelli, Niccolò. 1965. *Machiavelli, the Chief Works*. Trans. Allan Gilbert. Vol. 1. Durham: Duke University Press.

Martin, Elliott, and Susan Shaheen. 2011. "The Impact of Carsharing on House-hold Vehicle Ownership." *Access* 38:22–27.

McChesney, Fred S. 2001. "Snow Jobs." Library of Economics and Liberty, October 15. www.econlib.org/library/Columns/Mcchesneysnow.html (retrieved September 24, 2012).

Olsson, Marie, and Gerald Miller. 1979. *The Impact on Commuters of a Residential Parking Permit Program*. Washington, DC: Urban Institute.

O'Neill, Natalie. 2012. "Doormen Accused of Hogging Parking Spots in Slope 'Parking Ring.'" *Brooklyn Paper*, February 16.

Osgood, Andrea. 2010. "On-Street Parking Spaces for Shared Cars." *Access* 36:8–13.

Pesce, Anthony. 2007. "Apron Parking Restricts Disabled Students." *Daily Bruin*, July 30.

Rheault, Gina. 2001. "No Parking." Master's thesis, University of Massachusetts, Boston. www.arkone.org/noparking/index.htm (retrieved September 24, 2012).

Shoup, Donald. 2010. "Putting Cities Back on Their Feet." *Journal of Urban Planning and Development* 36 (3):225–233.

Shoup, Donald. 2011. *The High Cost of Free Parking*. Chicago: Planners Press.

Sibley, Susan. Forthcoming. "J. Locke, op. cit.: Invocations of Law on Snowy Streets." *Journal of Comparative Law*.

University of Michigan. N.d. "Stadium History." www.umich.edu/stadium/history/ (retrieved September 24, 2012).

Viser, Matt. 2007. "Some Dig In for Spots They Dug Out." *Boston Globe*, December 27.

Wilson, Woodrow. 1918. *President Wilson's State Papers and Addresses*. New York: Review of Reviews Company.

# Conclusion: Deepening the Understanding of Informal Urbanism

Anastasia Loukaitou-Sideris and Vinit Mukhija

We started this book with the objective of better comprehending informality and its settings in U.S. cities. Our interest was piqued by the belief that the early twenty-first-century city cannot be fully understood without documenting and comprehending the landscapes of informality. As Nabil Kamel explains in his chapter, these come about from "opportunistic, calculated, and autonomous actions by local actors to redefine and renegotiate space outside of the realm of legal use of the built environment." In the twenty-first century, the landscapes of informality are omnipresent in our cities. They often occur in defiance of rules, ordinances, and regulations, out of necessity, or because of opportunity. The frequency of such landscapes, even in the abundantly wealthy and regulated cities of the Western world, indicates that they are neither anomalies nor aberrations. Indeed, they compose the informal city that coexists, interacts, competes, overlaps with, and complements its formal counterpart. Scholars keen to comprehend contemporary cities with all their complexities and contradictions must acquire a better understanding of informal urbanism and its sociospatial consequences.

As urban planning educators, we also believe that our profession's response, or lack thereof, to informality is frequently misguided by a variety of misconceptions about it. Admittedly, informality challenges planners' rational practices and regulatory conventions. But in the end planners cannot afford to ignore, persecute, or even romanticize it. Nor can they treat the diverse settings and activities of informal urbanism homogeneously, simply devising universal policies and regulations to address them. Context matters in urban planning, and it may matter even more in addressing informal activities.

The preceding chapters have provided insights about different facets of informal urbanism through case studies of diverse informal activities and settings in cities and regions across the country. Collectively, the chapters add to a growing literature that dispels many of the misconceptions surrounding informality and suggests lessons for planners, urban designers, and policymakers. Even though previous research has challenged many of the myths about informality, they stubbornly persist in the conventional wisdom. In this concluding chapter we highlight these misconceptions and summarize the lessons we have learned from the book's contributors, including the implications of informal urbanism for planning education and research.

## Misconceptions and Myths

A common misconception about informality is that *it is primarily associated with the developing world; to the extent that it appears in the developed world, it is always in the context of poor neighborhoods and marginalized populations.* However, most Americans living in cities are quite familiar with the settings and landscapes described in the book— the front yard that transforms into a minibazaar on the weekends, the taco truck that serves fast food on the roadside, the street corner where day laborers congregate in search of work, the community garden where neighbors go to cultivate crops and plants, the garage that has been converted into residential or commercial space, and so on. And while it is true that informality is often associated with poor neighborhoods and marginalized populations because it offers them opportunities for survival, it is also encountered in a much wider spectrum of neighborhoods and diverse urban settings, and can benefit or burden both poor and wealthy households.

As an informal innovation to address the need for affordable housing, colonias are typically developed in poor and underserved parts of the metropolitan fringe (Ward's chapter). But colonias are not the only form of informal housing in the United States. Unpermitted second units in single-family homes are an informal response to the lack of affordable housing too, as well as offering households a source of additional income or the convenience of more space. For these reasons, perhaps, Vinit Mukhija finds second units distributed all over the city of Los Angeles. While some of them are rudimentary shacks offering substandard housing conditions, others represent significant financial investment by their owners. Similarly, and as Mark Vallianatos explains, *loncheras* have traditionally served and continue to serve a primarily immigrant population that has few food options. But they have been increasingly complemented by gourmet food trucks that also operate in affluent neighborhoods. Donald Shoup discusses how informal on-street parking markets benefit wealthy apartment owners and their doormen in New York and San Francisco. And Margaret Crawford details how visiting garage sales has become a weekend pastime for low- and middle-income individuals alike.

A second myth is that *formal and informal activities and settings are always distinct and rigidly separated.* As we explain in the book's introduction, informality theorists have long questioned the dualist concept of formal versus informal economies, emphasizing instead their interdependent and overlapping nature (Bromley 1978). A similar interdependence exists between the spaces of formal and informal urbanism. For example, elements of the built environment of the formal city can help sustain informality. As Jacob Avery explains, the casino halls and bus terminals of Atlantic City provide a sustaining habitat for the unhoused residents there. And as Margaret Crawford shows, binaries such as private/public or formal/informal seem to dissolve in the inclusive and open space of a garage sale. Similarly, as Ginny Browne, Will Dominie, and Kate Mayerson illustrate through the food carts of Portland, the lines between the formal and the informal, the permitted and the unpermitted, are not always clear-cut in the built environment.

A third misconception is that *informality is an ephemeral construct.* As Michael Rios explains, informality involves "the appropriation of public and private land for a range of purposes and informal activities that defy land use norms, zoning requirements, and the law." For this reason, informal settings are much more vulnerable to termination. However, the ubiquity of many informal activities shows that the informal *practices* are not transitory, even if some specific settings are. There are a number of reasons for this. For one, as Peter Ward explains, informality can be a rational response when it provides opportunity for someone to acquire an asset that the formal market fails to deliver. Secondly, informality persists because it offers economic opportunities— as in the case of street vending (Kettles's chapter; Vallianatos's chapter), day labor (Valenzuela's chapter), or urban agriculture (Covert and Morales's chapter)—sustenance in the case of homelessness (Avery's chapter; Ehrenfeucht and Loukaitou-Sideris's chapter), or a right to the city in the case of disenfranchised populations (Kamel's chapter; Rios's chapter). Third, there is a synergy between formal and informal activities and spaces. For example, informality may create vibrancy in urban settings by repurposing abandoned or obsolete lots into community gardens (Hou's chapter), or street food districts (Browne, Dominie, and

Mayerson's chapter), or by introducing mixed uses in a single-use area (Crawford's chapter).

While these examples identify several positive outcomes of informality, the notion that *informality is always a virtue or has only positive consequences* is also flawed. Being outside the realm of regulation and government oversight not only results in revenue losses for the state but can lead to increased vulnerability, exploitation, and unhealthy conditions for those undertaking the informal activity or consuming its products, and to nuisances for their neighbors. In some cases, the use of space for informal activities by some groups can lead to the exclusion of others (Loukaitou-Sideris and Ehrenfeucht's chapter; Shoup's chapter). This is why a number of case studies show that, depending on the informal activity and context, formalization and regulation may be a positive prospect (Covert and Morales's chapter; Mukhija's chapter; Valenzuela's chapter; Ward's chapter).

While several authors recommend some form of formalization through ordinances and permits, the belief that *legalization and regulation can adequately respond to all aspects of informality* is also misleading. For one, the transformation from unregulated and informal to fully regulated and formal is frequently fraught with conflict between proponents and opponents, winners and losers (Covert and Morales's chapter). Moreover, and as many case studies seem to attest, the application of conventional regulatory norms that work well for formal activities may have devastating effects on informal activities. This is because regulatory actions at times embody an "irreconcilable tension" that can harm those undertaking informal activities (Ehrenfeucht and Loukaitou-Sideris's chapter). Additionally, while formalization may bring legitimacy and protection, it may simply make no economic sense for many in the informal economy. Lastly, selective enforcement of regulations on the part of authorities may result in inequitable outcomes (Loukaitou-Sideris and Ehrenfeucht's chapter). Thus, a "brown" immigrant sidewalk vendor selling fruit or orange juice is likely to attract more regulatory and punitive attention from the authorities than "white" youngsters selling lemonade on their neighborhood sidewalk. Here, the impulse to regulate is more connected with the socioracial attributes of participants than with the characteristics of the informal activity per se.

### Lessons Drawn

The last few observations raise an important practical question: how can planners, urban designers, and policymakers better understand and respond to urban informality and its spatial settings? As we noted in the introduction, our intellectual position is closely aligned with the reformist approach, and we advocate an active role for governments and civil society in upgrading informal activities. The premise of this book is that planners can no longer ignore informality but should play a key role in understanding and responding creatively and justly to its different facets. Indeed, the recognition of informality in U.S. cities should have significant effects on the scholarship, education, and practice of planning and urban design. For example, the acknowledgment of informal jobs, housing, and public spaces should help broaden the conventional policy focus from its emphasis on job creation, new housing construction, and new public space development to also include job improvement, housing adaptation and upgrading, and the enhancement of existing public spaces to better accommodate informal activities. We also hope that, in addition to the conventional emphasis on legal responses, the spatial lens used by physical planners and urban designers can play an important role in addressing and managing informality.

The preceding chapters have provided insights into the challenges and opportunities of the informal city and have discussed its policy and design implications. Rather than repeating the chapter-specific recommendations, this concluding chapter identifies some cross-cutting lessons, including advice for education and research.

One significant lesson drawn from the variety of informal activities and diverse settings and issues detailed is that informal urbanism is complex and at times contradictory in nature. There are different stakeholders involved and both potential winners and losers. Another key characteristic of informal activities is their interaction and relationship with formal institutions, including local regulations and markets. These interactions and local conditions help define the complex nature of informality. It is important for planners, designers, and policymakers to understand the nuances of the specific sociospatial contexts they are dealing with, or as Michael Rios puts it, to "contextualiz[e] marginality and emplac[e] informality" before deciding on a design, action, or policy.

To address the complexity of multiple interests and conflicting issues, a number of authors call for planners and policymakers to become mediators, acting as the professionals who can build bridges between different stakeholders. Urban agriculture in Kansas City, community gardens in Seattle, and the food cart pods in downtown Portland were all enabled by partnerships between formal institutional actors and grassroots-based social groups. In addition to developing mediation skills, planners will need to understand both the intricacies of formal regulations and the nature of informal activities in order to effectively span the world of formal and informal institutions, and help stakeholders dependent on informal activities for survival.

As Peter Ward observes, outlawing or criminalizing informality is rarely successful. And while some regulation is necessary to protect the health and safety of the general public, many existing laws and ordinances make absolutely no room for informality and other unexpected activities. Planners and policymakers, as Ward notes, should consider regulation and policy intervention that "seek to work within the realms of informality, not exclusively outside it." For this reason, various chapters raise the need for "creative," "benign," and "flexible" regulation, or "mud," as Gregg Kettles calls a law's purposeful ambiguity that allows some discretion to regulators. In addition, as Abel Valenzuela suggests, planners, policymakers, and communities also need to consider alternative institutional arrangements, such as worker centers, that can help regulate informal activities without preventing them.

## A Spatial Lens for Informality

Explicitly or implicitly, the chapters in the book have also argued for a spatial understanding of informality, and have documented the physical attributes of many informal locations and settings. Informal activities are inherently spatial (Ogbu 2012), and individuals or groups need to occupy space to perform a variety of important activities. Nevertheless, informal urbanism has mostly failed to attract the attention and skills of urban designers (Mukhija 2011). Instead, people are left to their own means and devices, or "tactics," in adapting, adjusting, and making space for informal activities (Kamel's chapter). This failure to accommodate the spatial needs of informality can lead to conflict—when one group occupies the space of another—or to unsafe, hazardous, and marginalized environments.

In the 1980s, economist and Nobel laureate Amartya Sen pioneered the capability approach, arguing that the well-being of persons should not only focus on their resources but also on the opportunities they have to carry on their lives in the way they value (Sen 1985; Robeyns 2006). But are there spatial arrangements that can help participants of informality enhance their capabilities? A basic premise of this book is that a spatial perspective is necessary not only to document but also to respond to informality. In other words, planners and urban designers should offer creative spatial solutions that accommodate, integrate, or allow informal settings to coexist and even contribute to their formal counterparts (Rios's chapter; Ehrenfeucht and Loukaitou-Sideris's chapter). Michael Rios argues that progressive urban designers cannot avoid questions of aesthetics. They need to be proactively involved in defining support for an aesthetic that accepts informality and its perceived disorder. They need, he adds, to be engaged in *revelation* (uncovering the invisible and understanding the informal), *negotiation* (finding a middle ground to blur or soften the boundaries between formal and informal urbanism), and *imagination* (creatively envisioning new forms or adapting existing ones to accommodate informal activities). Different spatial strategies may be needed for different circumstances and sociospatial contexts. Nevertheless, we want to take Rios's promptings one step further and sketch some ways that planners and urban designers can respond to informality by creating a more inclusive urban commons, which enhances the capabilities of its participants.

For one, the design and creation of a supportive public infrastructure may go a long way toward lessening hardships incurred by those participating in informal activities. It would also help to ameliorate the nuisances and negative externalities produced by informality. For example, creating public rest stops with showers and toilets for homeless denizens (Ehrenfeucht and Loukaitou-Sideris's chapter) can give relief to those without shelter, and at the same time keep municipal sidewalks clean from human excrement. Connecting colonias to municipal water systems not only lifts a huge economic and health burden from colonia residents, but also protects public health from the spread of diseases caused by contaminated water (Ward's chapter). Building worker centers benefits day laborers by providing them with safe and hassle-free spaces to congregate and get training or other resources, and can also benefit potential employers and lessen conflicts between local residents and day laborers (Valenzuela's chapter). The provision of such public infrastructure is not inexpensive, but its absence may be more costly.

Second, where formal and informal activities coexist, design and policy should seek to lessen conflict between them. Conflict is frequently generated by a lack of appropriate or available space that forces informal activities to occupy territory used by formal activities. Conflict is also generated when informal activities are perceived as creating nuisances for others. Creatively identifying underutilized space that can host informal activities, enhancing this space through design, and tweaking the regulatory framework to accommodate such activities may not only ameliorate conflicts but even create a public amenity, as the case of Portland's food cart pods demonstrates (Browne, Dominie, and Mayerson's chapter). Nuisances such as litter, noise, and odors can be addressed through a series of sensible regulations that hold informal participants responsible for cleanliness, removal of trash, good sanitation, and operating during established and agreed-upon business hours.

Third, where formal and informal activities are rigidly separated, creative design could soften the edges and build bridges and middle grounds. In the early twenty-first century, divisions between formal and informal are propagated by the increasing economic inequality of cities. Such divisions are often accentuated by design, through the creation of sharply demarcated borders, abrupt discontinuities, and walled, fenced, or gated boundaries (Loukaitou-Sideris 2012). Softer edges and boundaries in the form of transitional zones, such as a small public park where formal and informal activities coexist, may act as connecting links. While design solutions cannot solve poverty and inequality, they should not help further stigmatize it.

Lastly, because informal activities are spread differently in urban space, have different impacts on different neighborhoods, and may be appreciated, tolerated, or disparaged depending on the neighborhood context and circumstances, a spatially decentralized decision-making approach may be more appropriate than regionwide or citywide umbrella policies. Thus, a citywide ban on sidewalk vending may not make sense in some neighborhoods, where vendors provide important retail services. Similarly, garage sales, second units, or urban agriculture may be highly appreciated in some neighborhoods but disliked in others. While citywide regulations are important for matters pertaining to health and safety, other issues relating to where and when informal activities can take place may sometimes be better resolved at the neighborhood level, by neighborhood councils or other local groups. This privileging of residents, however, can be problematic. It can perpetuate exclusionary tendencies and unbalanced power dynamics. For example, it is unlikely that most neighborhoods would enthusiastically agree to create spaces for the homeless. Decentralized and neighborhood-level policies may work well only in cases where neighborhoods have a clear gain from informal activities.

## Future Scholarship

Lastly, we turn to the possible contributions of future scholarship. By studying and explaining the nature, underlying logic, and diversity of urban informality to a larger public, researchers can help build a bridge between formal and informal urbanism. Presently, the landscapes of informal urbanism remain largely unexplored by planning and design scholars. In popular perception they are often seen in negative terms: as spaces of marginality that are ignored at best or contested and reviled at worst. We need more in-depth inquiries into the characteristics and sociospatial attributes of different informal activities, better estimates of the locations and scale of informality (where it appears, how frequently, and at what intensity), and more inductive studies to identify under what conditions informality benefits or hurts vulnerable populations. Researchers need to help explain informality, and also assist in developing appropriate responses to it. To this end, we need more research on the different regulatory responses to informal activities (from formalization to alternatives to formalization), as well as research on spatial solutions to satisfactorily accommodate informal activities. Comparative analyses and lessons learned from different domestic and international cities can help reveal such good practices. As we suggested in the introduction, this can be a fruitful area of collaboration between scholars in developed and developing countries.

In the end, the informal city cannot be ignored, because it occupies the spaces of everyday life and interacts and overlaps with the settings and institutions of the formal city. Informal urbanism is an inherent part of U.S. cities and has become relevant for an increasing number of social groups that are affected by it in both positive and negative ways. It deserves to be recognized, understood, and responded to by planners, policymakers, and urban designers in ways that reduce conflicts and enhance human capabilities. This book represents only a preliminary step in this direction.

## References

Bromley, Ray. 1978. "Introduction—The Urban Informal Sector: Why Is It Worth Discussing?" *World Development* 6 (9–10):1033–1039.

Loukaitou-Sideris, Anastasia. 2012. "Addressing the Challenges for Urban Landscapes: Normative Goals for Urban Design." *Journal of Urban Design* 17 (4):467–484.

Mukhija, Vinit. 2011. "Urban Design for a Planet of Informal Cities." In Tridib Banerjee and Anastasia Loukaitou-Sideris, eds., *Companion to Urban Design*: 574–584. London: Routledge.

Ogbu, Liz. 2012. "Reframing Practice: Identifying a Framework for Social Impact Design." *Journal of Urban Design* 17 (4):573–589.

Robeyns, Ingrid. 2006. "The Capability Approach in Practice." *Journal of Political Philosophy* 14 (3):351–376.

Sen, Amartya. 1985. *Commodities and Capabilities.* Amsterdam: North-Holland.

# Contributors

Jacob Avery is an assistant professor in the Department of Sociology, University of California, Irvine, where he is working on a book about street life in Atlantic City. Previously he was a postdoctoral fellow at the University of Michigan's National Poverty Center. His primary research interests include urban poverty and inequality, social service provision, culture, social interaction, and fieldwork methods. He holds a Ph.D. in sociology from the University of Pennsylvania.

Ginny Browne received her master's in urban and regional planning from the University of California, Los Angeles. Her interests are in community economic development and housing. She is a project coordinator with the Participatory Budgeting Project, a nonprofit organization in California.

Matt Covert received an M.S. in environment and resources from the Nelson Institute for Environmental Studies at the University of Wisconsin-Madison. He wrote his master's thesis on developing regimes of urban agriculture land use policy in the American West. Currently he is a planning researcher for 1000 Friends of Wisconsin, a statewide planning advocacy organization, while working toward an M.S. in urban and regional planning.

Margaret Crawford is a professor of architecture in the College of Environmental Design at the University of California, Berkeley. Her research focuses on the evolution, uses, and meaning of urban space. She is known for her work on everyday urbanism, a concept that encourages the close investigation and empathetic understanding of the specifics of daily life as the basis for urban theory and design. Crawford is the author of *Nansha Coastal City: Landscape and Urbanism in the Pearl River Delta*

(Harvard University, Graduate School of Design) and *Building the Work-ingman's Paradise: The Design of American Company Towns* (Verso), as well as the coeditor of *The Car and the City: The Automobile, the Built Environment, and Daily Urban Life* (University of Michigan Press) and *Everyday Urbanism* (Monacelli Press). She holds a Ph.D. in urban planning from the University of California, Los Angeles.

**Will Dominie** currently works as a planner challenging spatial health inequities at the Contra Costa County Public Health Department. He has spent the last ten years working for environmental, racial, economic, and gender justice, providing research support to the Los Angeles Bus Riders Union, working for racial and environmental justice with Urban Habitat, and contributing research and political education to support Causa Justa :: Just Cause's work for self-determination and the right to the city. He holds a master's degree in urban and regional planning from the University of California, Los Angeles.

**Renia Ehrenfeucht** is an associate professor and chair of the Department of Planning and Urban Studies at the University of New Orleans. She currently conducts research on shrinking cities and on the production and meaning of public space and the specificity of sidewalk. Ehrenfeucht is the coauthor of *Sidewalks: Conflict and Negotiation over Public Space* (MIT Press). She holds a Ph.D. in urban planning from the University of California, Los Angeles.

**Jeffrey Hou** is an associate professor and chair of Landscape Architecture in the College of Built Environments at the University of Washington. His research, teaching, and practice focus on engaging marginalized communities and citizens through community design, design activism, and cross-cultural learning. He has worked with indigenous tribes, farmers, and fishers in Taiwan, neighborhood residents in Japan, villagers in China, and inner-city immigrant youths and elders in North American cities, in projects ranging from conservation of wildlife habitats to rebuilding of indigenous villages and design of urban open space and streetscapes. Hou is the editor of *Insurgent Public Space: Guerrilla Urbanism and the Remaking of Contemporary Cities* (Routledge). He holds a Ph.D. in environmental planning from the University of California, Berkeley.

**Nabil Kamel** is an assistant professor in the School of Geographical Sciences and Urban Planning at Arizona State University. His research explores the relationship between the built environment and institutional structures in cities to address social and environmental issues associated with urban development. His current projects include urban design strategies for sustainable development, transit-oriented development, urban simulation, housing market analysis, and long-term post-disaster recovery. He holds a Ph.D. in urban planning from the University of California, Los Angeles.

**Gregg Kettles** was deputy counsel to former Los Angeles Mayor Antonio Villaraigosa and is a visiting professor at Loyola Law School. He also sits on the Los Angeles Food Policy Council. He is a cofounder of the Open Air Market Network, an Internet-based forum for discussing the functions, importance, and variety of street markets and merchants. His research focuses on the legal aspects of street vending, street food, and other kinds of commerce in public space. He holds a J.D. from Yale University.

**Anastasia Loukaitou-Sideris** is a professor of urban planning in the Luskin School of Public Affairs at the University of California, Los Angeles. Her research focuses on the public environment of the city: its physical representation, aesthetics, social meaning, and impact on the urban resident. Her books include *Urban Design Downtown: Poetics and Politics of Form* (University of California Press) and *Sidewalks: Conflict and Negotiation over Public Space* (MIT Press). She is also the coeditor of *Jobs and Economic Development in Minority Communities* (Temple University Press) and *Companion to Urban Design* (Routledge). She holds a Ph.D. from the University of Southern California.

**Kate Mayerson** is a program manager at Los Angeles Neighborhood Initiative, a nonprofit organization that stimulates neighborhood revitalization with catalytic community improvement projects. She received her master's in urban and regional planning at the University of California, Los Angeles, where her research focused on regulatory models of informal land uses, including research on secondary dwelling units, medical marijuana collectives, and a capstone project on street vending legislation.

**Alfonso Morales** is an associate professor in the Department of Urban and Regional Planning at the University of Wisconsin. He studies public marketplaces and street vendors and the role they fill in economic development. Morales is the coeditor of *Street Entrepreneurs: People, Place,* *and Politics in Local and Global Perspective* (Routledge) and *Renascent Pragmatism: Studies in Law and Social Science* (Ashgate). He holds a Ph.D. from Northwestern University.

**Vinit Mukhija** is an associate professor of urban planning in the Luskin School of Public Affairs at the University of California, Los Angeles. His research focuses on informal housing and slums in developing countries and Third-World-like housing conditions (including colonias, unpermitted trailer parks, and illegal garage apartments) in the United States. His work also examines how planners and urban designers in both developing and developed countries can learn from the everyday and informal city. Mukhija is the author of *Squatters as Developers? Slum Redevelopment in Mumbai* (Ashgate). He holds a Ph.D. from the Massachusetts Institute of Technology.

**Michael Rios** is an associate professor of urban design and community planning in the Landscape Architecture Department at the University of California, Davis. He also directs the Sacramento Diasporas Project which provides policy-relevant and community-based research related to the region's migrant and refugee populations. Rios's research focuses on the intersection between marginality, urbanism, and public space, with particular interest in placemaking as an assemblage of different practices involving negotiations of belonging, authorship, and power. Rios is the coeditor of *Diálogos: Placemaking in Latino Communities* (Routledge). He holds a Ph.D. from Pennsylvania State University.

**Donald Shoup** is Distinguished Professor of Urban Planning at the University of California, Los Angeles, where he has served as chair of the Department of Urban Planning and as director of the Institute of Transportation Studies. His book *The High Cost of Free Parking* shows how better parking policies can improve cities, the economy, and the environment; a growing number of cities have adopted his recommendations. He is a Fellow of the American Institute of Certified Planners and an honorary professor at the Beijing Institute of Transportation Research. He holds a Ph.D. in economics from Yale University.

**Abel Valenzuela Jr.** is a professor of urban planning and Chicano studies at the University of California, Los Angeles. His research is primarily concerned with the issues faced by minorities and immigrants in the United States, including immigration and labor markets, poverty and inequality, and immigrant settlement patterns and related services. At UCLA, he directs the Center for the Study of Urban Poverty. Valenzuela is the coeditor of *Prismatic Metropolis: Inequality in Los Angeles* (Russell Sage Foundation) and *Immigration and Crime: Ethnicity, Race, and Violence* (New York University Press). He holds a Ph.D. from the Massachusetts Institute of Technology.

**Mark Vallianatos** is an adjunct professor at Occidental College and the policy director of Occidental's Urban and Environmental Policy Institute. His research focuses on food access, transportation, and goods movement. Before moving to the Los Angeles region he worked on international trade and environmental issues in Washington, D.C. Vallianatos is the coauthor of *The Next Los Angeles: The Struggle for a Livable City* (University of California Press). He holds a J.D. from the University of Virginia.

**Peter M. Ward** is a professor in the Department of Sociology and in the Lyndon B. Johnson School of Public Affairs at the University of Texas at Austin, where he has also served as director of the Mexican Center of the Institute of Latin American Studies. His research focuses on Latin American urbanization, low-cost and informal housing, land markets, social policy, and local government and Mexican politics. Ward has written and edited twelve books, among them *Colonias and Public Policy in Texas: Urbanization by Stealth* (University of Texas Press), *Housing, the State and the Poor: Policy and Practice in Latin American Cities* (Cambridge University Press), and *Self-Help Housing: A Critique* (Mansell Publishing Company). He holds a Ph.D. from the University of Liverpool.

# Index

## Urban and Industrial Environments

Series editor: Robert Gottlieb, Henry R. Luce Professor of Urban and Environmental Policy, Occidental College

Catherine Tumber,
*Small, Gritty, and Green: The Promise of America's Smaller Industrial Cities in a Low-Carbon World*

Sam Bass Warner and Andrew H. Whittemore,
*American Urban Form: A Representative History*

John Pucher and Ralph Buehler, eds.,
*City Cycling*

Stephanie Foote and Elizabeth Mazzolini, eds.,
*Histories of the Dustheap: Waste, Material Cultures, Social Justice*

David J. Hess,
*Good Green Jobs in a Global Economy: Making and Keeping New Industries in the United States*

Joseph F. C. DiMento and Clifford Ellis,
*Changing Lanes: Visions and Histories of Urban Freeways*

Joanna Robinson,
*Contested Water: The Struggle against Water Privatization in the United States and Canada*

William B. Meyer,
*The Environmental Advantages of Cities: Countering Commonsense Antiurbanism*

Rebecca L. Henn and Andrew J. Hoffman, eds.,
*Constructing Green: The Social Structures of Sustainability*

Peggy F. Barlett and Geoffrey W. Chase, eds.,
*Sustainability in Higher Education: Stories and Strategies for Transformation*

Isabelle Anguelovski,
*Neighborhood as Refuge: Community Reconstruction, Place Remaking, and Environmental Justice in the City*

Kelly Sims Gallagher,
*The Global Diffusion of Clean Energy Technology: Lessons from China*

Vinit Mukhija and Anastasia Loukaitou-Sideris, eds.,
*The Informal American City: Beyond Taco Trucks and Day Labor*

Printed in the United States
by Baker & Taylor Publisher Services

incomes in 1960 may be consistent with very different growth prospects, so they can hardly be taken as similar technologies. In this sense, the alternative split, based upon 1990 wealth, may reflect much better these technological differences. The good fit for the last subsample (column 5) is somehow surprising if we consider the rather implausible parameter values we obtain in the context of Solow technology. To analyse this puzzle we have run unconditional convergence regressions for the five subsamples. The unconditional model fits much worse than the conditional one among poor countries and generates a very low convergence speed. The unconditional rate is about a half of the conditional one; this holds regardless of whether we define the poorest countries in 1960 (0.9 versus 2.1) or in 1990 (1.1 versus 2.2). The correlation among the initial conditions and the steady state is strong and positive among poor countries; the lower the initial conditions the lower the steady state. In the rich countries subsamples (columns 3 and 5) things look different. When we choose the countries on the basis of their position in 1960, the unconditional model fits slightly worse, but produces a higher rate of convergence than the *conditional* one (4.1 versus 2.4). Unlike the other subsamples, in this case the correlation among initial conditions and the steady state is, if anything, negative. Finally, when we choose the richest countries in 1990, the steady state variables become irrelevant. The absolute and relative rates of convergence are similar, and the fit does not improve substantially. This result, together with the implausible parameter values for this subsample, casts some doubts on the adequacy of the augmented Solow model at this disaggregate level. Information about technological constraints adds nothing to the simple unconstrained unconditional model. We shall return to the implications of this result once we analyse the pooled sample.

## 5    Pooling

### 5.1    Results for the whole sample

Cross-section results, such as the ones presented in the previous section, are illustrative in many ways of the long-run behaviour of the OECD economies; nevertheless, there is an alternative use for our information. There are several advantages in exploiting the time series dimension of our data set. First, the way in which long-term growth and shorter-term fluctuations are isolated is somewhat arbitrary; it is true that the time span needed for growth forces to become effective is long and it is advisable not to draw conclusions from annual data. A popular intermediate approach consists of taking shorter period averages as representative of the long-run path of the economy; this cancels out some uninteresting cyclical movements but still leaves some room for time varying shocks to affect the growth process. It is important to remember that convergence applies only to the neighbourhood of the steady state. Five-year averages probably capture steady-state changes that can be hidden in the analysis of the preceding section using 30-year averages. We have chosen a 5-year period split with the break points at 1960, 1965, 1970, 1975, 1980 and 1985. This amounts to reformulating the model as

$$\ln y^i_{T+t^*} = B_1 + \phi T + \beta^{-1} \left[ \alpha \ln(s^{i*}_{kT}) + \gamma \ln(s^{i*}_{hT}) - (\alpha+\gamma) \ln(n^{i*}_T + \phi + \delta) \right] + \nu_{iT}$$

(16)

$$\ln y^i_{T+\tau} - \ln y^i_T = \phi\tau + \left(1 - e^{-\lambda\tau}\right) \left[ \ln y^i_{T+t^*} - \ln y^i_T + \phi t^* \right] + \eta_{iT} \qquad (17)$$

or in linear format,

$$\ln y^i_{T+\tau} - \ln y^i_T = \pi_0 + \pi_1 \ln y^i_T + \pi_2 \ln(s^{i*}_{kT}) + \pi_3 \ln(s^{i*}_{hT}) + \pi_4 \ln$$
$$(n^{i*}_T + \phi + \delta) + \pi_5 T + \epsilon_{iT} \qquad (18)$$

where $i = 1, 2, \ldots, 24$, $T = 1960, 1965, \ldots, 1985$, $\tau = 5$.

The second advantage of the model in (16), (17), (18) is that it enables us to improve our understanding of the relationship between growth and medium term macroeconomic performance. In the pooled sample we can carry out some tests of structural stability on the convergence model. Growth rates have been far from homogeneous along the sample period in the OECD. Many countries grew very fast until 1973 and then entered a deep recession until 1986. This raises two related issues as far as the Solow model is concerned. The first is to what extent it is legitimate to expect the Solow model (or in general any model based on labour market equilibrium) to hold during periods of high unemployment. Moreover, we can also investigate whether the rate of convergence remains stable regardless of average growth. In other words, the question is whether OECD economies converge at the same speed during recessions or, rather whether richer countries fare better than poor ones in bad times, so that the distance between them is widened.

Finally, there are two ways in which the econometric specification can be improved, one of which we shall exploit here. So far we have relied on OLS estimates in the cross-sections. The reasons for doing that were twofold; first because of the difficulty of finding well-suited instruments, and second for comparison purposes, given that most of the work done in this area has followed this approach. In fact the size of the simultaneity bias is expected to be small in the cross-sections, given that only the last element in the full period average of each variable is simultaneously determined with the final year per capita income.[21] However, in the pooled sample, the potential bias is larger, because in this case it is one out of five (rather than one out of thirty) elements in the average which is simultaneously determined with the left-hand variable. In general we have estimated the models by non-linear instrumental variables. The instruments we have used are lags of endogenous variables and current and past values of macroeconomic indicators, such as public spending, inflation, and export growth. The model in (16), (17) and (18) could also be estimated allowing for time-invariant individual country effects.[22] In fact the null of the same constant term across countries has been imposed rather than tested at this stage,[23] and we shall proceed assuming that these effects do not exist, or at least that they are uncorrelated with the right-hand side variables to ensure consistency in the estimates in our pooling model.

The linear regression estimates in Table 9.6 partially confirm the results found in the cross-section model. The coefficient of initial income, $\hat{\pi}_1$, is negative and highly significant. With time dummies, the inclusion of steady-state variables improves the fit with a 10% fall in the standard error and a substantial increase in $R^2$. In this case the conditional model also yields a much higher convergence rate, with a 40% increase in $\hat{\pi}_1$, which again suggests a positive correlation among the initial conditions and the steady state. The parameter restrictions implied by the linearized Solow model are easily accepted by the data, as can be seen in the unchanged standard error (with a $p$ value of 9.5 and 51.2 in columns 5 and 6 respectively). Unlike the cross-section case, in the pooled data set without imposing restrictions on coefficients (not reported here) the human capital proxy is positive but not strongly significant, with a $t$-statistic below 1.8. As we shall see this result is heavily dependent on the specification chosen, so that the estimated elasticity of human capital must be carefully interpreted.[24]

Non-linear instrumental variables regressions are summarized in Table 9.7. In columns 1 to 3 we present the results of the joint estimation of both the steady state and the convergence equations with (column 1) and without (columns 2 and 3) imposing all cross-equation restrictions. The convergence equation in the fully restricted model (column 1) fits worse than the unrestricted linear one. The estimated parameter set yields some implausible values with $\hat{\alpha}$ lower than expected (0.16). The restriction imposed on $\phi$ is easily accepted and free estimation yields a point estimate around 0.03. Unlike the linear case, once we impose the cross-equation restrictions, human capital appears well signed and significant. The convergence rate is between 2.5 and 2.8, higher than the values

**Table 9.6    Linear models of convergence. Pooled data**

|  | 1 | 2 | 3 | $4^d$ | $5^d$ | $6^d$ |
|---|---|---|---|---|---|---|
| constant | 0.36 | −0.30 | −0.58 | 0.34 | −0.26 | −0.60 |
|  | (9.45) | (2.26) | (3.57) | (8.96) | (2.25) | (3.62) |
| $\log(Y^i_{60})$ | −0.10 | −0.11 | −0.12 | −0.08 | −0.10 | −0.11 |
|  | (6.18) | (8.38) | (6.02) | (5.26) | (7.67) | (6.60) |
| $\log(I/Y)^i$ |  | 0.12 | 0.13 |  | 0.11 | 0.12 |
|  |  | (5.59) | (6.35) |  | (5.57) | (5.81) |
| $\log(n+\phi+\delta)^i$ |  | −0.12* | −0.17* |  | −0.11* | −0.18* |
| $\log(s_h)^i$ |  |  | 0.04 |  |  | 0.06 |
|  |  |  | (1.67) |  |  | (2.33) |
| $\bar{R}^2$ | 0.322 | 0.420 | 0.387 | 0.396 | 0.479 | 0.462 |
| $\sigma$ | 0.066 | 0.061 | 0.059 | 0.062 | 0.058 | 0.055 |
| DW | 1.53 | 1.81 | 2.23 | 1.55 | 1.82 | 2.25 |
| $\chi^2_1$ |  | 1.07 | 0.21 |  | 2.78 | 0.43 |
| $\rho$ |  | 30.2% | 64.8% |  | 9.5% | 51.2% |

*Notes:* * Restricted parameter.
$^d$ Equation including time dummies.
Instruments: constant, $\log(Y^i_T)$, $\Delta\log(Y^i_{T-1})$, $\log(I/Y)^i_{T-1}$, $\log(Y^i)_{T-1}$, $\log(s_h)^i_T$ $\log(n+\phi+\delta)^i_{T-1}$, $(n+\phi+\delta)^i_{T-1}$, $(G/Y)^i_{T-1}$, $\pi^i_{T-1}$, $\Delta X^i_{T-1}$, trend or dummies.
Dependent variable $\log(Y^i_{90}/Y^i_{60})$. Sample $i$: 1, ..., 24. $T$: 1960, 65, ..., 85
Estimation method: instrumental variables.

obtained in the cross-section model. Similarly, the steady-state equation presents a poor fit. Moreover, the rejection of theoretical restrictions is overwhelming; the point estimates of $\alpha, \gamma$ and $\phi$ differ very much across equations and point to very different technological parameters, as can also be seen in the corresponding $\chi^2$ statistics, significantly higher than their critical value. The joint estimation of both equations without imposing the cross-equation restrictions in columns 2 and 3 reveals other explanations for the poor performance of the fully restricted model. Imposing cross-equation restrictions produces parameter values close to the ones obtained in the steady-state equation. When these restrictions are relaxed the fit of the convergence equation improves sharply and reaches the same statistics as the unrestricted linear model ($\hat{\sigma} = 0.059$). As in the cross-section model, the poor fit of this equation[25] as well as the conceptual difficulty of using average $(Y/L)_{T,T+\tau}$ as the steady-state proxy makes it advisable to focus on the convergence model.

In columns 4 to 6, we present three versions of the convergence equation which fit as well as their linear counterparts, and with reasonable DW

**Table 9.7**  Non-linear estimation of steady-state and convergence equations. Pooled data

|  | 1 | $2^{SS}$ | 3 | 4 | $5^d$ | $6^d$ |
|---|---|---|---|---|---|---|
| $B_1$ | −4.10 (5.62) | −4.17 (4.78) | | | | |
| $B_2$ | −4.48 (6.01) | | −5.28 (3.88) | −5.84 (4.00) | −7.10 (4.71) | −6.33 (3.81) |
| $\alpha$ | 0.16 (3.77) | 0.10 (1.91) | 0.34 (4.59) | 0.43 (5.07) | 0.38 (4.08) | 0.38 (6.06) |
| $\gamma$ | 0.41 (13.4) | 0.45 (12.4) | 0.27 (3.97) | 0.17 (3.01) | 0.26 (5.11) | 0.24 (3.79) |
| $\phi$ | 0.03 (3.03) | 0.01 (0.83) | 0.03 (3.19) | 0.02 (2.38) | 0.03 (2.65) | 0.02* |
| $\lambda$ | — | — | | | | 0.023 (5.76) |
| $\bar{R}^2$ | 0.310 | | 0.396 | 0.356 | 0.465 | 0.470 |
| $\bar{R}^2_{ss}$ | 0.505 | 0.507 | | | | |
| $\sigma$ | 0.063 | | 0.059 | 0.061 | 0.055 | 0.055 |
| $\sigma_{ss}$ | 0.287 | 0.286 | | | | |
| DW | | | | 2.19 | 2.29 | 2.26 |
| $\beta_{imp}$ | 0.43 | 0.45 | 0.39 | 0.40 | 0.37 | 0.38 |
| $\lambda_{imp}(\hat{\phi}=0.02)$ | 0.025 | 0.026 | 0.023 | 0.023 | 0.021 | |
| $\lambda_{imp}(\phi)$ | 0.028 | 0.022 | 0.028 | 0.024 | 0.024 | |

*Notes:* * Restricted parameter.
[d] Equation including time dummies.
Restrictions:  $\chi^2_1(\gamma) = 5.75\,(1.7\%)$; $\chi^2_1(\alpha) = 6.98\,(0.8\%)$; $\chi^2_1(\alpha, \gamma) = 7.25(2.7\%)$ $\chi^2_1(\alpha, \gamma, \phi) = 12.68\,(5.4\%)$
Instruments:  constant, $\log(Y^i_T), \Delta\log(Y^i_{T-1}), \log(I/Y)^i_{T-1}, \log(Y^i)_{T-1}, \log(s_h)^i_T$ $\log(n + \phi + \delta)^i_{T-1}, (n + \phi + \delta)^i_{T-1}, (G/Y)^i_{T-1}, \pi^i_{T-1}, \Delta X^i_{T-1}$, trend or dummies.
Dependent variable $\log(Y^i_{T+5}/Y^i_T)$. Sample $i$: 1, ..., 24; $T$: 1960, 65, ..., 85.
Estimation method: non-linear instrumental variables with robust errors.

values. In columns 4 and 5 technical progress is specified as a linear trend, and, in column 6, $\phi$ is set to 0.02. The model without time dummies (column 4) yields a slightly high $\hat{\alpha}$ and a much lower than expected $\hat{\gamma}$ (0.17). Again including time dummies improves the overall fit and brings the technological structure closer to what we obtained in the cross-section model ($\hat{\alpha} = 0.38, \hat{\gamma} = 0.26$). Finally, the direct estimation of $\lambda$ turns out to be fairly precise (column 6). In all cases, the convergence rate is within the range of values obtained in the cross-section model:

between 2.1% and 2.4%. The overall conclusion we can draw from these estimations is a value of $\lambda$ which is slightly higher than that found in the cross-section analysis, in the context of a convergence equation which has many similarities to the one estimated in the previous section. In fact these differences are controlled for, the pooling model becomes very similar to the cross-section one; in this case the point estimates of $B_2$, $\alpha, \gamma, \lambda$, and $\phi$ almost coincide.

### 5.2    Subsample estimates

In order to facilitate comparisons with the results in section 4, we have kept the same split among countries as in the cross-section model. As in that case, we have proceeded to estimate the model with and without steady-state variables to establish differences among conditional and unconditional convergence. In all cases we have chosen the linear trend specification for technical progress in order to be able to estimate $\phi$. In the time dummies model this estimate showed implausible values, and we are interested in testing whether there are significant differences in technology among country subsamples. Let us consider the conditional model first (Table 9.8). The exclusion of Turkey and Greece from the sample increases the rate of conditional convergence by more than 20% (from 2.2% to 2.8%), and improves the fit with a substantial fall in the standard error. As in the cross-section, the convergence model displays a much better fit as we exclude poor countries from the sample. The differences in estimated parameters among poor and rich countries according to their position in 1960 (columns 2 and 3 respectively) are striking. The relative size of $\hat{B}_2$ goes in the direction suggested by theory ($\hat{B}_2^P < \hat{B}_2^R$) pointing towards huge differences in efficiency in the use of productive factors in favour of the most advanced countries. There are not differences though in the estimated rate of labour augmenting technical progress ($\hat{\phi}$), which are not significantly different from 0.02. The discrepancy in the labour share is large and goes against what was expected; the point estimate of $\hat{\beta}$ for poor countries is 0.37 against 0.58 for the rich ones. Similarly, the convergence rate is higher when we exclude the poorest countries (3.2% versus 2.2%).

These results are largely confirmed if we take the alternative splitting criterion (per capita income in 1990). Again, the initial conditions and the scale effect (summarized in $\hat{B}_2$) are significantly better for rich countries. The estimated labour share is also much larger among richer countries, generating a conditional convergence rate of 4.6% against 2.4% among the poor ones. The estimated capital share is rather implausible for the rich countries sample; the point estimate is around

**Table 9.8  Subsamples: models of conditional convergence. Pooled data**

|  | $1^d$ | $2^d$ | $3^d$ | $4^d$ | $5^d$ |
|---|---|---|---|---|---|
| $B_2$ | −4.56 | −6.64 | −1.40 | −6.77 | 1.82 |
|  | (2.09) | (4.04) | (0.66) | (4.61) | (1.21) |
| $\alpha$ | 0.35 | 0.35 | 0.28 | 0.37 | 0.13 |
|  | (5.45) | (3.56) | (3.25) | (4.91) | (1.17) |
| $\gamma$ | 0.21 | 0.28 | 0.14 | 0.25 | 0.07 |
|  | (2.65) | (3.21) | (1.82) | (3.73) | (0.54) |
| $\phi$ | 0.03 | 0.022 | 0.018 | 0.027 | 0.02 |
|  | (2.11) | (1.68) | (1.98) | (2.49) | (1.82) |
| $\bar{R}^2$ | 0.464 | 0.440 | 0.454 | 0.474 | 0.502 |
| $\sigma$ | 0.052 | 0.059 | 0.042 | 0.054 | 0.048 |
| DW | 2.24 | 2.22 | 2.41 | 2.48 | 2.01 |
| $\chi_1^2(H_0 : \hat{\phi} = 0.02)$ | 0.40 | 0.02 | 0.02 | 0.42 | 0.001 |
| $p$ | 57.5% | 89.7% | 86.9% | 51.5% | 97.2% |
| $\beta_{imp}$ | 0.44 | 0.37 | 0.58 | 0.37 | 0.80 |
| $\lambda_{imp}(\hat{\phi} = 0.02)$ | 0.025 | 0.021 | 0.033 | 0.022 | 0.046 |
| $\lambda_{imp}(\phi)$ | 0.028 | 0.022 | 0.032 | 0.024 | 0.046 |

*Notes:* [*] Restricted parameter.
[d] Equation including time dummies.
Col. 1: excluding Turkey and Greece.
Col. 2: excluding the seven richest countries in 1960.
Col. 3: excluding the seven poorest countries in 1960.
Col. 4: excluding the seven richest countries in 1990.
Col. 5: excluding the seven poorest countries in 1990.
Instruments as in Table 9.7.
Dependent variable log $(Y^i_{T+5}/Y^i_T)$. Sample $i$: 1, ..., 24; $T$: 1960, 65, ..., 85.
Estimation method: non-linear instrumental variables with robust errors.

one-third of the value obtained for the OECD as a whole and is not even significantly different from zero. The same happens with the human capital share, suggesting failure of the constant returns to scale model for this group of countries. Unconditional convergence models in Table 9.9 confirm these differences and the caveats about the textbook Solow model interpretation of convergence. Given that the unconditional model is in general badly specified, we should not place very much trust in the point estimates. Nevertheless, the differences in $\hat{B}_2$, in columns 2 and 3 and in columns 4 and 5 go in the direction suggested by the technological non-convexities argument put forward earlier. The unconditional convergence

**Table 9.9    Subsamples: models of absolute convergence**

|                          | $1^d$   | $2^d$   | $3^d$   | $4^d$   | $5^d$   |
|--------------------------|---------|---------|---------|---------|---------|
| $B_2$                    | 2.16    | 1.38    | 2.28    | 0.50    | 2.22    |
|                          | (3.45)  | (0.67)  | (5.24)  | (0.25)  | (6.07)  |
| $\beta$                  | 0.44    | 0.19    | 0.60    | 0.19    | 0.70    |
|                          | (3.45)  | (2.98)  | (4.84)  | (3.39)  | (3.82)  |
| $\phi$                   | 0.03    | 0.04    | 0.03    | 0.05    | 0.03    |
|                          | (1.91)  | (1.36)  | (2.05)  | (1.54)  | (2.36)  |
| $\bar{R}^2$              | 0.305   | 0.124   | 0.363   | 0.185   | 0.452   |
| $\sigma$                 | 0.061   | 0.073   | 0.045   | 0.068   | 0.050   |
| DW                       | 1.95    | 1.86    | 2.09    | 1.83    | 2.06    |
| $\chi_1^2(H_0: \hat{\phi} = 0.02)$ | 0.38 | 0.02 | 0.04 | 0.02 | 0.05 |
| $\rho$                   | 53.5%   | 50.6%   | 55.8%   | 34.6%   | 36.7%   |
| $\lambda_{imp}(\hat{\phi} = 0.02)$ | 0.025 | 0.011 | 0.035 | 0.011 | 0.040 |
| $\lambda_{imp}(\hat{\phi} = 0.00)$ |       | 0.007 |       | 0.007 |       |
| $\lambda_{imp}(\hat{\phi})$ | 0.029 | 0.015 | 0.039 | 0.017 | 0.049 |

*Notes:* [*] Restricted parameter.
[d] Equation including time dummies.
Col. 1:    excluding Turkey and Greece.
Col. 2:    excluding the seven richest countries in 1960.
Col. 3:    excluding the seven poorest countries in 1960.
Col. 4:    excluding the seven richest countries in 1990.
Col. 5:    excluding the seven poorest countries in 1990.
Instruments as in Table 9.7.
Dependent variable log $(Y_{T+5}^i/Y_T^i)$. Sample $i$: 1, ..., 24; $T$: 1960, 65, ..., 85.
Estimation method: non-linear instrumental variables with robust errors. Steady-state variables not-included.

rate is almost zero among the poorer countries whereas it is as high as the conditional rate among the richer ones.

Taking together the results of these subsamples and those obtained in Section 4.2, we can trace a clear pattern. If we analyse just the group of non-rich countries at any point in time, the conditional model fits much better than the unconditional one, producing also a higher convergence rate. This means that the steady state has variation enough among these countries and that poorer countries move towards lower per capita incomes in the long run. Finally, the technological parameter set takes reasonable values, not too different from those obtained for the OECD as a whole. This pattern does not hold for the non-poor countries subsample. In this case, the convergence rate (whether conditional or unconditional) is much higher than the OECD average. On the other hand, the overall fit does not improve when we control for the accumulation rates and the convergence rate does not change either. On the basis of this result we may conclude that the steady state is uncorrelated with initial conditions in this subsample, or that this correlation is negative. However, the parameter estimated for this subsample takes some rather implausible values; under the maintained assumption of constant returns to scale, the labour share is far too large (between 0.7 and 0.8), and the return to human and physical capital are not even statistically different from zero. A formal test for a structural break obtained in Andrés and Boscá (1993) indicates that the constant returns technology might not be applicable to all countries in the OECD. This result, and the unimportance of the steady state, suggest that the strong convergence pattern among the richest countries in the OECD is not fully explained by the mechanism built in the Solow model.

## 5.3 Convergence and non-convergence across the sample period

Pooling data permits yet another way of analysing the data that sheds additional light on the structural stability of the growth process we are looking at. Perhaps the main advantage of the time series dimension in our sample is that it may be used to uncover possible structural breaks in the relevant parameters of the Solow model. 1960–90 is a very long period for technological parameters to remain unchanged; however it is not the time span of the data that we are interested in here. The issue we want to address is whether or not the speed of convergence itself bears any particular relationship with the average rate of growth. This means studying the convergence and growth processes across different episodes of the economic cycle. As was discussed in Section 3, we can identify two very different periods of macroeconomic performance among the OECD economies since 1960. These periods capture, better than a set of variables does, the changing performances of OECD economies in the post-war era: sustained and balanced growth until 1974 and a long-lasting recession thereafter until 1985. Since then, OECD economies have grown rather fast again, although they have experienced major macro-economic shocks.

In what follows we carry out the study of growth and convergence splitting the sample in two periods. Period I covers the first fifteen years of the sample, from 1960 until 1975, plus the latest period 1985–90; similarly, period II refers to 1975 to 1985. Given that our interest is mainly to analyse the relation between growth and convergence, we have chosen this split in order to isolate fast growth and low growth periods.

**Table 9.10　Convergence across different sample periods. Linear models**

|  | 1 | $2^d$ | $3^d$ | 4 | $5^d$ | $6^d$ |
|---|---|---|---|---|---|---|
| constant | −0.32 | −0.41 | −0.38 | −0.23 | −0.21 | −0.05 |
|  | (1.15) | (1.51) | (1.39) | (1.50) | (1.48) | (0.43) |
| $\log (Y_{60}^i)$ | −0.13 | −0.13 | −0.11 | −0.10 | −0.08 | −0.05 |
|  | (6.25) | (6.05) | (6.58) | (2.60) | (2.32) | (1.46) |
| $\log (I/Y)^i$ | 0.08 | 0.10 | 0.09 | 0.13 | 0.12 | 0.11 |
|  | (2.35) | (2.64) | (2.48) | (3.56) | (3.23) | (2.95) |
| $\log (n + \phi + \delta)^i$ | −0.15 | −0.17 | −0.19 | −0.06 | −0.05 | −0.04 |
|  | (1.68) | (1.91) | (2.10) | (2.39) | (2.25) | (1.82) |
| $\log (s_h^i)$ | 0.05 | 0.05 | — | 0.10 | 0.11 | — |
|  | (1.28) | (1.30) |  | (1.85) | (2.08) |  |
| $\bar{R}^2$ | 0.458 | 0.481 | 0.475 | 0.169 | 0.274 | 0.245 |
| $\sigma$ | 0.058 | 0.057 | 0.057 | 0.053 | 0.050 | 0.051 |
| DW | 2.39 | 2.29 | 2.24 | 2.66 | 2.54 | 2.48 |

*Notes:* [d] Equation including time dummies.
Cols. 1, 2 and 3, $T = 1965, 1970, 1985$.
Cols. 4, 5 and 6, $T = 1975$ and 1980.
Instruments as in Table 9.6.
Dependent variable $\log (Y_{90}^i/Y_{60}^i)$. Sample $i$: 1, ..., 24. Estimation method: instrumental variables.

In fact, we have proceeded to estimate equation (13) for the six sub-periods by simple OLS and found very different parameter estimates, that lead to high convergence rates from 1965 to 1975, and more moderate ones in 1960–65 and 1985–90. Conversely, estimated factor shares for periods 1975–80 and 1980–85 are rather different from the other estimates, leading to very low, or even zero, convergence rates and suggesting a genuine change in structural parameters. Some of the most remarkable differences among subsamples are somehow hidden in the linear fully restricted model and can be better shown in the context of the linear unrestricted version (14). In Table 9.10 we display some of the most interesting results. The comparison of simple linear models (column 1 versus column 4), reveals three important differences across periods. The fit of the unrestricted linear model in period I is much better than in period II. The standard error is 10% higher and the $\bar{R}^2$ is much lower in period II as compared with period I. In fact, the abnormally high DW casts some doubts on the adequacy of the Solow model for the low growth period. Turning to the estimated parameter values we see that $\hat{\pi}_1$ is also lower and less precisely estimated in the second sub-period. The

**Table 9.11** **Convergence across different sample periods. Non-linear models**

|  | 1 | $2^d$ | $3^d$ | 4 | $5^d$ | $6^d$ |
|---|---|---|---|---|---|---|
| $B_2$ | −3.79 | −4.17 | −3.76 | −14.4 | −15.2 | −14.9 |
|  | (2.64) | (2.96) | (2.33) | (3.31) | (3.14) | (3.04) |
| $\alpha$ | 0.35 | 0.33 | 0.32 | 0.43 | 0.41 | 0.38 |
|  | (3.75) | (2.48) | (3.56) | (3.81) | (3.90) | (3.74) |
| $\gamma$ | 0.19 | 0.22 | 0.21 | 0.33 | 0.36 | 0.39 |
|  | (2.76) | (3.06) | (2.69) | (3.51) | (4.00) | (4.43) |
| $\phi$ | 0.024 | 0.02* | 0.20* | 0.03 | 0.02* | 0.02* |
|  | (2.37) |  |  | (1.48) |  |  |
| $\lambda$ | — | — | 0.028 | — | — | 0.015 |
|  |  |  | (5.84) |  |  | (2.38) |
| $\bar{R}^2$ | 0.448 | 0.483 | 0.490 | 0.231 | 0.344 | 0.326 |
| $\sigma$ | 0.059 | 0.057 | 0.056 | 0.052 | 0.048 | 0.048 |
| DW | 2.41 | 2.32 | 2.30 | 2.81 | 2.65 | 2.59 |
| $\beta_{imp}$ | 0.47 | 0.45 | 0.46 | 0.25 | 0.23 | 0.240 |
| $\lambda_{imp}(\hat{\phi} = 0.02)$ | 0.027 | 0.026 | — | 0.014 | 0.013 | — |
| $\lambda_{imp}(\phi)$ | 0.030 | — | — | 0.016 | 0.015 | — |

*Notes:* [d] Equation including time dummies.
* Restricted parameter.
Cols. 1, 2 and 3, $T$ = 1965, 1970, 1985.
Cols. 4, 5 and 6, $T$ = 1975 and 1980.
Instruments as in Table 9.6.
Dependent variable log $(Y_{90}^i/Y_{60}^i)$ Sample $i$: 1, ..., 24. Estimation method: instrumental variables.

sum of coefficients $\hat{\pi}_2$ and $\hat{\pi}_4$ is also much higher in period II, which indicates a much lower convergence rate in this period. The change in the regression results in response to the inclusion of time dummies is also revealing of the remarkable differences between the two subsamples. Time dummies add very little explanatory power to the model in period I, whereas they contribute to a substantial improvement in the fit for the second period. The differences among $\hat{\pi}_1$ are now larger. When human capital is not considered, the model even predicts non-convergence. The human capital proxy is crucial in the second period, but seems almost non-significant in the first.

In Table 9.11 we proceed to estimate the non-linear model (13). Again the model displays a very poor fit for the second period when time dummies are not included (column 1 versus 4). Although the overall fit in both cases is similar to the linear version in Table 9.10, the imposition of parameter restrictions makes the estimation of $\gamma$ much more precise in period I, whereas the gain in the standard error of $\gamma$ is much more modest in period II. The rate of convergence in fast growth periods is twice as large as during the period of stagnation. The differences in estimated $B_2$ are also fairly substantial; this cannot be interpreted, as in the splitting across countries, as a 'threshold level effect' because we are taking observations at different points in time. A lower constant term in the recession period indicates that the fall in average growth inside the OECD cannot be accounted for by the evolution of the accumulation rates, and that the impact of short term macroeconomic shocks should be taken into account somehow to analyse the growth process during this period (see Andrés et al. 1994). Including time dummies (as in columns 2, 3, 4 and 6) improves the fit in both periods, but again much more clearly in the second one; the standard error falls by 10% and the $R^2$ increases over 50% in the latter case. Again the estimated $\alpha, \beta$ and $\gamma$ differ markedly across periods. The share of physical capital maintains its value, but the labour share declines sharply in the recession period (from 0.45 to 0.25) whereas the share of human capital increases. This casts some doubts on the interpretation of $\alpha$ and $\gamma$ estimates during deep recession periods, unless one is prepared to accept that capital is used more efficiently in slumps.[26] Estimated $\lambda$ values are again significantly different across periods, regardless of whether they are estimated directly (2.8 versus 1.5) or calculated from estimated parameters (2.6 versus 1.3).

These results show that the rate at which countries converge (towards their own steady states) is affected by the same sort of shocks that affect the average rate of growth. In other words, recessions seem to be particularly harmful for lagging countries. At the same time, some parameters are particularly sensitive to the sample split: in particular the share of human capital increases from 0.19 to 0.39 from one period to the other. As we saw in Section 3, the fall in the 1975–85 average growth rate was particularly large among the poorest countries in the sample.

To complete the analysis it is worth investigating whether the observed fall in the convergence rate is a general feature in the OECD sample or is due to the particularly poor performance of the lagging countries. In Table 9.12 we present several equations in which we have included time and country interaction dummies designed to address this issue. We consider three such dummies with coefficients $\gamma_2, \gamma_1^P$ and $\gamma_2^P$. The first one measures the possibility of a change in the rate of convergence during the second period for the OECD as a whole; the second and third dummies allow for differences in the convergence rate for the five poorest countries[27] in the sample during the first and the second period

Table 9.12 Convergence across different sample periods and different countries. Non-linear models

|  | $1^d$ | $2^d$ | $3^d$ | $4^d$ |
|---|---|---|---|---|
| $B_{21}$ | $-2.48$ | $-2.53$ | $-2.94$ | $-3.16$ |
|  | (1.54) | (1.75) | (2.66) | (3.08) |
| $B_{22}$ | $-2.55$ | $-2.60$ | $-3.01$ | $-3.16^*$ |
|  | (1.58) | (1.78) | (2.63) |  |
| $\alpha$ | 0.30 | 0.30 | 0.32 | 0.33 |
|  | (4.12) | (4.39) | (4.83) | (5.39) |
| $\gamma$ | 0.19 | 0.19 | 0.19 | 0.18 |
|  | (2.97) | (3.04) | (3.22) | (3.09) |
| $\lambda$ | 0.038 | 0.038 | 0.035 | 0.034 |
|  | (3.26) | (4.03) | (5.29) | (6.27) |
| $\lambda_2$ | 0.037 |  |  |  |
|  | (0.05) |  |  |  |
| $\lambda_1^p$ | $-0.11$ | $-0.12$ |  |  |
|  | (0.33) | (0.39) |  |  |
| $\lambda_2^p$ | $-1.33$ | $-1.33$ | $-1.39$ | $-1.00^*$ |
|  | (4.34) | (4.43) | (5.28) |  |
| $\phi$ | $0.02^*$ | $0.02^*$ | $0.02^*$ | $0.02^*$ |
| $\bar{R}^2$ | 0.486 | 0.491 | 0.484 | 0.504 |
| $\sigma$ | 0.054 | 0.054 | 0.054 | 0.053 |
| DW | 2.30 | 2.30 | 2.30 | 2.30 |
| $\chi_2^2(H_0: \lambda_2^p = -1.0: B_{21} = B_{22})$ |  |  | 4.12 |  |
| $\rho$ |  |  | 12.7% |  |

Notes: $^d$ Equation including time dummies.
Instruments as in Table 9.6.
Dependent variable log $(Y_{T+5}^i / Y_T^i)$. Sample $i$: 1, ..., 24; $T$: 1960, 65, ..., 85.
Estimation method: non-linear instrumental variables with robust errors.

respectively. The model also includes a different constant term for periods I and II. The model in column 1 shows some interesting differences with the basic model in Section 5.1. On the other hand, once we allow for differences in the convergence rate, there is some improvement in the fit. The difference in the constant term across periods becomes non-significant, which means that the right-hand side variables can account for the big fall in the average growth rate in the recession. Finally there is a substantial fall in both $\hat{\alpha}$ and $\hat{\gamma}$, with the corresponding increase in the implicit labour share (from 0.38 to 0.51). This increase is consistent with a substantial change in the average convergence rate to

3.8%, which is almost twice as large as the one we have obtained so far. Turning now to the stability analysis, only one of the new coefficients appears clearly significant, $\lambda_2^P$, while the others are not significantly different from zero.

Contrary to what the models in Table 9.11 suggest, there are no signs of a significant fall in the convergence rate among the rest of OECD countries in the 1975–85 decade. In fact, once we control for the evolution of the five poorest countries in the sample, this parameter shows no sign of structural instability. In column 2, the dummy for the second period is removed and we only control for the behaviour of the poorest countries in both periods. Again, there is no sign of a particularly poor performance of these countries in the period of fast growth, so that we are only left with the parameter $\lambda_2^P$ which turns out to be negative and strongly significant; the point estimate ($-1.39$) even suggests a negative convergence rate among these countries in the decade of low growth, although we cannot reject the hypothesis of $\lambda_2^P$ equal to one. This result implies that the causes of the extraordinary fall in the convergence rate among OECD countries during the recession are entirely attributable to the poor performance of the less advanced countries. These five countries, whose behaviour seems to be similar to the OECD average in periods of fast growth, have ceased to converge to their own steady state during the recession. It is important to bear in mind that conditional convergence (not only unconditional) is not operating any more among these countries. This implies that the impact of the negative shocks is not fully reflected in the behaviour of the accumulation rates, and that the fall in the growth rates in the less advanced countries ought to be explained in a broader empirical framework.

## 6    Conclusions

In this chapter we have estimated the augmented Solow model for OECD countries during the period 1960–90. We have proceeded to homogenize National Accounts data, using the official 1990 PPP series published by the OECD for each component of GDP. The use of this data source has the advantage that it is specially appropriate for comparing income levels between OECD countries without any alterations necessitated by the inclusion of non-OECD countries in the sample, as in the case of *PWT5* and its new version *PWT5.5* which are designed to provide comparable information over time about 138 and 150 countries respectively. Throughout the chapter we have kept the assumption of constant returns to scale technology as the appropriate framework to organize our discussion of the growth process in the OECD.

Unlike most previous studies, we have chosen to estimate the model taking full account of the theoretical parameter restrictions. Linear estimation gives some interesting hints, but non-linear models are well suited to the discussion of other implications of the Solow model. Exploiting the technological parameter restrictions we can get direct point estimates and $t$-statistics for the basic parameters of interest, and assess whether these restrictions are rejected by the data. The basic convergence equation has also been estimated jointly with the steady-state equation imposing the cross-equation restrictions. In the cross-section model, parameter estimates fall within the range suggested in previous work; the production function has similar factor shares {1/3, 1/3, 1/3}, and the rate of labour augmenting technical progress grows at the commonly accepted 2% rate. In this setting, the data are seen to accept fairly well the cross-equation restrictions so that convergence features are consistent with the implications of the Solow model. When pooled data are used, cross-equation restrictions are rejected and we must control for the sizeable differences in average growth rates over shorter periods; otherwise the pooling model presents remarkable differences from the cross-section model. Estimation by non-linear instrumental variables and controlling with time dummies, yields plausible point estimates, although the share of physical capital is higher than expected (around 0.45) and that of human capital slightly lower (0.2).

The rate of convergence is very robust to alternative estimation procedures and takes a value between 2.0 and 2.3, very much in the range of what previous studies have found. However, this value is not fully stable. When different splits are taken in the sample, the estimated rate of convergence changes substantially. In particular, the rate of convergence seems to be higher among the richer countries (defined according to their per capita income at different points in time). Subsample estimates also reveal remarkable differences with respect to goodness of fit and the adequacy of the Solow model. Estimated parameters are very different across subsamples, in a way suggesting the presence of technological non-convexities. Moreover, for the group of richer countries, the rate of convergence is very high despite the implausible values of the technological parameters. The estimated convergence rate is not stable either in the time dimension. In periods of fast growth (1960–75, 1986–90) this rate is twice as large as in recession times (1975–85). In these latter years, the rate of convergence is not even significantly different from zero in some specifications. Furthermore, the sharp fall in the goodness-of-fit statistics of the Solow model in the 1975–85 decade suggests that it is not well suited to fit the growth patterns of OECD countries during this period.

The overall picture that can be drawn from this exercise can be summarized as follows. The descriptive analysis contained in the data section has shown that $\sigma$-convergence has been important in OECD countries, although dispersion in GDP per capita has not decreased from the mid-1970s to the mid-1980s. Moreover, there are some significant differences between poor and rich countries related to $\sigma$-convergence. The lack of convergence of the poorest OECD countries has been also corroborated analysing the evolution of the GDP per capita distribution across time and, even controlling for differences in steady-state GDP per capita, poor countries did not converge from 1976 to 1985.

The human capital augmented Solow model explains growth and convergence among the OECD economies reasonably well over the 1960–90 period; the main parameter estimates are robust to alternative specifications as well as to different estimation methods, cross-section and pooling, OLS and two-stage non-linear least squares, etc. However, according with the descriptive analysis, a closer look reveals many features that remain to be explained. Convergence occurs at different speeds among different groups of countries; the estimated parameter is not stable across countries and the constant returns to scale restriction yields some implausible parameter values if we restrict our sample to the richer countries. Convergence seems to be a feature of fast growth times. During recessions, convergence is much slower or non-existent. This lack of convergence seems to be mainly a country-specific rather than a time-specific effect; controlling for the poor performance of the five lagging countries during the recession accounts for all the observed instability of the convergence rate. Finally, the model does not fit very well in shorter time periods of great macroeconomic turbulence. These issues deserve further research.

## NOTES

This chapter is part of the project 'Growth, Convergence and Macroeconomic Performance' carried out at the Ministry of Finance of Spain. A preliminary version of this paper was presented at the European Historical Economics Society Workshop on 'Long-Run Economic Growth in European Periphery' held in July 1993. We would like to thank José E. Boscá and David Taguas for helpful comments. This chapter was finished while Javier Andrés was visiting the Centre for Economic Performance at the LSE whose hospitality is gratefully acknowledged.

  1 An alternative method of contrasting the convergence hypothesis, based upon the notion of stochastic convergence and cointegration among per capita incomes across countries, has been suggested by Bernard and Durlauf (1991). Alternatively, the one-factor neoclassical growth model could be tested on the

basis of its long-run implications about the evolution of some aggregate time series (Neusser, 1991).

2  We could calculate a different $\lambda_i$ for each country. However, upon the imposition of the same technological parameters, this would lead to the unattractive result that economies with faster population growth mechanically present a higher speed of convergence. This is the reason we compute $\lambda$ from average population growth. When we partially relax this assumption we shall be able to compute different convergence rates across countries or group of countries.

3  Using the definition of $\lambda$, the implicit estimate is

$$\lambda_{\text{imp}} = \hat{\beta} \sum \left( n_i + \hat{\phi} + \delta \right) / I$$

4  In this chapter we use OECD data drawn from *National Accounts, 1960–1991* (1992). See Dabán and Doménech (1994) for a complete comparison between *PWT5*, *PWT5.5* and OECD data, for OECD countries. That paper also explores how the use of different data sources affect $\sigma$- and $\beta$-convergence. With both *PWT5* and *PWT5.5* $\sigma$-convergence decreases after the mid-1970s and there is even some evidence of an increase in the dispersion of GDP per capita level in OECD countries, which is not observed with OECD data. Convergence equations are also better fitted with OECD data, although technological parameters seem not to be sensitive to the use of these different data sources.

5  The ratio of the sum of both variables to GDP is included in *PWT5* data set as a series termed OPEN.

6  As it is mentioned in Dabán and Doménech (1994), comparing both *EKS* and Geary–Khamis OECD results for PPP in 1990 with national accounts data, we have detected a big discrepancy in Turkey's national accounts magnitudes. The estimated 1990 GDP per capita in OECD *Purchasing Power Parities, Vol I* and *Vol. II* publications differs significantly from that obtained dividing GDP from national accounts by its *EKS* or Geary–Khamis 1990 PPP, but not if we use the 1985 PPP extrapolation instead. For that reason, we have used Turkey's 1985 PPPs extrapolations to 1990, affecting only its GDP level for each year but not its rate of growth.

7  Turkey, Portugal, Greece, Ireland, Spain and New Zealand.

8  We also used enrolment rates in secondary education from MRW, obtaining worse results. In general there is a strong correlation between both measures of human capital, although we have observed severe discrepancies for some countries (e.g. Switzerland). Kyriacou estimates are available for 1965, 1970, 1975, 1980 and 1985, but for Austria, Belgium, Finland, The Netherlands, Norway and Switzerland there are some missing values that we have interpolated.

9  Later, in some non-linear specifications, we estimate $\phi$; as we shall see, the point estimate does not differ very much from the restricted value, 0.02.

10  The unconditional rate is the one obtained in the model without steady-state variables. This is not strictly correct as these equations may be mis-specified. Still, we carry out this exercise for comparison purposes.

11  See Blomström *et al.* (1993).

12  The convergence property is also built into some endogenous growth models for particular values of the technological parameters (Kelly, 1992).

13  For a similar approach see Holtz-Eakin (1992).
14  $\sigma_{iv.1.4} = 0.116$ versus $\sigma_{iv.2.4} = 0.110$ in the conditional model, whereas for the unconditional model $\sigma_{iv.1.1} = 0.172$ versus $\sigma_{iv.2.5} = 0.248$.
15  Actually, none of these procedures can be formally justified. An alternative method based on more solid grounds is tried in Andrés and Boscá (1993). At this stage we are merely interested in excluding from the sample the countries in each of the tails of the distribution at different points in time.
16  The results are fairly robust to the cut-off income level. We chose this split in order to avoid a sharp fall in the degrees of freedom, and also to allow for different countries in each group when we rank them according to their position in 1990.
17  The USA, Switzerland, New Zealand, Luxemburg, Sweden, Germany and the United Kingdom.
18  Turkey, Greece, Portugal, Spain, Japan, Ireland and Italy.
19  Helliwell and Chung (1992) also report sizeable differences in the constant term once their full sample is divided according to per capita income levels. These differences present the expected sign, the constant term being lower for low income than for high income groups of countries.
20  In this case the seven richest countries are: USA, Switzerland, Luxemburg, Canada, Germany, Japan and France. On the other hand, the seven poorest are: Turkey, Greece, Portugal, Ireland, Spain, New Zealand and United Kingdom.
21  Although this is not true for the steady-state equation.
22  The investigation of country-specific parameters is now in our research agenda; given the heavy non-linearity involved in (16) and (17) this is not a trivial task, in particular if this individual effect affects the parameter $\phi$.
23  Despite the fact that this constant term is statistically different among countries (Andrés and Boscá, 1993).
24  By its very nature the impact of $s_h$ upon growth only works over the long run. If this is the case, shorter-period correlations between human capital accumulation and growth may not be very strong.
25  This static relationship among time series processes is likely to be poorly specified; in fact the unreported DW statistic is consistently below 1 in this equation.
26  An alternative explanation in terms of omitted variable bias can be stated as follows: when unemployment is high and rapidly changing, the model in terms of per capita income is not properly specified. As unemployment rates are not included as regressors, the parameters may be biased.
27  Spain, Portugal, Ireland, Greece and Turkey.

## REFERENCES

Andrés, J. and J. Boscá, (1993), 'Technological Differences and Convergence in the OECD', D-93005, Dirección General de Planificación, Ministerio de Economía y Hacienda, Madrid.
Andrés, J., R. Doménech and C. Molinas (1994), 'Growth, Convergence and Macroeconomic Performance in the OECD Countries: A Closer Look', D-93003, Dirección General de Planificación, Ministerio de Economía y Hacienda, Madrid.

Barro, R. and X. Sala-i-Martin (1991), 'Convergence across States and Regions', *Brookings Papers on Economic Activity*, 1, 107–82.

Bernard, A. and S. Durlauf (1991), 'Convergence of International Output Movements', NBER Working Paper 3717.

Blomström, M., R.E. Lipsey and M. Zejan (1993), 'Is Fixed Investment the Key to Economic Growth?' NBER Working Paper 4436.

Dabán, T. and R. Doménech (1994), 'International and Intertemporal Comparisons of Real Product in the OECD: 1960–1990', D-93008, Dirección General de Planificación, Ministerio de Economía y Hacienda, Madrid.

Durlauf, S. and P. Johnson (1992), 'Local versus Global Convergence across National Economies', NBER Working Paper 3996.

Helliwell, J. and A. Chung (1992), 'Convergence and Growth Linkages Between North and South', NBER Working Paper 3948.

Holtz-Eakin, D. (1992), 'Solow and the States: Capital Accumulation, Productivity and Economic Growth', NBER Working Paper 4144.

Kelly, M. (1992), 'On Endogenous Growth with Productivity Shocks', *Journal of Monetary Economics*, 30, 47–56.

Kyriacou, G. (1991), 'Level and Growth Effects of Human Capital: A Cross-Country Study of the Convergence Hypothesis', C.V.STARR Working Paper 91-26.

Lucas, R. (1988), 'On the Mechanics of Economic Development', *Journal of Monetary Economics*, 32, 3–42.

Lucas, R. (1993), 'Making a Miracle', *Econometrica*, 61, 251–72.

Mankiw, N., D. Romer and D. Weil (1992), 'A Contribution to the Empirics of Economic Growth', *Quarterly Journal of Economics*, 107, 503–30.

Neusser, K. (1991), 'Testing the Long Run Implications of the Neoclassical Growth Model', *Journal of Monetary Economics*, 27, 3–37.

OECD (1985), *Purchasing Power Parities and Real Expenditures*, Paris.

OECD (1992), *Purchasing Power Parities and Real Expenditures*, Paris.

OECD (1992), *National Accounts, 1960–1991*, Paris.

OECD, *Economic Outlook. Historical Statistics*, Various issues.

OECD, *Labour Force Statistics*, Various issues.

OECD, *Main Economic Indicators*, Various issues.

Parente, S. and E. Prescott (1993), 'Changes in the Wealth of Nations' *Quarterly Review*, Federal Reserve Bank of Minneapolis, 17, 3–13.

Romer, P. (1989), 'Capital Accumulation in the Theory of Long Run Growth', R. Barro (ed.), *Modern Business Cycle Theory*, Cambridge, MA: Harvard University Press, pp. 51–127.

Sala-i-Martin, X. (1990a), 'Lecture Notes on Economic Growth (I): Introduction to the Literature and Neoclassical Models', NBER Working paper 3563.

Sala-i-Martin, X. (1990a), 'Lecture Notes on Economic Growth (II): Five Prototype Models of Endogenous Growth', NBER Working Paper 3564.

Solow, R. (1956), 'A Contribution to the Theory of Economic Growth', *Quarterly Journal of Economics*, 70(1), 65–94.

Summers, R. and A. Heston (1991), 'The Penn World Table (Mark 5): An Expanded Set of International Comparisons, 1950–88', *Quarterly Journal of Economics*, 106(2), 327–68.

# 10 On the historical continuity of the process of economic growth

THEO VAN DE KLUNDERT and
ANTON VAN SCHAIK

## 1 Introduction

From an empirical point of view economic growth is usually seen as a long-run process. Growth is conceived of as the trend in GDP over a substantial time span. Therefore, to explain growth by econometric techniques, one needs data for a large number of countries to apply cross-section analysis. The equation estimated contains the growth rate of GDP either in total or per capita as the dependent variable and a number of explanatory variables based on economic theory. There are basically two strategies that can be followed. First, the estimated equation may be derived from a theory of economic growth (e.g. Dowrick and Nguyen, 1989; Barro and Sala-i-Martin, 1992; Mankiw *et al.*, 1992). Second, a pool of explanatory variables, which come from different macroeconomic theories, may be considered, assuming that they can be entered independently and linearly (e.g. Kormendi and Meguire, 1985; Grier and Tullock, 1989; Barro, 1991; Levine and Renelt, 1992). In the latter case it is useful to sort out variables that really matter. As shown by Levine and Renelt (1992), by applying cross-section analysis for the period 1960–89 to a sample of about 100 countries, the number of robust explanatory variables with respect to real per capita GDP is rather limited.

This chapter looks at economic growth as a process of the medium as well as the long run. In studying growth, one has to eliminate the business cycle, but there is no compelling reason to assume that differences in growth rates across sub-periods must be averaged out to get the right picture. Therefore, the aim here is not only to show why growth rates differ between countries but also to investigate whether growth accelerates or decelerates over time. More specifically, we want to investigate whether there is historical continuity with respect to economic growth. Can economic growth before and after World War II be explained by the same growth equation? This approach calls for pooling cross-sectional data and time series data, going back in history as far as the availability of statistical sources allows. The equation estimated for this purpose is based on the growth theory of Scott (1989). The resulting equation is rather simple and could have been postulated right away, as implied by the results of Levine and Renelt (1992). However, for a proper understanding of the estimation results it seems desirable to make a short theoretical detour in Section 2. The data, estimation procedures and statistical tests are dealt with in Section 3, while the results of the regressions are discussed in Section 4. The chapter closes with some observations on the follow-up in our research programme.

## 2   Endogenous versus exogenous growth theory

Endogenous growth theories such as that of Scott (1989) intend to explain growth including technological progress, while exogenous theories leave room for an unexplained residual. The difference between these views can be illustrated by comparing Scott's theory with the neoclassical approach of Dowrick and Nguyen (1989), and Dowrick (1992).

Assuming a Cobb–Douglas specification, the neoclassical production function can be written in rates of change as

$$g = \alpha g_k + (1 - \alpha)g_l + \epsilon \tag{1}$$

where $g$, $g_k$ and $g_l$ denote the growth rate of output, capital input and labour input, respectively. The parameter $\alpha$ stands for the production elasticity of capital. Technological change is constant and is equal to $100\epsilon\%$ per year. Applying equation (1) to a cross-section of countries leads to unsatisfactory results because total factor productivity varies substantially across regions. A way out is to assume that technological knowledge converges in the sense that countries with lower GDP per capita but broadly similar socio-economic characteristics catch up with the leader, which is the USA in the twentieth century. Equation (1) may therefore be extended by introducing a catch-up variable ($cu$) in the form of the ratio of the initial level of labour productivity in each country in the sample ($y_0$) and the initial labour productivity level in the US ($y_{us}$) ($cu \equiv y_0/y_{us}$).

The introduction of a catch-up variable gives rise to additional observations. First, as argued by Inkster (1990), who supplied ample historical evidence for his view, the international transfer of knowledge is an ongoing process with countries exchanging ideas, hardware and skilled people on a bilateral base. If countries differ substantially in their level of development, transfers from 'leaders' to 'latecomers' may dominate, thus giving rise to catch-up, which can be identified by econometric methods. Second, a substantial difference in GDP per capita is a necessary but not a sufficient condition for catching up. In addition, the social and economic environment of the receiver should be similar to that of the source for the technology transfer to be fully 'indigenized' and therefore successful (e.g. Abramovitz 1989; Inkster, 1990). Adding a logarithmic catch-up variable and making the necessary transformations, Dowrick and Nguyen (1989) end up with the estimation equation

$$g = a_0 + \frac{a_1}{\kappa} \sigma + a_2 g_1 - a_3 \ln cu + \mu \tag{2}$$

where $\mu$ denotes a random error term and the positive defined coefficients $a_0$, $a_1$, $a_2$ and $a_3$ depend on the parameters of the original production function, a coefficient introduced to account for the impact of the catch-up variable, and the length of the time period ($T$) for which growth rates are defined. Intuitively, one would expect the absolute extent of catch-up to be stronger in the earlier years, so that the coefficient $a_3$ diminishes if $T$ increases. There is a similar impact on the other coefficients. More specifically, as shown by the authors, the coefficient on the growth of capital $a_1$ is an underestimate of the Cobb–Douglas parameter $\alpha$. Finally, it should be noted that because of missing estimates for the capital stock, the Harrod Domar identity $g_k = \sigma/\kappa$ is substituted in equation (1), with the share of investment in output denoted by $\sigma$ and the capital–output coefficient denoted by $\kappa$. (Depreciation of capital is ignored to simplify the argument.) In estimating equation (2) the authors have to assume that $\kappa$ is constant, which is inconsistent from a theoretical perspective.

The theory of endogenous growth of Scott (1989, 1991, 1993) is based on learning by doing and learning by watching. This places Scott's theory in line with endogenous growth theories developed independently (e.g. Romer, 1986). In Scott's theory, firms are conceived of as on-going concerns with sunk costs determining their position at each point in time. They have to decide how much will be invested to change the existing facilities and organizational capabilities and how much labour will be hired or fired compared with the volume of labour applied to run existing operations. In other words, firms have to decide on the volume of investment and the direction of technical progress simultaneously. In case of rationalization, emphasis is put on labour saving, while in case of expansionary investment, labour demand will usually increase. Growth is never a repetition of the old but implies qualitative change as firms cumulate knowledge by investing. Every act of investment induces a change in production capacity as well as a rise in the stock of existing knowledge, which can be tapped later on. As Scott (1993) states it: 'There are no diminishing returns to *cumulative* investment, because changing the world reveals fresh opportunities' (italics our own). Note that Scott uses a broad investment concept, including expenditure on R&D, outlays on organizational changes, some forms of advertising and the like. In this respect Scott's view parallels that of Chandler (1990), who points to the importance of 'three-pronged investment' in the history of economic growth: (1) investment in production facilities large enough to achieve cost advantages of scale and scope; (2) investment in product-specific marketing, distribution and purchasing networks; (3) recruiting and organizing of managers to coordinate and supervise production and distribution. With such a broad investment concept there is a measurement problem. However, as argued by Scott (1989, pp. 30–3), gross investment can be taken as a proxy for the true amount of investment because the omission of the outlays on R&D, marketing and improvement of the organization, etc., is counterbalanced by the inclusion in the definition of gross investment and some expenditures that should be classified as 'maintenance' instead of as true replacement investment. Maintenance and repair should be considered as current costs of production to prevent or offset physical deterioration of existing assets.[1]

The options for firms can thus be summarized by a *fundamental growth equation*

$$g = f(\sigma, g_1) \qquad f_1, f_2 > 0, \; f_{11}, f_{22} < 0 \tag{3}$$

where the symbols have the same meaning as before. Forward-looking firms maximize the present value of the cash flow for given time paths of wages, prices and interest rates. Depending on these time paths economic growth will be predominantly expansionary, requiring additional labour to realize plans, or more defensive, rationalizing on variable labour input. The theory bears a certain resemblance to the model of Kamien and Schwartz (1969), which combines the Kennedy–Weizsäcker innovation possibility frontier with the idea that investment expenditure can shift this frontier outward.[2]

There are three additional observations to be made. First, Scott's growth equation is concave in $\sigma$ and $g_1$, but when the curves are relatively flat a linear approximation may be acceptable in empirical work. Second, learning can be internal to the firm or can take the form of an externality. The theory can cope with externalities on a microeconomic level. The macroeconomic growth equation relates internal as well as external effects to gross investment as the primary engine of growth. Third, the growth equation may shift under the impact of special circumstances. The post-World War II situation in developed countries provided an almost ideal situation to imitate superior American ways of producing and distributing commodities. For this reason a catch-up variable as in Dowrick and Nguyen (1989) should be added for relevant periods.[3] The equation to be estimated can therefore be written as

$$g = b_0 + b_1\sigma + b_2g_1 - b_3 \ln cu + \mu \qquad (4)$$

where $\mu$ is a random error term and the constant $b_0$ is predicted to be zero, because technological change is fully endogenous in the model. In some studies convergence or catch-up is measured by including initial GDP per capita instead of $cu$ as an explanatory variable (e.g. Dowrick, 1992). This destroys the dimensional homogeneity of the estimation equation, so that the constant term cannot be interpreted as a pure measure for exogenous technological change. Consequently, Scott's theory of endogenous growth, implying that the constant term equals zero, cannot be properly tested. Equations (2) and (4) look similar, but the underlying theories differ substantially. Moreover, there is no need in Scott's theory to assume that the capital–output ratio is constant, because there is no need for a static neoclassical production function in the theory of economic growth. It should be noted that except for deviations caused by business cycles or temporary changes in X-efficiency for whatever reason, equation (4) applies for each sub-period within the entire period of observation.[4] There are no transitional dynamics apart from catching up, as is also true for some other macroeconomic models of endogenous growth with encompassing concepts of capital accumulation (e.g. Romer, 1986; Rebelo, 1991).

## 3   Estimation: data, procedure and statistical tests

For all sixteen countries the data on GDP and employment levels come from Maddison (1991). In the core sample the investment ratios are from Maddison (1992).[5] The investment series covers eight countries, which constrains the pool of observations of the core sample. Elimination of cyclical fluctuations is performed by calculating average exponential growth rates of output and labour input from peak to peak level.[6] Maddison reports employment levels for 1870, 1890, 1913, 1929, 1928, 1950, 1960, 1973 and 1989. For most countries these years show peaks in the level of output, so that it is justified to use them for this purpose. It is therefore possible to split the observation period (1870–1989) into eight sub-periods. Thus, in principle, the core sample consists of 64 observations. The series for Australia, the UK, Canada and the USA covers the whole period from 1870 onwards. Data are missing, however, for Germany, Japan, France and The Netherlands for the 'war period' 1938–50, whereas the Japanese series starts in 1890 and the Dutch series starts in 1913. This reduces the core sample to 57 observations. Contrary to Scott (1989), the observations are not weighted for country size or reliability. The growth rate of labour input is captured by two different measures: man-hours and persons. For the investment ratio, we take the mean value of annual observations. The catch-up variable is defined as GDP per man-hour (respectively per person) relative to (corresponding) labour productivity in the USA.

The core sample of $g$, $\sigma$, and $g_1$ and $cu$ recapitulates briefly the medium- and long-run tendencies in capitalist development.[7] Since 1870, all eight countries have been involved in a process of substantial growth measured in hours.[8] Output growth amounted to 3.3% a year on average, whereas employment, measured in hours, grew by 0.7%, and measured in persons by 1.2% a year. The average investment ratio was 13.4. Apart from inter-country differences, output and labour productivity growth have varied significantly over time. Compared with the inter-war era, all countries experienced an acceleration in the 1950s and the 1960s. After 1973, there has been a substantial and general deceleration, but not dramatic compared with pre-World War I evidence.

Estimation proceeds as follows. First, we tested the significance of country-specific factors by introducing country dummies. Stability over time of the coefficient of the investment ratio and the constant term was tested by adding dummies for all sub-periods with the exception of the 1950s and the 1960s. Stability over time of the coefficient of the catch-up variable was tested for all sub-periods. The test reveals that country-specific influences can only be assigned to Australia and that the coefficient of the investment ratio is stable over time, with the exception of the 'war period' 1938–50. Further, it appears that the catch-up variable is insignificant in the periods before 1950 and after 1973. This is illustrated by the equation in Table 10.1, where labour input growth is measured in man-hours. The catch-up variable is highly significant in the sub-periods 1950–60 and 1960–73. For all other sub-periods the catch-up variable can be eliminated.

The equations (1) in Table 10.2 and (1A) in Table 10.3 summarize the regression results after elimination of insignificant variables.[9] However, the post-1973 catch-up variable is shown to emphasize one of our main conclusions: catching up after 1973 is not significant. Deletion of this insignificant explanatory variable hardly changes the results as can be seen by comparing the equations (1) and (2) in Table 10.2 and the

**Table 10.1   Test on the significance of the catch-up variable, 1870–1989**

| OLS estimation of output growth $g$ on | Coefficient | $t$-value |
|---|---|---|
| Constant | 0.35 | 0.72 |
| Investment ratio ($\sigma$) | 0.13 | 2.95 |
| Growth rate of labour input ($g_l$)$^a$ | 0.87 | 8.93 |
| Catch-up (ln $cu_{1870}$) | −0.09 | −0.12 |
| Catch-up (ln $cu_{1890}$) | −0.13 | −0.31 |
| Catch-up (ln $cu_{1913}$) | −0.58 | −1.41 |
| Catch-up (ln $cu_{1929}$) | −0.14 | −0.35 |
| Catch-up (ln $cu_{1938}$) | −1.74 | −1.08 |
| Catch-up (ln $cu_{1950}$) | −2.32 | −6.18 |
| Catch-up (ln $cu_{1960}$) | −3.38 | −5.64 |
| Catch-up (ln $cu_{1973}$) | −0.22 | −0.23 |
| $\sigma$Dummy$_{1938-1950}$ | 0.16 | 2.49 |
| $\sigma$Dummy$_{Australia}$ | −0.06 | −2.71 |
| Number of observations ($N$) | 57 | |
| $\bar{R}^2$ | 0.86 | |

$^a$ Measured in hours worked.

that the offset is absent, whereas the equations in Table 10.3 imply a equations (1A) and (2A) in Table 10.3. Labour input growth is measured by man-hours (1) and persons (1A) respectively. Absolute $t$-statistics are shown in brackets.[10] Joint tests of zero restrictions on the coefficients of the deleted dummy variables yield $F$-values below the critical $F$-values at a 5% significance level. The remaining variables appear to be robust in the sense defined by Levine and Renelt (1992). The $t$-statistics show that all coefficients are highly significant (at the 0.005 probability level on a two-tailed test), with the exception of the constant term and the catch-up variable of the period 1973–89.[11] Additional tests indicate little or no evidence of serial correlation and heteroscedasticity. The equations explain about 87% of the variance of the dependent variable, so that there is no compelling reason to introduce additional explanatory variables.[12]

The distinction between the Tables 10.2 and 10.3 has to do with the fact that annual hours worked per person have been approximately halved since 1870 (see the Appendix). When hours of work are long, a reduction can generally be expected to result in some offsetting increase in output per man-hour. Scott (1989) mentions several studies showing that such an offset exists. Authors disagree, however, as to how much should be allowed for increased productivity as hours fall. That is the reason we

Table 10.2 Pooled regression with labour input in man-hours, 1870–1989

| OLS estimation of output growth $g$ on | (1) | (2) | (3) | (4) |
|---|---|---|---|---|
| Constant | 0.34 | 0.39 | 0.79 | 0.50 |
| | (0.73) | (1.00) | (2.79) | (1.73) |
| Investment ratio ($\sigma$) | 0.14 | 0.14 | 0.10 | 0.13 |
| | (3.46) | (4.33) | (4.78) | (5.82) |
| Growth rate of labour input ($g_l$) | 0.83 | 0.83 | 0.85 | 0.81 |
| | (9.04) | (9.57) | (11.37) | (11.26) |
| Catch-up 1950–60 (ln $cu_{1950}$) | −2.19 | −2.22 | −2.02 | −2.03 |
| | (6.37) | (7.10) | (9.16) | (9.64) |
| Catch-up 1960–73 (ln $cu_{1960}$) | −3.13 | −3.19 | −3.37 | −3.27 |
| | (5.76) | (7.07) | (11.42) | (11.58) |
| Catch-up 1973–1989 (ln $cu_{1973}$) | 0.19 | | | |
| | (0.21) | | | |
| $\sigma$Dummy$_{1938-1950}$ | 0.21 | 0.21 | 0.20 | 0.21 |
| | (5.13) | (5.18) | (5.14) | (5.55) |
| $\sigma$Dummy$_{Australia}$ | −0.06 | −0.06 | −0.05 | −0.06 |
| | (3.09) | (3.11) | (2.89) | (3.42) |
| $\sigma$Dummy$_{Scandinavia}$ | | | | −0.04 |
| | | | | (2.98) |
| Number of observations ($N$) | 57 | 57 | 84 | 84 |
| $\bar{R}^2$ | 0.87 | 0.87 | 0.86 | 0.87 |
| SE of regression | 0.72 | 0.71 | 0.69 | 0.66 |
| Serial correlation ($F$-statistic) | 0.16 | 0.17 | 0.04 | 0.62 |
| Functional form ($F$-statistic) | 1.18 | 1.25 | 0.00 | 0.37 |
| Heteroscedasticity ($F$-statistic) | 0.20 | 0.22 | 0.06 | 0.00 |

present both tables here. The equations in Table 10.2 implicitly assume complete compensation for change in hours. It is to be expected that the truth lies somewhere in between these extremes. As things stand now, statistical tests favour equation (1) over (1A).[13]

It is interesting to see whether our results are robust in case the core sample is extended or the growth equation is fitted to observations from a different data set. First, we extended the core sample by including eight additional countries as in Maddison (1991, 1992): Italy, Austria, Belgium, Denmark, Finland, Norway, Sweden and Switzerland. For Italy, we used the investment series of Rossi et al. (1992), which starts in 1890.[14] For the other countries the investment ratios are derived from the OECD National Accounts, which begin in 1950.[15] Altogether, the core sample is extended to 84 observations. The results are presented in equations (3) and (4) of Table 10.2 and the equations (3A) and (4A) of Table 10.3. In equations (4) and (4A) a common dummy variable is

Table 10.3   Pooled regression with labour input in persons, 1870–1989

| OLS estimation of output growth $g$ on | (1A) | (2A) | (3A) | (4A) |
|---|---|---|---|---|
| Constant | −0.07 | −0.13 | 0.20 | −0.09 |
| | (0.15) | (0.33) | (0.68) | (0.32) |
| Investment ratio ($\sigma$) | 0.11 | 0.12 | 0.09 | 0.13 |
| | (2.68) | (3.68) | (4.23) | (5.44) |
| Growth rate of labour input ($g_l$) | 1.07 | 1.06 | 1.09 | 1.05 |
| | (8.36) | (8.89) | (11.03) | (11.09) |
| Catch-up 1950–1960 (ln $cu_{1950}$) | −2.77 | −2.73 | −2.60 | −2.59 |
| | (6.95) | (7.53) | (10.46) | (11.02) |
| Catch-up 1960–1973 (ln $cu_{1960}$) | −3.72 | −3.62 | −3.54 | −3.44 |
| | (5.60) | (6.51) | (10.15) | (10.41) |
| Catch-up 1973–1989 (ln $cu_{1973}$) | −0.30 | | | |
| | (0.28) | | | |
| $\sigma$Dummy$_{1938–1950}$ | 0.14 | 0.14 | 0.13 | 0.14 |
| | (3.15) | (3.23) | (3.21) | (3.63) |
| $\sigma$Dummy$_{Australia}$ | −0.07 | −0.07 | −0.07 | −0.07 |
| | (3.39) | (3.43) | (3.42) | (4.03) |
| $\sigma$Dummy$_{Scandinavia}$ | | | | −0.04 |
| | | | | (3.22) |
| Number of observations ($N$) | 57 | 57 | 84 | 84 |
| $\bar{R}^2$ | 0.86 | 0.86 | 0.85 | 0.88 |
| SE of regression | 0.76 | 0.75 | 0.71 | 0.67 |
| Serial correlation ($F$-statistic) | 0.47 | 0.45 | 0.09 | 1.50 |
| Functional form ($F$-statistic) | 0.84 | 0.74 | 0.01 | 0.10 |
| Heteroscedasticity ($F$-statistic) | 0.28 | 0.31 | 0.01 | 0.67 |

applied to all Scandinavian countries. This dummy variable appears to be significant. Separate dummies for the Scandinavian countries give *grosso modo* the same outcome. As appears by comparing equations (2) and (4), with respectively, equations (2A) and (4A), the results obtained for the core sample are robust with respect to an extension of the sample along the lines set forth by Maddison.

Second, the fundamental growth equation was tested applying the post-World War II data set by Summers and Heston (1991). Oil-producing countries were eliminated, as were small countries (less than one million inhabitants) resulting in a sample of 245 observations (95 countries and three time periods if available). Applying OLS results in:

$$g = -0.16 + 0.12\sigma + 0.77g_l - 0.79\ln cu_{1950} - 0.80\ln cu_{1960} + 0.09\ln cu_{1973}$$
$$(-0.24)\ (5.66)\ \ (5.45)\ \ (-3.41)\ \ \ \ \ \ \ (-4.33)\ \ \ \ \ \ \ (0.46)$$

$$\bar{R}^2 = 0.25,\ N = 245$$

Absolute $t$-statistics are shown in parentheses. Labour input is measured in persons, so that the result should be compared to equations (2A) and (4A) in Table 10.2. Here again the main results of our analysis stand upright: (1) technological change is endogenous; there is no indication of an autonomous factor; (2) catching up is limited to the 1950s and 1960s; there is no catch-up after 1973. The impact of the explanatory variable $cu$ from 1950 to 1973 is less than in the Maddison samples, as may be expected in a sample with very heterogeneous countries. Moreover, the equation explains only 25% of the variance of the dependent variable. A distinction between different growth clubs would undoubtedly improve these results (e.g. Dowrick and Gemmell, 1991; Dowrick, 1992). However, for our purpose there is no need to go into so much detail.

The robustness of our results can also be investigated by introducing a measure of investment in human capital as an additional explanatory variable. Investment in human capital or schooling differs substantially before and after World War II and may thus explain part of the acceleration in economic growth from 1950 to 1973.[16] To account for this possibility equation (4) of Table 10.2, which now includes the catch-up variable for the last sub-period, is reestimated by including a proxy for human capital investment:

$$g = 0.17 + 0.13\sigma + 0.82g_1 - 2.12 \ln cu_{1950} - 3.45 \ln cu_{1960} + 0.47 \ln cu_{1973}$$
$$\quad (0.45) \quad (4.94) \quad (11.17) \quad (-8.811) \quad\quad (-9.92) \quad\quad (-0.80)$$
$$\quad + 0.22\sigma D_{38-50} - 0.05\sigma D_{Aus} - 0.04\sigma D_{Scandinavia} - 0.13 \ln SEC$$
$$\quad (5.79) \quad\quad (-2.49) \quad (-3.02) \quad\quad (-1.58)$$
$$\bar{R}^2 = 0.87, \ N = 84$$

Investment in human capital is approximated by $SEC$, the Secondary School Enrollment Ratio as used by Barro (1991) and Levine and Renelt (1992).[17] It appears that our claim about the insignificance of the constant term (endogenous growth) and the significance of catching up from 1950 to 1973 stands up to this additional test very well. The human capital variable $\ln SEC$ is not statistically significant at the 10% level and does not improve the overall fit of the equation. For this reason we do not go further into the subject.

## 4   Discussion of the results

As appears from regression equation (2) in Table 10.2 we found the process of economic growth to be steady over eight countries and eight distinct sub-periods since 1870, interrupted only by some events like

World War II and the impact of convergence towards the USA in productivity and lifestyle during the 1950s and 1960s. As observed before, the explained variance of our growth equation (2) is 87%,[18] while the coefficients on the investment ratio (0.14) and the growth rate of working hours (0.83) are highly significant and robust.[19] The constant term does not differ significantly from zero, so that the hypothesis of endogenous growth cannot be rejected.

The robustness of the growth equation over time and across countries is a remarkable phenomenon. It points towards a *normal pattern* of investment and growth since the second industrial revolution, which started around 1870 (Chandler, 1990). As exceptions confirm the rule, it is rewarding to look at deviations from the normal pattern. There are two minor deviations. First, it is evident that the period including World War II was one of high turbulence. It should be recalled in this connection that data for this period refer only to countries which did not suffer from foreign occupation (Australia, Canada, UK, USA). The higher productivity of investment during this period can, therefore, be explained in terms of an increase in X-efficiency. Second, the growth performance of the Australian economy is below the mark. Although this underperformance should be studied in more detail to warrant definitive conclusions, our rough estimate is that the isolated geographical location, protectionist policies and small domestic market size may have hampered a full integration in the industrializing world economy.[20]

The major exception with respect to continuity in the process of economic growth was of course the process of catching up *vis à vis* the US economy in the 1950s, which became even somewhat stronger in the 1960s. As documented in Maddison (1991), Abramovitz (1989) and others, this golden era of economic growth in Western Europe is quite unique. It is not necessary to recapitulate the factors that caused this exceptional development in detail. However it is remarkable that catching up in the 1960s was more pronounced. Post-war relocations and adjustments were complete by then and massive foreign investment from the USA to Europe speeded up the transfer of technological and managerial knowledge. However, what needs to be stressed is that the European economies were back on the historical track after 1973. Catching up is no longer a relevant issue, despite a remaining gap in productivity levels compared with the USA, as presented in the Appendix. There are at least two factors which may be of some help explaining this robust result. First, catching up should not be regarded as a linear and mechanical process. Before World War II, European countries such as France and Germany had substantially lower productivity levels than did the USA, but the catch-up variable is insignificant for this period, as shown in Section 3. This result confirms the view of Abramovitz (1989) and Inkster (1990) that catching up requires adequate preconditions in terms of institutions and cultures to be effective. Moreover, countries may grow differently by choosing specific technological trajectories, as shown for instance by Chandler (1990) in his description and comparison of economic growth in the UK and the USA from 1870 to 1948. Second, looking at the post-World War II experience, macroeconomic stability differs in the period before and after 1973. According to Boltho (1982) and Maddison (1991), this may explain to a large extent the difference in growth performance across these periods, leaving less mileage for the catch-up hypothesis. Although this proposition seems exaggerated and the causality could perhaps be reversed, business cycles and the resulting uncertainties after 1973 may be partly responsible for a failure to realize what may have been left in terms of a potential for catch-up. Uncertainty may lead to a lower investment ratio, but that would not be enough to explain the irrelevance of catching up after 1973. To explain what is at stake one has to assume that firms invested relatively less heavily in risky up-front technological improvements in times of higher uncertainty.

Extension of the core sample by including post-war data for another eight countries as in Maddison (1991)[21] leads to a significant but still small constant term as shown by regression equation (3) in Table 10.2. The coefficient of the investment ratio declines compared with that of equation (2), so that investment is less productive in the larger sample ($N = 84$). Inspection of the residuals reveals that the problem is mainly due to the relatively weak growth performance of the Scandinavian countries.

Introducing a dummy variable for the set of Scandinavian countries brings the result more in line with the smaller sample ($N = 57$), as appears to be the case in equation (4).[22] The question of why the Scandinavian countries underperform must here, to a large extent, be left unanswered. Boltho (1982) explains sharply above-average investment ratios in Finland and Norway by their very low population densities which require much higher infrastructure investment and by the composition of their industrial output, heavily concentrated in highly capital-intensive semi-manufactures. However this may be, our growth equation (4) compares well with the result obtained for a smaller sample of countries, equation (2). This reinforces our earlier conclusion that economic expansion in the West can be characterized by a normal pattern of investment and growth, which is robust over time and across countries.

If employment is measured in persons instead of in hours, the results are not fundamentally different (see Table 10.3). The coefficient on the growth rate of labour input is somewhat higher, because the effects of structural labour time reductions are now not taken into account. The growth rate of persons employment correlates almost perfectly with the growth rate of output. The higher coefficient on $g_l$ has a slightly depressing effect on the productivity of investment, while the constant term is much lower in this case. There is, consequently, no indication for exogenous technological change. Endogenous growth theory explaining technological change as a cumulative learning process fits the facts satisfactorily. It remains to be seen which measure of labour input is most suitable for explaining economic growth. Ideally, one would like to have a quality-adjusted standard of hours worked. However, lacking such data the robustness of results for changes in the measurement of labour input is reassuring, as one would expect that a correct measure of labour input sits somewhere between labour input in hours and in persons.

The question may be raised whether our analysis is vulnerable to the critique of De Long (1988) with respect to applying the Maddison data set. According to De Long, there may be selection bias with respect to countries, because countries with relatively high GDP per capita levels in 1870 that did not make it in terms of economic growth afterwards are excluded from the sample (for instance Argentina, Chile, Spain, Portugal). The original sample is therefore biased, because it favours convergence. Moreover, measurement errors of GDP per capita in 1870 create the appearance of convergence where it does not exist in reality. Both points are well taken but do not seriously affect our analysis. Selection bias is not relevant, because we do not study convergence since 1870 but rather present an estimate of the fundamental growth equation showing that catch-up became relevant only after World War II. Measurement errors may play a role, but it is unlikely that by taking these into account the conclusion of no catch-up in the pre-World War II period would be changed.

It is instructive to compare our results with the outcomes obtained by authors studying catching up in similar terms, i.e. Scott (1989), Dowrick and Nguyen (1989), and Crafts (1992) (see Table 10.4). Scott's results are mainly based on his own data for the USA, the UK and Japan starting at different years in the nineteenth century for different countries and ending the estimation period in 1973. There is a strong emphasis on USA data because weights are applied based on country size, length of the sub-periods and statistical reliability.[23] The insignificant constant term is suppressed in the regression equation preferred by Scott. An important difference with our results is that we found the coefficient of the investment ratio to be stable over time, while Scott introduces a dummy variable on $\sigma$ for the post-World War II period. According to Scott there

Table 10.4    Comparison with other regression results

| OLS estimation of $g$ on | Table 10.2 (2) | Scott (1989) | Table 10.3 (2A) | Dowrick (1989) | Crafts (1992) |
|---|---|---|---|---|---|
| Constant | 0.39 (1.00) | | −0.13 (0.33) | | 6.10 (5.23) |
| Investment ratio ($\sigma$) | 0.14 (4.33) | 0.05 (2.01) | 0.12 (3.68) | 0.06 (2.54) | 0.09 (4.69) |
| Labour input ($g_1$) | 0.83 (9.57) | 0.90 (8.11) | 1.06 (8.89) | 0.58 (3.74) | 0.86 (7.75) |
| Catch-up (ln $cu_{1950}$) | −2.22 (7.10) | | −2.73 (7.53) | −2.01 (9.67) | −1.35 (4.94) |
| Catch-up (ln $cu_{1960}$) | −3.19 (7.07) | | −3.62 (6.51) | | |
| $\sigma$Dummy$_{1950-1973}$ (Scott) | | 0.08 (3.61) | | | |
| $\sigma$ ln $cu$Dummy$_{1950-1973}$ (Scott) | | −0.05 (3.23) | | | |
| Dummy 1950s (Crafts) | | | | | 1.45 (5.27) |
| Dummy 1960s (Crafts) | | | | | 2.28 (8.24) |
| Reconstruction (Crafts) | | | | | 1.28 (1.72) |
| Reconstruction squared (Crafts) | | | | | −1.28 (2.51) |
| Number of observations | 57 | 26 | 57 | 24 | 70 |
| $\bar{R}^2$ | 0.87 | 0.89 | 0.86 | 0.83 | 0.83 |

was an autonomous increase in technological change (an upward shift of the fundamental growth equation) after 1950. This shift can be explained by pointing to an increase in communication between both sides of the Atlantic after the war. Such an increase in communication and exchange of information could have stimulated international knowledge spillovers, thus raising the productivity of investment on a world-wide scale. However, there seems to be no need for such an interpretation if one considers a longer post-war time period and if catching up is treated in the usual way. Multiplication of the catch-up variable by $\sigma$ as in Scott (1989) detracts from catching up.[24] This is compensated for by the post-war time dummy on $\sigma$. Apart from this, the post-war regression coefficients of Scott's equation are remarkably close to the results we found, as appears from Table 10.4.

Dowrick and Nguyen (1989) obtain different but significant coefficients for the investment ratio and the growth rate of labour input by applying cross-country data from the Summers and Heston data set for the period 1950–85. The constant term is not reported. Catching up relates to the entire period under consideration. In addition, Dowrick and Nguyen (1989) test for parameter stability by splitting the sample period into three sub-periods: 1950–60, 1960–73 and 1973–85. The catch-up variable appears to be significant in all sub-periods, but the coefficient of the investment ratio becomes insignificant for the last sub-period if coefficients are not restricted to being equal across sub-periods.

Crafts (1992) extends the analysis of Dowrick and Nguyen by including data for the sub-periods 1900–13 and 1923–38 (eleven countries) based on Maddison (1982). Labour is measured in hours worked, which compares with our equation (2) in this respect. Catch-up extends over the entire post-war period from 1950 to 1988. The catch-up variable has a smaller impact than in Dowrick and Nguyen, but part of the higher post-World War II growth performance is explained by reconstruction variables à la Dumke (1990). Despite this extension, dummies for the 1950s and 1960s are required in order to get a good fit. Crafts explains this increase in productivity by referring to the possibility of long swings in economic growth, on the one hand, and by the impact of trade liberalization in those years, on the other hand. Here, as in Scott, the problem seems to be how to reconcile pre-war and post-war data on economic growth. However, the problem may well be that catching up in the 1950s and 1960s is not given proper weight by the procedure chosen.

The idea of 'back to normal', as implied by our regression results, explains the growth slowdown after 1973 in the European countries and Japan rather well, as inspection of the residuals in Table 10.5 shows. The slowdown in the USA remains nevertheless partly unexplained. We predict a US growth rate of 3.5% for the period after 1973, which is too high compared with the actual growth rate of 2.7%. In contrast, our predictions for the 1950s and 1960s are too low. A hint of an explanation may be found in the relevance of mutual technological spillovers analysed in a different historical context by Inkster (1990). According to this view the US economy may have profited from feedback effects related to the catch-up in other countries. When catching up came to an end the USA may have suffered a decline in international technological spillovers. There may of course be different reasons for a productivity slowdown in the USA, but it remains to be seen whether the negative residual in the last period foreshadows a structural deviation from the general pattern of economic growth. What this example reveals is that it is rewarding to study in detail country-specific and period-specific

**Table 10.5    The proximate causes of growth (equation (2)) in percentages**

| | Period | Actual growth rate ($g$) | Explained by $\sigma$ | $g_1$ | Other factors | Un-explained |
|---|---|---|---|---|---|---|
| *Germany* | | | | | | |
| 1 | 1870–1980 | 2.384 | 1.553 | 0.412 | | 0.028 |
| 2 | 1890–1913 | 3.177 | 1.908 | 1.076 | | −0.196 |
| 3 | 1913–1929 | 1.203 | 1.612 | −0.145 | | −0.653 |
| 4 | 1929–1938 | 3.779 | 1.324 | 1.136 | | 0.928 |
| 5 | 1950–1960 | 7.966 | 2.196 | 0.854 | 2.684 | 1.841 |
| 6 | 1960–1973 | 4.373 | 2.388 | −0.675 | 2.513 | −0.242 |
| 7 | 1973–1989 | 2.051 | 1.977 | −0.493 | | 0.177 |
| *Japan* | | | | | | |
| 8 | 1890–1913 | 2.505 | 1.548 | 0.617 | | −0.050 |
| 9 | 1913–1929 | 3.698 | 1.973 | 0.207 | | 1.127 |
| 10 | 1929–1938 | 3.594 | 1.842 | 1.002 | | 0.360 |
| 11 | 1950–1960 | 8.827 | 2.720 | 2.476 | 4.239 | −0.998 |
| 12 | 1960–1973 | 9.606 | 3.609 | 0.393 | 5.102 | −0.110 |
| 13 | 1973–1989 | 3.927 | 3.242 | 0.557 | | −0.262 |
| *France* | | | | | | |
| 14 | 1870–1890 | 1.281 | 1.312 | −0.083 | | −0.338 |
| 15 | 1890–1913 | 1.658 | 1:413 | −0.082 | | −0.061 |
| 16 | 1913–1929 | 1.865 | 1.521 | −0.419 | | 0.372 |
| 17 | 1929–1938 | −0.394 | 1.645 | −2.641 | | 0.211 |
| 18 | 1950–1960 | 4.566 | 1.864 | −0.010 | 2.023 | 0.299 |
| 19 | 1960–1973 | 5.408 | 2.308 | 0.101 | 2.256 | 0.351 |
| 20 | 1973–1989 | 2.324 | 2.025 | −0.603 | | 0.513 |
| *Netherlands* | | | | | | |
| 21 | 1913–1929 | 3.647 | 2.017 | 0.619 | | 0.620 |
| 22 | 1929–1938 | 0.327 | 1.893 | 0.372 | | −2.328 |
| 23 | 1950–1960 | 4.611 | 2.469 | 0.359 | 1.729 | −0.337 |
| 24 | 1960–1973 | 4.832 | 2.686 | −0.331 | 1.961 | 0.125 |
| 25 | 1973–1989 | 1.991 | 1.988 | −0.289 | | −0.098 |
| *Australia* | | | | | | |
| 26 | 1870–1890 | 4.495 | 0.950 | 3.611 | | −0.456 |
| 27 | 1890–1913 | 2.561 | 0.797 | 0.544 | | 0.828 |
| 28 | 1913–1929 | 1.291 | 0.938 | 0.009 | | −0.045 |
| 29 | 1929–1938 | 2.057 | 0.801 | 0.765 | | 0.099 |
| 30 | 1938–1950 | 3.481 | 0.773 | 1.053 | 2.194 | −0.930 |
| 31 | 1950–1960 | 4.043 | 1.454 | 1.024 | 0.891 | 0.283 |
| 32 | 1960–1973 | 5.210 | 1.521 | 2.148 | 1.183 | −0.032 |
| 33 | 1973–1989 | 3.125 | 1.405 | 1.264 | | 0.066 |
| *UK* | | | | | | |
| 34 | 1870–1890 | 2.048 | 0.905 | 0.513 | | 0.238 |
| 35 | 1890–1913 | 1.763 | 0.951 | 0.588 | | −0.167 |

**Table 10.5** *(contd)*

| | | | | | | |
|---|---|---|---|---|---|---|
| 36 | 1913–1929 | 0.705 | 0.719 | −0.614 | | 0.209 |
| 37 | 1929–1938 | 1.895 | 0.806 | 0.805 | | −0.106 |
| 38 | 1938–1950 | 1.626 | 0.754 | −0.508 | 1.173 | −0.183 |
| 39 | 1950–1960 | 2.865 | 1.530 | 0.460 | 1.250 | −0.766 |
| 40 | 1960–1973 | 3.159 | 1.930 | −0.579 | 1.850 | −0.431 |
| 41 | 1973–1989 | 1.949 | 1.896 | −0.099 | | −0.237 |
| *Canada* | | | | | | |
| 42 | 1870–1890 | 3.061 | 1.516 | 1.220 | | −0.065 |
| 43 | 1890–1913 | 4.952 | 2.068 | 1.640 | | 0.853 |
| 44 | 1913–1929 | 2.797 | 1.848 | 0.999 | | −0.440 |
| 45 | 1929–1938 | −0.035 | 1.407 | −0.127 | | −1.705 |
| 46 | 1938–1950 | 5.779 | 1.454 | 0.379 | 2.263 | 1.293 |
| 47 | 1950–1960 | 4.581 | 2.373 | 1.205 | 0.653 | −0.041 |
| 48 | 1960–1973 | 5.446 | 2.408 | 2.115 | 0.746 | −0.212 |
| 49 | 1973–1989 | 3.601 | 2.174 | 1.498 | | −0.460 |
| *USA* | | | | | | |
| 50 | 1870–1890 | 3.983 | 1.327 | 1.974 | | 0.292 |
| 51 | 1890–1913 | 3.897 | 1.484 | 1.364 | | 0.658 |
| 52 | 1913–1929 | 3.100 | 1.533 | 0.544 | | 0.632 |
| 53 | 1929–1938 | −0.708 | 1.333 | −1.760 | | −0.671 |
| 54 | 1938–1950 | 5.076 | 1.360 | 1.525 | 2.117 | −0.316 |
| 55 | 1950–1960 | 3.252 | 1.703 | 0.637 | | 0.522 |
| 56 | 1960–1973 | 3.951 | 1.764 | 1.222 | | 0.574 |
| 57 | 1973–1989 | 2.671 | 1.799 | 1.265 | | −0.783 |

deviations from the normal growth pattern, even if these deviations are not statistically significant. This holds *a fortiori* if genuine outliers are found. Fortunately, there are very few of them in the post-war period. The main exception is German output growth in the 1950s, which is underexplained in our main equation (6.1% versus 8%). This 'reconstruction' effect for the German economy is well documented in Dumke (1990). Looking at a clustering of negative or positive residuals for the post-war period as a whole, it can be concluded that France does very well, while UK performance lies below average. These results correspond with the findings of Dowrick and Nguyen (1989) and Crafts (1992).

Catching up set aside, the relative contribution of investment and employment varies greatly between countries and periods. In general the investment ratio has a larger impact than the growth rate of employment. In the post-war period, the influence of $g_1$ is most marked for Australia, Canada, the USA and Japan. Demographic factors (population growth, migration and rising participation rates) may be held responsible for this difference with the European countries (see the Appendix). These observations merely make a start in explaining why growth rates differ. A more comprehensive explanation should include institutional factors as well as differences in national economic policies. Our econometric analysis could serve as a framework for a more detailed description of economic growth in individual countries and single periods, especially so if the sample for estimating the fundamental growth equation can be extended by including more nations as well as additional pre-World War II data.

## 5    Conclusion

This chapter makes the case for the idea of a normal pattern of economic growth, which is robust over time and across nations if proper account is taken of exceptional situations and special circumstances. This idea is reminiscent of a normal pattern of sectoral development analysed by Chenery and Syrguin (1975). The advantage of these models is that idiosyncratic developments can be detected in a rigorous way. However, too many idiosyncracies may spoil normality. There is a delicate balance between exceptions and the rule in our analysis as well as in Chenery's approach of sectoral developments. From these observations follow two important lessons, which set the agenda for further research. First, additional effort should be spent to refine the estimation of the fundamental growth equation. This requires improvement and extension of data, especially with respect to growth before World War II. It could be worthwhile, moreover, to consider different subdivisions of time with respect to countries, for which the initial and terminal points of business cycles are not synchronized. Second, our analysis could be applied to explain sectoral growth rates and deviations from the normal pattern at a disaggregated level. As developments on a sectoral level may differ substantially from the aggregate picture (e.g. Wolff, 1992), such an extension shows great promise.

## Appendix

*I    Observations (1870–1989) with labour input man-hours*

| | Period | $g$ | $g_1$ (hours) | $g-g_1$ | $\sigma$ | $cu$ |
|---|---|---|---|---|---|---|
| *Germany* | | | | | | |
| 1 | 1870.0 | 2.3841 | 0.49382 | 1.8903 | 11.4690 | 0.50664 |
| 2 | 1890.0 | 3.1777 | 1.2895 | 1.8881 | 14.0838 | 0.53747 |
| 3 | 1913.0 | 1.2037 | −0.17426 | 1.3780 | 11.9000 | 0.49533 |
| 4 | 1929.0 | 3.7793 | 1.3616 | 2.4177 | 9.7778 | 0.41991 |
| 5 | 1950.0 | 7.9662 | 1.0239 | 6.9422 | 16.2100 | 0.29890 |
| 6 | 1960.0 | 4.3739 | −0.81003 | 5.1839 | 17.6308 | 0.45520 |
| 7 | 1973.0 | 2.0517 | −0.59095 | 2.6426 | 14.5933 | 0.64432 |

| | Period | $g$ | $g_1$ (hours) | $g-g_1$ | $\sigma$ | $cu$ |
|---|---|---|---|---|---|---|
| *Japan* | | | | | | |
| 8 | 1890.0 | 2.5055 | 0.74031 | 1.7652 | 11.4261 | 0.20537 |
| 9 | 1913.0 | 3.6986 | 0.24828 | 3.4503 | 14.5688 | 0.18454 |
| 10 | 1929.0 | 3.5948 | 1.2009 | 2.3939 | 13.6000 | 0.21589 |
| 11 | 1950.0 | 8.8279 | 2.9677 | 5.8602 | 20.0800 | 0.14848 |
| 12 | 1960.0 | 9.6061 | 0.47124 | 9.1349 | 26.6385 | 0.20236 |
| 13 | 1973.0 | 3.9275 | 0.66769 | 3.2598 | 23.9333 | 0.45784 |
| *France* | | | | | | |
| 14 | 1870.0 | 1.2814 | −0.099901 | 1.3813 | 9.6900 | 0.55896 |
| 15 | 1890.0 | 1.6585 | −0.099296 | 1.7578 | 10.4315 | 0.53757 |
| 16 | 1913.0 | 1.8650 | −0.50290 | 2.3679 | 11.2312 | 0.48387 |
| 17 | 1929.0 | −0.39467 | −3.1654 | 2.7707 | 12.1444 | 0.47990 |
| 18 | 1950.0 | 4.5667 | −0.013043 | 4.5798 | 13.7600 | 0.40235 |
| 19 | 1960.0 | 5.4083 | 0.12156 | 5.2868 | 17.0385 | 0.49334 |
| 20 | 1973.0 | 2.3247 | −0.72308 | 3.0478 | 14.9467 | 0.70299 |
| *Netherlands* | | | | | | |
| 21 | 1913.0 | 3.6475 | 0.74220 | 2.9053 | 14.8890 | 0.68950 |
| 22 | 1929.0 | 0.32759 | 0.44612 | −0.11853 | 13.9778 | 0.73975 |
| 23 | 1950.0 | 4.6110 | 0.43036 | 4.1806 | 18.2300 | 0.45934 |
| 24 | 1960.0 | 4.8323 | −0.39691 | 5.2293 | 19.8308 | 0.54112 |
| 25 | 1973.0 | 1.9910 | −0.34683 | 2.3378 | 14.6800 | 0.76820 |
| *Australia* | | | | | | |
| 26 | 1870.0 | 4.4953 | 4.3279 | 0.16740 | 12.7800 | 1.3228 |
| 27 | 1890.0 | 2.5610 | 0.65284 | 1.9082 | 10.7217 | 0.99820 |
| 28 | 1913.0 | 1.2919 | 0.011004 | 1.2809 | 12.6125 | 0.92655 |
| 29 | 1929.0 | 2.0571 | 0.91795 | 1.1392 | 10.7780 | 0.77321 |
| 30 | 1938.0 | 3.4814 | 1.2624 | 2.2190 | 10.4083 | 0.75265 |
| 31 | 1950.0 | 4.0439 | 1.2279 | 2.8160 | 19.5600 | 0.66969 |
| 32 | 1960.0 | 5.2100 | 2.5742 | 2.6359 | 20.4615 | 0.69037 |
| 33 | 1973.0 | 3.1255 | 1.5149 | 1.6106 | 18.9000 | 0.70084 |
| *UK* | | | | | | |
| 34 | 1870.0 | 2.0480 | 0.61521 | 1.4328 | 6.6850 | 1.0446 |
| 35 | 1890.0 | 1.7631 | 0.70562 | 1.0575 | 7.0261 | 1.0129 |
| 36 | 1913.0 | 0.70519 | −0.73580 | 1.4410 | 5.3125 | 0.77619 |
| 37 | 1929.0 | 1.8953 | 0.96470 | 0.93060 | 5.9556 | 0.66544 |
| 38 | 1938.0 | 1.6262 | −0.60890 | 2.2351 | 5.5667 | 0.63590 |
| 39 | 1950.0 | 2.8657 | 0.55225 | 2.3134 | 11.3000 | 0.56964 |
| 40 | 1960.0 | 3.1595 | −0.69452 | 3.8541 | 14.2462 | 0.56031 |
| 41 | 1973.0 | 1.9497 | −0.11963 | 2.0693 | 14.000 | 0.67095 |
| *Canada* | | | | | | |
| 42 | 1870.0 | 3.0619 | 1.4632 | 1.5987 | 11.1900 | 0.64243 |
| 43 | 1890.0 | 4.9520 | 1.9600 | 2.9861 | 15.2652 | 0.64180 |
| 44 | 1913.0 | 2.7977 | 1.983 | 1.5993 | 13.6437 | 0.75124 |
| 45 | 1929.0 | −0.035769 | −0.15312 | 0.11735 | 10.3889 | 0.65725 |
| 46 | 1938.0 | 5.7797 | 0.45457 | 5.3251 | 10.7333 | 0.58444 |
| 47 | 1950.0 | 4.5812 | 1.4444 | 3.1368 | 17.5200 | 0.74516 |

| | Period | $g$ | $g_1$ (hours) | $g-g_1$ | $\sigma$ | $cu$ |
|---|---|---|---|---|---|---|
| 48 | 1960.0 | 5.4467 | 2.5346 | 2.9122 | 17.7769 | 0.79167 |
| 49 | 1973.0 | 3.6018 | 1.7955 | 1.8063 | 16.0467 | 0.83166 |
| *USA* | | | | | | |
| 50 | 1870.0 | 3.9836 | 2.3656 | 1.6180 | 9.7950 | 1.0000 |
| 51 | 1890.0 | 3.8979 | 1.6351 | 2.2627 | 10.9565 | 1.0000 |
| 52 | 1913.0 | 3.1007 | 0.65237 | 2.4484 | 11.3187 | 1.0000 |
| 53 | 1929.0 | −0.70822 | −2.1101 | 1.4019 | 9.8444 | 1.0000 |
| 54 | 1938.0 | 5.0766 | 1.8276 | 3.2490 | 10.0417 | 1.0000 |
| 55 | 1950.0 | 3.2527 | 0.76402 | 2.4887 | 12.5700 | 1.0000 |
| 56 | 1960.0 | 3.9517 | 1.4648 | 2.4869 | 13.0231 | 1.0000 |
| 57 | 1973.0 | 2.6713 | 1.5170 | 1.1543 | 13.2800 | 1.0000 |

## II    Observations (1870–1989) with labour input persons

| | Period | $g$ | $g_1$ (persons) | $g-g_1$ | $\sigma$ | $cu$ |
|---|---|---|---|---|---|---|
| *Germany* | | | | | | |
| 1 | 1870.0 | 2.3841 | 0.80437 | 1.5797 | 11.4690 | 0.50271 |
| 2 | 1890.0 | 3.1777 | 1.5881 | 1.5895 | 14.0838 | 0.53284 |
| 3 | 1913.0 | 1.2037 | 0.59869 | 0.60506 | 11.9000 | 0.49134 |
| 4 | 1929.0 | 3.7793 | 1.2050 | 2.5743 | 9.7778 | 0.40951 |
| 5 | 1950.0 | 7.9662 | 2.1106 | 5.8555 | 16.2100 | 0.37078 |
| 6 | 1960.0 | 4.3739 | 0.28587 | 4.0880 | 17.6308 | 0.52773 |
| 7 | 1973.0 | 2.0517 | 0.13011 | 1.9215 | 14.5933 | 0.67697 |
| *Japan* | | | | | | |
| 8 | 1890.0 | 2.5055 | 1.0384 | 1.4671 | 11.4261 | 0.20397 |
| 9 | 1913.0 | 3.6986 | 0.81711 | 2.8815 | 14.5688 | 0.18334 |
| 10 | 1929.0 | 3.5948 | 1.0733 | 2.5215 | 13.6000 | 0.21792 |
| 11 | 1950.0 | 8.8279 | 2.2717 | 6.5562 | 20.0800 | 0.17227 |
| 12 | 1960.0 | 9.6061 | 1.2635 | 8.3426 | 26.6385 | 0.26132 |
| 13 | 1973.0 | 3.9275 | 0.96038 | 2.9672 | 23.9333 | 0.55810 |
| *France* | | | | | | |
| 14 | 1870.0 | 1.2814 | 0.20657 | 1.0748 | 9.6900 | 0.55537 |
| 15 | 1890.0 | 1.6585 | 0.19633 | 1.4622 | 10.4315 | 0.53391 |
| 16 | 1913.0 | 1.8650 | 0.24163 | 1.6234 | 11.2312 | 0.48071 |
| 17 | 1929.0 | −0.39467 | −0.79670 | 0.40202 | 12.1444 | 0.47068 |
| 18 | 1950.0 | 4.5667 | 0.023370 | 4.5433 | 13.7600 | 0.41507 |
| 19 | 1960.0 | 5.4083 | 0.74160 | 4.6667 | 17.0385 | 0.52742 |
| 20 | 1973.0 | 2.3247 | 0.13573 | 2.1890 | 14.9467 | 0.72510 |
| *Netherlands* | | | | | | |
| 21 | 1913.0 | 3.6475 | 1.6407 | 2.0068 | 14.8890 | 0.68950 |
| 22 | 1929.0 | 0.32759 | 0.52545 | −0.19786 | 13.9778 | 0.71385 |
| 23 | 1950.0 | 4.6110 | 1.1739 | 3.4371 | 18.2300 | 0.54323 |
| 24 | 1960.0 | 4.8323 | 0.82213 | 4.0102 | 19.8308 | 0.61829 |
| 25 | 1973.0 | 1.9910 | 1.1153 | 0.87570 | 14.6800 | 0.78341 |

| Period | | $g$ | $g_1$ (hours) | $g-g_1$ | $\sigma$ | $cu$ |
|---|---|---|---|---|---|---|
| *Australia* | | | | | | |
| 26 | 1870.0 | 4.4953 | 4.6480 | −0.15265 | 12.7800 | 1.3144 |
| 27 | 1890.0 | 2.5610 | 0.95069 | 1.6103 | 10.7217 | 0.99140 |
| 28 | 1913.0 | 1.2919 | 1.2092 | 0.082769 | 12.6125 | 0.92050 |
| 29 | 1929.0 | 2.0571 | 1.0711 | 0.98598 | 10.7780 | 0.70619 |
| 30 | 1938.0 | 3.4814 | 2.4337 | 1.0477 | 10.4083 | 0.77017 |
| 31 | 1950.0 | 4.0439 | 1.6274 | 2.4165 | 19.5600 | 0.65929 |
| 32 | 1960.0 | 5.2100 | 2.8425 | 2.3675 | 20.4615 | 0.67960 |
| 33 | 1973.0 | 3.1255 | 1.8080 | 1.3175 | 18.9000 | 0.69716 |
| *UK* | | | | | | |
| 34 | 1870.0 | 2.0480 | 0.92330 | 1.1247 | 6.6850 | 1.0517 |
| 35 | 1890.0 | 1.7631 | 1.0012 | 0.76185 | 7.0261 | 1.0194 |
| 36 | 1913.0 | 0.70519 | 0.12341 | 0.58178 | 5.3125 | 0.78185 |
| 37 | 1929.0 | 1.8953 | 1.0584 | 0.83693 | 5.9556 | 0.64695 |
| 38 | 1938.0 | 1.6262 | 0.61222 | 1.0140 | 5.5667 | 0.69912 |
| 39 | 1950.0 | 2.8657 | 0.78632 | 2.0793 | 11.3000 | 0.59741 |
| 40 | 1960.0 | 3.1595 | 0.26594 | 2.8936 | 14.2462 | 0.59714 |
| 41 | 1973.0 | 1.9497 | 0.40612 | 1.5436 | 14.0000 | 0.65961 |
| *Canada* | | | | | | |
| 42 | 1870.0 | 3.0619 | 1.7724 | 1.2895 | 11.1900 | 0.64243 |
| 43 | 1890.0 | 4.9520 | 2.2690 | 2.6830 | 15.2652 | 0.64180 |
| 44 | 1913.0 | 2.7977 | 1.7207 | 1.0769 | 13.6437 | 0.75124 |
| 45 | 1929.0 | −0.035769 | 0.61057 | −0.64634 | 10.3889 | 0.67324 |
| 46 | 1938.0 | 5.7797 | 1.5485 | 4.2313 | 10.7333 | 0.63489 |
| 47 | 1950.0 | 4.5812 | 1.9206 | 2.6606 | 17.5200 | 0.78507 |
| 48 | 1960.0 | 5.4467 | 2.9184 | 2.5283 | 17.7769 | 0.82783 |
| 49 | 1973.0 | 3.6018 | 2.2193 | 1.3824 | 16.0467 | 0.86605 |
| *USA* | | | | | | |
| 50 | 1870.0 | 3.9836 | 2.6776 | 1.3060 | 9.7950 | 1.0000 |
| 51 | 1890.0 | 3.8979 | 1.9372 | 1.9607 | 10.9565 | 1.0000 |
| 52 | 1913.0 | 3.1007 | 1.3241 | 1.7766 | 11.3187 | 1.0000 |
| 53 | 1929.0 | −0.70822 | −0.71534 | 0.0071223 | 9.8444 | 1.0000 |
| 54 | 1938.0 | 5.0766 | 2.6741 | 2.4025 | 10.0417 | 1.0000 |
| 55 | 1950.0 | 3.2527 | 1.1611 | 2.0916 | 12.5700 | 1.0000 |
| 56 | 1960.0 | 3.9517 | 1.8121 | 2.1396 | 13.0231 | 1.0000 |
| 57 | 1973.0 | 2.6713 | 1.9499 | 0.72140 | 13.2800 | 1.0000 |

*III Participation rates (Part) and annual hours worked per person (Hours)*[25]

| | Year 1 | Year 2 | Part in year 1 | Part in year 2 | Hours in year 1 (000s) | Hours in year 2 (000s) |
|---|---|---|---|---|---|---|
| *Germany* | | | | | | |
| 1 | 1870.0 | 1890.0 | 26.1528 | 24.4573 | 2.9410 | 2.7650 |
| 2 | 1890.0 | 1913.0 | 24.4573 | 25.8339 | 2.7650 | 2.5840 |

| | Year 1 | Year 2 | Part in year 1 | Part in year 2 | Hours in year 1 (000s) | Hours in year 2 (000s) |
|---|---|---|---|---|---|---|
| 3 | 1913.0 | 1929.0 | 25.8339 | 29.4058 | 2.5840 | 2.2840 |
| 4 | 1929.0 | 1938.0 | 29.4058 | 30.9286 | 2.2840 | 2.3160 |
| 5 | 1950.0 | 1960.0 | 42.3424 | 47.0478 | 2.3160 | 2.0810 |
| 6 | 1960.0 | 1973.0 | 47.0478 | 43.6717 | 2.0810 | 1.8040 |
| 7 | 1973.0 | 1989.0 | 43.6717 | 44.5798 | 1.8040 | 1.6070 |
| *Japan* | | | | | | |
| 8 | 1890.0 | 1913.0 | 50.6650 | 49.8355 | 2.7700 | 2.5880 |
| 9 | 1913.0 | 1929.0 | 49.8355 | 46.3791 | 2.5880 | 2.3640 |
| 10 | 1929.0 | 1938.0 | 46.3791 | 44.9227 | 2.3640 | 2.3910 |
| 11 | 1950.0 | 1960.0 | 43.0434 | 47.8983 | 2.1660 | 2.3180 |
| 12 | 1960.0 | 1973.0 | 47.8983 | 48.3987 | 2.3180 | 2.0930 |
| 13 | 1973.0 | 1989.0 | 48.3987 | 49.7742 | 2.0930 | 1.9980 |
| *France* | | | | | | |
| 14 | 1870.0 | 1890.0 | 46.3059 | 48.3325 | 2.9450 | 2.7700 |
| 15 | 1890.0 | 1913.0 | 48.3325 | 48.7956 | 2.7700 | 2.5880 |
| 16 | 1913.0 | 1929.0 | 48.7956 | 48.9207 | 2.5880 | 2.2970 |
| 17 | 1929.0 | 1938.0 | 48.9207 | 44.7307 | 2.2970 | 1.8480 |
| 18 | 1950.0 | 1960.0 | 47.0002 | 43.1420 | 1.9260 | 1.9190 |
| 19 | 1960.0 | 1973.0 | 43.1420 | 41.6286 | 1.9190 | 1.7710 |
| 20 | 1973.0 | 1989.0 | 41.6286 | 39.4801 | 1.7710 | 1.5430 |
| *Netherlands* | | | | | | |
| 21 | 1913.0 | 1929.0 | 37.8001 | 38.8461 | 2.6050 | 2.2600 |
| 22 | 1929.0 | 1938.0 | 38.8461 | 36.4882 | 2.2600 | 2.2440 |
| 23 | 1950.0 | 1960.0 | 40.7356 | 40.3099 | 2.2080 | 2.0510 |
| 24 | 1960.0 | 1973.0 | 40.3099 | 38.3213 | 2.0510 | 1.7510 |
| 25 | 1973.0 | 1989.0 | 38.3213 | 41.4169 | 1.7510 | 1.3870 |
| *Australia* | | | | | | |
| 26 | 1870.0 | 1890.0 | 38.8889 | 50.3058 | 2.9450 | 2.7700 |
| 27 | 1890.0 | 1913.0 | 50.3058 | 40.3028 | 2.7700 | 2.5880 |
| 28 | 1913.0 | 1929.0 | 40.3028 | 36.8199 | 2.5880 | 2.1390 |
| 29 | 1929.0 | 1938.0 | 36.8199 | 37.5435 | 2.1390 | 2.1100 |
| 30 | 1938.0 | 1950.0 | 37.5435 | 42.3016 | 2.1100 | 1.8380 |
| 31 | 1950.0 | 1960.0 | 42.3016 | 39.5620 | 1.8380 | 1.7670 |
| 32 | 1960.0 | 1973.0 | 39.5620 | 43.3321 | 1.7670 | 1.7080 |
| 33 | 1973.0 | 1989.0 | 43.3321 | 46.3078 | 1.7080 | 1.6310 |
| *UK* | | | | | | |
| 34 | 1870.0 | 1890.0 | 39.1329 | 39.3864 | 2.9840 | 2.8070 |
| 35 | 1890.0 | 1913.0 | 39.3864 | 40.6712 | 2.8070 | 2.6240 |
| 36 | 1913.0 | 1929.0 | 40.6712 | 41.4609 | 2.6240 | 2.2860 |
| 37 | 1929.0 | 1938.0 | 41.4609 | 43.8329 | 2.2860 | 2.2670 |
| 38 | 1938.0 | 1950.0 | 43.8329 | 44.4771 | 2.2670 | 1.9580 |
| 39 | 1950.0 | 1960.0 | 44.4771 | 46.2547 | 1.9580 | 1.9130 |
| 40 | 1960.0 | 1973.0 | 46.2547 | 44.6113 | 1.9130 | 1.6880 |
| 41 | 1973.0 | 1989.0 | 44.6113 | 46.7468 | 1.6880 | 1.5520 |

| | Year 1 | Year 2 | Part in year 1 | Part in year 2 | Hours in year 1 (000s) | Hours in year 2 (000s) |
|---|---|---|---|---|---|---|
| *Canada* | | | | | | |
| 42 | 1870.0 | 1890.0 | 34.7707 | 37.5339 | 2.9640 | 2.7890 |
| 43 | 1890.0 | 1913.0 | 37.5339 | 39.3832 | 2.7890 | 2.6050 |
| 44 | 1913.0 | 1929.0 | 39.3832 | 39.4265 | 2.6050 | 2.3990 |
| 45 | 1929.0 | 1938.0 | 39.4265 | 37.4754 | 2.3990 | 2.2400 |
| 46 | 1938.0 | 1950.0 | 37.4754 | 36.6164 | 2.2400 | 1.9670 |
| 47 | 1950.0 | 1960.0 | 36.6164 | 33.9717 | 1.9670 | 1.8770 |
| 48 | 1960.0 | 1973.0 | 33.9717 | 40.0643 | 1.8770 | 1.7880 |
| 49 | 1973.0 | 1989.0 | 40.0643 | 47.8665 | 1.7880 | 1.6730 |
| *USA* | | | | | | |
| 50 | 1870.0 | 1890.0 | 36.8876 | 39.5997 | 2.9640 | 2.7890 |
| 51 | 1890.0 | 1913.0 | 39.5997 | 39.9282 | 2.7890 | 2.6050 |
| 52 | 1913.0 | 1929.0 | 39.9282 | 39.3488 | 2.6050 | 2.3420 |
| 53 | 1929.0 | 1938.0 | 39.3488 | 34.5598 | 2.3420 | 2.0620 |
| 54 | 1938.0 | 1950.0 | 34.5598 | 40.4877 | 2.0620 | 1.8670 |
| 55 | 1950.0 | 1960.0 | 40.4877 | 38.2989 | 1.8670 | 1.7950 |
| 56 | 1960.0 | 1973.0 | 38.2989 | 41.2399 | 1.7950 | 1.7170 |
| 57 | 1973.0 | 1989.0 | 41.2399 | 47.8461 | 1.7170 | 1.6040 |

## NOTES

We are grateful to Angus Maddison for providing us with a data diskette on time series of investment ratios. We should also like to thank Sjak Smulders and the participants of the CEPR Workshop 'Interpreting Economic Growth' in Berlin (June 1993) for useful comments on an earlier version of the chapter.

1 To illustrate his point, Scott (1989) mentions replacements for a fleet of taxis which are included in gross investment, because they are lumpy, whereas they should be included in maintenance.

2 As shown in Diederen (1993), the Kamien–Schwartz model can easily be adapted to a model of endogenous growth similar in spirit to the model of Scott.

3 Scott (1989) accounts for catch-up in a somewhat different manner by premultiplying the catch-up variable in equation (4) by $\sigma$. This result comes from the specification of the growth equation as an investment programme contour that shifts along a *radius* under the impact of different factors (dummies, catch-up, etc.).

4 Sub-periods should be of approximately equal length to allow for a uniform impact of catching up across the sample.

5 From Maddison (1991): Table A.2, *Gross Domestic Product in 1985 UK Relative Prices (adjusted to exclude impact of boundary changes)*, Table C.8, *Total Employment, 1870–1989* and Table C.9, *Annual Hours Worked per Person, 1870–1989*. From Maddison (1992): *Gross Non-Residential Fixed Investment as % of GDP, 1870–1988*. The missing figures for France (1870–

1938) were derived by scaling the time series for Gross Fixed Investment as % of GDP. The missing figures for Germany (1870–1924) were obtained by adjusting the series of Hoffman (1965) to that of Maddison. The investment ratio for The Netherlands (1913–29) is the average of 1921–29. The investment ratios of the sample are the annual averages of 1871–90, 1891–1913, 1914–29, 1930–38, 1939–50, 1951–60, 1961–73 and 1974–88.

6 Alternatively, trend growth rates of employment and output could be estimated by, for instance, piecewise linear trend regression. Complete time series for employment are lacking, however, so that we have to rely on comparing peak levels.

7 The data of the core sample are presented in the Appendix.

8 There are only three out of 57 cases with negative output growth: France, Canada and the USA in the 1930s. See the Appendix.

9 The bottom of the table shows the $F$-statistics of the Lagrange multiplier test of residual serial correlation, the Ramsey RESET test using the square of the fitted values as additional explanatory variable and a test on heteroscedasticity based on the regression of squared residuals on squared fitted values.

10 White's heteroscedasticity-consistent $t$-statistics (not reported here) deviate only slightly from the $t$-statistics in the tables.

11 This holds for equation (1) in Table 10.2. For equation (1A) in Table 10.3, the coefficient of the investment ratio is significant at the 0.01 probability level.

12 Potential additional variables are human capital accumulation and the share of exports in GDP. The impact of human capital could not be tested because adequate proxy variables are not easily available before World War II. The share of exports in GDP proved to be statistically highly insignificant and of the wrong sign. In this connection it should be recalled that the growth equation (3) is concave in $\sigma$ and $g_1$. However, both investment ratio squared and labour input growth squared are not significant.

13 To check for a simultaneous equation bias equation (2) in Table 10.2 is reestimated by applying 2SLS. This results in: $g = 0.24 + 0.15\sigma + 0.83g_1 - 2.17\ln cu_{1950} - 3.08\ln cu_{1960} + 0.21\sigma D_{38-50} - 0.06\sigma D_{aus}$, $\bar{R}^2 = 0.87$. As the differences with OLS estimation in Table 10.2 are very minor no further use is made of instrumental variables.

14 Gross Non-Residential Fixed Investment comes from adding the time series on Public Works and Machinery Equipment in current prices. This is related to GDP at market prices from the same paper. The average investment ratios are 8.4 (1890–1913), 10.7 (1913–29), 11.3 (1929–38), 14.2 (1950–60), 15.3 (1960–73) and 16.0 (1973–89).

15 Source: OECD (1970), (1990) and (1992).

16 This hypothesis was suggested by N. Crafts in discussing an earlier version of the chapter.

17 For each sub-period the (initial) Secondary Enrollment Rate is the ratio of the number of pupils in secondary schools and population in age group 15–19 calculated from Mitchell (1982, 1992, 1993). For Canada $SEC$ is approximated by the USA enrolment rates.

18 This is reduced to 82% in case of $g - g_1$ as independent variable. Other empirical growth studies (Barro, 1991; Mankiw *et al.*, 1992) explain $g - g_1$ instead of $g$. This reduces the $t$-value for $g_1(t = 1.89)$ on the RHS of equation (2). In the case of equation (2A) the coefficient of $g_1$ then becomes insignificant ($t = 0.50$). This result (population growth is not robust), which is stressed by

Levine and Renelt (1992), actually depends on measuring labour input growth in persons and choosing labour productivity as the variable that has to be explained.

19 Robustness of the results here refers to the tests reported in Section 3.

20 If the Australian economy is included without a dummy, the constant term in the regression equation and its $t$-value become higher as should be the case when observations relating to a lower growth curve are combined with observations relating to the normal pattern.

21 Notice that for Italy also pre-war data have been added to the core sample.

22 The dummy is one in each post-war sub-period (multiplied by $\sigma$) for Denmark, Norway, Sweden and Finland and zero for the other countries. As explained in note 18, the introduction of dummies for underperforming countries also reduces the constant term.

23 Scott defends this by pointing at heteroscedasticity in the unweighted regression. Testing for heteroscedasticity of our results does not reveal serious problems of this kind (see Section 3).

24 Applying Scott's procedure to our data (1870–1973) results in:

$$g = 0.175 + 0.166\sigma + 0.817g_1 - 0.106\sigma \ln cu_{50} - 0.119\sigma \ln cu_{60} + 0.20\sigma D_{38-50} - 0.07\sigma D_{Aus}$$
$$\quad (0.33) \quad (3.62) \quad (7.89) \quad (-4.98) \qquad (-4.66) \qquad (4.50) \qquad (-2.88)$$

$$\bar{R}^2 = 0.86, \ N = 49$$

All coefficients are significant except the constant term. As appears from this equation, the influence of catching up on growth is reduced substantially. It is about 20% of the impact in our equation (1).

25 Part $\equiv$ total employment (persons)/total population.

# REFERENCES

Abramovitz, M. (1989), 'The Catch-up Factor in Postwar Economic Growth', *Economic Inquiry*, 1–18.

Barro, R.J. (1991), 'Economic Growth in a Cross Section of Countries', *Quarterly Journal of Economics*, **106**, 407–43.

Barro, R.J. and X. Sala-i-Martin (1992), 'Convergence', *Journal of Political Economy*, **100**, 223–51.

Boltho, A. (1982), 'Growth', in A. Boltho (ed.), *The European Economy. Growth and Crisis*, Oxford: Oxford University Press.

Chandler, A.D. (1990), *Scale and Scope. The Dynamics of Industrial Capitalism*, Cambridge, MA: Belknap Press of Harvard University.

Chenery, H.B. and M. Syrguin (1975), *Patterns of Development: 1950–1970*, Oxford: Oxford University Press.

Crafts, N. (1992), 'Productivity Growth Reconsidered', *Economic Policy*, **15**, 387–414.

Diederen, P. (1993), *Technological Progress in Enterprise and Diffusion of Innovations*, Maastricht: Universitaire Pers.

De Long, J. Bradford (1988), 'Productivity Growth, Convergence, and Welfare: Comment', *American Economic Review*, **78**, 1138–54.

Dowrick, S. (1992), 'Technological Catch Up and Diverging Incomes: Patterns of Economic Growth 1960–88', *Economic Journal*, **102**, 600–10.

Dowrick, S. and N. Gemmell (1991), 'Industrialisation, Catching Up and Economic Growth: A Comparative Study Across the World's Capitalist Economies', *Economic Journal*, **101**, 263–75.

Dowrick, S. and D.-T. Nguyen (1989), 'OECD Comparative Economic Growth 1950–85: Catch-Up and Convergence', *American Economic Review*, **79**, 1010–30.

Dumke, R.H. (1990), 'Reassessing the Wirtschaftswunder: Reconstruction and Postwar Growth in West Germany in an International Context', *Oxford Bulletin of Economics and Statistics*, **52**, 451–91.

Grier, K.B. and G. Tullock (1989), 'An Empirical Analysis of Cross-National Economic Growth, 1951–80', *Journal of Monetary Economics*, **24**, 259–76.

Hoffman, W.G. (1965), *Das Wachstum der Deutschen Wirtschaft Seit der Mitte des 19. Jahrhunderts*, Berlin.

Inkster, I. (1990), 'Mental Capital: Transfer of Knowledge of Technique in Eighteenth Century Europe', *Journal of European Economic History*, **19**, 403–41.

Kamien, M.I. and N.L. Schwartz (1969), 'Induced Factor Augmenting Technical Progress from a Microeconomic Viewpoint', *Econometrica*, **37**, 668–84.

Kormendi, R.C. and P.G. Meguire (1985), 'Macroeconomic Determinants of Growth: Cross-Country Evidence', *Journal of Monetary Economics*, **16**, 141–63.

Levine, R. and D. Renelt (1992), 'A Sensitivity Analysis of Cross-Country Growth Regressions', *American Economic Review*, **82**, 942–63.

Maddison, A. (1982), *Phases of Capitalist Development*, Oxford: Oxford University Press.

Maddison, A. (1991), *Dynamic Forces in Capitalist Development*, Oxford: Oxford University Press.

Maddison, A. (1992), 'A Long-Run Perspective on Saving', *Scandinavian Journal of Economics*, **94**, 181–96.

Mankiw, N.G., D. Romer and D.N. Weil (1992), 'A Contribution to the Empirics of Economic Growth', *Quarterly Journal of Economics*, **107**, 407–37.

Mitchell, B.R. (1982), *International Historical Statistics: Africa and Asia*, New York: Macmillan (Stockton Press).

Mitchell, B.R. (1992), *International Historical Statistics: Europe*, New York: Macmillan (Stockton Press).

Mitchell, B.R. (1993), *International Historical Statistics: The Americas*, New York: Macmillan (Stockton Press).

OECD (1970), *National Accounts 1950–1968*, Paris.

OECD (1990), *National Accounts 1976–1988*, Vol. II, Paris.

OECD (1992), *National Accounts 1960–1990*, Vol. I, Paris.

Rebelo, S. (1991), 'Long-Run Policy Analysis and Long-Run Growth', *Journal of Political Economy*, **99**, 500–21.

Romer, P.M. (1986), 'Increasing Returns and Long-Run Growth', *Journal of Political Economy*, **94**, 1002–37.

Rossi, N., A. Sorgato and G. Toniolo (1992), 'Italian Historical Statistics: 1890–1990', Unpublished Paper, University of Modena and University of Venice.

Scott, M.F. (1989), *A New View of Economic Growth*, Oxford: Oxford University Press.

Scott, M.F. (1991), 'Obsolescence and the Analysis of Economic Growth', Paper presented for the World Bank.

Scott, M.F. (1993), 'Explaining Economic Growth', *American Economic Review Papers and Proceedings*, **83**, 421–5.

Summers, R. and A. Heston (1991), 'The Penn World Table (Mark 5): An Expanded Set of International Comparisons, 1950–1988', *Quarterly Journal of Economics*, **106**, 327–68.

Wolff, E.N. (1992), 'Productivity Growth and Capital Intensity on the Sector and Industry Level: Specialization Among OECD Countries, 1970–1988', Paper prepared for the MERIT conference, 'Convergence and Divergence in Economic Growth and Technical Change', 10–12 December 1992, Maastricht.

# 11 Europe's Golden Age: an econometric investigation of changing trend rates of growth

NICHOLAS CRAFTS and TERENCE C. MILLS

## 1 Introduction

The main aim of this chapter is to provide estimates of trend rates of growth in output per person based on modern methods of time series analysis. This is of interest for several reasons:

(i) we can obtain more reliable estimates of changes in trend growth and their statistical significance than hitherto;
(ii) this will allow us to put both the Golden Age of European growth in the earlier post-war period and the more recent slowdown into a long-run context;
(iii) in investigating whether the hypothesis of a unit root in output per person can be rejected, the results obtained inform not only statistical debate but also throw light on controversies in growth theory.

Our analysis is based almost entirely on the standard set of long-run data provided by Maddison (1991). To this we add only the recent estimates for Spain constructed by Prados (1993). The Maddison data have been used by a number of econometricians interested in unit root and segmented trend models and keen to avail themselves of long runs of data: see, for example, Ben-David and Papell (1993), Duck (1992) and Raj (1992).

These authors engage the data from the standpoint of the econometrics literature and, in particular, the debate triggered off by Perron (1989), who argued that the failure to allow for adverse exogenous shocks, such as the Great Crash of 1929 and the 1973 oil crisis, had led researchers erroneously to fail to reject the unit root hypothesis for USA GDP. In contrast, our analysis is informed by the economic history literature and a European perspective which tends to argue for more shocks and to recognize positive as well as negative interruptions to the time series.

415

Thus, Maddison himself (1991) continues to write in terms of epochs in growth. He sees the World Wars as interruptions to the growth process with a successful reconstruction of what became the OECD economies ushering in a Golden Age of growth between 1950 and 1973, when the stagflationary shocks of the 1970s intervened. It seems clear that he regards all these as exogenous shocks, rather than realizations from the tail of the distribution of the underlying data generating process of the time series. Modelling which does justice to this view clearly must allow for more than one break of trend.

A very well-known historical view was put forward by Janossy (1969) and has been much discussed by writers on West Germany, as Dumke (1990) reminds us. Janossy emphasized that the phase of super growth after World War II primarily reflected reconstruction, and argued that there would be a return to growth on a historically normal path. The path that Janossy envisaged can be thought of as an exogenously given natural rate of growth based on a constant rate of Harrod-neutral technological progress (Janossy, 1969, pp. 44, 98–9). In principle, this is testable but in practice the statistical methods used have been crude and have led to conflicting and unsatisfactory results (Dumke, 1990, pp. 457–61). We offer an explicit test of the Janossy hypothesis based on the rate of growth of real GDP per person.

More recently, Abramovitz (1986) has also reviewed long-run European growth, in his case explicitly in a catch-up and convergence framework. Like Maddison, he suggested that the era of reconstruction after World War II created a newly favourable environment for growth, but he also argued for enhanced social capability for catch-up in the 1950s and 1960s together with a greater facility for technology transfer from the leading country, the USA, to Europe. These last arguments have been endorsed and expanded in an influential article by Nelson and Wright (1992).

The hypothesis common to these authors is that, while there might be a phase of abnormally rapid growth during reconstruction, the eventual growth path for European countries would involve a superior performance to that which might have been forecast on the basis of early twentieth century experience. This allows two variants of the pure Janossy hypothesis which we also test. The first of these, which might be called a 'modified Janossy' hypothesis, sees the eventual growth rate returning to its original size but with income levels on a higher path than would previously have been possible, rather than on the same path as Janossy supposed. The second version, which might be called a 'reverse Janossy' hypothesis, predicts that when growth returns to normal it will be along a trend growth path which can be extrapolated back to the point at which interruption occurred but which exhibits faster growth than would have been possible before the interruption. Both these variants would reflect the greater accumulation of technological capability in Europe in the post-war world. The precise algebra of these specifications is spelt out in Section 2 below.

Writers like Abramovitz and Maddison operated within the framework of traditional growth theory. The new growth theory offers a range of models of endogenous growth in which there are constant returns to the accumulation of (broad) capital. The archetype of these models can be found in Rebelo (1991). In this case we would expect to find a unit root in GDP as, for example, shocks to the investment rate have permanent effects on growth rather than the transitory impact of the traditional Solow model which underlies the trend-stationary Janossy hypothesis. We thus test the unit root hypothesis against the alternative of a segmented trend model.

## 2    Empirical tests and results

As stated in the Introduction, our database is taken from Maddison (1991) and Prados (1993) and comprises annual observations on output per person for seventeen countries: all series end in 1989 and the different starting dates, the earliest being 1860, are recorded in Table 11.1 (all tests and models were also applied to output as well, with almost identical results: many of these are reported in Mills and Crafts, 1994). Logarithms of the data are used in all the empirical exercises reported below.

Conventional (augmented) Dickey–Fuller tests, reported in Table 11.1, suggest that all series contain a single unit root except the USA, which rejects the unit root null hypothesis in favour of a trend-stationary alternative at less than the 5% significance level.

Of course, such a conclusion is unsurprising if, rather than the alternative to the unit root null being a trend-stationary process, it is a segmented trend. Campbell and Perron (1991, Rule 4) show that the power of these unit root tests goes to zero as the sample size increases when the trend function contains a shift in the slope!

The discussion in the Introduction suggests that the relevant alternative to consider here is indeed a segmented trend-stationary process, but one in which there is more than one break in the trend. We interpret the Maddison hypothesis as specifying breaks in trend at 1914, 1919, 1939, 1950 and 1973. Moreover, we regard these break points as being exogenously determined and consequently they are used for *all* series: we thus avoid the problems of pre-testing bias that have been a major criticism of Perron's (1989) testing approach. Note that if there is more

**Table 11.1  Unit root tests: output per person. Augmented Dickey–Fuller tests**

| | Start | $x$ | | $\nabla x$ | |
| | | $\tau_\tau$ | $\hat{\rho}$ | $\tau_\mu$ | $\hat{\rho}$ |
|---|---|---|---|---|---|
| Australia | 1870 | −1.37 [2] | 0.965 | −10.64 [0] | 0.015** |
| Austria | 1870 | −1.61 [0] | 0.950 | −10.06 [0] | 0.063** |
| Belgium | 1870 | −1.04 [1] | 0.978 | −5.02 [4] | 0.118** |
| Canada | 1870 | −2.93 [1] | 0.895 | −8.16 [0] | 0.270** |
| Denmark | 1870 | −1.57 [2] | 0.950 | −10.72 [0] | 0.003** |
| Finland | 1870 | −1.47 [4] | 0.968 | −6.12 [3] | 0.077** |
| France | 1870 | −2.03 [3] | 0.947 | −5.47 [4] | 0.099** |
| Germany | 1870 | −1.90 [2] | 0.935 | −8.94 [1] | −0.161** |
| Italy | 1870 | −1.66 [1] | 0.963 | −8.35 [0] | 0.247** |
| Japan | 1885 | −1.17 [0] | 0.970 | −9.23 [0] | 0.080** |
| Netherlands | 1900 | −2.47 [1] | 0.893 | −7.16 [1] | 0.030** |
| Norway | 1870 | −1.06 [0] | 0.979 | −10.17 [0] | 0.54** |
| Spain | 1860 | −0.56 [1] | 0.991 | −9.21 [0] | 0.190** |
| Sweden | 1870 | −1.72 [5] | 0.968 | −4.88 [4] | 0.175** |
| Switzerland | 1899 | −1.08 [1] | 0.984 | −5.57 [0] | 0.462** |
| UK | 1870 | −0.92 [4] | 0.974 | −6.65 [2] | 0.118** |
| USA | 1870 | −4.04 [1]* | 0.826 | −6.59 [3] | −0.025** |

*Notes:* $\tau_\tau$ is computed from a regression of $x_t$ on a constant, $t$, $x_{t-1}$ and $k$ lags of $\nabla x_t$: the value of $k$ is shown in brackets [·]. $\tau_\mu$ is computed from the regression of $\nabla x_t^2$ on a constant, $\nabla x_{t-1}^2$ and $k$ lags of $\nabla^2 x_t$. $\hat{\rho}$ is the coefficient on the lagged dependent variable in both regressions. * and ** denote significance at the 0.05 and 0.01 levels respectively. $x$ is the logarithm of output per person: all samples end in 1989.

than one break in trend but only a single break is fitted then, again from Campbell and Perron's Rule 4, the power of a unit root test still goes to zero as the sample size increases.

Thus, with $x_t$ denoting the logarithm of output per person, the segmented trend model can be written as

$$x_t = \gamma_0 + \gamma_1 t + \sum_{i=2}^{6} \gamma_i D_{it} + u_t \tag{1}$$

where $D_{it} = (t - T_i) \cdot 1(t > T_i)$, $1(\cdot)$ is the indicator function and $T_i = 2, \ldots, 6$ correspond to the break years 1914, 1919, 1939, 1950 and 1973. Following Campbell and Perron (1991), the unit root hypothesis can be tested by estimating the regression (1), obtaining the residuals $\hat{u}_t$ and using the $t$-statistic for testing $\pi = 0$ in the auxiliary regression

$$\nabla \hat{u}_t = \pi \hat{u}_{t-1} + \sum_i \delta_i \nabla \hat{u}_{t-1} + a_t \qquad (2)$$

where enough lags of $\nabla \hat{u}_t$ are included to ensure that $a_t$ is white noise. The distribution of the test statistic, $t_\pi$, under the null depends upon the sample size and the number and placing of the breaks $T_i$ and thus it can only be obtained by Monte Carlo simulation. For each series, we obtained the empirical distribution of $t_\pi$ by assuming that $x_t$ was generated by a random walk with a drift given by the sample mean of $\nabla x_t$ and simulating this process five thousand times, each time fitting the model (1) and calculating $t_\pi$ from (2).

The unit root tests so calculated are shown in Table 11.2 and lead to a number of rejections of the unit root null: it is rejected at the 5% significance level in favour of the segmented trend model for Austria, Belgium, Denmark, Finland, France, Japan, Sweden, and the UK, and at the 10% level for Germany, The Netherlands, Norway and the USA, but not for Australia, Canada, Italy, Spain or Switzerland.

However, it is well known that unit root tests of this type have notoriously low power against an alternative of a maximum autoregressive root that is large but nonetheless smaller than unity. Such an alternative is particularly plausible here, for it allows fairly long, perhaps cyclical, movements away from a long-term trend path. We thus supplement the Dickey–Fuller statistic with three further pieces of information: the estimated maximum autoregressive root, $\hat{\rho} = 1 + \hat{\pi}$, the Phillips and Ploberger (1994) Bayesian posterior odds in favour of a unit root, and the number of sample autocorrelations of $\hat{u}_t$ that are observed before the sample autocorrelation function becomes non-positive, a statistic that has been shown by Leybourne (1994) to be a particularly simple and robust test for a unit root.

These are all reported in Table 11.2 as well and provide convincing evidence that, in fact, *all* output per person series are stationary around a segmented trend: no roots are estimated to be greater than 0.83, the Bayesian posterior odds in favour of there being a unit root are all extremely small, and the number of positive autocorrelations of $\hat{u}_t$ that are observed before a negative value is encountered are all much smaller than would be expected if there were unit roots present in each series.

Given these findings, we may then assume that, as in (2), the error $u_t$ can be modelled by an autoregressive process:

**Table 11.2  Unit root tests against the segmented trend alternative: exogenous breaks**

|  | $t_\pi$ | $\hat{\rho}$ | Bayesian posterior odds | $c$ |
|---|---|---|---|---|
| Australia | −4.15 | 0.83 | 0.011 | 5 |
| Austria | −5.53** | 0.63 | <0.001 | 3 |
| Belgium | −5.55** | 0.73 | 0.012 | 4 |
| Canada | −4.91 | 0.70 | 0.003 | 4 |
| Denmark | −5.89** | 0.64 | 0.001 | 4 |
| Finland | −7.07** | 0.41 | <0.001 | 3 |
| France | −5.90** | 0.69 | <0.001 | 4 |
| Germany | −5.28* | 0.51 | <0.001 | 3 |
| Italy | −4.52 | 0.79 | 0.048 | 5 |
| Japan | −6.02** | 0.25 | <0.001 | 2 |
| Netherlands | −5.03* | 0.67 | 0.099 | 4 |
| Norway | −5.41* | 0.53 | <0.001 | 4 |
| Spain | −4.17 | 0.76 | 0.020 | 5 |
| Sweden | −6.28** | 0.59 | <0.001 | 4 |
| Switzerland | −4.61 | 0.75 | 0.016 | 4 |
| UK | −6.11** | 0.61 | <0.001 | 3 |
| USA | −5.23* | 0.66 | <0.001 | 3 |

*Notes:* The test statistic $t_\pi$ and the estimator $\hat{\rho} = 1 + \hat{\pi}$ are as defined in the text (see equations (1) and (2)). * and ** denote significance at 10% and 5% levels, respectively, with critical values computed via Monte Carlo simulation as discussed in the text. The Bayesian posterior odds are defined as $1/BLR$, where $BLR$ is the Bayes model likelihood ratio criterion of Phillips and Ploberger (1994). $c$ is the number of positive sample autocorrelations of $\hat{u}_t$ observed before a non-positive value is encountered. Using the table of critical values given in Leybourne (1994), all $c$ values reject the null of a unit root at the 1% significance level.

$$u_t = \rho u_{t-1} + \sum_i \delta_i \Delta u_{t-i} + a_t \qquad (3)$$

Equations (1) and (3) can then be jointly estimated, and trend rates of growth across segments calculated as $\sum_{i=1}^{k} \gamma_i$ for the $k$th segment (the period up to the first break at $T_2 = 1914$ being the first segment, etc.). The order of the autoregression for $u_t$ was determined individually for each country using goodness-of-fit criteria.

Table 11.3 reports these estimated trend rates of growth. The maintained hypothesis that the Golden Age (the fifth segment, 1951–73) showed faster growth in European countries than earlier or later peacetime

**Table 11.3  Estimated trend rates of growth of output per person: predetermined breaks, unrestricted model**

| % p.a.<br>Segment $k$ | $T_1$–1914<br>1 | 15–19<br>2 | 20–39<br>3 | 40–50<br>4 | 51–73<br>5 | 74–89<br>6 |
|---|---|---|---|---|---|---|
| Australia | 0.36 | 0.31 | 0.62 | 2.08 | 2.32 | 1.90 |
| Austria | 1.31** | −4.44** | 1.29** | −0.32 | 5.50** | 1.83** |
| Belgium | 0.90** | −0.63 | 1.01 | −0.17 | 3.90** | 2.09** |
| Canada | 2.46** | −0.05 | 0.89 | 3.98* | 2.47 | 2.91 |
| Denmark | 1.77** | −0.39* | 1.58 | 0.91 | 3.46** | 1.59** |
| Finland | 1.45** | −1.71** | 3.25** | 1.56** | 4.12** | 2.83** |
| France | 0.96** | 0.85 | 0.78 | 0.70 | 4.92** | 1.42** |
| Germany | 1.47** | −2.19* | 2.91 | 3.28 | 5.11** | 1.26** |
| Italy | 1.47** | 3.16 | 0.21 | 1.01 | 5.31** | 2.05** |
| Japan | 1.48** | 3.35 | 1.95 | −2.76** | 8.03** | 2.70** |
| Netherlands | −0.42 | 6.02 | −0.08 | 0.84 | 4.16* | 0.95* |
| Norway | 1.13** | 2.45 | 2.28 | 1.96 | 3.49** | 3.48 |
| Spain | 0.87** | 2.22 | −0.15 | −0.66 | 4.95** | 1.56** |
| Sweden | 1.52** | −3.04** | 3.03** | 2.63 | 3.42* | 1.62** |
| Switzerland | 0.57 | 2.02 | 1.69 | 3.28 | 2.91 | 0.84** |
| UK | 1.04** | −1.47** | 1.56** | 1.20 | 2.24* | 1.83 |
| USA | 1.70** | 1.58 | 0.86 | 3.76* | 1.54* | 1.89 |

*Notes:* $T_1$ is the series starting date (see Table 11.1); * and ** denote that a change in trend growth at the break $T_k$ is significant at the 5% and 1% levels, respectively, i.e. that $\gamma_k = 0$ is rejected at these levels.

periods is not rejected (omitting Switzerland, which was neutral), with the exception that Norway and the UK do not experience a slowdown after 1973 (both countries were, of course, favoured by North Sea oil). In general, the estimated trend growth rates for European countries during 1951–73 are a lot higher than those estimated for other periods and the label Golden Age does seem to be justified. As might be expected, a similar comment applies to Japan but not to the North American countries, which are, of course, not eligible for a phase of rapid catch-up growth.

However, while there is a clear case for treating the break points at 1914, 1919, 1939 and 1950 as exogenous and relevant to all countries, treating the final break at 1973 in the same fashion is rather more contentious. Janossy-type views of the world would perhaps envisage an earlier endogenous slowdown as reconstruction was completed. For example, in Germany this might often be located in the literature in the mid-1950s (Dumke, 1990). This breakpoint might also be expected to vary in timing across countries, as also might a slowdown based on the

**Table 11.4   Unit root tests against the segmented trend alternative: endogenously determined final break**

|  | $\hat{T}_6$ | $t_\tau$ | $\hat{\rho}$ | Bayesian posterior odds | $c$ |
|---|---|---|---|---|---|
| Australia | 1975 | −4.00 | 0.78 | 0.006 | 5 |
| Austria | 1957 | −6.23 | 0.40 | <0.001 | 2 |
| Belgium | 1974 | −5.58 | 0.65 | 0.30 | 4 |
| Canada | 1954 | −5.47 | 0.69 | <0.001 | 3 |
| Denmark | 1969 | −5.98 | 0.55 | 0.007 | 4 |
| Finland | 1974 | −7.09 | 0.51 | <0.001 | 3 |
| France | 1957 | −6.58 | 0.62 | <0.001 | 4 |
| Germany | 1955 | −6.62 | 0.25 | <0.001 | 2 |
| Italy | 1969 | −4.62 | 0.75 | 0.027 | 4 |
| Japan | 1970 | −6.14 | 0.19 | <0.001 | 2 |
| Netherlands | 1955 | −5.42 | 0.60 | 0.061 | 3 |
| Norway | 1954 | −5.52 | 0.53 | <0.001 | 4 |
| Spain | 1973 | −4.17 | 0.76 | 0.005 | 5 |
| Sweden | 1971 | −6.26 | 0.54 | <0.001 | 4 |
| Switzerland | 1970 | −4.08 | 0.73 | 0.007 | 4 |
| UK | 1973 | −6.11 | 0.61 | <0.001 | 3 |
| USA | 1958 | −5.51 | 0.67 | <0.001 | 3 |

*Notes:* The test statistics are as in Table 11.2, except that they are computed from equations (1) and (2) with the regressor $D_6$ defined using the estimated break point ($\hat{T}_6$) recorded in the first column.

exhaustion of catch-up opportunities. We therefore wish to reconsider our initial results in the light of estimates obtained by allowing the final breakpoint to be determined endogenously for each country. This will permit an examination of the robustness of the findings in Tables 11.2 and 11.3 and also provide a suitable framework within which to test the various Janossy hypotheses.

We can determine the final break point endogenously by jointly fitting equations (1) and (3) for a range of final break years, using, for example, a minimum residual variance criteria (for a statistical justification of this approach, see Gallant and Fuller (1973)). Table 11.4 thus reports the final break points obtained for each country after searching over the interval 1951 to 1980, along with the same information about the presence of a unit root, *conditional* on this endogenously determined break, as was given in Table 11.2. Significance levels are not reported for the Dickey–Fuller statistics because of the conditional nature of the test, but it is clear from this information that, once again, all series appear to be stationary around a segmented trend.

It is equally clear, however, that when the final break point is endogenously determined, the countries fall into two groups: those with a break in the early 1970s (which includes 1969), and those with a break occurring in the mid-1950s. This latter group contains the 'European' countries – Austria, France, Germany, The Netherlands and Norway – and North America.

Conditional upon the rejection of a unit root in favour of the segmented trend alternative (with endogenously determined final break), we may then test the various Janossy hypotheses, since they place restrictions on the coefficients of the segmented trend function. After the final break, the trend model becomes

$$x_t = \gamma_0 + \gamma_1 t + \sum_{i=2}^{6} \gamma_i(t - T_i) + u_t$$

which can be written as

$$x_t = \gamma_0 + \gamma_1 t + \left(\sum_{i=2}^{6} \gamma_i\right) t - \sum_{i=2}^{6} \gamma_i T_i + u_t$$

If $\Sigma\ \gamma_i = 0$, output *growth* returns to pre-1914 rates, i.e. the path of $x$ is *parallel* to the trend level extrapolated from 1914: this is the modified Janossy hypothesis. Conditional upon this restriction, the path of $x$ will be the *same* as the extrapolated path if $\Sigma\ \gamma_i T_i = 0$: this is the pure form of the Janossy hypothesis. These restrictions are tested for, along with the restriction $\gamma_i = 0$, $i = 2, \ldots, 6$, i.e. that there are *no* shifts in trend, in Table 11.5. This latter restriction is rejected conclusively for all countries: breaks in trend are thus endemic.

The modified Janossy 'return to growth rate' hypothesis is not rejected by Canada, Denmark, Spain, Sweden, Switzerland, and the USA. Conditional upon the acceptance of this hypothesis, the pure Janossy 'return to growth path' hypothesis is not rejected by Denmark and the USA.

The 'reverse Janossy' hypothesis has the backwards extrapolated final trend meeting an earlier segment at a break point. On inspection of the fitted trends, seven countries appeared to be candidates for such a hypothesis: Finland, Germany, Japan and Italy with a 'join' point at 1914, and Austria, France and The Netherlands with a join point at 1939. A join point at 1914 ($T_2$) implies the linear restriction $\sum_{i=3}^{6}\gamma_i(T_2 - T_i) = 0$, whereas a join point at 1939 ($T_4$) implies that $\gamma_5(T_4 - T_6) + \gamma_6(T_4 - T_6) = 0$ must hold. Tests of these restrictions for the above seven countries are presented in Table 11.6, where it is seen that for no country can they be rejected.

**Table 11.5    Tests of segmented trend restrictions**

|  | $\sum \gamma$ | $p(\gamma = 0)$ | $p(\sum \gamma = 0)$ | $p(\sum T\gamma = 0)$ |
|---|---|---|---|---|
| Australia | 1.57% | 0.0000 | 0.033 | 0.0001 |
| Austria | 1.96% | 0.0000 | 0.0000 | 0.84 |
| Belgium | 1.02% | 0.0000 | 0.070 | 0.0003 |
| Canada | 0.48% | 0.0000 | 0.18 | 0.027 |
| Denmark | 0.11% | 0.0000 | 0.71 | 0.27 |
| Finland | 1.30% | 0.0000 | 0.0005 | 0.0000 |
| France | 1.87% | 0.0000 | 0.0000 | 0.0072 |
| Germany | 1.35% | 0.0000 | 0.0000 | 0.0000 |
| Italy | 1.06% | 0.0000 | 0.10 | 0.0089 |
| Japan | 1.95% | 0.0000 | 0.0004 | 0.0000 |
| Netherlands | 2.87% | 0.0000 | 0.10 | 0.21 |
| Norway | 2.29% | 0.0000 | 0.0000 | 0.0000 |
| Spain | 0.73% | 0.0000 | 0.16 | 0.0000 |
| Sweden | 0.20% | 0.0000 | 0.14 | 0.0000 |
| Switzerland | 0.20% | 0.0001 | 0.84 | 0.12 |
| UK | 0.80% | 0.0000 | 0.006 | 0.0003 |
| US | 0.27% | 0.0000 | 0.38 | 0.76 |

*Notes:* $\sum \gamma = \gamma_2 + \ldots + \gamma_6$. $p(\gamma = 0)$ is the $p$-value testing the null hypothesis $\gamma_2 = \ldots = \gamma_6 = 0$, $p(\sum \gamma = 0)$ is the $p$-value testing the null hypothesis $\gamma_2 + \ldots + \gamma_6 = 0$, and $p(\sum T\gamma = 0)$ is the $p$-value testing the null hypothesis $\sum_{i=2}^{5} (T_6 - T_i(\gamma_i = 0)$

**Table 11.6    Tests of the 'reverse Janossy' hypothesis**

| | $p\left( \sum_{i=3}^{6}\gamma_i(T_2 - T_i) = 0 \right)$ |
|---|---|
| Austria | 0.53 |
| Germany | 0.10 |
| Italy | 0.95 |
| Japan | 0.99 |

| | $p\left( \gamma_5(T_4 - T_6) + \gamma_6(T_4 - T_6) = 0 \right)$ |
|---|---|
| Finland | 0.75 |
| France | 0.48 |
| Netherlands | 0.53 |

*Notes:* $p\left( \sum_{i=3}^{6}\gamma_i(T_2 - T_i) = 0 \right)$ is the $p$-value testing the null hypothesis $\sum_{i=3}^{6}\gamma_i(T_2 - T) = 0$; $p\left( \gamma_5(T_4 - T_6) + \gamma_6(T_4 - T_6) = 0 \right)$ is the $p$-value testing the null hypothesis $\gamma_5(T_4 - T_6) + \gamma_6(T_4 - T_6) = 0$.

**Table 11.7   Trend rates of growth**

| % p.a. | $T_1$–1914 | 15–19 | 20–39 | 40–50 | 51–$T_6$ | ($T_6$+1)–89 |
|---|---|---|---|---|---|---|
| Australia | 0.41 | 0.41 | 0.41 | 2.22 | 2.22 | 2.22 |
| Austria | 1.35 | −4.81 | 1.48 | −2.08 | 11.36 | 3.14 |
| Belgium | 0.69 | 0.69 | 0.69 | 0.69 | 3.60 | 2.08 |
| Canada | 2.47 | 0.72 | 0.72 | 3.66 | 3.66 | 2.47 |
| Denmark | 1.92 | 1.03 | 1.03 | 1.03 | 3.61 | 1.92 |
| Finland | 1.45 | −1.72 | 3.24 | 1.61 | 4.06 | 2.86 |
| France | 0.96 | 0.96 | 0.96 | −0.97 | 9.34 | 3.03 |
| Germany | 1.53 | −3.12 | 3.30 | 0.71 | 13.89 | 3.12 |
| Italy | 1.15 | 1.15 | 1.15 | 1.15 | 5.26 | 2.57 |
| Japan | 1.61 | 2.22 | 2.22 | −3.21 | 8.50 | 3.40 |
| Netherlands | 0 | 5.57 | 0 | 0 | 8.47 | 2.65 |
| Norway | 1.16 | 2.22 | 2.22 | 2.22 | 3.44 | 3.44 |
| Spain | 1.02 | 1.02 | −2.21 | −2.21 | 5.03 | 1.02 |
| Sweden | 1.47 | −2.61 | 2.83 | 2.83 | 3.59 | 1.47 |
| Switzerland | 1.05 | 1.05 | 1.81 | 3.11 | 3.11 | 1.05 |
| UK | 1.03 | −1.27 | 1.46 | 1.46 | 2.08 | 2.08 |
| USA | 1.74 | 1.74 | 0.76 | 3.51 | 1.74 | 1.74 |

*Notes:* $T_1$ is the series starting date (see Table 11.1); $T_6$ is the endogenously determined final break point (see Table 11.4).

Table 11.7 reports the estimated trend rates of growth across segments for each country after all acceptable restrictions have been imposed on the models (1) and (3), i.e. the pure, modified or reverse Janossy restrictions plus any zero coefficient restrictions that are found to be appropriate, which thus eliminate any statistically insignificant shifts of trend. For the European countries whose break points are not found in the mid-1950s, all our previous remarks about the validity of the term 'Golden Age of growth' still hold. For the early break point countries (Austria, France, Germany and The Netherlands), comparison of Tables 11.3 and 11.7 suggest that the true model may be a slowing in the 1950s at the end of reconstruction and another slowing in the 1970s as catch-up peters out. An attempt was therefore made to investigate this possibility. Conditional upon the five breaks already established, a search for a sixth break within the period 1966 to 1980 was undertaken. Using a similar approach to that employed above, breaks were identified at 1973 for Germany, 1974 for France and Holland, and 1977 for Austria. On estimation of the extended models, all estimated break coefficients were negative, thus implying that there was indeed a slowing down in the 1970s for these countries. However, in every case, these coefficients were statistically insignificant, so that the importance of this slowing down is questionable. Overall, then, the exceptional nature of European growth in the 1950s and 1960s remains highly visible, but we are reminded that in some cases reconstruction was responsible for supergrowth in the early 1950s.

## 3    Implications of the results

In this section we review the ideas discussed in Section 1 in the light of Section 2's results. It turns out that we have obtained an interesting but somewhat mixed picture that does not provide unqualified support for any of the competing views.

First, it should be emphasized that our results amount to a rejection of the unit root hypothesis in favour of a segmented trend-stationary alternative. This evidence is contrary to what would be expected on the basis of assuming an endogenous growth model of the Rebelo (1991) type where there are constant returns to the accumulation of reproducible factors of production. In particular, it is important to note that this finding applies both in the case where 1973 is treated as an exogenous breakpoint and where the post-1950 breakpoint is found endogenously.

Second, it is clear that these results are quite different from those obtained by time series analysis in the 1980s. Other recent studies have considered one break in trend and have found frequent rejections of the unit root null, although not across the board. Thus, at conventional levels of significance, Duck (1992) was able to reject the unit root null for GDP in seven countries out of nine, Ben-David and Papell (1996) in eight countries out of sixteen for both GDP and GDP per person, and Raj (1992) in six out of nine countries for GDP per person. Perron (1994), whose discussion and battery of tests is the most exhaustive, eventually rejected a unit root in GDP for seven countries out of eleven. Since the data series used in all these studies are virtually the same, it seems that the key difference is our investigation of several, rather than simply one, break in trend.

Third, our results strongly suggest the value of a perspective on the properties of GDP that is not confined to USA experience, analysis of which has dominated much of the econometrics literature. Figures 11.1 to 11.4 underline this point.

Fourth, although the pure Janossy hypothesis cannot be rejected for the USA, it is generally rejected. All European countries except Denmark are found to have higher output per person during the post-war period than would have been predicted by extrapolating the pre-1914 trend growth rate.

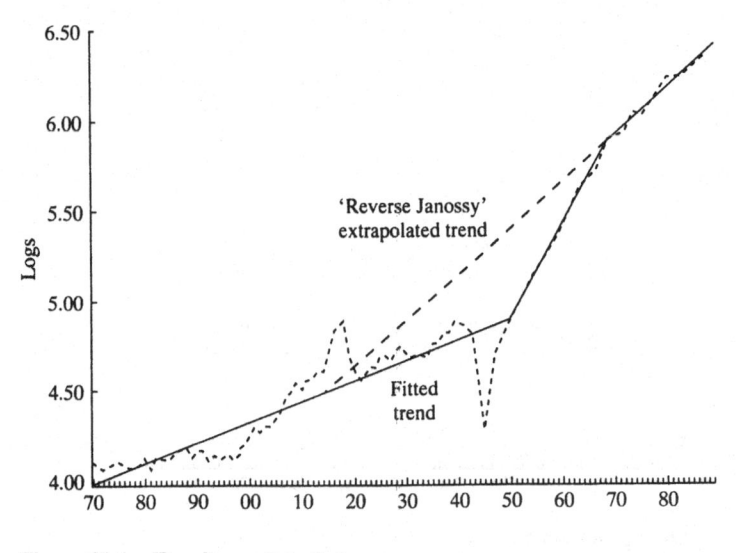

**Figure 11.1   Trend growth in Italy**

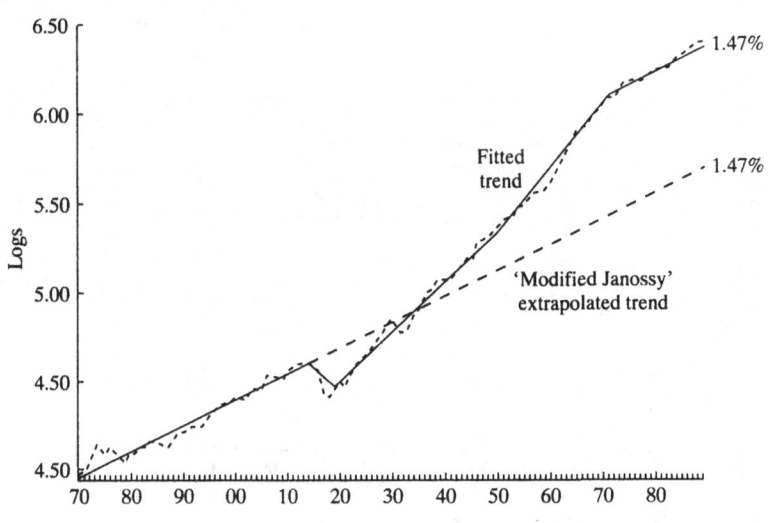

**Figure 11.2   Trend growth in Sweden**

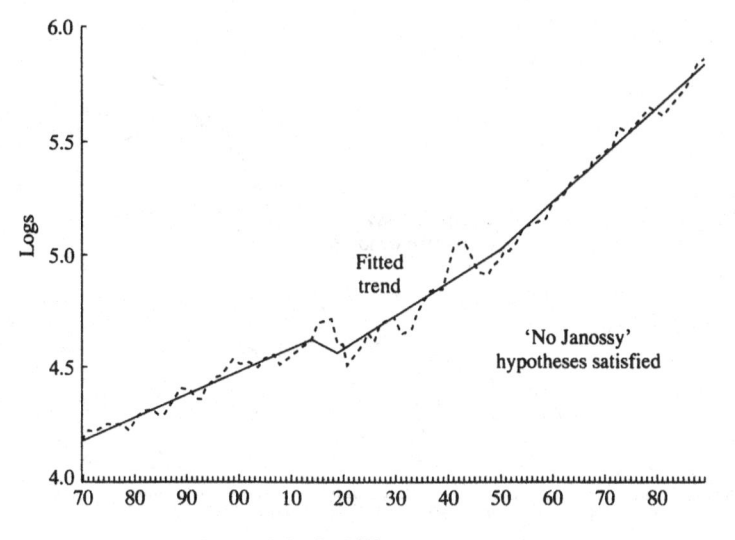

Figure 11.3    Trend growth in the UK

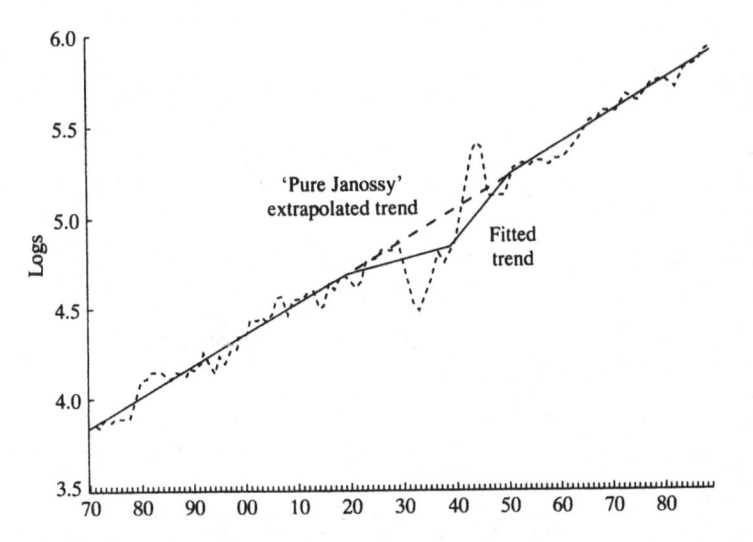

Figure 11.4    Trend growth in the USA

Table 11.8   Levels of GDP/hour worked relative to the
USA (USA = 100 in each year)

|  | 1913 | 1973 | 1989 |
|---|---|---|---|
| Australia | 93 | 70 | 78 |
| Austria | 48 | 59 | 74 |
| Belgium | 61 | 64 | 86 |
| Canada | 75 | 83 | 92 |
| Denmark | 58 | 63 | 68 |
| Finland | 33 | 57 | 67 |
| France | 48 | 70 | 94 |
| Germany | 50 | 64 | 80 |
| Italy | 37 | 64 | 79 |
| Japan | 18 | 46 | 61 |
| Netherlands | 69 | 77 | 92 |
| Norway | 43 | 64 | 90 |
| Sweden | 44 | 76 | 82 |
| Switzerland | 51 | 67 | 68 |
| UK | 78 | 67 | 80 |

Source: derived from Maddison (1991); data for Spain not
available.

Fifth, nevertheless we cannot reject the modified or reverse Janossy
variants (whose implications are captured in Figures 11.1 and 11.2,
respectively) in a total of ten European countries. This suggests that
Janossy's emphasis on the importance of reconstruction to early post-
war growth is valuable, even though his suggestion of a constant
'historically normal' rate of growth based on a traditional neoclassical
natural rate model is not generally valid.

Sixth, the proposition that, in most cases, much more than simple
recovery from wartime retardation of growth and productivity was
involved in the fast European growth of the Golden Age is borne out by
the evidence on relative productivity levels reported in Table 11.8. In all
countries, except Australia and the UK, output per hour worked in both
1973 and 1989 was higher relative to the USA than in 1913. All in all, the
Nelson and Wright (1992) view seems to be supported by these data.
Post-war reconstruction of the European economy can be identified as a
positive shock leading 'exceptionally', as Abramovitz put it (1986, p.
395), to the coming together of various elements required for rapid
growth by catching up to levels of productivity relative to the USA
hitherto unattainable.

## 4   Concluding comments

The main thrust of our results is easy to summarize. With regard to historical questions, we believe that there is strong econometric support for the idea of a Golden Age of European growth in the early post-war period. We would also argue that, in looking at this European experience, it is important not only to think in terms of catch-up growth which reduced technology gaps, but also to take account of reconstruction. With regard to econometric practice, we suggest that research into growth trends needs to take seriously the possibility that long-run series exhibit several breaks in trend.

## REFERENCES

Abramovitz, M. (1986), 'Catching-Up, Forging Ahead, and Falling Behind', *Journal of Economic History*, 36, 385–406.

Ben-David, D. and D.H. Papell (1996), 'The Great Wars, the Great Crash and the Unit Root Hypothesis: Some New Evidence about an Old Stylized Fact', *Journal of Monetary Economies* (forthcoming).

Campbell, J.Y. and P. Perron (1991), 'Pitfalls and Opportunities: What Macro-economists Should Know about Unit Roots', in O.J. Blanchard and S. Fisher (eds.), *NBER Macroeconomics Annual*, Vol. 7, Cambridge, MA: MIT Press.

Duck, N.W. (1992), 'Evidence on Breaking Trend Functions from Nine Countries', University of Bristol Discussion Paper No. 92–341.

Dumke, R.H. (1990), 'Reassessing the Wirtschaftswunder: Reconstruction and Postwar Growth in West Germany in an International Context', *Oxford Bulletin of Economics and Statistics*, 52, 451–90.

Gallant, A.R. and W.A. Fuller (1973), 'Fitting Segmented Polynomial Regression Models Whose Join Points Have to be Estimated', *Journal of the American Statistical Association*, 68, 144–7.

Janossy, F. (1969), *The End of the Economic Miracle*, White Plains: IASP.

Leybourne, S.J. (1994), 'Testing for Unit Roots: A Simple Alternative to Dickey–Fuller', *Applied Economics*, 26, 721–30.

Maddison, A. (1991), *Dynamic Forces in Capitalist Development*, Oxford: Oxford University Press.

Mills, T.C. and N.F.R. Crafts (1994), 'Modelling Changing Trend Rates of Output Growth: Unit Roots, Segmented Trends and Common Features', Hull Economic Research Paper 214.

Nelson, R.R. and G. Wright (1992), 'The Rise and Fall of American Technological Leadership', *Journal of Economic Literature*, 30, 1931–1964.

Perron, P. (1989), 'The Great Crash, the Oil Price Shock, and the Unit Root Hypothesis', *Econometrica*, 57, 1361–401.

Perron, P. (1994), 'Trend, Unit Root and Structural Change in Macroeconomic Time Series', in B.B. Rao (ed.), *Cointegration for the Applied Economist*, London: Macmillan.

Phillips, P.C.B. and W. Ploberger (1994), 'Posterior Odds Testing for a Unit Root with Data-Based Model Selection', *Econometric Theory*, 10, 774–808.

Prados de la Escocura, L. (1993), 'Spain's Gross Domestic Product, 1850–1990: A New Series', Discussion Paper No. D-93002, Ministerio de Economia y Hacienda, Madrid.

Raj, B. (1992), 'International Evidence on Persistence in Output in the Presence of an Episodic Change', *Journal of Applied Econometrics*, 7, 281–93.

Rebelo, S. (1991), 'Long Run Policy Analysis and Long Run Growth', *Journal of Political Economy*, 99, 500–21.

van de Klundert, T. and van Schaik, A. (1993), 'On the Historical Continuity of the Process of Economic Growth', CEPR Discussion Paper No. 850.

# Index